F. E. PEACOCK PUBLISHERS, INC.

ITASCA · ILLINOIS

The New SOCIAL STUDIES

Analysis of Theory and Materials

MARK M. KRUG
UNIVERSITY OF CHICAGO
JOHN B. POSTER
NORTHEASTERN ILLINOIS STATE COLLEGE
WILLIAM B. GILLIES, III
EVANSTON TOWNSHIP HIGH SCHOOL

Preface

The progress made in rethinking and revitalizing the social studies instruction in elementary and secondary schools in recent years, has been truly remarkable. Today, one is fully justified to speak of the New Social Studies. Several factors comprise and justify the use of the word "New."

We will list them, not necessarily in order of preference:

1. Innovative and searching inquiry into the social studies curriculum, including objectives, philosophy and rationale.

2. An intelligent search for new methods of instruction.

3. A systematic and imaginative effort to find new approaches and new ways of teaching history, geography, sociology, anthropology, economics and political science on the elementary and high school level.
   The most exciting element in this endeavor is the joint cooperation, and active collaboration of academicians and social studies educators and teachers.

4. The publication by social studies projects of new teaching materials and the careful testing of same in a variety of schools.

5. An important effort to broaden the traditional history courses by an infusion of social science concepts and modes of inquiry.

All this is no mean achievement. Obviously, not all new approaches and materials are equally valid or equally worthy of use in schools. The authors are convinced that the social studies profession now needs an objective, searching, sympathetic, but critical evaluation of the new social studies materials. Basically, we intend to see to what extent the materials meet the objectives set for them by their creators and how valuable they are for classroom instruction. This is the purpose of this book.

We have, because of reasons of space, had to omit consideration of some very worthy social studies projects. This omission is in no way a reflection on their value.

MARK M. KRUG
JOHN B. POSTER
WILLIAM B. GILLIES, III

Contents

Introduction

Although truth-in-packaging legislation may aid the beleaguered house-holder, it is not likely to benefit the consumer of curriculum materials. In the education marketplace, the tradition of *caveat emptor* prevails. Researchers and specialists speak glibly of the "excitement" generated in subject-fields by the new wave of revisionism, but teachers, teacher trainers, and curriculum consultants may justifiably feel harassed rather than excited. Selective change of course content is readily accepted and mastered by school personnel; multi-dimensional change affecting curricular traditions, pedagogical practices, staff relationships, and generally, the school's role in society is likely to prove overwhelming.

The authors of this volume hope to aid history and social science educators and teachers in the school systems of the nation in at least one area of flux, by preparing systematic analyses of the most celebrated offerings of the major producers in the "new" social studies. Our purpose, therefore, is "to provide a basis for selection among already developed curricular instruments." [1]

This chore of clarification is made more difficult by the diverse assumptions and starting points of the authors of the materials surveyed. To achieve some reasonably reliable evaluation of the almost bewildering variety of recently published social studies materials, it is necessary to use some "dependable methods for discerning the intentions of educators, for analyzing the implicit values of a curriculum, for observing personal interactions in the classroom, for surveying the perceptions of community leaders, and so on." [2]

Fortunately, our undertaking does not entail an inclusive, longitudinal evaluation. We are not attempting an exhaustive study of the worthiness

---

[1] Robert E. Stake, "An Emerging Theory of Evaluation: Borrowings from Many Methodologies," paper presented at a symposium on "The Role of Evaluation in National Curriculum Projects," 1967 Annual Meeting of the American Educational Research Association, New York.

[2] Ibid., p. 5.

of given materials in all environments. We are not engaging in premature comparisons of student performance in experimental and control treatment groups. Certainly we are not attempting to judge whether or not the new materials have permanent value and usefulness. We do seek to illuminate the salient features, implicit and explicit, of the products under consideration and, thus, to increase the ability of curriculum consumers to identify those materials which may help in making social studies instruction more effective.

Before we present the design we have used in examining the new social studies, we must pause to inspect a convention of the field of evaluation which might prejudice our analysis. A useful and justifiable tenet of orthodox evaluation theory holds that objectives should be expressed behaviorally, that is, learners should be able to demonstrate operationally that they have changed in the manner desired. This convention inhibits the tendency of curriculum designers to establish grandiose, but nebulous, claims for their creations. All too often, however, the convention also promotes the production of curriculum instruments which deal only with unconnected and seemingly irrelevant collections of data.[3] This latter point deserves further elaboration.

The demand that all objectives be stated behaviorally raises two questions:

1. Can all higher cognitive processes be overtly demonstrated in a school situation?
2. Will teachers be tempted to deal only with the most easily documented behaviors such as recognition and recall?

Our first question has special relevance for the new social studies because in the new curriculum the emphasis is often placed on the production of heuristic self-starters, i.e., intrinsically motivated discoverers. A crucial operation in the process of discovery is the "self-loop." The required sentience might be defined as the Socratic ability to see one's self as an actor while acting. According to Bruner, the self-loop represents "a separate and special problem in discovery—discovering what it is you've been doing and discovering it in a way that has productive power to it." [4]

---

[3] Sorenson states, "We know that instead of such high-sounding slogans as 'transmitting the cultural heritage,' 'educating citizens for democracy,' and 'developing the individual's potential,' we must develop objectives defined in terms of changes in pupils' behavior or in the products of student behaviors. We must also be careful that, in rigorously setting behavioral goals, we do not slip into triviality." Garth Sorenson, "A New Role in Education: The Evaluator," *Evaluation Comment*, Newsletter of University of California, Los Angeles, Center for the Study of Evaluation of Instructional Programs, 1, no. 1 (January, 1968): 3.

[4] Jerome S. Bruner, "Some Elements of Discovery," in *Learning by Discovery: A Critical Appraisal*, Lee S. Shulman and Evan R. Keislar, eds. (Chicago: Rand McNally & Co., 1966) p. 104.

Perhaps Bloom was speaking of the same phenomenon as Bruner when he noted that, "One of the major threads running through all the taxonomy appears to be a scale of consciousness or awareness." [5]

Heightened consciousness may be a legitimate curricular objective, but it poses problems for evaluation. There is an epistemological difference between awareness and awareness of something.[6] How can the child prove awareness? As curriculum developers attempt to achieve higher process desiderata they find it harder to specify behavior which corresponds to the desired objectives.

Our second question, regarding teacher behavior, has long worried educators. There seem to be many ways to distort or misuse the behavioral objective convention. It is, for example, widely recognized that, "Practically all teachers have considerable confidence in their ability to build tests of knowledge. Because of the simplicity of teaching and evaluating knowledge, it is frequently emphasized as an educational objective out of all proportion to its usefulness or its relevance for the development of the individual." [7]

The stricture on posing objectives in behavioral terms can be converted into a tacit resolution to strive only for those classroom goals, the attainment of which can be readily exhibited. In other words, a commonsensical admonition can become a dogma which coincides with and reinforces the proclivity of some teachers to omit from their instruction all but the most obvious elements of education. Ralph Tyler has observed that:

History is sometimes regarded and taught as a body of proven facts, rather than an account which is a subject of continuing inquiry and reinterpretation in the light of new information and knowledge.
As another example, geography is sometimes considered to be a listing of places on a map, sometimes a subject for explaining the location of peoples and industries in terms of climate and other physical features.[8]

In light of both the questionable logic and practical consequences of requiring overt behaviors to legitimate educational objectives, the occasional

---

[5] *Taxonomy of Educational Objectives, Handbook 1: Cognitive Domain,* Benjamin S. Bloom, ed. (New York: David McKay Co., Inc., 1956), p. 63.

[6] This point is well treated in Clive Beck's "The Question of Knowledge in Curriculum Inquiry," a paper delivered at the 1968 American Educational Research Association Convention, Chicago. See also Martin Haberman, "Behavioral Objectives: Bandwagon or Breakthrough," *Journal of Teacher Education,* Spring, 1968, and Clifford Houston and Stephen E. Hodge, "An Affective Behaviors Project Report," occasional paper, Rocky Mountain Educational Laboratory, Inc.

[7] *Taxonomy of Educational Objectives, Handbook 1: Cognitive Domain,* p. 34.

[8] Ralph Tyler, "An Assessment: The Edge of the Future," Wesley Sowards, ed., *The Social Studies: Curriculum Proposals for the Future, Cubberley Conference, Stanford University,* 1963 (Chicago: Scott, Foresman & Company, 1963) p. 122.

failure of the authors of the new social studies materials to specify appropriate behaviors must not be considered *prima facie* evidence of a serious shortcoming. Criticism of new materials for lack of orthodoxy, overlooks the possibility that some of the objectives of the new curricular offerings may be difficult to express in behavioral terms. But it is clear that these recent offerings do not content themselves with simply demanding, "The recall of specific and isolable bits of information." [9]

Happily, recognition of the inequities involved in forcing new generation packages into old generation molds appears to be growing. Goodlad and Tyler have both attempted to respond to the evolving revisionist challenge. Goodlad advises that:

Current emphasis on "structure of the disciplines" in curriculum planning offers promise for delineating the substantive element in an objective more precisely and usefully. Interestingly, although most current curriculum reformers endorse the concept of structure in their planning, few make any effort to be precise by formulating educational objectives in which the structural elements to be developed are made clear. However, their emphasis on concepts, principles, values, laws, and so forth is illustrative of their concern for emphasizing something substantive in the curriculum that is more powerful than facts alone. Their accompanying stress on inquiry, discovery, and induction, also suggests the kinds of behavior elements to be sought.
A little digging into the curriculum plans and products of such enterprises as those of the School Mathematics Study Group, the Physical Sciences Study Committee, the Science Curriculum Improvement Study, Project Social Studies and others, enables one, sometimes with considerable difficulty, however, to ferret out the kinds of behavioral and substantive elements that personnel in these projects might include in carefully-defined statements of educational objectives.[10]

Tyler, in the revision of his once definitive *Basic Principles of Curriculum and Instruction*, is sensitive to new thrusts and orientations.

Learners can understand the structure of the discipline, that is, the question it deals with, the kind of answers it seeks, the concepts it uses to analyze the field, the methods it uses to obtain data, and the way it organizes its inquiries and findings. When they (the learners) gain this understanding of

[9] *Taxonomy of Educational Objectives, Handbook I: Cognitive Domain*, p. 63.
[10] John I. Goodlad, with Maurice N. Richter, Jr., *The Development of a Conceptual System for Dealing with Problems of Curriculum and Instruction* (Report of an inquiry supported by The Cooperative Research Program of the Office of Education, U.S. Department of Health, Education, and Welfare. Contract No. SAF-8024, Project No. 454 [with the University of Chicago]. Report processed and forwarded by University of California, Los Angeles, and Institute for Development of Educational Activities), p. 50.

the structure, they learn more effectively and efficiently the content involved in it. *Hence I now seek to explore the nature of knowledge and structure of an area before deriving and formulating objectives involved in that area.* [emphasis added] [11]

This lengthy digression is an attempt to explain the omission from our analytic design of a convention which is widely revered. Since the question of by whose standards ye shall be judged is preeminent here, our decision to abandon the requirement that objectives be stated behaviorally may be interpreted as reflecting our determination to meet the revisionists on their own grounds.

Tyler and Klein have suggested a number of categories of properties which may serve as indicators to particular consumers of the assets and liabilities of prospective curricula. Among the considerations they list are: rationale, appropriateness, effectiveness, conditions, and practicality. Some of the qualities they subsume under each rubric follow:

Rationale:
The producer should present documentation about the value of the objectives formulated. For example, what is the basis for thinking that objectives having to do with understanding the structure of the disciplines are important?

Appropriateness:
The kind of student for whom the materials are designed should be specified. Characteristics such as age, sex, prerequisite skills, socioeconomic class should be reported.

Effectiveness:
Manuals should cite sources of available evidence to document any claims made about effectiveness and efficiency.

Conditions:
The manual must indicate the qualifications of the teacher which are required to use the materials effectively.

Practicality:
The guide must indicate which instructional materials are required and whether any of the instructional materials can be reused. Where supplementary materials are to be used, these should be described along with statements of initial and maintenance cost.[12]

---

[11] Ralph Tyler, "New Dimensions in Curriculum Development," *Phi Delta Kappa,* 48, no. 1, (September, 1966): 26.
[12] Louise L. Tyler and Francis Klein, *Recommendations for Curriculum and Instructional Materials* (Los Angeles: University of California, 1967). In *Recommendations for Curriculum and Instructional Materials,* Tyler and Klein elaborate these points much more completely.

It ought to be noted that Tyler and Klein are interested not only in materials, but also in the characteristics of the students, teachers, and districts where the materials will be used. Utilization of the Tyler and Klein guidelines will help to provide answers to some of the questions raised by Stake (see page 10). Individual projects, under the pressure of externally imposed deadlines, may not furnish formally all of the data previously listed. We have attempted therefore to either report the pertinent data in those instances where it is presented by the materials designers, or to extrapolate answers regarding questions of rationale, effectiveness, and so forth from the materials themselves.

Characteristics of materials especially pertinent to the social studies have been identified by Morrisett and Stevens.[13] These authors arrange their critical concerns in seven categories. Some of the headings are similar to those of Tyler and Klein, but several introduce additional valuable considerations.

Descriptive Characteristics:
One of the easiest tasks in curriculum analysis, but certainly not unimportant, is describing the curriculum materials and ideas. Consideration should be given to the characteristics of the textual materials (pages, cover, color, title, durability, size of print, illustrations, etc.) . . .

Structure of the Curriculum Materials:
Structure is the relationship of the components of a subject to each other. The analyst must be concerned with both the substantive and the affective structure of a curriculum.
Affective goals are common in social studies curricula, as shown by the prevalence of terms such as "respect," "appreciate," and "good citizenship." However, an explicit structure of goals and attitudes showing how they are related to each other in complimentary and conflicting ways and how they are related to the curriculum materials is rare.

This latter point is especially important when analyzing the new social studies generation of broad-gauge materials. Clearly some attitudes are antecedent to certain goals. An attitude of skepticism or doubt is a precursor of the goal labeled critical thinking. In our analysis we will attempt to discover and report curricular affective, as well as cognitive, structures.

Thus far we have presented seven areas for investigation germane to our analytic task. To review for a moment, they are: (1) rationale, (2) descriptive or impressionistic properties, (3) structure—cognitive and affective, (4) appropriateness, (5) effectiveness, (6) conditions, and (7) practicality. The last four headings refer to the fit or match between

---

[13] Irving Morrissett and W. William Stevens, Jr., "Curriculum Analysis," *Social Education,* 31, no. 6 (October, 1967): 483–89.

individual children, teachers, schools, districts and materials. We have mentioned that where information is not provided by curriculum designers we shall suggest likely outcomes in the light of our own experience.

We have been using the word curriculum to mean a body of intended learnings in a discrete course. Some consumers will be primarily concerned with the broader curriculum—the intended learnings in all the courses offered by the school. These consumers will wish to know the philosophical and psychological foundations of proferred packages. They will be concerned with integrating social studies material with materials used in other courses.

A reasonable format for deducing materials-laden assumptions about philosophy and psychology is furnished by Venable in *Philosophical Foundations of the Curriculum*.[14] According to Venable we should explore the curriculum's apparent view of the child, subject matter, learning process, and teaching agency. Venable categorizes possible results of this exploration within the framework of essentialism, idealism, pragmatism, and realism. Venable has adapted the Tylerian grid to benefit consumers instead of developers. His codification of deduced data may be too simple and clear-cut to actually represent the complexities of sophisticated curricula, but his identification of areas for study is most helpful.

We will include implied assumptions about views of the child and the teaching agency in our explication of project rationales. Views of the subject matter and the learning process will be included in our descriptions of posited cognitive and affective structures.

It seems to be important not to confuse evaluative criteria with the categories of evaluation. A statement of objectives, for example, is only meaningful if the reader is equipped with some conception of desirable knowledge, beliefs, and skills. Since our stated purpose is to provide the consumer with a basis for selection among already developed curricular instruments, it is necessary to appreciate the pluralistic value structure of American society. Statements regarding the nature of man, civilization, and the good life, have to be judged pragmatically, i.e., in the light of the consequences likely to result from adherence to the philosophies exhibited in such statements. Put in more simple terms, the new social studies ought to exhibit faith in the basic worth of the individual and a desire to comprehend the contemporary human condition and an intent to improve it. Curriculum rationales which meet these general criteria, though they may be deficient in other aspects, must be deemed respectable.

Likewise in judging overt or covert statements of cognitive and

---

[14]   Tom C. Venable, *Philosophical Foundations of the Curriculum* (Chicago: Rand McNally & Co., 1967).

affective structure, our criteria must skirt personal preferences on the continuum from behaviorism to conceptualism or the continuum from deduction to induction. What we can insist upon is that curriculum makers continue throughout their products to manifest their allegiance to the position that they, or the major portion of their materials, proclaim. Logical consistency is, therefore, a fundamental criterion.

What about consideration of match or fitness between materials and local circumstances? If we possess insights concerning materials and some experience with prevailing norms in student ability, teacher training, and curricular expenditure, we can make reasoned estimates about appropriateness, effectiveness, conditions, and practicality. The basic criterion under which we subsume our determinants of fit is feasibility.

In our organizational format we have divided the projects under study into two groups—integrative and disciplinary. The characterization is suggested by Bellack and is easily justified by even a cursory examination of the materials.[15]

---

[15] Arno Bellack, "Structure in the Social Sciences and Implications for the Social Studies Program," in *The Social Studies: Curriculum Proposals for the Future,* Wesley Sowards, ed. (Chicago: Scott, Foresman & Company, 1963).

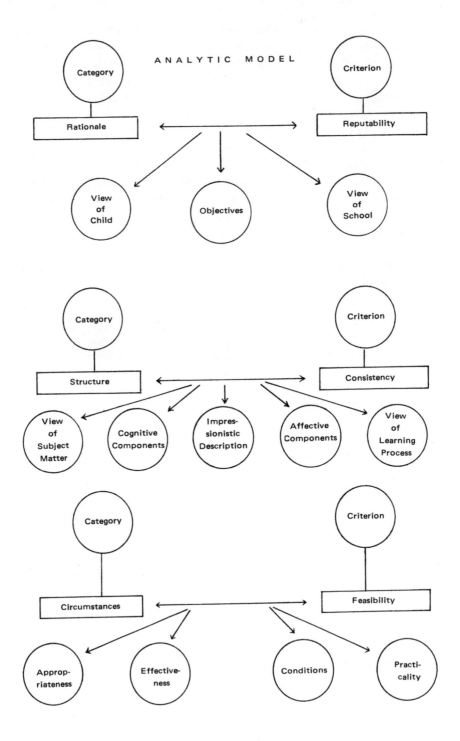

ANALYTIC MODEL

PART I

Prologue

Social Sciences and History — The Narrowing Gap: Implications for Social Studies*

THE AUTHORS

A variety of reasons and factors have contributed to the growing rapprochement and to the improving prospects for fruitful collaboration between history and the social sciences. The most important of these was the gradual recognition by leading social scientists that their respective disciplines are not as purely scientific as originally claimed and the frequently expressed conviction by prominent historians that they need and value the use of social science concepts and modes of inquiry in their work. More and more historians have declared themselves ready to explore new ways of looking at man, the ultimate object of their study, in order to gain a better understanding of the nature of man and his behavior in the past.

The impressive growth of the social sciences and their great diversification, make it hazardous and unwise to generalize too much about new trends and new orientations. However, one may perhaps be bold enough to indicate a few trends in a major social science like sociology which if viewed, on the whole, may explain the growing affinity, and the greatly improved prospects for fruitful collaboration between history and sociol-

---

* From *Social Education*, vol. 29, no. 8, December, 1965. Reprinted by permission of the publisher, from Mark M. Krug, *History and the Social Sciences* (Waltham, Massachusetts, Blaisdell Publishing Company, a Division of Ginn and Company, 1967).

ogy. Some sociologists have expressed the view that the stress in traditional, Weberian sociology on recurrent social patterns, on the concepts of order, stability and social equilibrium, have been rather one-sided. Conflict and disequilibrium, these sociologists maintain, are as important in the story of human society as order and equilibrium. Lewis Coser and others have suggested that Marx may have been completely wrong in stating that the fate of men is determined by their relation to the productive power of the society, but he made a contribution to modern sociology by his emphasis on the mutable nature of human society.

A substantial and vocal group of sociologists has urged in recent years a shift from micro-sociology to macro-sociology. They call for a broad analysis of large societal issues, like the issue of peace and war and race relations. "The focus of social analysis," wrote its chief protagonist, Professor Amitai Etzioni of Columbia University, "and its *raison d'être*, are the problems of the age, the application of sociology to the understanding of society, its major sub-collectives, and a society's place in more encompassing communities. . . . Social analysis is concerned with applying [sociological] concepts to the evolution of a world community, the redistribution of social wealth, efforts to advance the growth of civil rights, the development of 'have not' nations, etc." [1]

Obviously, such an ambitious program of social analysis and social action cannot be squared with the view of traditional sociology which postulated "freedom from value-judgment." [2] Seeking some authority for his view that the sociologist, because he knows more about society than other observers, should be committed to societal issues and ought to express his concern about them, Etzioni observes that Max Weber was careful to make a clear distinction between a *wert-frei*, or value free and a *wert-loss*, or valueless approach. A sociologist who is *wert-frei* withholds his judgment and lets his facts and findings speak for themselves, while a *wert-loss* sociologist does not have any values. Professor Etzioni obviously suggests that sociologists today have the duty to present their data objectively, but they should not hesitate to support social analysis aimed at the betterment of society through the maintenance of peace, of racial equality and world cooperation. He thinks that sociology has paid too much attention to low-level, concrete social problems and has neglected the larger societal issues. "We will not learn much about the anatomy of elephants," Etzioni concluded, "by studying that of fruit flies. Hence, we ought to

---

[1]   Amitai Etzioni, "Social Analysis as a Sociological Vocation," *The American Journal of Sociology*, 70 (March, 1965): 614–15.

[2]   See Introduction by Robert K. Merton to Harry M. Johnson's, *Sociology, A Systematic Introduction* (New York: Harcourt, Brace & World, Inc., 1960), p. 2.

continue to study small groups for their own sake and for the light they cast on social behavior in general, we ought to invest more of our resources in macroscopic sociology." [3] Another sociologist, Professor Robert Bierstedt of New York University, while basically agreeing with Etzioni's premise that sociologists have often "contented themselves with trivialities and have not taken into their purviews the larger problems that surround them," took issue with his assertion that sociologists are better equipped to analyze and deal with the larger problems confronting contemporary society than editors, journalists and commentators. Bierstedt maintained that such commentators as Walter Lippmann and James Reston have few peers in social analysis among the professional sociologists. "It would be even more embarrassing," he continued, ". . . if we were to discover that undergraduate training in history, philosophy, constitutional law, or even English literature provides a better background for social analysis than sociology does." [4]

The new trend in sociology as represented by Etzioni, Bierstedt, and the colleagues who share their views, greatly improves the prospects for fruitful collaboration between history and sociology. Concern for larger societal problems like integration, peace and war, will result in a confrontation with the truly complex nature of human society and will make the formulation of broad generalizations difficult, if not impossible. Macrosociology is bound to play havoc with the inclination for scientific predictions of future behavior and future developments on social and political crises. In the study of macro-sociology, the role of the unique and the specific will loom rather large. All this is bound to draw the sociologist and the historian closer together.

Even more important in this rapprochement is the growing respect between the sociologists and historians. Pioneering sociologists used historical sources to illustrate and substantiate their theoretical concepts and generalizations, the founders of modern sociology, like Max Weber and Emile Durkheim, advocated that sociology as an analytical science try to explain contemporary social institutions in terms of the functions they serve and not in terms of their historical development. The dwelling on the unique features of a particular social system was actually thought to be detrimental to a sound study of societal problems. Many sociologists have in the past and many still do, select and arrange historical data without regard to their chronological sequence, in order to demonstrate a coherent sociological analysis and insight.

---

[3] Etzioni, "Social Analysis," p. 617.
[4] Robert Bierstedt, "Comment," *The American Journal of Sociology*, 70 (March, 1965): 623.

Few sociologists and historians would now agree with the sarcastic remark of an English sociologist, Donald G. MacRae, who remarked that "Sociology is history with the hard work left out; history is sociology with the brains left out." [5] Two important volumes, both published by a happy coincidence in 1964, testify to the growing affinity between history and the social sciences. What is even more important, they indicate many promising avenues for fruitful collaboration. The two books are *Sociology and History* and *American History and the Social Sciences*.[6] The first book includes contributions of a number of sociologists who employ sociological concepts for the illumination and sounder analysis of events and periods in history and those sociologists who use historical data to illuminate and test the validity of sociological concepts, models and theories. Among the former are such eminent sociologists as E. Digby Baltzel, Werner J. Cahnman and Sigmund Diamond, while the latter are represented by Alvin Boskoff, Thomas F. O'Dea and Ernest Manheim.

The credo of the editors contains a declaration that the coming together of history and sociology has become possible and desirable because sociologists have grown wary of generalizations based on doubtful evidence which is often severely restricted in time and place and historians feel the need to broaden the scope of their investigations by comparing analogous situations and by the formulation of broader concepts and generalizations. The interest of the historian in the unique and the interest of the sociologist in the general can be bridged, the editors assert, because "it is desirable and possible to attain some measure of understanding of specific events and related periods; it is also desirable and possible to discover the extent to which explanations applicable to one situation may be extended to comparable situations from other times and places." [7] This is a cautious and wise statement which social studies teachers may well take to heart. It would suggest to them an approach to the teaching of historical events and of generalizing concepts from the social sciences not in an unrelated and disjointed way, but by a sensible fusion of both, when fusion is logical and possible. The new sociology, the editors state, must steer its course between the Scylla of rigid generalization and the Charybdis of sheer empiricism.[8] "We believe," Cahnman and Boskoff wrote, "that the ways in which history and sociology are similar and

[5]   Donald G. MacRae, "Some Sociological Prospects," *Transactions of the Third World Congress of Sociology* (London: The Congress, 1956) 8: 302.

[6]   Werner J. Cahnman and Alvin Boskoff, eds., *Sociology and History* (New York: The Free Press, 1964); Edward N. Saveth, ed., *American History and the Social Sciences* (New York: The Free Press, 1964).

[7]   Cahnman and Boskoff, eds., in "Sociology and History: Reunion and Rapprochement," in *Sociology and History*, p. 3.

[8]   Ibid, p. 11

complementary are as significant as the avowed differences, and that the specialized scholar ought to pause occasionally and look about to see whether his strivings and findings are in line with the general concerns of mankind." [9]

Among the many contributions to the volume, Professor Alvin Boskoff's paper represents an important example of fruitful collaboration between history and sociology. Boskoff examines the concept of a transitional society by the use of two historical case studies, Greece in the fourth and fifth centuries, B.C., and Rome in the third to the eighth centuries, A.D. He finds that the Greek society in the fourth and the fifth centuries, B.C., suffered from social indecision caused by an unresolved conflict between oligarchy and democracy, the fruitless rivalry between Sparta and Athens, and the confusion over conflicting ideas of practical realism and utopian escapism.

The Roman society in the third to the eighth century, A.D., was, according to Boskoff, also a transitional society, because it was beset by a number of unresolved social crises. These included the problem of imperial succession which became the toy of the legions, and the growing disorganization of the Roman army which became demoralized by politization. In addition, agriculture became stagnated by the escape of peasants to the cities and trade and industry were severely hampered by lack of a clear economic policy.

In his essay on "Religion and Nationality," Cahnman uses sociological insights to explain the peculiar position of non-Moslems, particularly of Jews and Christians in the Ottoman Empire. They were tolerated, allowed to profess their faith, but they were considered tenants who had to pay tribute for themselves and their land to the Moslem state. Cahnman also considered the lack of a clear boundary between religion and nationality in Islam and in Judaism. He finds the answer in the social pattern of the Mid-Eastern region where conditions of tribal law prevented social stratification and where the ancient custom of adoption and naturalization prevailed. In Islam, there was also the concept of Moslem brotherhood which encouraged conversion of peoples of many nationalities, races and colors.[10]

American History and the Social Sciences gives ample proof that many historians see great benefits in a close working relationship with social scientists. However, while they are ready to acknowledge the value of empirical social research, they remain unwilling to take seriously the far-reaching claims made by some social scientists for their respective

---

[9]   Ibid.
[10]   Cahnman and Boskoff, eds., *Sociology and History,* pp. 271–80.

disciplines. The historian is ready to acknowledge the contributions made by political science in the development of rigorous research designs and to the application of precise methods of analysis to the study of political behavior. Such a systematic study of politics and government has been of great help in many historical studies. But few historians will accept this claim made for political science by Professor Peter H. Odegard, former President of the American Political Science Association:

There is a new look in the study of politics.... No longer a hostage to history, and freed at last from its bondage to the lawyers as well as from the arid schematism of the political taxonomists, political science is in the process of becoming one of the central unifying forces for understanding why we behave like human beings. [11]

When television audiences throughout the nation are intently watching distinguished political scientists differ diametrically in the diagnosis and prognosis in Viet Nam, in the analysis of relations between India and Pakistan and between Russia and China, and when almost every month a political upheaval takes place in the world which puzzles political scientists as much as historians, it is rather difficult to take such exaggerated claims seriously. A more realistic political scientist, Professor Heinz Eulau, observed that "... Professor Odegard's picture is still more in the nature of a snapshot of a possible future than of a richly painted canvas." [12]

Arthur Schlesinger, Jr., addressing a meeting of the American Sociological Association in Washington in 1962, discussed frankly the historian's dilemma in his relationship to the social sciences. Schlesinger gratefully acknowledged his debt as a historian to the sociologists who have as he put it, "so vastly broadened my own intellectual horizons and refined my conception of the historical enterprise." [13] He stated that he is in fact prejudiced in favor of the empirical social research aimed at devising inquiries and experiments which often make it possible to bring about a better understanding of human behavior and societal processes and changes. But Schlesinger cautioned that the historian and the social scientist part ways when the latter suggests that the empirical method of inquiry is the only path to the understanding of social phenomena of the present and of the past and that social wisdom can be gained only through analytical quantitative analysis. Polls are useful, but they are often

---

[11]   Bert Hoselitz. ed., *A Reader's Guide to the Social Sciences* (New York: The Free Press, 1959).

[12]   Ibid.

[13]   Edward N. Saveth, ed., *American History and the Social Sciences*, p. 52.

misleading and unreliable and the quantitative method of inquiry in history would ignore many important psychological and philosophical variables. "For an indefinite future," Schlesinger concluded, "I suspect humanism will continue to yield truths about both individual and social experience which quantitative social science research could never reach." [14] It is of course one thing to assert that the quantitative method of empirical research cannot illuminate all, or even major historical events, and it is another, not to acknowledge the usefulness of this method in the exploration of many problems in historical research.

Professor Edward N. Saveth, the editor of the volume *American History and the Social Sciences* suggested that the traditional historical method of verifying data would profit greatly from the use of insights that the social scientists have gained on the nature of man. Such concepts as, class, role, mobility, and decision-making, may be of great help to the historian in his work.

In spite of the growing influence of econometricians in the discipline of the economics, there is evidence which suggests the existence of large areas of cooperation between history and economics. W. W. Rostow suggested that the study of the problem of economic growth may become a fruitful meeting ground between history and economics. "The study of economic growth," Professor Rostow wrote, "would force historians to theorize about whole societies and economists would be compelled to attempt a thorough analysis of the political, social and cultural forces that affect economic growth.[15] Another indication of the increasing possibilities for collaboration between history and economics, is the readiness of leading economists to acknowledge the existence of widely publicized differences in their discipline over the best ways to attain continued economic growth, the relation of interest rates to inflation, or the best method of preventing economic recesssions or depressions. Basically, economists are obviously at crossroads on the issue of how economic growth is to be maintained. One group argues that maximum growth depends largely upon the incentive system developed and maintained by the private sectors of the nation's economy. Such an encouragement of the incentive system calls for a minimum of government intervention and spending and allows the consuming public to keep most of its income. The other interest rate, governmental subsidies and large welfare programs aimed a great deal of government intervention, through the juggling of the school of economists believes that continued economic growth necessitates at increasing productivity.

---

[14] Ibid., p. 536.
[15] W. W. Rostow, "Economics" in *American History and the Social Sciences*, pp. 25–38.

This basic disagreement in the discipline of economics may well bring historians and economists closer to each other. It seems clear that general economics, with the possible exception of econometrics, cannot make very serious claims as to the reliability of its predictions. What economists, and for that matter, other social scientists can do, is to indicate certain trends which under a specific set of conditions may materialize in the future. Whether the trend will actually materialize or not, depends upon the emergence or the non-emergence of a number of unforeseen and unforeseeable variables. What is even more important, the sharp conflict among several schools of economists points to the inescapable conclusion that the root of the disagreements lies not in purely economic issues, but belongs to the realm of values. As Professor Seymour Harris of Harvard University, put it: "But the major disagreements on welfare programs revolve around non-economic issues. To what extent, for example, should the well-to-do subsidize the relatively underprivileged? Some will hold that old people who are unemployed or without savings deserve their fate, either because they have not worked hard enough or they have not been thrifty." [16] Obviously, these are moral questions which have nothing to do with the findings of an analysis of economic questions by the use of the quantitative empirical method of inquiry. The Medicare program for elderly people and federal programs to fight poverty have had an important effect on the economy of the country, but they must be discussed primarily in moral and humane terms. Disagreements among economists, Harris continued, "arise both in strictly economic analyses and in the application of different value systems to economic problems." [17] On the basis of this acknowledgment, historians who must set for themselves the task of apprising the economic problems in the broad content of the political, social and cultural structure and values, and the economists who are largely concerned with the problem of distribution of limited resources, can find a large area of fruitful cooperation.

Setting aside for a moment the question of whether economics should be taught as a separate subject of instruction or be integrated in the study of history, civics, and government in the general framework of the social studies, the purpose in the teaching of economics is to impart to the students a general economic understanding. Such an economic understanding would give the students a knowledge of the ways in which our society and some other societies manage their productive human and natural resources. The basic scarcity of resources necessitates an understanding of how fully and efficiently they are used and what proportion

---

[16] Seymour E. Harris, "Economics" in *High School Social Studies Perspectives.* Erling Hunt, ed. (Boston: Houghton Mifflin, 1962) p. 7.
[17] Ibid.

these resources are distributed among the many segments of the population. Both in totalitarian and democratic countries, the role of the government in the allocation and use of scarce resources is an important subject of exploration. One economist, Ben W. Lewis, sensibly argues that economic understanding is essential to the survival of our society. "I argue simply," he wrote, "that the demonstrated capacity of our democratic political economy to perform, and hence its capacity to survive, will be substantially affected in the years ahead by the extent to which our people become equipped to face up to public economic issues with an understanding of 'what it's all about' and 'how to get on with the job'." [18] Professor Lewis, who is a member of the National Task Force on Economic Education, which drew up a set of guidelines for the teaching of economics on the high school level, is open-minded on whether these guidelines should be taught as straight economics or be integrated in the study of history and government. If economics is to be taught as part of other courses, he urges that economics be integrated explicitly and imaginatively by competent teachers.

Richard Hofstadter, the foremost writer in American intellectual history has repeatedly acknowledged his debt to social science and especially sociological insights and concepts which in his view, greatly enhance the "speculative richness of history." In his volume, *The Age of Reform: From Bryan to F.D.R.*, which won the Pulitzer Prize, Hofstadter applied relevant aspects of the method of sociological research to the study of Populism and Progressivism. He found such sociological and psychological concepts as status anxiety, self-deceiving image, role, and role playing, alienation and social mobility very useful in tracing the sources of social conflict in the latter part of the nineteenth century and in the better understanding of the character of the leaders of the Populist Rebellion, of the Progressive Movement and of the prominent Muckrakers. The Populists, Hofstadter suggested, failing to understand the true cause of the agricultural depression, projected their animosities and grievances on "alien" forces, Wall Street, New Yorkers, English capitalists and Jewish bankers. The split personality, the paranoic tendencies of many of the Populist leaders became clear when such leaders of the People's (Populist) Party as Thomas Watson and Ben Tillman became bitter Negro haters. As for the Progressive leaders, most of whom came from the clergy, the law and the universities, Hofstadter asserted that their reform crusades were an expression of resentment against the loss of status to the newly rich industrialists and the new breed of politicians representing the grow-

[18] Ben W. Lewis, "Economics" in *The Social Studies and the Social Sciences*, Sponsored by the American Council for Learned Societies and the National Council for the Social Studies, (New York: Harcourt, Brace & World, 1962), p. 115.

ing political strength of ethnic blocs in the big cities. Using a sociological term, Hofstadter spoke of "the status revolution."

Professor Hofstadter is convinced that the modern historian must maintain a close contact with the social sciences primarily because the social sciences have made impressive achievements, developed techniques of inquiry and accumulated a body of substantive findings, intellectual concerns and professional perspectives which can serve to enrich the work of the historian. "Questions associated with social status, social mobility, differences and conflicts between generations, child-rearing in its relation to culture, the sociology of knowledge and of the professions," Hofstadter wrote, "are questions which he [the historian] might properly take upon himself, and which are interwoven with his traditional concerns. It seems inevitable, too, that some of the discoveries made by modern social research about current mass political behavior and political influence will revise some of the historian's assumptions about political behavior of the past." [19] Hofstadter was careful to state that for him these new social science perspectives were useful only as an addition to the traditionally rich and varied methods of historical analysis.

William L. Langer and H. Stuart Hughes seem to be fascinated by the potential contribution of psychoanalysis to history and especially to the field of biography. They agree that historians have, on the whole, ignored what Erik Ericson has defined as "the fateful function of child-hood in the fabric of society." Professor Hughes sees a great affinity be-tween historians and psychoanalysts. "For the historian as for the psycho-analyst," he writes, "an interpretation ranks as satisfactory not by passing some formal scientific tests, but by conveying our inner conviction. For both plural explanations are second nature. . . . Indeed, for both of them the word 'cause' is admissible only if defined with extreme flexibility. . . . For both deal in complex configurations, searching for a thread of inner logic that will tie together an apparent chaos of random words and actions." [20] Hughes suggested that at least some Ph.D. candidates in history should go through the process of psychoanalysis to be prepared to use psychoanalytical insights in their historical investigations.

A number of historians have recently testified to the debt they owed to psychology and psychiatry for the better understanding of the subjects of their inquiries. David Donald has acknowledged the great benefit he derived from frequent consultations with psychiatrists in the course of writing *Charles Sumner and the Coming of the Civil War*. He was

---

19 Richard Hofstadter, "History and the Social Sciences" in *Varieties of History*, Fritz Stern, ed. (Cleveland: World Publishing Co., 1956).

20 H. Stuart Hughes, *History as Art and Science* (New York: Harper-Row, 1964) p. 47.

especially grateful for the psychological insights which led him to a better understanding of Sumner's complex character and especially his puzzling reaction to the assault on him by Congressman Brooks. An important event in the life of another Civil War personality, Lyman Trumbull, is also impossible to answer by the usual mode of historical inquiry. In 1871, Trumbull did all in his power to obtain the nomination for the Presidency of the newly organized Liberal Republican Party. When, however, the nomination was in his grasp, he suddenly, without any explanation, either at the time or subsequently, lost all interest and did practically nothing to assure his nomination at the party's convention in Cincinnati. On the contrary, this able and experienced politician behaved like a bumbling neophyte in politics. [21] The plausible explanation for this enigma can be found in the psychological concept of dual personality which allows for contradictory drives in one human being. Psychology has taught us to accept the bizarre fact that one may idolize Willie Mays and hate all Negroes. Trumbull wanted the nomination because he was ambitious and thought himself well fitted for the White House, but he loathed campaigning and shuddered at addressing large crowds. Thus, his seemingly inexplicable last minute paralysis becomes quite understandable.

The rapprochement between history and the social sciences has become easier because historians are occasionally willing to admit that there are weaknesses in the traditional historical method of investigation of the past. Lee Benson, a University of Pennsylvania historian, has convincingly argued that the use of a classification system, favored by the social sciences, would help to undermine the long-standing dominance of economic determinism in American historiography. "By providing a framework for ordering data in some systematic and logical fashion," Benson wrote, "it brings into focus relationships among empirical data that are not readily apparent." [22] In analyzing the American voting behavior, Benson illustrated the advantages of the classification system. He classed the voting patterns under three main categories, (1) Pursuit of political goals by individuals or groups, (2) Individual or group fulfillment of political roles and, (3) Negative or positive orientation in reference to individuals or groups. The advantage of Benson's approach should be clear to any high school social studies teacher who ever attempted to teach and to make sense from the erratic behavior of American voters.

The tendency of some historians to rely too much on what may be called "footnote evidence" is a cause for legitimate concern. Too often a

---

[21] Mark M. Krug, *Lyman Trumbull: Conservative Radical* (New York: Thomas Yoseloff, 1965).

[22] Lee Benson, "A Tentative Classification for American Voting Behavior," in *Sociology and History*, pp. 415–21.

rather irrelevant footnote reference to a single private letter is used as supportive evidence for a generalization. Take for instance this example chosen from an otherwise superior work of historical research. The author, writing about the later years of William Jennings Bryan, makes the broad statement that the oratorical talents of Bryan in the 1920's had not diminished to any great extent. He wants his reader to believe that the silver-tongued orator from the Platte was as good a speaker in 1920 and in 1925 as he was during his memorable campaign against McKinley in 1896. This indeed is a far-reaching statement. How does he go about proving it? He does it by citing in a footnote a single excerpt from a letter to Bryan written in 1923, by a man who was in his audience. The man wrote: "I shall never forget your speech at Ogden. . . . A Republican sat by my side and made slighting remarks about you and your ideas before you began to speak. He was cold-blooded and cynical. His slurs began to weaken after you had spoken five or ten minutes and inside of twenty minutes you had him cheering lustily and even stamping his feet. I have never heard anything so masterful as that speech." [23] This is a very interesting letter, but it assuredly does not prove the generalization about the unimpaired oratorical powers of William Jennings Bryan in the later 1920's.

Some of the younger historians who acknowledge the importance of the unique and the specific in history, and who reject the idea of predictions in history are nevertheless convinced that the emphasis on detail in historical writing almost wittingly discourages even a limited applicability to the future. Too often, results of historical investigations are presented in such detail and with such dull monotony that even a foundation for a broader analysis is lacking. Martin Duberman complained that, "No bit of information is too small to be worth having when used creatively as part of a larger mosaic, but all too frequently detail is elaborated in vacuo, the dead specifics of past action tirelessly rehearsed for themselves alone, without reference to a broader framework which might rescue them from antiquarianism." [24]

Historians often and with justice complain that the special professional jargon developed by their colleagues in the social sciences makes some of their work incomprehensible to the uninitiated. Social scientists may with equal justice, object to the footnote tedium and dreary detail of many of the historical monographs which appear in the historical scholarly

---

[23] Lawrence W. Levine, *William Jennings Bryan: 1915–1925* (New York: Oxford University Press, 1965), p. 186.

[24] Martin Duberman, "The Limitations of History," *The Antioch Review*, Summer, 1963, p. 286.

journals. Reading some of these contributions to historical research, a bored reader may sometimes also be inclined to ask: "So what?"

No one, however, would either be bored or have any doubts about the great value of Crane Brinton's *The Anatomy of Revolution*. No better example of the best utilization of social science concepts and methodology in history can be found in the historical literature of recent years. Brinton set for himself a deceptively simple task. Being the good historian that he is, he was quite aware of the unique and the specific in the major revolutions in history, but he decided to establish "as the scientist might, certain first approximations of uniformities" in the course of four successful revolutions, the English Revolution of the 1640's, The American Revolution, the French Revolution and the Bolshevik Revolution.[25] The author disclaimed any desire to write a sociology of revolution and cautioned against any attempt to extend his conclusions to all revolutions. He was not ready to predict, on the basis of his study when and where the next revolution would break out.

Brinton found the social science approach which he used in his study a very useful one. Without the use of graphs, charts and statistical correlations, but relying on his superb knowledge of the evidence, and using a common-sense comparative technique, Brinton tested a number of generalizations concerning the four revolutions which he studied. He found some of them wanting and others quite reliable.

One major generalization which Brinton has formulated for himself and which postulated a pattern of uniformity among the leaders of the four revolutions, proved to be unsupportable. The leaders of the Puritan, French, American and Russian Revolutions proved to be a varied lot. Some were aristocrats, others middle class professionals and still others proletarians. "To sum up," Brinton concluded, "it should by now be clear that it takes almost as many kinds of men and women to make a revolution as to make a world." [26] However, a number of "lower" type generalizations were supported by evidence. All revolutions were led by a minority of dedicated leaders who were conscious and very proud of their small numbers. Cromwell was proud of the relatively small number of his Saints and Lenin was exalted by his select group of Bolsheviks. The revolutionary leadership group in all four revolutions was not only small, but it also was fanatically dedicated.

Among the other generalizations which Brinton found valid on the basis of his analysis of the four revolutions were the following:

---

[25] Crane Brinton, *The Anatomy of Revolution* (New York: Random House, 1952), p. 6.

[26] Ibid., p. 126.

a. Revolutions are not started by starving, miserable people. The revolutions under study, came at the time when the respective societies were economically on the upgrade.
b. A mass desertion of the existing regime by intellectuals has preceded all four revolutions.
c. The pre-revolutionary governments were inefficient and unwilling or unable to make the necessary reforms.
d. Many in the ruling group have lost faith in their own ability to govern and have come to lose faith in their own traditions and values.

Crane Brinton's study combined excellent narrative history with a systematic search of patterns of similarity by the use of social science insights and perspectives. It indicated how much promise there is in a meaningful working relationship between the historian and his colleagues in the social sciences.

In an excellent statement on "Sociology and The School Curriculum," Professor Robert Perucci, of Purdue University, wrote:

If the resources of sociology are to be used to help our youth understand the world in which they live, the curriculum must reflect our current knowledge about (1) the nature and importance of individual and social values, (2) how values shape institutions, groups and organizations, (3) how men react with one another through the various positions and roles they assume in groups and organizations, and (4) how the interaction between the individual and society may result either in the preservation of the modification of the values and institutions of society. This article describes these fundamental ideas and relationships. [27]

Perucci maintained that the basic ideas of sociology can be used in the social studies curriculum at all levels, either in separate sociology courses or to enrich the students' understanding of history.

Since anthropology claims an interest in man, his works and his thoughts at all times and in all places, its affinity to history is obvious. Like history, anthropology is interested in all aspects of human life in all places in all times. The differences lie in the points of emphasis and methodology. Anthropology is a study devoted to the scientific understanding of men as a whole through the comparative study of man in particular groups. There are two main branches of anthropology, physical and cultural. Physical anthropology is concerned with the biological origins of man, with the evolution of man from other forms of animal life. Cultural anthropology concentrates on man's behavior in society, both shared and learned.

---

[27]   Robert Perucci, "Sociology and the School Curriculum," in *Social Science Education Consortium Newsletter*, vol. 1, no. 2 (July, 1963).

The essential method of investigation in anthropology is the field study, the collection of data in the field about peoples and cultures and the organization of this data in a systematic way which would aid our understanding of many societies. As we have observed in the previous chapter, cultural anthropologists, intent on the preservation of objectitvity in their studies and guarding against ethnocentric "judgments" of other cultures, have been rigidly careful not to inject subjective value statements in their work. Recently a number of anthropologists have produced highly praised field studies which have not been value-free. Three themes emerge from cultural anthropology, one, the basis in nature of the unity of man, two, the existence of human diversity within the total human pattern and third, the universality of the process of cultural change.

The close ties between history and anthropology stem primarily from the fact that much of the research in anthropology, and especially in physical anthropology and in archeology, which is a branch of cultural anthropology, is as scientific and as artistic as is history. A physical anthropologist and an archeologist, just as an historian, rely on available data and on creative imagination. It would indeed be difficult to term physical anthropology a hard science. It abounds in conjectures and the controversies in which its celebrated practitioners engage are sharp and vocal. Consider for instance these excerpts from a paper on "Human Beginnings" written by one of America's leading physical anthropologists:

... We know virtually nothing about the precise way in which this tool-using and tool-making propensity of man became an established attribute of his ... When and how this primate adjustment to partially upright posture became converted into a fully erect one is still obscure.
... We cannot therefore, assert with confidence that man's ancestors took to ground living because of burgeoning intellectual equipment. [28]

It is clear that the physical anthropologist because of scarcity of data must, like the historian, often rely on his best educated guesses in the formulation of his conclusions. Archeology, which is called pre-history in Europe, is also as scientific and as non-scientific as history. Chemical carbon analysis has been of great help in dating ancient documents, but even this process is not absolutely reliable. Archeologists, for instance, are still locked in a bitter dispute about the exact origin of the Dead Sea Scrolls.

Two important voices have been recently raised which promise a closer relationship between historians and anthropologists. The dean of anthropologists in Great Britain, Professor Evans-Pritchard, has pointed out that anthropology, especially cultural and social anthropology, have come so

---

[28] Harry L. Shapiro, "Human Beginnings" in *Man, Culture and Society,* Harry L. Shapiro, ed. (New York: Oxford University Press, 1956), pp. 4, 5 and 7.

close to history that a complete merger of the two disciplines is within the realm of probability. Both the anthropologist and the historian have become aware that "any event has the characteristics of uniqueness and generality and that in an interpretation of it both have to be given consideration. If the specificity of a fact is lost, the generalization about it becomes so general as to be valueless. On the other hand, events lose much, even all of their meaning, if they are not seen 'as having' some degree of regularity and constancy, as belonging to a certain type of event, all instances of which have many features in common." [29]

Margaret Mead argued recently that there is a special bond between anthropologists and historians, not shared with other scientists and social scientists. While scientists have a single-minded devotion to abstract concepts, generalizations and patterns of similarity which they test by repetitive experimentation, the historian and the anthropologist work with a concrete material, whether this be an ancient document or a tribal initiation ceremony. The loving preservation of the detail, Margaret Mead suggested, is a unique and unifying feature of history and anthropology. Traditionally "historians and anthropologists have been distinguished from one another," Professor Mead wrote, "by the materials which they have studied: the historian dealing with past periods and the anthropologist with primitive peoples. This distinction is fast becoming obsolete, as both are turning their attention to contemporary problems of the great civilizations of the world—including our own.[30] This statement may be a bit overdrawn and would probably be challenged by many practicing members of both disciplines, but it undoubtedly faithfully represents the new trends in both history and anthropology.

How important is this discussion about the relationship of history and the social sciences for the social studies teacher? It is hoped that he will draw several conclusions from this review.

First, the growing affinity between history and the social sciences has become possible, and prospects for a meaningful collaboration have become brighter because historians have become less dogmatic about their refusal to make generalizations and social scientists have generally become wary about exaggerating the value of empiricism in the formulation of broad generalizations. Dr. Gordon W. Allport of Harvard University warned, in an address to the American Psychological Association, against the dangers of "galloping empiricism." [31] Empiricism, objective experimentation and

[29] Quoted in Thomas C. Mendenhall, "Social Studies, History and the Secondary School," *Social Education*, April, 1963, p. 203.

[30] Margaret Mead, "Anthropology," in *American History and the Social Sciences*, pp. 90–91.

[31] *New York Times*, September 7, 1965, p. 28.

analysis he said, "dashes forth like a headless horseman." Too often, Allport complained, social science researchers over-generalize for a limited and specific study. A most vigorous attack on the dogmatic scientism of his own colleagues in political science came from Hans J. Morgenthau of the University of Chicago. In his brilliant volume, *Scientific Man Versus Power Politics*, Morgenthau argues that while scientism has given man a technical mastery over nature, it has failed to answer the most basic questions of human existence. Social science generalizations are only indicative of certain possible trends which materialize only when certain developments and conditions occur. "What can be stated scientifically," Morgenthau writes, "in way of prediction on the basis of a 'social law' is merely that, given certain conditions, a certain social trend is more likely to materialize than are others. . . ." Professor Morgenthau points out that there is a fundamental distinction between natural and social phenomena and problems. Problems in the natural sciences are either solvable at a particular time or they are not. Once solved, they stay solved. This is not true of the social problems. "Social problems," Morgenthau concludes, "such as marriage, education, equality, freedom, authority, peace, are of a different kind. They do not grow out of temporary limitations of knowledge or temporary insufficiencies of technical achievement—both of which can be overcome by the progressive development of theory and practice. They are the result of those conflicts in which selfishness and the lust for power, which are common to all men, involve all men." [32]

Second, historians in an increasing number have become convinced that the use of a social science concept like status, social mobility, consensus, cultural change and alienation can be of great value to a better understanding of a historical event or a personality. This realization holds great promise for social studies teachers in the teaching of United States history, world history or civics and government. The concept of status politics may well make the teaching of basic motives of political behavior more explicable and more interesting. The concept of balance of power as applied, let us say to Europe on the eve of World War I, will make that tangled period more understandable and of more interest to our students.

Third, the increasing complexity of our society and the ever-present danger to its survival, is turning the attention of historians and social scientists to contemporary problems. Richard Hofstadter may have been right when he said that "the next generation may see the development of a somewhat new historical genre, which will be a mixture of traditional history and the social sciences." [33] However, one would be wise to assume

---

[32] Hans L. Morgenthau, *Scientific Man Versus Power Politics* (Chicago: University of Chicago Press, 1965), pp. 136, 215.

[33] Richard Hofstadter, "History and the Social Sciences" in Stern, op. cit., p. 363

that there will still be many genres of historians in the coming generations.

Fourth, historians and the social scientists have come to abandon in an ever increasing measure the sterile, pseudo-scientific approach to values in their investigation. There is an awareness that morally neutral history and valueless social science have weakened the spirit of personal responsibility for the betterment of human society. The practitioners of history and of the social sciences are beginning to appreciate the importance of the moral relevance of their scholarship to a society direly in need of intellectual and ethical guidance. This point has a great bearing on the work of the social studies teacher who is called upon to deal with ever larger numbers of "controversial issues." The only way that he can deal safely and intelligently with these problems is not by refusing to take a stand, but by insisting on high standards in the inquiry stages of any complex problem. Once he is able to establish a reputation for scholarship and scrupulous adherence to free inquiry, his personal position on controversial issues which he should not hesitate to reveal at the last stage of the investigation, will be respected.

What remains to be discussed is the need for caution lest the opportunities for the infusion of social science concepts and methodology in the high school social studies be oversimplified. It is essential to realize that the term *social sciences* is becoming more and more complex. Too many people who should know better, and far too many social studies teachers use the term social sciences as if the boundaries among the social sciences and between the social sciences and the natural sciences were clear and definite. There also prevails a widespread illusion that the scholars in the social sciences are agreed upon a set of concepts and generalizations which are ready and waiting to be used by teachers in their social studies classrooms. It is likewise repeatedly assumed by those who write about the new social studies curricula that each of the social sciences has one particular and generally accepted mode of inquiry which can and should somehow be put to use in social studies instruction. Finally, there is the dangerous, and almost ridiculous assumption, that it is the duty of the high school social studies teacher to "integrate" in his classroom instruction, concepts, insights learnings and methods of inquiry of the social sciences. These are dangerous illusions which have already caused a lot of grief in the field of social studies.

Even our brief review has indicated that there are very considerable differences in the question of concepts, basic aims of the discipline and the methods of inquiry within each of the social science disciplines. There are traditional economists and the econometricians. There are the positivist and behavioristic political scientists who put their faith in quantitative analysis and there are their colleagues who rely on old-fashioned analysis of politics and politicians, and, there is the deepening cleavage between the macro-sociologists and the micro-sociologists. The prospect is that the tremendous accumulation of research and the refinement of many methods of inquiry will even more accentuate the differences and cleavages in each of the social science disciplines. It makes little sense and it is even irresponsible to suggest that a high school teacher should integrate the social sciences when even the scholars in one field have not succeeded in finding and in formulating the integrated principles of their own discipline. In fact, most scholars would agree that such an attempt at integration was impossible of achievement and unnecessary.

Finally, the glib talk about the grandiose plan for the inclusion of the social sciences in the social studies curriculum ignores the fuzziness of the lines of demarcation between the natural and the social sciences. A few examples will suffice to illustrate this point. Many psychologists are convinced that their discipline belongs to the natural sciences. Many physical anthropologists, concerned primarily with the biology of man, look upon themselves as natural scientists, while cultural and social anthropologists just as firmly see themselves as social scientists. In economics, the econometricians see themselves as hard-nosed scientists, unlike their colleagues, the classical economists, whom they consider rather old-fashioned social scientists.

These cautionary injunctions should in no way weaken the determination of social studies teachers to intelligently choose from the social sciences those concepts, insights and modes of inquiry which would help him in more effective instruction of the story of man and toward a better understanding of the human society, cultures and civilizations. The framework for the selective utilization of insights from the social sciences must be determined in view of the needs of high school students and the recognized objectives of the social studies.

History, because of its total concern with human experience and its rather ill-defined boundaries, can and should serve as a common body of knowledge for the other social sciences. Social science concepts and modes of inquiry would add a new and promising dimension to the teaching of history by making all history, as taught on the high school level, conform to Croce's famous statement that all history is contemporary history. A fruitful collaboration between history and the social sciences will bring about a greater motivation, more depth and dynamics in high school social studies.

CHAPTER II

A New Frame
for the Social Studies *

C. ARNOLD ANDERSON

Thoroughgoing reorganization of social studies curricula in American high schools is long overdue. The lag between those courses and the state of knowledge in the parent disciplines is greater than for other parts of the curriculum. The importance of reducing this lag is underlined by the recent advances in the teaching of mathematics and science. The steady widening of national responsibilities abroad and growing disharmonies in national life, such as racial tensions, call for new efforts to increase the social competence of citizens.

It would be stultifying to set out to cope with this challenge by insinuating "junior" social science courses from each of the conventional academic disciplines into secondary time tables. Only myopic specialists who will not face the intricacies of curriculum building could so define the task. Even if the time could be found for a gamut of such specialized courses, that evasive policy would flout the aim of generality that is central to secondary education. It also would make the social studies courses even more unattractive and less manageable for the less-than-brilliant pupils than they are today.

---

* From *The School Review*, vol. 72, no. 4 (Winter, 1964), by permission of The University of Chicago Press and the author.© 1964 by The University of Chicago.

The awesome and diversified assortment of materials now available cannot be covered by any impartial allocation of time to a series of autonomous subjects, however broad the interests or training of teachers. The materials must be compressed to manageable limits. The products of twentieth-century scholarship in both history and the social sciences must be selectively sampled and organized in accordance with novel and cogent rules, as a few venturesome schools—and the better English sixth forms— are already demonstrating.

I would favor retaining for history the key place in the social studies. And there seems no escaping a survey of all human history, even though special attention is given to national history. Broadening conceptions of what history is needed to understand the contemporary world call for new approaches. The crucial components of the invaluable and truly revolutionary output by social scientists of the past generation also must be made available to secondary pupils. These findings doubtless seem bewilderingly heterogeneous to historians: each discipline is a sprawling world of data, conclusions, and unfamiliar concepts, unfairly called jargon. But these findings are relevant to the life of citizens. They are also the foundations for whole new families of professions and technologies.

There is no need to await a new curriculum theory; most such theories rest on shaky foundations and are of debatable utility except to guide us in adjusting materials to pupils' maturity and abilities. A sounder guide to the restructuring of social studies courses will emerge, not from looking at "life," but rather from finding out what the social sciences have to say and the methods on which they rest.

There is a logic implicit in the relationships among these contributing disciplines that will be invaluable in choosing representative topics and appropriate illustrative materials. As distinguished from history, the social sciences are marked by the operation of "analytical abstraction." Each discipline investigates an aspect of social relationships, to explore which it has worked out a guiding conceptual scheme. Each discipline has its appropriate ways of collecting and analyzing data, ways that are rooted in the particular scheme of abstracting from full-bodied reality that is its hallmark. It is no longer acceptable, for example, to tell pupils that economics deals with "how men make a living," for economists do not conceive their concern to be identified with men's subsistence activities. It is equally antiquarian to present sociology as "the study of community life." Only reliance upon modern social science will permit us to bring the social studies up to the new standards set by science teaching.

Nor are pupils' interests a helpful guide to curriculum construction. To aim at preparing children for their later lives by "familiarizing" them with how adults "live" is a platitude that offers no prescription. Few adults perform chemistry experiments, but we teach chemistry to many pupils. Because pupils will marry is insufficient reason to teach homemaking in social studies, and it is doubtful whether "family relationships" courses do much good. The economist is not qualified to teach people how to manage their personal finances. If those kinds of topics are not organized into the extracurriculum they are perhaps most suitably handled by a new breed of counselor. It is the learning that will not be done under the influence of extra-school agencies that should preoccupy the social studies teacher. Appeals to the present concerns and future "interests" of pupils should serve mainly to entice them to come to grips with more fundamental topics, more fundamental in relation to an adequate cognitive map of the world of men. Understanding the basic processes by which society operates should be the aim, and for this purpose we need to turn our backs on the misleading concreteness of the newspaper world. It can be taken for granted that pupils will read newspapers and watch the TV news; they do not need "current events" or subscriptions to *Time*.

The aim of the social studies is not to help pupils "identify" with life. Empathy is an exquisite outcome of education, to which all subjects make their contribution. But it is upon literature and language courses—and hopefully upon a reconstructed art program—that we must rely to give pupils skill in identifying with human nature in varied situations. A besetting temptation in social studies courses is to engage in "slumming," reading about or visiting melodramatic scenes and problem areas. This familiarity has its place, but today it is well inculcated by the mass media. The social studies have the more difficult task of preparing pupils to deal with the normal complexities of the situations facing contemporary societies. The descriptive materials of these courses will play their part in nourishing empathy, but a greater contribution lies in teaching the skills of conceptualizing through which minds are opened to different premises and patterns of action.

It is equally unsuitable to turn a social studies class into an arena for the exchange of personal opinions. Science courses give pupils respect for the objective world that exists apart from and independent of their opinions about it. Lacking an understanding of principles of behavior, debates and the reading of controversial materials for their own sake will downgrade social science. More important is to demonstrate that human actions follow stable patterns, that these are predictable in the large, and that they can be objectively analyzed. The approach to social behavior through specialized disciplines conceals the broad area of agreement among them, for specialists do not write and argue about the core of agreed principles. Values are not more incompatible with knowledge in the social studies than in bacteriology. Pupils need to learn how to obtain data that bear upon human situations and how to select the proper tools to analyze the historical roots and social processes at work with the same ruggedness they display in science courses.

DISTINCTIVE OBSTACLES FOR THE SOCIAL STUDIES

Contemporary events steadily enlarge the number of societies we need to know about, as do the advances in historical scholarship. Both influences are graphically illustrated by the intrusion of African and southeast Asian nations into the headlines and into the policy papers of officials. Meanwhile, time keeps adding to the historian's subject matter, and the projections of social research findings backward make further additions. The recognized interconnections among societies that generate "important" events multiply. The range of societies and topics whose history is important for understanding the world of tomorrow grows accordingly.

If one omits the Hellenistic period from a history course, a major link to our past is obliterated and discussion of later links is crippled. If one ignores some of the small and "unimportant" countries to reduce the material, there is a double loss.[1] One then cannot account for some of the major steps in human progress, and pupils get no comprehension of the singular problems, adjustments, and contributions of the small peoples.

History, in contrast to the sciences, cannot be summarized in compact formulas; it cannot be compressed in newer and better generalizations that render earlier one superfluous. Even in the social sciences we as yet have few generalizations cutting across many areas, as does the inverse square law in physics. Yet the social sciences resemble the physical sciences in having hierarchies of principles. Condensation in social science is more a practical than a theoretic difficulty; such conceptual integration as we possess is difficult to present at the high school level—partly because few have tried it.

The science teacher can confine his attention to the successes of his predecessors, but in the human sciences men's failures are as important as their successes. Moreover, the verbal nature of social science and history materials hinders packing much information into brief compass. Extensive reading is necessary also to exemplify social science generalizations, and insofar as one deals with ethnographic or historical concreteness detailed description is of the essence.

Social processes are largely "invisible," yet pupils must learn to conceptualize these processes in order to "see" them. Few topics can be exemplified by experiments; essential forces cannot be isolated as dramatically as in an experiment on expansion of metals. There are deep emotional resistances to abstracting from human actions, in part because we have not

---

[1] Importance of countries has little meaning when one ceases to define history in political terms.

learned how to teach this skill. Reiteration and description are needed to inculcate generalizations. How illuminate the connection between psychological insecurity and ethnic prejudice? How demonstrate the influence of comparative advantage upon international trade? How trace out the relations of public officials to pressure groups without descending to muckraking?

Though extensive documentation is needed for each principle, pupils have nevertheless to learn that such extensive reading is not like fiction—an illusion widely fostered by literature teachers. Social science analysis often clashes with common sense and with sentimental attachments. The subject matter of the social sciences is the texture of our lives, and interference with accustomed orientations is resisted. For example, expectations for the behavior of modern women are incompatible with patriarchal traditions, but few (even among women) will acquiesce in the demonstration of that incompatibility. For these and related reasons high school teaching of social studies has typically proceeded at too low a level of conceptualization, and in this deficiency may lie an important reason for its poor assimilation by pupils as compared with their learning of physical science.[2]

THREE FRAMEWORKS FOR THE SOCIAL STUDIES CURRICULUM

It is desirable to give explicit and moderately even attention to three perspectives: the temporal, the spatial, and the social.

The Temporal Framework

This perspective will receive principal attention. It is the most familiar one to social studies teachers. Here is where the most drastic condensation of traditional course content is called for in order to assimilate new materials. And it is in this connection that the most creativity will be needed to work out new relationships between history and the social sciences. I would concede history pride of place, or even sole place, were such a choice inescapable—if only because other influences upon children today are so lacking in time depth. But that choice need not be made.

The temporal framework is not solely a preoccupation with sequence. History, as written or taught, does not consist of trends (one of the social scientists's abstractions) but of events clustered and linked in complex patterns. Among the aspects of these patterns, succession is peculiarly

---

[2] There seems also to be a factor of pupil maturity that affects ability to cope with social studies materials; if so, this may constitute a further reason for caution in trying to inject specialized social science courses into the subcollege years. It may not be an unrelated fact that social scientists choose their careers later than natural scientists. Certain traits of personality may be needed to display as much adeptness with social as with physical data. The familiar propensity of the public to interfere with social studies teaching both influences the selection of topics and requires more time and skill in their exposition.

important to be sure, just because of man's reliance upon a social heritage. Especially since the invention of writing, men cannot act significantly without consciously taking account of how their predecessors conducted themselves.[3]

Any event is woven of many threads in a pattern that is never duplicated at any other time or place. Only history, among the social disciplines, is fully sensitive to the uniqueness of the configurations of actions and circumstances: the "accidents" of experience and contact, personal creativity, the intrusions of circumstances. Appreciation of the ways events coalesce and dissolve should be one of the prime aims of the social studies, not to be confused with the collections of named men and dates. It is configuration, even more than singularity, that one thinks of in this connection.

The why of events is not specified by their configuration, however, and is only dimly suggested by their succession. The more that historical accounts are truncated, as they must always be in large measure, the greater the temptation to fall back upon what is virtually mere succession enlivened by factitious melodrama. The missing explanatory element must be supplied from the principles created by the social scientists: the common or general processes whose conjuncture it is the historian's task to elucidate. There are broad patterns of human actions, recognizable recurrences in diverse time-place settings. On the level of individual psychology historians have always relied upon universal processes to explain the motives of their actors. It is the recurrences on the societal level and in group interaction that have been lacking in the history books, as will be spelled out in more detail below.

In the temporal context there is another kind of configuration, however: epochs or interlocked chains of events over long spans of time. Epochs are the acts in one of mankind's dramas. They are characterized by recurrent and congruent kinds of happenings, even by trends. Though epochs are constructs devised by historians, they are not identified arbitrarily. The social scientist also assists in their definition, largely by his delineation of trends and of the transformations in the structures of processes with which he is particularly concerned. Epochs have a more abstract character than do events and to a greater degree they are the constitutive terms by which we seek to bring order into our comprehension of large "time chunks."

Implicit in the temporal perspective are certain methodological con-

---

[3] A particularly impressive analysis of the social implications of literacy is found in J. Goody and I. Watt, "The Consequences of Literacy," *Comparative Studies in Society and History,* 5 (1963): 304–45.

tributions to education over and above the frequently mentioned techniques of document interpretation and the construction of narrative. These methods are no less essential than the "facts" of history and they are adequately taught by no other discipline. Four are selected for comment:

(1) Pupils need to learn something of how past occurrences become items of present knowledge to historians. One reads that Alexander explored India, that the Romans imported wheat from Egypt, that the horse-collar developed in a particular period and locality. Seldom is an attempt made to demonstrate the complex process by which such "facts" have come down to us through time. All "pastness" tends to remain a homogeneous blur; events of two millenia ago have the same cognitive standing in pupils' minds as events in the Cleveland administration. How occurrences came to be recorded, how the record was preserved, disinterred, dated, collated, and interpreted is just as basic training in "learning to learn" as the procedure of a chemistry experiment. The interplay between the presentness of past events and their pastness is a vital part of the human experience.

(2) Only from historians can we procure the chronologies of events, the leads and lags of epochs, the "stages" of great movements, such as gothic architecture, and the simultaneous successions of civilizations. In part this entails learning masses of "mere facts," inescapable in truncated and simplified schemata; substantively this is one of the basic contributions of history. But the management and comprehension of chronologies is an essential methodology. The diverse chronologies used in other civilizations (or imposed by us upon their events) and the methods by which these chronologies are made equivalent need to be explained, together with the history of the emergence and alteration of the frameworks themselves. The combination of this methodology with the simplified plots of the various societies' histories can convey some understanding of contemporaneity and the before-afterness of events. From such knowledge comes that most rare product of historical study: appreciation of anachronism and synchronism.

(3) A third contribution is the demonstration of the nature of epochs. There is a complex logic in the ways historians synthesize events in large time clusters, whether contemporaries were conscious of the wholeness of the periods in which they lived or not. Broad categories of events and interrelated series of changes—such as are dealt with in the separate chapters of textbooks: government, religious life, economy, etc.—comprise the components of these epochs. Equally important is to distinguish the wholeness of an epoch as we now see it from the way it was perceived by the people of that time. In so many ways we know more about the lives of men in past periods than they did because we can see events in the context of the epoch. We evaluate the homogeneity as well as the individuality of

past clusters of events through our perception of the themes pervading the texture of a period; here again the social scientists' assistance in identifying trends is of service. The conception of epochs is helpful also in examining the impingements of societies upon each other. It was not, for example, just that a certain state of affairs existed in India when Europeans intruded; those affairs were part of an Indian epoch and of an English one and the encounter was affected by the natures of those epochs.

(4) Perhaps most important of all, the history teacher needs to guide pupils to an appreciation of the particularity of events. This is several tasks in one. It is not merely that events differ: the constitutional situation for the crowning of Henry VIII differed from that for Elizabeth I. It is especially difficult to show that events are wholes, new weavings of actions and conditions reflecting other things going on at the same time and things that had happened previously or particular aspects of past events. This appreciation is especially important for learning to share the historian's great skill: selective exposition of total situations. One has to learn how singular sequences of happenings converge at a particular time and place to become an interactive whole with its own individuality. There is a delicate balance in this exposition between disguising trends and the social scientists' processes as specific events and telling a story wherein all the basic questions of causation are evaded. History is not mythology nor is its study a memorization of beads on the string of time. To expose how chains of causation are built up and dissolved by new chains of causes requires drawing upon the principles that it is the social scientists' task to create. For the elements in an event are also parts of the various subsystems of relationships in a society. The teachers may emphasize how agricultural depression weakened the feudal lords in the face of royal ambition, but that depression is also part of an economic nexus just as the tension between king and lords was part of a political system that had its own dynamics quite apart from any economic circumstances. Paradoxically, careful attention to the particularity of events offers the opportunity for giving full attention to the patterns of social relationships underlying the events.

The Spatial Framework

This is the most difficult of the three frameworks to clarify. The difficulty arises in large degree from the fact that for a generation geography has played little part in the education of scholars. The relationships between geographers and other social scientists have become not only aloof but even hostile due to the timeworn battles about "geographical influences." Meanwhile, newer and more analytical work in "spatial science" is little known.[4]

---

[4] See W. Bunge, *Theoretical Geography* (Lund: Gleerup, 1962).

A more mundane difficulty arises, however, from the fact that the content of "geography" is indefinitely expansible in descriptive terms, as is that of history. In the schools, too, a common tendency persists to use geography as a skeleton on which to hang materials more suitably dealt with by other disciplines such as economics or sociology. Textbooks commonly exemplify the assumption that anything happening in a locality should be included in the geographer's description of that locality.

Basic to any reliance upon a spatial framework as one of the organizing principles for the social studies is a firm grounding in the locational coordinate system, illustrated on the simplest level by the grid of longitude and latitude. Familiarity with the named places that have been the scenes of human history and that recur in today's headlines is as essential as familiarity with the major plots in human history. Placement of the political units of the world and their correlation with the major cultural areas and with the gross physical map are elementary literacy.

It is important also to teach the nomenclature of the physical world, the rudiments of landforms, and the associated logic of physical geography and its dependence upon alternative methods of transportation. It is more difficult to present the implications of locality features, for example, the constraints of a locality upon communication or settlement patterns. Adeptness in these matters might be regarded as parallel to skill in recognizing anachronisms in history.[5]

Beyond the vocabulary and grammar of world geography, that discipline has a special contribution to make by its stress on the particularities of physical and cultural landscapes. Each landscape has its individuality, in which lies an importance transcending the outmoded preoccupation with geographical influences. Unique combinations of location and physical features and man-made transformations in them contribute to the events that lie at the center of the historians' attention. By focusing upon the logic of cultural landscapes, it is easier to avoid the temptation to make encyclopedic surveys of life here, there, or elsewhere. Moreover, the creation of cultural landscapes and the systematic spatial patterning of social relationships are bound up with the social processes that are the concern of the generalizing social sciences, economics for example.

In recent years there has developed a new convergence between geography and the other social sciences, resting upon new mathematical techniques. The content of this new "spatial science" embodies and extends the older human ecology and major aspects of economics. This new discipline exemplifies a generalizing rather than an individualizing approach

---

[5] S. Mitsuhashi, "Conceptions and Images of the Physical World," *Comparative Education Review*, 6 (1962): 142–47.

to geograhic and related phenomena. It stresses the spatial patterning of human affairs: processes of communication and infusion, hierarchical relationships among communities, and ordered patterns within and between cultural landscapes.

The Social Framework

This approach can be summed up in four broad themes, each with several corollaries.

(1) The most basic characteristic of man as a social being is that he lives by his social heritage rather than being predetermined in action by biological heredity. This is, of course, the prime reason for including history in the curriculum, apart from the esthetic values to be satisfied by its study. From this characteristic arises the uniqueness of the cultures that men build, which is a reason to give special attention to our own heritage as distinct from that of other peoples. It follows that summary generalizations will not substitute for acquaintance with other cultures though the generalizations are no less important than such ethnographic familiarity. In practice only representatives of the world's many cultures can be given attention but this attention should not be limited to those cultures upon which our own has primarily been based.

(2) Besides being the creature who must learn how to act, man displays "conduct" in his modes of acting: values are the fundamental determinants of human activity. This is to say much more than that behavior is guided by custom. It presupposes a more "intellectual" conception of behavior, and it offers an occasion to concern ourselves with the great intellectual and religious systems of mankind. For those teachers who fear that the social sciences are so scientific that they leave out "values," this is an entry point for historical data on the continuity of the great institutional structures of values: churches, law, social movements, or currents of ideas.

(3) There are certain requisites for societal existence. The patterns of human behavior are at bottom responses to universal necessities arising from the life of society. Social life presupposes control over nature through cooperative activities for subsistence, control over individual impulses and group conflicts for the sake of social order, protection against the psychological anxieties of existence, procedures for decision-making and authority, and so on. Satisfying these requisites gives rise to the structural and procedural universals in human existence, from the study of which we derive the analytical principles for understanding human society. These requisites are the "handles" with which the specialized social sciences take hold of their data; their discussion offers avenues for introducing social science generalizations and methods into the curriculum.

(4)   For the social sciences, in contrast to history, it is less the uniqueness of cultures than the commonality of processes by which they are built, maintained, and changed that is important.[6] Interaction between individuals and groups is patterned; human relationships have just as definite a structure as a crystal does. It is these orderly patterns, recurring in essentials in all societies, that form the solid foundations for human existence and are the mold within which "events" take shape. Much of human history indeed is repetition unless one defines history as what does not repeat. Though the penchant for thinking in terms of instincts is less common among today's pupils, that social behavior is something more than "customs vary" is a more subtle idea. It is difficult to teach children that interaction is patterned. Yet starting from the idea of values controlling action it is not too difficult to take up the processes of acquiring and changing social roles. The next step to principles of social stratification and "organization theory" is more difficult, especially when one tries to include some ideas from economics about market processes, incidence of costs and benefits, and marginal analysis. Still more difficult is the next step to demonstrations of the integrative factors in groups and societies; here economics concepts are again essential: conflict generation and resolution, group accommodation, etc. Links back to the first point mentioned in this section can be developed by stressing the role of diffusion in human history. And though diffusion is most easily demonstrated in connection with material traits, it can be exemplified also in many examples from social behavior ranging from the diffusion of ceremonies (as Christian rites) to electoral practices or Roman conceptions of authority.

There are numerous interconnections of topics, interest in which is shared by historians and at least some of the social sciences. It is not suggested that all these topics, as listed here, would be suitable for secondary school classrooms, but they offer clues for those who plan new courses to ways in which integration can be fostered. Thus, the counterpoint of stability and change relates to geographic space, social space, social trends, and historic time. Interdependencies of social structures are of central concern not only to historians but also to specialists in spatial science, economics, political science, anthropology, or sociology. The interplay of value attitudes and decision processes can be dealt with from any of several viewpoints and with diverse illustrative material.

The sociologist's or anthropologist's knowledge of behavior patterning contributes to the economist's understanding of constraints on decisions and

---

[6] Suitable materials for demonstrating this approach are readily available. Today we can play down the examples from primitive societies, for such information has become widely familiar. Integration with history will be easier if illustrations are chosen from "historical" societies.

of preference functions. The economist shares with other social scientists an interest in flow of human behavior, growth curves, and decision theory. Certainly work on decision theory should throw new light on some familiar historical puzzles, such as dynastic policy. Geographers, historians, and all the social scientists must reckon with the influence of diffusion upon processes of change and development.[7]

Each of the social sciences has developed a distinctive way to identify the data it can work with, standardized procedures for collecting those data and for making them answer the questions posed. Each has its "grammar" of concepts for organizing and explaining the data. It is entirely feasible to give pupils practice in data collection, including instruction in the logic of sampling; working such practice into lesson plans has become easier since historians have begun to use some of the same techniques. It is possible also to teach pupils something of how social scientists use their analytical abstractions, distinguishing from the historian's way of going about his tasks. A historical account can be shortened and simplified by omissions and telescoping; yet the thread of the story remains intact and meaningful. It is assumed that the story would not be changed in basic plot but only in detail by including more facts and by "thickening" the exposition. Social scientists simplify the world they deal with in a different way. They do not prepare a précis; rather they use lenses of different colors with which to look at human actions. Each specialist scrutinizes only threads of a certain color in the "seamless web," but what he sees is a meaningful configuration. As a "lens" he uses a particular principle of abstraction to view that "aspect" of conduct he has been trained to understand. An economist observes the processes by which groups allocate their scarce resources among alternatives to maximize certain desired outcomes. The sociologist focuses on recurrent social relationships: for example, domination in an army, in a factory, in a boys' gang. Even with all the talk about integrating the social sciences, one seldom has difficulty in identifying an author as economist or sociologist by recognizing the system of conceptual abstractions he employs.

Suggested Ways of Selecting Historical Materials

It is frivolous to ask whether high school pupils should study ancient or modern history, that of Latin America or the Far East. Both present-day events and their historical roots in all parts of the world now play their part in American lives. These are not novel intrusions from an outer world but a progressively closer linking of histories that never were as independent

---

[7] No special attention is given here to psychology; part of that field is treated in biology and part in various sections of social studies, not to mention the (perhaps heretical) discussions in literature courses.

as we pretended to believe. Not only contemporary African politics but African history deserves its place in the curriculum. It is not mainly the contemporary revolution in China that demands attention but the epoch in Chinese history that is giving a particular pattern to the heightened interaction. As a few professional historians are so belatedly demonstrating, we must try to deal with world history, not just a composite of histories of various parts of the world. So comprehensive a set of historical materials can be dealt with, however, only by recourse to a drastic but carefully structured selection. In the organizing of historical materials for such new courses, the social scientists can be of some help.

Neither "societies" nor their histories interact. It is economic, political, and cultural relationships between various segments and agents of societies that link together area and national histories. The identification of these relationships and their analysis within their respective disciplinary frameworks can help to guide the historians in their own selection and organizing of materials. This is, after all, one implication of teaching "social" history: the religious, as well as the economic and political, history of nineteenth-century Europe underlies the emergence of Africa onto the center of the stage today.

The need for a broader approach can be illustrated by contrasting the various "histories" offered to the conscientious reader. If one reads a standard history of the Western world, then reads Linton's *Tree of Culture*, and then the Oxford history of technology he quickly perceives that the pictures presented have almost no congruence and few points of contact. If he perseveres to read a legal history, a history of political thought, and a history of art he will be further convinced that "history" is at most partial and, as normally taught, an illusory affair. The treatment of Greece, for example, in Linton and in the history of technology gives an impression of relating quite a different society than the one we have become familiar with. But the sweep of the cultural history portrayed by Linton would seem to be the necessary foundation for other accounts and, from our present position, to leave out technological history is to exaggerate the distinctiveness of our own epoch.

It should be possible to relate these several kinds of history. Moreover, one of the advantages of giving more attention to cultural history (in Linton's sense) and to technological history is the opportunity supplied for demonstrating the persisting and recurrent interconnections of societies. The flow of cultural influences is one of the main themes in any approximation to world history. It is equally possible to link in other great themes: the emergence of science, great social movements, major ideologies. As the strictly historical part of the curriculum is broadened in such ways, the hitherto predominant political themes take on new depth. And the possibilities to bring in the analysis of type situations favored by the social scientist become more numerous.

However broadly we look at the history of mankind and no matter how much assistance the social sciences offer, the historian cannot be relieved from the task of teaching the main plots or themes of the major parts of mankind. In American schools, doubtless, treatment of sixteenth-century Chinese history will be more schematic than for sixteenth-century English history. Teaching will be more schematic for periods when "less happened," though this distinction raises difficult problems in measuring the rate of social change that have been barely touched by sociologists. But it would be irresponsible to linger over trivialities of American history while ignoring sweeping transformations of civilization in the Far East. To take account of the shifting foci of salient events is desirable. But to balance topics from one and another society's history of mankind calls for a nice judgment. There has to be a drastic condensation of the materials pupils must read: mainly we must present landscapes, not etchings.

There would seem to be no escape from relying upon handbooks and paperback condensations of the scholar's library. We can imitate some of the compact manuals so favored in European schools and we can build out the tables of parallel chronology into compact handbooks. Historians possess the expository skill to prepare adequate summaries to serve as the backbone of new social studies courses, without affronting the dignity of history teachers.

As was made clear earlier in discussing "the temporal framework" one aim in the present discussion is to make it possible for the historians to bring their special techniques and insights to pupils in a more persuasive manner. Any suggestion that the condensed historical summaries proposed above would be only rags and tatters of history is rejected. Such condensed history is a necessary body of knowledge for pupils today, but it is also the foundation on which detailed historical analysis can rest.

In building the strictly historical part of the curriculum, it is feasible to concentrate attention—apart from the broad overview—upon certain kinds of historical situations or cases, with particular attention also to comparisons and contrasts. Only a few examples are given; many pages could be devoted to extending the list and justifying the choices, but here the principle of selection is of main concern.

Selected examples of the diffusion of technology would have particular appeal to contemporary pupils. It would be easy to choose examples of important migrations of peoples. The process by which major cultural centers rose and were displaced can be documented from many fresh scholarly studies. The dynamic interrelationships among economic centers would offer many similarities and differences to the previous topic. The spread of religious or political ideologies calls for similar techniques but different sorts of data. The rise of new social classes in turn taps still a different kind of data. The transformation of a family system under the influence of urbanization or industrialization brings the historian into closer touch with his social science colleagues. Or one might focus upon the process by which a society polarizes into a state of civil war, the emergence of a nation-state, the outbreak of multi-party warfare. Innumerable examples of the impact of civilized upon simpler peoples come to mind. Alternatively, one could deal with the seventeenth-century English and nineteenth-century American civil wars, various examples of revolution, or a comparison of Roman expansion with European intrusion into Africa. The rise of industry in southern New England can be compared with the shift of industry to the English midlands. Episodes in ancient Greek history can be compared with contemporary political disturbances. Such examples offer opportunities to examine events in different civilizations.

These kinds of topics also facilitate drawing social science materials into the social studies courses. According to the cases chosen, the principal auxiliary discipline would be economics or political science or sociology, but always in close association with history. Devoting a part of the course to such analyses has two special advantages. It offers a logical opportunity, as mentioned, for linking social science analysis with history. Since treatment of these cases would be intensive and draw upon more than one discipline, the number of topics would be few, but those chosen can reflect the special interest or competence of the teachers. The second advantage is that it would be possible to exemplify at the same time those special techniques and insights of the historian discussed earlier.

The argument for integrating materials from the social sciences with materials from history, rather than merely adjoining bits and pieces from these subjects, may merit further elaboration. In essence I am arguing for building social science analysis into event analysis. The usual historical account, when dealing with events more complex than those of personal actions supplies few explanations. Yet sound explanations for complex events must draw upon the generalizations of the social scientist. Especially in textbooks, historians' explanations tend to be *ad hoc* and commonplace; often this suffices because the writer was not trying to look at the "processes" that are the main concern of social science. By the same token the historian is commonly superficial, perhaps at times counterbalanced by the social scientists' irrelevancy. But as historians try to deal with more complex sets of materials they are tending to borrow the social scientists' methods; explanations become more general and less limited to statements of "what happened." In turn social scientists have been learning, or relearning, to appreciate the value of historians' work as sources of data. Events happen because individuals or groups act in response to the forces it is the business of economist or sociologist or some other colleague to explain, but the conjuncture of these forces calls for an interpretative technique in which the historian is a specialist. The historian remains superficial in analyzing events transcending personal relationships unless he relies upon general principles of human interaction; the creative historian weaves these principles into his explanation. The pedagogic problem is to integrate these several sources of explanation into lessons suited to given types of pupils. The aim is to teach why things happen as well as to recount what happened. A high order of constructive skills is called for to provide both a broad overview of human history and detailed explanation of selected episodes or situations.

It is from respect for the unique contribution of history to education that this brief for new patterns of integration between history and social science is being set forth. We can ignore the social sciences in secondary schools no more than we can ignore the physical sciences. Given the emerging struggle among professional disciplines and the increasingly instrumental approach to curriculum building, unless historians play their part in inventing new kinds of social studies courses the rapid recession of history in those curricula can be predicted confidently.

The proposed integration is feasible though its achievement will be difficult. Its achievement, even though not in the particular format proposed here, would constitute a breakthrough in this sector of secondary education. In this reorganization the historian must carry a major share of the task and the responsibility, even though the portion of time given to his materials will diminish. He has the task of summarizing human history. He must show that men always live in particular situations, not at the center of a field of abstract forces, that events and periods have wholeness as well as particularity. And he can play a leading part in selecting those topics for intensive analysis in which the contributions of social scientists can be of greatest utility. He will, however, have to cease trying to be a specialist in American or British history and become a teacher of world history. He will have to make a greater display of his knowledge of historical method and logic. It is to be hoped that he will invite the social scientist into collaboration, for if the latter must force his way into the classroom the schools and pupils will be the losers.

There is no blinking the fact that any serious reorganization of social studies curricula is going to involve a painful reorientation of the teachers. New kinds and levels of competence will be needed. But there is much to be said for undertaking the development of a new kind of teacher along with new kinds of sources.

A no less painful realignment of the relationships among the social science professional bodies will be called for. Those relationships are commonly either hostile or aloof. The teachers in the secondary schools and the administrators should make every effort to insist that the various professional groups face up to the problems of the schools rather than functioning as lobbyists for intellectual vested interests.

PART II

Disciplinary Approaches

CHAPTER III

Anthropology

1   MALCOLM COLLIER AND EDWIN S. DETHLEFSEN *

Anthropology in the Pre-Collegiate Curriculum

College and university people often think of secondary curricula as watered-down college courses. Some express a related concern that studying a subject in high school somehow takes the edge off the "real thing," which the student should first encounter in college. According to this view, economics taught in high school would satiate rather than whet a student's interest in that discipline. There are certainly shortcomings in secondary school studies, but these are not among them. The real threat is that traditional secondary school social studies courses may blunt forever the student's interest in social data through sheer boredom produced by inept and inadequate exposure to the social sciences rather than too little or too much.

It is our observation that high school students consistently rate social studies low on their scale of interests. Among the factors responsible for low interest are the remoteness and unreality of the social data presented, the passiveness and non-involvement of the students with the data, and the methods used in covering the data. Conventional social studies courses present masses of facts with few glimpses of the theoretical principles needed to understand them. We believe the social sciences can and should

* Malcolm Collier is Director of the Anthropology Curriculum Study Project, Chicago, Ill.; Edwin Dethlefsen is a writer and consultant for that Project, and Unit Director for "The Study of Early Man." ACSP is supported by the National Science Foundation, and sponsored by the American Anthropological Association.

The article is based on material prepared in 1965 as part of an experimental course, "The Study of Early Man," published in *Human Organization*, vol. 27. no. 1 (Spring 1968). Reprinted by permission of the authors and the journal.

provide secondary social studies curricula with the needed conceptual framework.

Whether or not the social sciences can indeed bring enduring light and interest to the high school curriculum remains to be seen, but present attempts in this direction show promise. Curriculum improvement projects in geography, sociology, economics, political science, and anthropology have been under way for several years. In varying degrees these efforts are made on the assumption that there are disciplined ways of looking at social data and that high school students are capable of comprehending and using them profitably in studies of human history and human behavior. Certainly the Anthropology Curriculum Study Project has assumed that anthropology can contribute to high school studies both in content and in pedagogy. It has further assumed that:

If high school education marks, for the moment, the minimal education we expect of all citizens, then it must be said that the capacity to think systematically about man's nature, his many societies, the whole career of his species, has not been included in our definition of the educated citizen. Knowledge of man produced by the disciplined researches of social scientists has not been generally available to public school students. The high school graduate who has been taught to expect regularities in the affairs of the physical universe will never have heard of the search for regularities in the affairs of men. But the schools seem to be on the threshold of offering access to such understandings, ready in effect to *democratize a social scientific comprehension of man.* It will be in the context of such a development that Anthropology may find a role in the schools.[1]

The development of this contribution involves four steps: (1) Selection of some of the most significant topics from the rich mass of anthropological information and understanding; (2) Identification of the specific relevance of each topic to the high school student's own experience with the world; (3) Isolation of the essential aspects of each topic; and (4) Development of methods for helping the student grasp and use the data and concepts needed to understand the selected topic.

The materials which follow illustrate the four points. They are taken from the 1965 version of "The Study of Early Man" teaching materials developed by the Project. The total unit, which is about eight weeks long, is designed for ninth or tenth grade students. It includes readings and activities regarding race that occupy several days within the larger sequence.

It can be argued that adults should know something about race formation and classification. The criteria by which most adults identify the

---

[1]   Robert G. Hanvey, "Anthropology in the Schools," *Educational Leadership,* 22, no. 5 (February, 1965): 313.

peoples of the world and classify them into national or racial groups are unclear and implicit where it is most important that they be clear and explicit. Development of this topic begins with an effort to have the students make explicit what they already know or believe about race. This is done in order to establish a baseline of present knowledge (or lack of it) from which they can work toward new understandings. The teacher is given specially prepared materials to supplement his own information and to help him guide students through the related lessons. We present the following excerpts from the experimental teacher's guide as an example of the level and depth at which an anthropological topic may be approached in a high school social studies class.

SAMPLE PAGES FROM "THE STUDY OF EARLY MAN" UNIT [2]

(The example begins with a brief exposition on race to provide a frame of reference to the teacher.)

Race is not an easy term to define, particularly in the case of our own species. Biologists use it more or less interchangeably with subspecies when they are talking about other animals or plants. There may be some plausibility in referring to Hottentots, Eskimos, Pygmies, Ainu, or a few other more or less reproductively isolated human populations as races in the biological sense of the term. They may indeed have considerable with-group uniformity with respect to the physical characteristics by which we may attempt to distinguish them.

But the great numbers of men and their mobility render the present concept of the human group as divisible into races as useless except for the specialist interested in studying human adaptations and evolutionary prehistory. The specialist knows that wherever large human populations occur there has been so much genetic mixture that variation is too great for racial descriptions to have any real meaning, except in a purely statistical sense. What are observed are the tag ends of environmental adaptations, many of which may be shared by quite unrelated peoples who simply have existed in similar environments for very long periods of time.

In the last few thousands of years men have so learned to control their environments that at present almost anyone can live almost anywhere with little or no naturally selective disadvantage. The result is that the greater proportion of the world's peoples have so mingled their genes that populations can be differentiated only by gene frequencies that compare proportions of populations exhibiting a given trait. . . . The concept of race, under such circumstances, cannot intelligently be applied to individuals. . . .

---

[2] Teaching Plan, "The Study of Early Man," ACSP 1965 Experimental Version, pp. 68–74.

One need remember ... that not only is it practically impossible to describe a "typical" member of a race but that there are untold numbers of people who defy such categorization.

Furthermore, one can easily become too arbitrary about his bases for racial classification of individuals. It is easy to say that a man with "slanty eyes" is a "Mongoloid." But if three of his four grandparents were, in fact, "Caucasoid," and "slanty eyes" happened to be one of the few traits inherited from the fourth, such a categorization is scientifically ridiculous and philosophically without rationale.... Defining such a race socially is, of course, a different and much simpler matter. The membership of any "race" is defined by those people who claim membership in it.

Human races are hardly valid as biological units, being so arbitrarily based, but the term is probably with us to stay, despite the protestations of scientists and humanitarians, so it behooves us to develop sufficient understanding of its "meaning" (and the problems of its definition) to talk about it intelligently. This is an area of knowledge/folklore where, for the moment at least, a lack of assurance may be a good thing; so one of the main purposes of the following suggestions is to make students a little more conscious of the difficulties involved in defining the term.

Although the following suggestions are given by "days," there is more than can be done in the time allowed. What to condense or leave out must be a matter of judgment in context—what do you want to emphasize that ties in with later sections of the unit or ties up earlier ones? As a last resort some exercises can be described rather than performed. Discussion of some readings can be handled more speedily by means of worksheets, and you will no doubt see a number of instances where points can be made with less ado.

Before the first session, give the students the following list of questions. Answers may be written and handed in the next day (Day 1):

How many races are there?
How can you tell them apart?
What is a race?
Of what race are you? How do you know?

Day 1.—(Assignments are collected and the class listens to a tape in which other youngsters attempt to answer the first three questions above and to identify by race the photographs of four people. The class looks at the photos while listening. The class attempts to identify the people in the photos after hearing the variety of identifications on the tape, and are asked what criteria they are using. They then are asked to differentiate between physical and cultural criteria.)

Work with the class to construct a chart of the "major races" on the blackboard. Elicit agreement as to ". . . what we shall consider for the time being to be the major races," and list them down one side. Across the top list the physical traits which will be referred to for "distinguishing characteristics," calling upon the class for the terms, but making sure some continuous variables are included, such as skin color, eyes, lips, nose, etc. Draw lines to make boxes in which will be placed the appropriate objectives When the chart is finished, it should bear some resemblance to this:

	Skin	Lips	Hair	Form	Nose	"X"	"Y"
"White"	white						
"Oriental"	yellow	thin	straight				
"Negroid"	brown	thick	kinky		flat		
etc.	etc.	etc.	etc.				

In helping to construct the chart be relatively uncritical of students' choices, but demand that the adjectives be reasonably specific. Sooner or later, the students should themselves remark, "But some 'whites' have kinky hair," or make similar comments. At this point you should begin to ask for other exceptions, e.g., "Do all Negroes have thick lips?" and so on. After a while it will be clear that the chart needs revision. Some of the adjectives will need to be changed from specific to more inclusive. . . . Don't be dismayed if the whole activity begins to bog down in disagreement—this is what should happen. If the class is too agreeable, press them with questions using combinations of characteristics—"Do all 'whites' have white skin, thin lips, wavy hair, straight noses . . .?" "What about the 'new race' of Hawaiians?" (This is a cross among Japanese, Chinese, occidentals, and natives.) "How long have races been mixing?" "Is the American Negro different?" But it is not yet time for conclusions.

Having students prepared with pencils and paper, begin to show the set of slides of peoples of the world.[3] Refer to the slides only by number, asking that the students name from the chart the race of each person shown. (If there are no more than three races on the chart, let students locate the people geographically, rather than "race" them.) They should write their conclusions beside the corresponding slide number. Show the 23 full-face views only. When the slides have been shown, discuss what the students have written to see the extent of disagreement. Show the pictures (slides) again, this time the 23 profile views. See how many instances of mind-changing have occurred and how much disagreement there is now.

---

[3]   The complete set includes 23 full-face and 23 profile views of young adults from all continents, from all over the world. The pictures cannot be reproduced here but are easy to imagine—standard "peoples of the world" but wearing modern "Western" clothes.

Now tell the class where each of the slide people came from, emphasizing that the examples were chosen at random, not for the purpose of fooling students. Exhibit the "tape" photos again and tell where these people live.

Discussion: Egypt is part of the UAR. Are Egyptians "Whites," "Negroes," or what? If "Negroes" (or whatever), do they fit all the adjectives in the chart? Apply similar questions to other people shown, reviewing slides as necessary.

For homework, read "Genetic and Environmental Influences on Body Measurements," from *The Human Species*, by F. S. Hulse.[4]

Day 2.—Discuss the homework reading from the standpoint of the influence of environment and genetics on some of the factors listed on the chart. Nose shape is, for example, illustrated and discussed in the reading, as are body form, stature and weight. Get the class to try to elaborate on the environmental reasons for these "racial" differences, and to speculate on some of the others.

Referring again to the homemade race chart, you should begin to bring out the point that many of the characteristics listed, such as skin color, represent continuous variables—that is why it is so difficult to draw a line between two races, if a single characteristic of this sort is used. A light "Negro" may be considerably lighter than a dark "white."

Let the class think of themselves as a population, and measure the frequency and range of some continuously variable characteristic. Height is probably easiest to measure though skin color may be more interesting and fun to chart, provided there are not individual students whose extreme position in the range might embarrass them too much. The latter can be measured by means of a good photographic light meter held no more than three inches from the inside (lightest part) of the forearm, about three inches below the point of the ulna (inside point of the elbow). Be careful that the light source is always the same distance from the spot measured and that its angle and that of the light meter are constant with respect to each skin surface measured. Using an arbitrarily chosen meter range, chart the distribution of skin shades in the class. (See below for the "point.")

If a good meter cannot be obtained, or if for any reason the measurement of skin shade is impracticable, measure stature instead. This is best done with the student standing against a smooth, vertical surface to which a yardstick has been attached vertically, its lower end forty inches from the floor. If possible, have the students remove shoes and stand with back to wall, straining erect but on flat feet with shoulders back and chin tucked

---

4 [Frederick S. Hulse (New York: Random House, 1963).]

in. Using a cigar box or small pasteboard box hold it flush against wall and ruler, and bring it down to top of student's head for a reading. This should be done firmly so as to eliminate the effect of high hairdos. Then add forty inches to the reading on the yardstick and write each height on a 3 × 5 card. Boys' cards should be a different color from girls'.

In a vertical column on the bulletin board list intervals of two inches (or three, if you have less than twenty students) from the lowest to the highest heights recorded. Attach the cards in horizontal rows by the interval in which each card falls. Rows near center of range will be longest and, if class is large enough, there will be a fairly even distribution of cards above and below this mode. (If the boys are of an age to be well into their adolescent growth spurt, the distribution may be bimodal, with a different distribution for girls. If not, or if there are very tall girls or very short boys, it may be best not to use separately colored cards to avoid embarrassment for them.) There will be relatively few cards near the extremes of the height range.

Conclusions to be reached:
1. In any population there is a range of variation with respect to any variable characteristic.
2. Most individuals are more or less "average," but a description of the "average" does not truly describe the whole population.

Discuss height and hair color as a combination, or if you charted skin shade, combine this with height. Do these variables vary together?

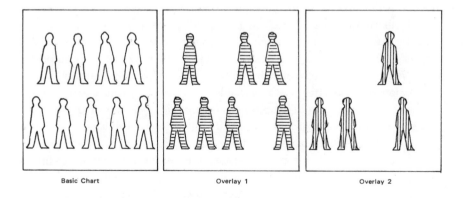

| Basic Chart | Overlay 1 | Overlay 2 |

FIGURE 1. Overhead Transparency No. 11.

Conclusion: Persons who are "average" in one respect may be quite extreme in another. Refer back to the race chart and discuss it critically in the light of the above conclusions.

For homework, read "Biological Adaptations to Culture," from *The Human Species*, by F. S. Hulse.

Day 3.—Using the Population OHT # 11 (Overhead Transparency # 11 consists of a basic chart and two overlays. In the original, the basic chart shows four rows of six figures each. Each overlay represents a particular characteristic, and when superimposed on the basic chart, the proportion of that characteristic in the total population appears.) pound home the point made that traits in a population vary independently of one another. . . . If horizontal lining (Overlay 1) is "typical" of this population, that does not signify that all members in good standing have horizontal lines. If vertical lines (Overlay 2) are also "typical" this means neither that those with horizontal lines also have vertical lines nor that those without horizontal lines lack vertical lines.

Conclusion: While it may be possible to describe particular races for some purposes, the descriptions must be understood to apply only to populations, not to their members as individuals.

While the Amerind "race" is indeed "typified" by presence of Diego antigen, it is nevertheless a fact that many Amerinds lack this trait. Similarly, while the Alpine "race" is characterizable as blond, it contains a great many brunettes . . . and so on.

Use OHT # 2 (Overhead Transparency # 2 is a map of Europe zoned and color-coded to show percentage of light eyes in the population: (100-90), (90-80), (80-70), etc.) to make the point that races, if they must be defined, are best defined on the basis of *trait frequency*. This eliminates the problem of racial categorization of individuals. We can characterize the Northern European "race" as having 50 percent or more light eyes, and the African "race" as having 49 percent or less of light eyes. With respect to this one trait any individual could be either a Northern European or an African, for there would be no way of telling which; but any given population is immediately distinguishable as not Northern European or not African. (One might add parenthetically that it is usually a good deal easier to say who is not of a given race than it is to say who is.)

Discussion: What are some of the causes of these "racial" differences? It should be brought out here that, as seen in the homework reading, cultural factors are very much involved.

Distribute the matrimonial ads of the *Bombay Times* (see below) and have the students discover some of these cultural influences. It might be fun to discuss mating preference in our own society.

MATRIMONIAL

MATRIMONIAL CORRESPONDENCE invited for Matriculate Punjabi Khatri girl, 21, beautiful, slim, well-versed in household. Decent marriage. Apply Box 23032 The Times of India, Bombay 1. A38144 (X)

MATRIMONIAL CORRESPONDENCE is invited from well settled boys for a fair Kerala Brahmin girl of 21, studied up to Matric. Please reply to Box 23948 The Times of India, Bombay 1. A39072 (X)

PARENTS OF EDUCATED AND DOMESTICALLY TRAINED Parsee girl, aged 22, invite matrimonial correspondence from well placed Parsee bachelors of respectable family. Write in details Box 23376, The Times of India, Bombay 1. A38466 (X)

PARENTS OF CUTCHI SWETAMBER Murtipujak Jain civil engineer, aged 26, invite matrimonial proposals from parents of healthy educated Gujarati girl, Jan Bania preferred. Early marriage. Please reply with particulars. Box 2292 The Times of India, Bombay 1. A38036 (X)

RESPECTABLE, WELL PLACED Christian gentleman, 40, employed in reputed foreign firm, seeks suitable match. Apply Box 23944, The Times of India. Bombay 1.

SUITABLE MATCH FOR GUJARATI Kapol Banja home-loving girl, age 22, passed SSC. Well settled Gujarati preferred. Write full particulars Box 23630, The Times of India, Bombay 1. A38715 (X)

SUITABLE MATCH WANTED: (a) Kerala Brahmin girl 26, very fair, employed, only daughter Pooram, Atreya Gotram; (b) Boy 28, Cost Accountant earning 300 monthly in reputed firm Bharadwaja Gotram Pooratem. Reply Box 23860. The Times of India, Bombay 1. A38979 (X)

WANTED IMPRESSIVE, TALL, FAIR, preferably Medical Graduate Maharashtrian Brahmin bride from respectable family, prepared to go abroad, for healthy, handsome, Maharashtrian, 28, foreign qualified. Government of India Service. Apply with horoscope, to Box 23856. The Times of India, Bombay 1. A38946 (X)

Is natural selection also involved? Allow further speculation on this, then assign (for homework) reading of "Historical Distribution of Racial Varieties." Distribute also the following worksheet to be filled out in conjunction with the reading:

Characterize, if you can, each of the following human groups:
1. American Indians
2. Arctic peoples
3. Eastern Asians
4. Pacific Islanders
5. East Indians
6. Africans

7. Caucasoids
8. Central Asians

For each of ten subgroups (subheadings in article) of your choice, decide on one characteristic that may be adaptive, and explain why you think so.

Day 4.—Discussion: How may natural selection have been influential in the formation of races? Review the characteristics of some of the varieties Hulse describes and their possible adaptive value:

Eskimos—built for least heat loss
Melanesian and Africans—built for most heat loss (dark skin for protection from U-V radiation of equatorial sun)
Why are Pygmies small?
Why are Plains Indians, and some other savanna hunters, tall?
Why do temperate zone dwellers tan readily but have relatively light skins?
Why do very fair-skinned northerners tan not quite so readily?
And so on.

Discussion: Race and Intelligence
Why are humans more "intelligent" than other animals?
What is intelligence?
Why should any group of humans be more or less "intelligent" than another? (This is a very good argument for intellectual "equality.")

It should be pointed out that every human trait is ultimately a product of natural selection. This certainly applies to "intelligence." It is probably true that, generally speaking, there has occurred selection for particular kinds of specific intellectual abilities (perhaps in our society for mathematical reasoning), but there are as yet no valid criteria or methods for evaluating the innate learning capacity of any group of people in contrast to another. To say that all groups are equal in this respect because evidence to the contrary is lacking is, however, as logically fallacious as to assume the opposite. But a couple of points are worth making:

1. Since all human groups are capable of communicating clearly with one another, and with no other species of animal, they can't differ so very much in intellectual capacity.
2. For a Bushman to learn to stalk a kudi is easily as difficult as for a French cab driver to learn his way about Paris.
3. "Intelligence," if and when it is definable, is a continuous variable and cannot, therefore, ever be applied as a racial characteristic to individuals.

Assignment: Read "Technological Advances and Population Change."

Review and revise the first homework paper—questions on race. What is the difference between an Englishman and a Caucasoid? (Can a Negro be an Englishman?)

DISCUSSION AND CONCLUSION

The aim of these lessons is to convey more than just information about race formation and classification. The hope is, first of all, to involve the student by starting him with his own experience of the topic and then to help him place that experience in a context that provides new perspectives which may also be applicable to other areas of knowledge. In the case of the materials presented above, the problem is to make the student aware of the confusion of criteria in the conventional classification of peoples into "racial" groups. He may realize—by becoming aware of the criteria he himself customarily uses, and by trying to apply them systematically—that there can be no definitive grouping. He finds that he cannot assign the accepted "facts" into categories of similar and dissimilar objects.

In constructing the "race chart" and tabulating the variations among his classmates in height, skin color, nose shape and so on, he may come to see that the criteria chosen to describe a race are not mutually supportive; that they are often, in fact, continuous variables. This understanding will, hopefully, lead him to the realization that it is population and not individuals that determines the pattern of transmitted genetic traits. This is a basic and far from watered-down lesson in anthropology.

Because these ways of thinking have become clearer to him, the student has something more than mere data (which may become obsolete) with which to work. He may be able to apply such thought processes to other kinds of data and even, perhaps, to improve upon them.

Is is difficult to evaluate the effect of such lessons because the results desired most are behavioral objectives which elude most testing procedures. Interviews with students and teachers do not suggest that sweeping reforms have been initiated. They do demonstrate that students and teachers have become aware of certain qualities of teaching and learning. Teachers realize, some for the first time, that students can think. One teacher who had literally considered his students to be sponges, reported this realization with enthusiasm. Another teacher commented, "For the first time the students themselves were aware that they knew how to discuss something and realized that they were not just exchanging opinions." Another effect reported by one teacher was that ACSP materials had led (forced?) him to do more reading than he usually did in preparing for class.

Some students respond that they are relieved to be "allowed" to think. One said, "It made me have a good feeling—like I had done something worth doing and not just read it out of a book."

There are no panaceas in a situation as vast and differentiated as secondary education. But there is evidence that ACSP materials can help students and teachers who know what they need and can move others toward goals they otherwise might not have perceived.

2   THE AUTHORS

Anthropology Curriculum Study Project Materials

Anthropology, one of the social sciences competing for a substantial position in the curriculum of secondary schools, has recently emerged as a force with which to be reckoned. To a considerable extent this successful development is the responsibility of a dedicated group of scholars and educators under the overall direction of Malcolm Collier. Operating from its central headquarters at 5632 S. Kimbark Avenue, Chicago, Illinois, this organization has been creating for the past five years an ambitious program designed to acquaint the high school student with a unique way of viewing human society.

Those associated with the project have identified some national developments which have undoubtedly facilitated their undertaking. Margaret Fallers finds origins of the growing interest in anthropology in post-World War II awareness of the non-western world.[1] And Robert Hanvey, Curriculum Research Director of the Project, believes that the socially "touchy" aspects of the discipline (evolution, for example) have been made acceptable by the new inquiry approaches to the social studies. "Topics that a few years ago might have been thought too controversial," writes Hanvey, "have slipped into the curriculum, partly because they are new, partly because they are blessed by scholars, but also because they are cast in a mode presumed to be fashionably 'inductive'."[2] It appears also that increased public respect for the achievements of science and technology has been another factor which has encouraged support of the anthropology and other social science projects by the National Science Foundation.

[1] Margaret Fallers, "Introduction" for special Anthropology issue, *Social Education*, 32, no. 2 (February, 1968): 105.

[2] Robert Hanvey, "Social Myth v. Social Science," *Saturday Review*, November 18, 1967, p. 81.

The origin of ACSP goes back to the early 1960's when Malcolm Collier was appointed by the American Anthropological Association to investigate the state of anthropology in the secondary schools. The Anthropology Project has undergone a rigorous process of materials development, field-testing, revision and retesting. Although it is never completely satisfied with its results, and in its continual striving for perfection brings a high degree of integrity to its operation, a number of products are now in press or already available for public consumption. The key items for the secondary schools are *Patterns in Human History*, a semester course to be published in November of 1969 and *History as Culture Change*, a three week sampler of the Patterns course now available from the Crowell Collier and Macmillan Company. The latter (HACC) will be reviewed later in the chapter. But prior to that analysis a glance at some aspects of the project's rationale would be in order.

RATIONALE

Anthropology as conceived by the project lends a scientific method to the traditional historical approach employed in many high schools. In attempting to interpolate "analytic processes" into the social studies, the designers believe in "a social science perspective which prompts looking beyond crises and personalities for general significance and pattern" in human societies.[3] Some of these patterns are evolution, culture as adaptation, and the process of cultural change. In an early experimental case study of the Kwakiutal Indians of British Columbia, settlement forms, social organization, and the process of valuing are also considered to be patterns or societal regularities. Beyond the identification of such patterns students are urged to see how they relate to form complex social systems. Thus, Michael Greenebaum summarizes by writing that "pattern refers to the ways in which particular, discrete aspects of a society are linked to one another" and function "focuses on how a number of patterns are themselves related." [4]

In its earlier development the project applied the above viewpoint to the study of classical Athens. Again Greenebaum characterizes the project's outlook toward the discipline of history.

Candor, however, compels us to admit that classical Athens has rarely been taught as a living society; we are prone to dwell on the exemplary accomplishments of its outstanding statesman, thinkers, and artists rather than the social milieu in which they occurred. By focusing on Athenian society as a functioning whole, anthropology can give even greater significance to the

---

[3] "Anthropology Curriculum Study Project," *Newsletter*, Winter, 1968, p. 2.
[4] *Newsletter*, Fall, 1966, p. 4.

unique accomplishments of the Athenians by providing students with a realistic context in which to place them. [5]

Like most anthropologists the project personnel have also been concerned with the problem of ethnocentrism. Their approach is balanced and realistic in warning the teacher not to expect inordinate amounts of open-mindedness from the students. One is asked only to consider the notion that, while he may not like a society or recognize it as "good," he should view it as being basically human with its own rendition of cultural complexity. Rachel Reese Sady goes a step further and suggests that "ethnocentrism is not only inevitable, it is an appreciable force for good within society, strengthening group solidarity, bolstering morale, and going hand-in-hand with the values that give meaning to life." [6] Presumably, the overall philosophy involves student recognition of ethnocentrism and observation of the various ways, positive and negative, in which it operates.

The pedagogy of ACSP is largely inductive with emphasis placed on the drawing of inferences from raw data. Since this procedure is such a central part of the discipline of anthropology, the project has spent much time assessing its successes and failures in the classroom. *Anthropology Materials in Social Studies Courses: A Case Study—Day One* is an unusually candid glimpse of the reactions of trained observers, teachers, and students to "inquiry" methods in the social studies. For example, in one lesson dealing with the classification of questions into broad categories, one teacher replied to the student in the following way:

No, no, I don't think that's what you're really asking. How did they make their living really? Isn't that what you're asking? [7]

The observer correctly classifies the comment as being pseudo-induction and notes that the technique used was "what he the teacher imagined to be an inductive procedure." [8] Aware, then, of the difficulties of the pedagogy of the new social studies, the project through *Day One* warns practitioners that sometimes induction is simply not appropriate.[9] Nonetheless, the fact that induction is the most favored method perhaps prompted the reminder that ACSP is not trying "to make amateur archeologists, anatomists, or any other 'ists' out of the students." [10] Some students, however, may not be

---

[5] Ibid.

[6] Rachel R. Sady, *Teacher's Manual for Kiowa Years* (New York: Crowell Collier and Macmillan, Inc., 1968), p. 9.

[7] *Anthropology Materials in Social Studies Courses: A Case Study—Day One* (Anthropology Curriculum Study Project, 1967), p. 17.

[8] Ibid., p. 39.

[9] Ibid., p. 43.

[10] Ibid., p. 5.

totally convinced by that claim when confronted with the project materials. And this possibility raises the important and related issue of motivation.

How can the Bushmen of the Kalahari be made relevant to the jet-age American? Despite the hackneyed nature of the problem and the anguish that educators may experience in seeking to solve it, the project recognizes it and meets it with varying degrees of success. The *Day One* booklet acknowledges the need to avoid the banality of "emotionally-chilling" experiences. And the methods utilized by the project are designed to deal with the crucial difficulty posed by the exotic side of anthropology. Jerome Bruner writes in *Toward a Theory of Instruction* that "the most persistent problem in social studies is to rescue the phenomenon of social life from familiarity without at the same time making it all seem 'primitive' and bizarre." [11] Solutions he offers such as the use of comparison and hypothesis-making are extensively employed by ACSP. Moreover, the danger of using the exotic for its own sake is explicitly recognized. As Rachel Reese Sady puts it:

Its impact is likely to be a head-shaking wonder at the oddity of the ways of man; using it is justified only if there is an immediate attempt to see the sense that these kinds of behavior make in the societies in which they occur.[12]

And Robert Hanvey provides a practical example of her dictum when he writes "in a Philadelphia suburb a teacher hands out reprints of matrimonial advertisements from the *Bombay Times*; class begins on a note of ribald hilarity but ends with a serious discussion of caste as it effects biological diversity." [13] In this spirit anthropology can stimulate curiosity while avoiding the fun and games syndrome so damaging to the credibility of the social studies. But the extent to which the project has succeeded in solving the relevance problem can best be judged by inspecting the materials themselves.

THE MATERIALS

In developing materials ACSP has undergone a long process of evolution. Some of the early experimental units of 1963–65 never have been commercially published. However, portions of "The Study of Early Man" and "The Great Transformation" (1966–67) have been incorporated

---

[11] Jerome Bruner, *Toward a Theory of Instruction* (Cambridge: Harvard University Press, 1966), p. 92.

[12] Rachel Reese Sady, "Anthropology and the Idea of Mankind" (Council for the Study of Mankind), p. 18.

[13] Robert Hanvey, "Anthropology in the High Schools," *Educational Leadership*. 22, no. 5 (February, 1965): 1.

into the Crowell Collier and Macmillan courses currently aimed at the secondary school market. Although this review will center on *History as Culture Change*, brief analyses of two project paperbacks will be included. Those two case studies are *The Great Tree and the Longhouse: Culture of the Iroquois* by Hazel W. Hertzberg and *Kiowa Years: Study in Culture Impact and Profile of a People* by Alice Marriott.

In particular the Hertzberg work has been singled out for high praise by professional anthropologists, one of whom cited its "dazzling" scholarship. The study involves a comparison between American and Iroquois culture and reveals some interesting facets of our national Indian policy. According to Kurt Johnson, who briefly describes the book in a bibliographical study for ACSP, one realizes that "it is impossible to understand the meaning to the Indian of the loss of his land to the Europeans, until one understands how the Indian himself regarded his land." [14] Hertzberg skillfully probes the conception the Iroquois formed about his natural environment.

The accompanying Teacher's Manual offers a potentially fruitful way of dealing with the problems of ethnocentrism. After suggesting that class members identify objects in the classroom that would have little or no meaning to a person from another culture, it adds:

An interesting exercise is to have the students write reports of a school event, such as a baseball or football game, from what they conceive to be the point of view of someone from another culture.[15]

Perhaps most important is the extreme readability of the study which makes it suitable for both junior and senior high school use. At times the writer reaches heights of philosophical eloquence. Note, for example, the questions about human nature posed by the following quotation:

And yet the question remains, as it does for so many other peoples: why were the Iroquois so kindly in peace yet so terrible in war? How did the face of the gentle farmer or the quiet hunter become transformed—for those who had the misfortune to be the Iroquois enemies—into the bloody visage of death? [16]

Alice Marriott's *Kiowa Years* is another excellent study dealing explicitly with the problem of culture change. Especially vivid are the

---

[14] Kurt Johnson, *Two Dozen Anthropology Books: A Selected Bibliography for High School Libraries and Social Studies Courses* (ACSP), p. 6.

[15] Hazel W. Hertzberg, *Teacher's Manual for The Great Tree and the Longhouse* (New York: Crowell Collier and Macmillan, Inc., 1967), p. 11.

[16] Hazel W. Hertzberg, *The Great Tree and The Longhouse: The Culture of the Iroquois* (New York: Crowell Collier and Macmillan, Inc., 1967), p. 83.

sections dealing with the modern Indian's confrontation with the white man's world. The Teacher's Guide indicates that the student might "contrast the scene at the trading post when Sitting Bear and White Shell Woman stare astonished at the stores on the shelves, and their pleasure in making their purchases, with the later scene when Sitting Bear bitterly disagrees with Kicking Bird about following the white man's more settled ways...." 17 Although the reading level of the book for the student is more suited to junior high use, a senior high instructor working with the Teacher's Manual can challenge his students with many problems relating to social change full of import for today. Both of the paperbacks are excellent examples of the high level of quality characterizing the ACSP endeavors.

History as Culture Change as a three week course is designed to accommodate schools that are unable or unwilling to make room for semester courses in Anthropology. The course "moves quickly to the consideration of a very important step in the evolution of culture—the food-producing revolution and the changes in human societies ushered in by that revolution." 18 To some extent it has the purpose of compensating for a long-standing omission in social studies curricula. Attention is directed to the "hinterland" and "peasant societies" on whose production of food "cities are parasitic." Although the course does not advocate ignoring civilization and the city, it is quite reasonable in pointing out the tendency to overlook areas of society which do not leave behind spectacular historical wake.

The teaching plan for each day provides a list of materials, suggested procedures, and student objectives followed by a summary for that day and teaching background materials. In no sense, however, are these resources intended to program the teacher. ACSP is never patronizing toward the teacher and encourages him to weave what is provided into his own teaching style.

True to its inductive rationale, the course begins by exposing the student to a map of an unidentified anthropological site. The student is asked to come up with questions and inferences about the life of the people who occupied the represented location. Later, he will write a short paper drawing together his insights in a "reasonable reconstruction" of "what life on the site may have been like." The exercise, of course, introduces the problems of anthropology and archeology to the student, and he is warned

---

17   Rachel Reese Sady, *Teacher's Manual,* for *Kiowa Years:* p. 18.

18   Anthropology Curriculum Study Project, *History as Culture Change: An Overview Teaching Plan* (New York: Crowell Collier and Macmillan, Inc., 1968), p. iii. Except as otherwise noted, subsequent quotes in the materials section are drawn from this teaching plan.

that the "ways of doing and thinking about things" of the people occupying the site "may have been quite different from ours." Closure is then provided by presenting the findings of professionals to the student for comparison with his own. At this point the student discovers that the site was occupied by the Bushmen of the Kalahari Desert in Africa and views a filmstrip about them narrated by Richard Lee of Harvard University. Although the desert background in many of the pictures gives one a slightly parched feeling over the long run, the presentation of Kalahari life is done in excellent detail. It is a long filmstrip, and, because it is sufficiently provocative to elicit student comments, the teacher may have to hustle to complete a showing in a short period. When the Bushmen segment of the course is completed, the student may realize that his inferences were "influenced by . . . past experience or impressions of what prehistoric people or natives ought to be like."

The next major portion of the course concerns "evidence of change in man and culture during the Pleistocene Age." Inferential techniques are applied to an examination of prehistoric tool development. Portions of this section are quite sophisticated. The suggestion that a stone tool is "one of the earliest information storage devices" makes possible a link to the technological aspects of our age and a potentially exciting discussion. Here the project lets the student compare skull size to changes in tool complexity. A colorful set of overlay transparencies gives a vivid representation of one aspect of human physical evolution. The class then takes up the problem of biological selection.

The project's explanation of the difficult concept of natural selection is the clearest presentation of that term we have ever encountered. Although the story depicting the effects of a flood in "Mouseville" on its population may seem corny to the current generation, the narrative and its accompanying diagrams are very illuminating.

A transition from hunter-gatherers to village life is accomplished by an investigation of Jarmo, a food-gathering site of ancient Iraq. It is here that the pattern-function motif of the rationale appears in its most explicit form. The class analyzes Jarmo "as a system by drawing lines connecting categories that seem to be related." Some of the categories are size of settlement unit, tool kit, economic roles, food sources, magic and religion.

The course moves on to a highly inductive glimpse of river valley civilization, which proceeds by a study of old tablets from Sumer, models of which are part of the HACC materials kit. The student can let his imagination roam as he inspects the facsimile of a historical artifact. In supplying a tactile element to social studies instruction, the project is experimenting with a technique that may have much to offer, especially to marginal readers.

The finale of HACC deals with a current problem of tremendous import—modernization in traditional societies all over the world. A case study of Hasanabad, a peasant village in Iran, is the major focus of this part of the course. After the student completes this investigation the book of student readings provided by the designers proves very useful. An excellent account by Robert Redfield of civilization's effect on a Mexican village provides data for a comparison with the Hasanabad experience. Thus, the phenomenon of culture change is seen from differing perspectives. The painful adjustment that many societies have to make to change is a "kind of suffering that millions of people . . . of the world are experiencing today. For that reason it is worth knowing about, worth puzzling about."

Another possibility for a provocative parallel is mentioned by the teaching plan.

Students may be able to extrapolate from their knowledge of peasant adaptation to the outside world to fairly accurate (or at least thought-provoking) parallels between socially adaptive behavior of peasants and the socially adaptive behavior of urban ghetto dwellers.

But the Manual cautions: "Do not press this topic if students do not react positively to it." We were puzzled by this caveat and think some clarification is needed at that point. What constitutes a positive reaction? And what about this topic has led the project to insert an admonition?

Some prospective users of HACC may feel initially that a lot of historical ground is covered in three weeks. We do not feel that this is a very substantial problem; moreover, the project acknowledges openly the inadequacies of any overview. Let us move now to consider some more important matters that may relate to the feasibility of the ACSP endeavor.

Feasibility

The overall format and quality of the project materials are impressive. However, as with any ambitious curriculum creation, some difficulties may arise in implementation. And these should be noted in passing.

Some of these problems are physical and economic in nature. For example, project personnel readily admit that it may be difficult to keep the cost of their materials down. When one inspects thoroughly what is included in the HACC course alone, it is not difficult to understand why. That packet comes complete with two filmstrips, a series of model artifacts, records, transparencies, teacher's guides and readings. Small schools and large may feel a pinch, for material of this quality simply cannot be produced cheaply. Some physical plants, too, may not be ideally suited to handle the audio-visual portions of the course due to poor facilities for room darkening and a myriad of other factors. Kurt Johnson has noted somewhat wryly that it never hurts to carry extra bulbs for overheads and filmstrip projectors, as well as extra long extension cords.

Other challenges evolve out of the project's inductive pedagogy. Although the directors, as has been earlier pointed out, do not preclude the use of expository methods, the inescapable fact remains that the materials with which the student is presented are heavily inductive. And mere awareness of the difficulties involved does not insure a solution to those problems. It would appear that the drawing of inferences followed by comparisons is somewhat overused in the HACC course. Too much induction raises the problem of lack of variety. But it also contains some frustration for the student. The ever-present tension between the freedom of speculation encouraged in the student, the actual findings of scholars, and the fact that the teacher often does not know whether a question can be definitively answered may often prove overbearing for the student who needs the security of more control and structure.

At times the project appears overly-confident in its ability to make the social studies come alive for the student. The following statements seem a bit optimistic:

1. We hope this unit will produce a new generation of Hellenophiles.
2. The materials in this unit present the Athenians as living human beings rather than as marble statues.
3. It should help the students to forget about the Indian as a barrier to frontier expansion and to think about him as an example of humanity.
4. Recognize that although traces left by past peoples are bone dry the people were not. Rather, they were as alive, complex, interesting, and human as people we know now.

But there is no point to quibble about objectives. The project deserves high praise for using non-verbal stimuli such as site maps and Venus figurines. Although questions are always raised about the relevance of "stones and bones" anthropology, we feel that ACSP's attempt to provide tactile materials for the stimulation of curiosity and imagination will open avenues to many different ability levels. Students from a wide variety of high schools and ability groups have reacted positively to the materials.

ACSP has put the burden of proof on student reception in the classroom situation—hard as that may be to assess accurately.[19] Thus, the project has shown a commendable tendency to trust the teacher and to believe in fact that its materials are often handled best by good teachers with little formal training in the discipline of anthropology. Those involved in this

---

[19] *Newsletter,* Fall, 1966, p. 1.

curriculum venture do not talk down to the classroom teacher. They do, however, understand the difficulties posed by their discipline and offer helpful hints on how one can say "I don't know" with constructive results.[20]

Most important is the fact that the project has shown itself to be very adaptable. It judiciously modifies its approach on the basis of the feedback it receives. For example, an exercise on dating by examining tree rings was eliminated for being too esoteric and irrelevant to the high school student. In its continued search for perfection and for constructive relevance and in its articulation of the usefulness of comparison as a classroom technique, the Anthropology Curriculum Study Project has offered a valuable contribution to the New Social Studies.

---

[20] Ibid., p. 3.

CHAPTER IV

Geography

3   ROBERT B. MCNEE

The Education of a Geographer *

This paper concerns the last five years of my education; it is about what
I have learned, or think I have learned, about the reform of geographic
education while associated with the High School Geography Project. When
I first became associated with the project, I knew quite a bit about
geography as a scholarly discipline, though not as much as I thought I did.
I didn't think I knew very much about geographic education, despite some
experience with the question of curriculum planning in the New York City
school system. And I was right. But now it is five years later and I have
had a wide variety of experiences with geographic education, thanks
particularly to the High School Geography Project. Just what have I learned
from all those experiences? The problem is no longer the lack of sufficient
experience on which to build generalizations. The problem now is to sort
out the experiences into meaningful patterns, to organize, to generalize, in
short, to find meaning in the experiences. The purpose of this paper, then,
is to present my tentative conclusions about the most significant considerations in geographic educational reform in terms of a simplified model or
schema.

My problem is similar to that faced by the students in the Settlement
Theme Course of the High School Geography Project. Learning by
"discovery" or inductive learning is a central theme in the course, just as
it is in many of the other courses being developed in current curriculum
reform projects. Over and over, in unit after unit, the student has direct

---

* From *The Journal of Geography,* vol. 67, no. 2 (Feb., 1968), pp. 70–75 by
permission of the author and the journal.

experience with geographic data. From time to time he is asked to form tentative conclusions or preliminary generalizations about these data. In arriving at his tentative conclusions, he uses many geographic models, both "classic" and "new." He is not encouraged to consider the relationships thus described as "laws" or ultimate "truths." Rather, he is led to consider the models as useful devices—nothing more—for organizing his thinking about the data. It is in that spirit that I am presenting here my tentative model of geographic educational reform.

I arrived at my choice of a model only very gradually. It is characteristic of almost any non-repetitive task that we understand what we are attempting to do much better after we have begun to do it. We learn as we go along. At first I was preoccupied with the details of what I was learning. But as more and more experiences with the High School Geography Project poured in upon me, I increasingly felt the need to organize these experiences in my mind, to give them meaning. I believe this is a very common experience for all of us, though much of the organizing and generalizing in our minds may occur below the level of our conscious awareness. I think all of us feel the need to organize our new experiences and that characteristically we tend to do this in terms of previous learnings. It was a foregone conclusion, no doubt, that a geographer such as myself would sooner or later think of the diffusion model as an appropriate one to use in organizing such experiences. I believe that all of us tend to try to organize the data pouring in on our consciousness in terms of both formal and informal "models" or schema carried in our heads. We tend to try out the data available on the various models stored in our mental "storage and retrieval systems" until we find a model which satisfies us as giving the best "fit," the most meaningful organization of the data. In any case, I gradually came to feel that the diffusion model or origins-and-dispersals model gave the best "fit," or gave the most meaning to the experiences I was having.

Let me be more specific. I am not thinking in terms of a complex mathematical model which states relationships with great precision. Instead, I am thinking in terms of a very simplified conceptual model. In such a simple diffusion model, one may think in terms of a specific point or points of origin on the earth's surface for an idea or an artifact. One thinks, then, in terms of that artifact or idea gradually spreading outward over the surface of the earth from its point of origin, being widely and rapidly adopted in some directions, but being accepted more slowly or even rejected in other directions. Why do not ideas find equal acceptance in all directions from their point of origin? Why is the spatial advance of an idea irregular rather than circular? Obviously, because the resistances or barriers are not of equal strength in all directions. If one wishes to increase the rate of spread of an idea or artifact, one must clearly identify these resistances and find means of overcoming them.

Now let us consider the problem of improving the teaching of geography in terms of this simple, general model. The first task is to identify the points of origin for geographic ideas and artifacts. I think it is fair to say that few geographers are very creative in a fundamental sense. Many of us can elaborate and develop an idea once it has been born. But few of us can create basic ideas. This fact need not disturb us too much, since this simply means that we are as other men, since time began. Most geographic ideas, then, originate in the minds of a handful of key thinkers. Characteristically, such key thinkers are found in the leading graduate schools, though there have been some conspicuous exceptions, such as Mark Jefferson. But such ideas do not spread very rapidly until they are taken up by the leading graduate schools. From the graduate schools, the ideas spread, through publication and face-to-face contact. Gradually, they spread to undergraduate instruction, being modified and elaborated in the process. Some undergraduate teachers are trainers of teachers. Characteristically, teacher trainers are more concerned with the dissemination of ideas than their initial creation. They often develop some highly effective and ingenious means of dissemination. Significant elaborations and embellishments of the original ideas occur in the process. Sometimes there are hybridizations between the new ideas and the old. (Such hybridization produces a few outstanding offspring and many monstrosities.)

But hybridized or not, the ideas spread gradually to the teacher trainees and hence ultimately to the students in the elementary and secondary classrooms. As long as there are key thinkers to produce new ideas and as long as these ideas spread rapidly, the subject remains vital and alive. Otherwise, the subject gradually atrophies, decays, and dies out.

But what of resistance to the new ideas? Undoubtedly, the primary resistance is the emotional resistance to change within every individual, from the resistances to change which keep the key thinker from developing many of the good ideas which emerge in his mind, on to the emotional resistances among those with whom he seeks to share the few ideas which he has allowed himself to develop. To remain whole individuals, we can accept new ideas—our own or those of others—only very slowly, allowing abundant time to relate the ideas to established patterns within our make-up. There are social or cultural resistances, too, in which the group accepts new ideas very slowly because to do otherwise might disrupt the cohesion of the group. Group cohesiveness is largely based on shared ideas, including values, and hence new ideas may be perceived as a threat to the group. Effective teaching might be defined as the development of appropriate strategies for the overcoming of such emotional resistances to new ideas.

There are some interesting resistance patterns associated with particular teaching roles in the thinker-to-pupil transmission chain. For example, those closest to the key thinkers in a field may so enjoy their role as an elite "in-group" that they really do not want to share the new ideas with others. Even as they praise the new ideas extravagantly, they may block diffusion by cloaking the new ideas in mystery, jargon, and double-talk. Similarly, the trainers of teachers often resist new ideas vigorously. One must remember that any college teacher has a very heavy investment of years of study in the established "body of knowledge." Like experts generally, a college teacher may seek avidly to add to his "store" of factual and technical knowledge while actively resisting fundamentally new ideas which might require a basic restructuring of his internal knowledge system. The less one knows about a subject, the easier it is to accept new ways of organizing the subject; the more one knows, the harder to accept fundamentally new structurings. Perhaps this is why most college teachers sound more like "priests" than "prophets." It is emotionally easier to chant the oft-repeated "truths" than it is to subject these "truths" to searching criticism in the light of a new vision of "truth."

But even if the new ideas have reached the teacher trainers and revolutionized their thinking, even if they are able to diffuse these ideas among their teacher trainees, these ideas may be slow to reach the pre-college classroom. Newly trained teachers have the same reasons for resisting new ideas that the teacher trainers have. In addition, there is a very powerful group influencing the classroom behavior of the teacher. This group can be called the "gatekeepers." Gatekeepers include state legislatures (which often specify courses in the curriculum) and the state offices of education (which often specify the curriculum rather rigidly and may even specify what books may be used). Local school administrators and curriculum specialists are also gatekeepers. In terms of the spread of the ideas of any particular discipline, such as geography, the role of both administrators and curriculum specialists is a highly conservative one. They cannot possibly keep up with all of the new ideas emerging in all of the disciplines under their jurisdiction, particularly not in the present time of a "knowledge explosion." But even if they were to be such supermen that they could accomplish this, they are restrained by their social role. They are, and they ought to be, mediators among the various groups competing for the mind and emotions of the child. They must heed the voice of the local community, which tends to resist new ideas for the same reasons as the teacher trainers and trainees. They must develop a coherent curriculum by harmonizing and adjudicating the competing claims of the various disciplines, each of which characteristically has a restricted view of the whole of knowledge and the whole educational process. They must protect the child from over-zealous parents, communities which stress community needs at the expense of individual needs, and over-zealous curriculum reformers from the various disciplines (quite possibly, this includes myself and several others associated with the High School Geography Project).

Perhaps the publishers are the most powerful gatekeepers of all today. Their gatekeeping role is rooted in the implications for economic survival of mass publishing, mass selling, and low per-unit profits. To be economically successful, a new text must win wide and rapid acceptance. A publisher can afford to publish a few texts with a narrow appeal, but he dare not do this too often or he perishes. To win rapid and wide acceptance, a text should have every appearance of modernity but little of its substance. It is imperative that it be attractively illustrated according to the prevailing mode and it should be filled with the latest figures on such key things as quebracho production. But the framework of ideas within which quebracho production is analyzed should be widely familiar, tried and true. Pupils in classrooms are the greatest captive market in the world. Though they are the ultimate consumers of texts, their views toward texts are seldom definitive. Instead, it is the classroom teachers, the curriculum specialists, the administrators, and the state offices of education who must be won over to a new text. In turn, these text selectors tend to derive their ideas about the nature of a discipline and the ideas coursing within it from other existing texts, rather than from professional journals or monographs, correspondence with professional geographers, or face-to-face contact. Thus "geography" to them tends to be what the publishers guess the market demands rather than what professional geographers think "geography" is. Is it any wonder that the gap between "geography" as understood by Johnny in the tenth grade and geography understood by a professional geographer is great indeed?

From this formidable array of resistances to new ideas, one might assume that no new ideas would ever diffuse outward all the way from the few key thinkers to the pupils in the classroom, or, that the diffusion of any idea would require generations to accomplish. Fortunately, this is not entirely true. Powerful ideas have a way of overcoming powerful resistances. A few of the disseminators along the way are extraordinarily skillful at overcoming resistances.

Still, the gap between "geography" as known to professional geographers and "geography" as learned by most high school students had grown alarmingly wide by 1960. This problem of a serious idea gap was not unique to geography. Indeed, the same general kind of gap existed in almost every school subject. The basic objective of most of the curriculum reform projects of the last decade, including the High School Geography Project, has been to narrow that gap, to find some means of overcoming the established resistances. For the first time, the Federal Government lent its prestige and gave broad financial support to an effort to overcome at least temporarily the chief resistances to idea-diffusion. For the first time, professional associations such as the Association of American Geographers accepted a responsibility to encourage the spread of ideas throughout the school system. Professional organizations such as the Association of American Geographers have always accepted responsibility for the primary phases of idea-diffusion, i.e., the diffusion of ideas among research minded college geographers. The principal purpose of journals, such as the *Annals*, has been to stimulate the diffusion of geographic ideas within the "inner circle" or "hard core" of geography. One of the principal purposes of annual meetings has been to spread ideas through the reading of papers and other face-to-face contact. But now, with the High School Geography Project, the Association of American Geographers has joined the National Council for Geographic Education and similar groups in accepting responsibility for encouraging the spread of ideas all along the line from key thinkers to the uninitiated pupil in the classroom.

The resistances of the past are still there and they are formidable indeed. However, in developing its materials, the High School Geography Project has "leap-frogged" over many of these resistances. It has put research geographers in direct contact with the pupils and their teachers in their classrooms. The project has found the pupils and teachers hungry for challenging ideas. They seem willing and eager to try out ideas still considered too "new," too "revolutionary," or too "disturbing" by many teachers of undergraduates. That is, the High School Geography Project has not sought simply to diffuse the ideas in last year's college textbook to the high schools. Instead, it has sought to diffuse the very best ideas of modern geography as understood in the leading graduate schools, whether these ideas are generally considered "new" or "old."

In developing its materials, the High School Geography Project has broken, at least temporarily, the "textbook barrier." Though some of the materials being produced by the High School Geography Project resemble, in format, the text materials of the past, the project as a whole is not bound by a narrow textbook tradition. Instead, every phase of the settlement theme course is being viewed as a diffusion challenge, as a challenge to develop new and ingenious means to put ideas across. For example, the intra-city unit uses a plastic model to teach urban land use patterns and accessibility as well as using more traditional means (readings, pictures, etc.). Similarly, the manufacturing unit uses role-playing in a location game to teach both the least-cost and maximum-demand approaches to industrial location analysis. Likewise, the nature of agricultural geography is brought home by a decision-making game in which the students pit themselves against the vagaries of the weather and the market. Other units of the course have similarly challenging devices as well as traditional ways of spreading geographic ideas. The course as a whole is a fascinating amalgam of ingenious teaching devices new and old. In short, the High School Geography Project materials are distinguished by (1) a stress upon up-to-date geographic ideas, (2) a stress on new ways of diffusing those ideas, as a result of (3) bringing research geographers into direct contact with high school classrooms and thus bypassing many of the resistances which have blocked the diffusion of geographic ideas in the past. In general, I believe that the High School Geography Project has been highly successful in the initial phases of its operations, the production of effective teaching materials.

Increasingly, the High School Geography Project has been broadening its concern to include not only the production of materials but also to other phases of the "resistance to diffusion" problem. After the materials have been tested thoroughly in representative schools and appropriately revised, they will be ready for mass diffusion. But will the classroom teachers and the gatekeepers accept these materials or will they resist any sort of geography which does not fit their necessarily restricted view of the field? Only time will tell. Much attention is now being devoted within the project to teacher training programs, arrangements with publishers, special institutes, and means of reaching special gatekeeper groups such as administrators, curriculum supervisors, and the like. Insofar as the ultimate consumers, the students themselves, have any say in the matter, I expect the new idea and the new materials to be widely and enthusiastically received.

However successful the High School Geography Project or similar curriculum reform projects may ultimately be, it is important to recognize how profoundly conservative such projects basically are. A truly revolutionary curriculum advance would be one which in some way basically and permanently altered existing patterns of idea diffusion. The project does not do this. The barriers to diffusion that produced the idea-gap of the sixties remain, largely unaltered. The project has temporarily leap-frogged over these barriers without dislodging them. Therefore new and perhaps more serious idea-gaps will develop in the future unless the High School Geography Project, or similar vehicles of change, continue to permit the same leap-frogging of ideas, or, unless more revolutionary mechanisms are developed to attack more directly the underlying problem of resistances to change deeply imbedded in human personalities and the whole educational and social order. Viewed in terms of this simple diffusion model, the problem of the reform of geographic education is without end.

If any conceptual model, such as this one, is taken too seriously for too

long a period of time it loses its value. I would not want this simple analysis to be taken too seriously. Through the use of a simple diffusion model
I have been able to give meaning to many of the understandings emerging
as I associated with the High School Geography Project. Yet in the process
of fitting the data of my experience to the model, I have begun to see
weaknesses in the model. My current dissatisfaction with the model centers,
I think, in the linear, one-directional movement of ideas which is assumed
in the model. Reality is much more complex than that. In the real world,
the "feedback" of ideas all along the line is immensely important. The
"thinker" I have described does not live in isolation. He is affected by the
reception granted his ideas. Similarly, the teacher trainers do more than
simply transmit or diffuse the ideas of the thinker. They affect the thinker
by the feedback they give to him and they in turn are affected by the
feedback from their pupils. And so on. Hence it is quite apparent that
really to understand the problem of reforming geographic education one
would have to construct a much more complex conceptual model. And this
model would be one involving feedback, as in a systems model (or, better,
an inter-systems model). But I do not feel I know enough at this time
about either systems models or about geographic education to attempt such
a thing. Perhaps one day I will. But, in any case, I am convinced from my
experience with the High School Geography Project that the feedback
from research geographers actually working directly with pupils and
teachers in classrooms will have profound long range effects on the
discipline itself. American geography will never be the same again.

4   THE AUTHORS

High School Geography Project-An Evaluation

The High School Geography Project (HSGP) originated in 1961 as an
outgrowth of the concern of certain members of the Association of
American Geographers (AAG) and the National Council for Geographic
Education (NCGE) with the state of geographic instruction in secondary
schools. Geographers who attempted to observe such instruction reported
that all too frequently geography as a clearly delineated subject or as a
contributor of identified concepts to hybrid courses was either not included

in the curriculum or was offered as a sop to low ability students. These geographers further noted that often, when geography was taught, the course framework and the information included in it were so archaic as to render them worthless.

"When a high school senior is awarded his graduation diploma, what does he know about those parts of the world where well over half the world's people live—the Near East, the Far East, Southeast Asia, Africa South of the Sahara?" asked Henry Warman in a lament characteristic of many geographers. "How can a student obtain such information when the standard high school courses in the social studies, or social sciences, are Civics, American History, World History, and Problems of Democracy?" [1]

Ironically, social studies has traditionally been conceptualized as an amalgamation of history, government, and geography, but, as geographers have discovered, in many social studies classrooms, geography has always been the first casualty in the triumvirate. According to Randall Anderson, geography's perceived content was unappealing to social studies theoreticians in the crucial era when social studies was being developed. "During the formative period in secondary education, when the social science subjects were being selected on the basis of their social, civic, and economic contributions, secondary school geography was being refined by eminent geographers as a physical science." [2]

The results for high school geography of the philosophical divergence between social studies curriculum developers and geographers became readily apparent. "As time went on," Warman tells us, "the content of the physical geography course was incorporated into an Earth Science course; the economic geography course was commonly downgraded until only the poorest students elected it." [3]

Many conscientious efforts to win actual acceptance for geography were made through the years by geographic educators, but it was not until an era of more general curriculum ferment arose that sufficient resources could be mobilized for a sanguine assault on the curriculum status quo.

In 1958, the AAG and the NCGE established the Joint Committee on Education. This Committee was entrusted with the task of "improving the status of geography," and "promoting geography as a discipline, particularly in the secondary school system." [4] The Committee skirted several thorny

---

[1] Henry J. Warman, "Additional Challenges and Responsibilities," in *selected Experiences: High School Geography Project*, Clyde Kohn, ed., Geographic Education Series   4, Publications Center, National Council for Geographic Education (Dubuque: William C. Brown Company, Publishers, 1964), p. 40.

[2] Randall C. Anderson, "Trends in Geography Instruction," *The Bulletin of Secondary School Principals*, no. 316 (February 1967), p. 16.

[3] Henry J. Warman, *Selected Experiences*, p. 40.

[4] Clyde F. Kohn, "Introduction," *Selected Experiences*, p. viii.

issues, leaving them unresolved, until the High School Geography Project was established. This probably was a wise procedure considering the strong likelihood that schisms at that time would have impeded the reform movement's incipient momentum. The committee was able to recommend that geographic instruction in secondary schools be the first target for improvement. Subsequently, the Ford Foundation's Fund for the Advancement of Education provided initial financing for the creation of the High School Geography Project.

Focus

The director of the HSGP in its nascent years, 1961–1963, was Professor William D.. Pattison. The Joint Committee mandated the Project to "improve the content of courses in geography at the freshman-sophomore level," and to "develop new instructional materials for use in these courses." [5]

The original intention of the Joint Committee and, therefore, of the HSGP, was to create a model filmed course, hence the word "demonstration" in the early HSGP literature. The first Project newsletter announced, "Action directed toward creation of a year demonstration course in high school geography has begun. Planned in five steps, a developmental program now under way aims at production of filmed or taped sequences which, together with study guides, maps and other materials, will assist the classroom teacher. . . ." [6] It soon became apparent, however, that the materials and techniques necessary for a high quality demonstration course could be the basis for a new, widely disseminated, geography curriculum.

In order to design new instructional materials and eventually a new two semester geography course, the Project leaders had to decide what the boundaries of the discipline known as geography were and if a mainstream of geographic inquiry existed. Naturally, there were many divergent views on these questions.

Geography, like so many other profitable and suggestive fields for research, might be termed an exploding discipline.[7] Physical geography rubs shoulders with cultural, political, urban, historical, transportational, economic and other brands of geography. Geographers themselves have debated the proper frontiers of geography and some have wondered if the interstices between geography and other disciplines were not properly the preserves of the other disciplines.

---

[5] Clyde Kohn, *Selected Experiences*, p. viii.

[6] High School Geography Project, *Newsletter*, no. 1 (January, 1962), p. 1.

[7] For a full description of the extent of the explosion see Preston E. James and Clarence F. Jones, eds., *American Geography: Inventory and Prospect*, Association of American Geographers (Syracuse: Syracuse University Press, 1954).

After many discussions within the Project staff and between members of the staff and other interested geographers, Pattison was able to propose a unique resolution of the conflict. Pattison postulated four historic thrusts in geography. He dubbed them: (1) the spatial tradition concerned with mapping, location, and movement; (2) the area studies tradition dedicated to study of unique aspects of regions; (3) the man-land tradition oriented to the relationships between societies and the earth; and (4) the earth-science tradition involving research into the physical properties of the earth.[8] This formulation Pattison later entitled "The Four Traditions of Geography." The immediate contribution of Pattison's insight to the Project's work was a philosophical foundation for the inclusion in curriculum materials of the findings of many geographic schools of thought, and an expansion rather than a contraction of the content and impact of secondary school geographic education. Pattison's solution to the problem allowed him to achieve an overview of the discipline in which:

The four traditions though distinct in logic are joined in action. One can say of geography that it pursues concurrently all four of them.... It is to be hoped that through a widened willingness to conceive of and discuss the field in terms of these traditions, geography will be better able to secure... inner unity and outer intelligibility, ... and that thereby the effectiveness of geography's contribution to American education and to the general American welfare will be appreciably increased. [9]

The next problem which confronted the Project was posed by the question of whether geography would be better served by deploying itself in high schools under the aegis of physical science or social science. At the research level, geography has a foot in either camp as "The Four Traditions" testifies. Nevertheless, the Project was faced with the necessity of arriving at an either/or decision. The answer involved not only theoretic issues, but practical considerations as to the best starting point for the innovators and innovations. Some geographers felt "that consignment to social studies implies exclusion from the earth-science courses," while others were convinced "that geography cannot find adequate breadth of opportunity if confined either to an earth science or to a social studies program." [10] Indeed geographers are fond of terming geography the "bridge" between social science and physical science. Unfortunately, at the secondary school level, this interdisciplinary formulation is apparently

---

8   William D. Pattison, "Changing Attitudes and the High School Geography Project," *Selected Experiences*, p. 36.
9   William D. Pattison, "The Four Traditions of Geography," Professional Paper. no. 25, National Council for Geographic Education, May, 1964, p. 216.
10   HSGP, *Newsletter*, no. 3 (April, 1963), p. 4.

difficult if not impossible to implement. Even geographic educators admit that traffic on the bridge appears to be one way, with social scientists using geography to learn about physical science rather than the other way around.[11]

In time, however, it became apparent to the HSGP staff that the decision on the place of geography in the social studies curriculum was not theirs to make. School administrators and teachers were accustomed to thinking of geography as part of the previously mentioned social studies trinity of history, government, and geography. Though geography could legitimately be presented as a physical science and though geography, in fact, had often ceased to exist in social studies programs, its image as a ward of the social studies remained. "Whatever the appropriate position of geography in general may be," the staff conceded, "HSGP itself is looked upon as a social studies project *by persons and organizations outside the field of geography*, almost without exception." [12]

The realization that geography would be offered, whatever its revised content as part of the social studies, produced considerable anxiety in geographers. They were fearful of the fatal embrace of history and history teachers. In order to emphasize geography's independent stance the HSGP staff repeatedly stressed two themes in their pronouncements:

1. Notwithstanding its assumed social studies role, HSGP has at all times aimed to include in its course definite units demonstrating the earth science capabilities of geography. [13]
2. Although some units of study might be included in World History courses, it is not possible to accomplish the objectives set forth in the High School Geography Project in a course that does not extend a full year. [14]

The alliance with earth science not only functioned as a defense against the claims of history, but helped appease those geographers who felt that geography in its pristine form must be physical.

If a school offered Earth Science followed by a course in Geography, it was suggested that this sequence be offered in the 8th-9th grades, or 9th-10th grades. If both were offered in the same year, then closer cooperation between teachers was suggested.[15]

---

11   Lillian W. Stimson, "Geography," *The Social Sciences: Foundations of the Social Studies,* John V. Michaelis and A. Montgomery Johnston, eds. (Boston: Allyn and Bacon, Inc., 1965), p. 83.

12   HSGP, *Newsletter,* no. 3, p. 4.

13   Ibid.

14   Henry J. Warman, *Selected Experiences,* p. 42.

15   Ibid., p. 41.

The demand for a specific two-semester course in geography rather than a construct or hybrid course utilizing concepts from several of the social sciences was, perhaps justified by some of the staff's experiences during the first year of trial use of certain units. Jumping ahead for a moment to this period, we can witness the realization of the staff's fears when in meetings with cooperating instructors, they noted that "a few of our teachers tended to subscribe to a widespread history-biased view that secondary school geography finds its principal raison d'être in the improvement of a student's background for education in history. For them the fixing of place locations was of major importance." [16] The fact that many teachers called upon to teach geography are unrepentant history majors has remained a critical problem of the HSGP.

When the actual work of preparation of materials was at hand, two closely allied questions had to be considered by the staff: (1) Would the prototypic course's orientation be primarily topical-systematic or regional? (2) What would be the pedagogic philosophy of the course? Although we are not able to document our assertion, the authors think it likely that the answer to the latter question influenced strongly the answer to the former.

In attempting to examine some of the factors which *may* have influenced the staff's outlook on pedagogic creeds, it will be useful to introduce several lengthy but illuminating passages. A most provocative article by Jerome S. Bruner appeared in Vol. 29 of the 1959 *Harvard Educational Review*. In this article, Bruner obliquely approached the teaching of geography.

One experiment which I can report provides encouragement. It was devised and carried out by the research group with which I am associated at Harvard in collaboration with teachers in the fifth grade of a good public school. It is on the unpromising topic of the geography of the North Central States and is currently in progress, so I cannot give all of the results. We hit upon the happy idea of presenting this chunk of geography, not as a set of knowns, but as a set of unknowns. One class was presented blank maps, containing only tracings of the rivers and lakes of the area as well as the natural resources. They were asked as a first exercise to indicate where the principal cities would be located ....

I will never forget one young student, as he pointed his finger at the foot of Lake Michigan, shouting, "Yippee, *Chicago* is at the end of the pointing down lake," and another replying, "Well, O.K., but Chicago's no good for the rivers and it should be here where there is a big city (St. Louis)." These

---

[16] *Response Paper: Suggestions From Teachers Associated with the High School Geography Project,* Joint Committee on Education of the Association of American Geographers and the National Council for Geographic Education. August, 1963, p. 34.

children were thinking and learning was an instrument for checking and improving the process.[17]

Robert B. McNee has since advised that, "Geographers can and should adopt many of the ideas of instruction being advocated by Jerome Bruner. . . . It is more important that the student learn to think like a geographer than it is for him to know a lot about the earth. Learning to think like a geographer means many things, but above all, it means absorbing the conceptual structure of the discipline." [18]

The structure of the discipline approach, stressing as it does the promulgation of separate courses, might well have appealed to geographers who feared the violation of their field in a forced submission to an overarching historical orientation. It should be added, however, that many research geographers, not concerned with curriculum management problems in the secondary schools, had consistently assumed that geography deserved at least a two-semester undiluted treatment. The Joint Committee, for example, assumed the desirability of a distinct two-semester geography course.

The term "structure" implies some constancies, some recurring phenomena or patterns.[19] Thus, the structural pedagogic approach harmonized with one major thrust in modern geography—the emphasis on systemization. Gilbert F. White, one of the founding fathers of the HSGP succinctly explained this emphasis.

The new exploration of the earth centers on understanding how and why the main elements in the landscape—the landforms, water, climate, vegetation, and soils, and the towns, crops, roads, and other works of man—differ in distribution from place to place. It asks what regularities there are in these distributions.[20]

The search of some modern geographers for regularities coincided with the search of some modern educators for structure. The two trends may have reinforced one another as the HSGP staff determined to adopt a systematic-structural approach. Certainly, the staff must have been desirous of utilizing whatever techniques available which seemed capable of ending the popular perception of geography as "an unpromising topic."

---

[17] Jerome S. Bruner, "Learning and Thinking," *Harvard Educational Review*, 29 (1959): 187–88.

[18] Robert B. McNee, "Good-By to Heavea Braziliensis and All That," *Introductory Geography: Viewpoints and Themes*, Commission on College Geography, (Washington Association of American Geographers, 1967), p. 31.

[19] See, for example, Joseph J. Schwab, "The Concept of the Structure of a Discipline," *The Education Record*, vol. 43, no. 1 (January, 1962).

[20] Gilbert F. White, "Rediscovering the Earth," *The Bulletin of the National Association of Secondary School Principals*, no. 316 (February, 1967), p. 2.

TRIALS

One of the most admirable qualities of the HSGP is its candor. Throughout the developmental period reports and materials have been made available to those who wished them regardless of the fact that these documents often vividly portray the travail involved in curriculum construction by committees.

By the beginning of the 1962–1963 academic year the HSGP had arranged to have the teaching loads of ten classroom teachers reduced to one class a day so that these teachers could develop at least two experimental units to fit into the framework of their regular geography courses. The units were to be consistent with the "structure" enunciated in the Advisory Paper.[21] Not all of the cooperating teachers had majored in geography, but each teacher was assigned an adviser, a geographer usually connected with a college or university in the vicinity of the cooperating teacher's school.

At the end of the 1962–1963 academic year the opinions of some of the cooperating teachers were collected in the *Response Paper*. The teachers recapitulated the arguments of professional geographers and geographic educators heard earlier by the Joint Committee and the HSGP. Teachers divided over the question of the importance of the memorization of place names versus structural or "theoretic" knowledge. Debate also centered on the question of a topical versus a regional approach. Issues resulting from consideration of these two questions involved the value of discovery learning and the legitimacy of the use of models, games, and role playing.

The surprising finding of the first school trials was not that certain teachers had reservations about a structural-systematic organization, but that most of those teachers involved were unreservedly sympathetic to the new construct. While some social studies teachers were not amenable to dispensing with so much of that aspect of geography, place names and location, which seemed so obviously its central core, others, displaying their heritage of Deweyan pragmatism, comfortably accepted a problem-centered formulation. These teachers approved of the inquiry or discovery technique which was interlaced with the structural systematic framework, perhaps because of their own "activities-process" background. At any rate, according to Robert Hanvey, "New programs are judged very critically in terms of their inquiry quotient," [22] and the HSGP orientation towards inductive

---

[21] *Advisory Paper for Teachers Associated with the High School Geography Project,* Joint Committee on Education of the Association of American Geographers and the National Council for Geographic Education, August, 1962.

[22] Robert G. Hanvey, "Social Myth vs. Social Science," *Saturday Review,* November 18, 1966, p. 81.

learning may have aided it in the course of the debate over place-name versus theoretic knowledge.

In the *Response Paper* the staff narrator remarks, "Inevitably, the teachers entered into contention over the relative merits of regional and topical organization of instruction. . . . Most of them compromised combining the two modes in one way or another." [23] This solution was to some degree imitated by the staff itself, as exemplified by the Japan unit.

One great strength of a topical approach was that it lent itself more easily than did a regional approach to the use of models and games. The debate over the regional vs. topical question took an unexpected turn when the staff and policy committee realized that some of the high school teachers had hit upon the same device which Bruner had reported elementary school teachers using. These teachers constructed model regions which contained only those features and relationships which corresponded to a typical concept. The students, in some cases, discovered the concept by participating in a game. Then the students verified their hypothesis by applying it to an extent region previously selected by the teacher.

The teachers who represented the social studies tradition liked this style of instruction because it was learning based on activity. All the teachers who used this technique liked it because of the dramatic student reaction to it. The teachers appreciated exuberant evidence of concept attainment and seemed to derive a visceral reinforcement from it. They concluded that what the students enjoyed were the "pleasures of predictive power." [24]

Insofar as they were aware of this adventuresome trend among the teachers, the new HSGP staff which took over the operation in 1963 may have been encouraged in implementing the topical-systematic approach. Such encouragement must have been valuable for them as, day by day, the implications of their approach were perceived by not altogether sympathetic colleagues.

If we think of a course of study as a finite body of information to be conveyed in a fixed amount of time, it becomes clear that whenever information is added to the course of study, information also must be withdrawn from it. When the HSGP staff placed data regarding geography's syntactical and substantive tools (using Schwab's formulation) [25] in their course, they could not include as much traditional geographic content as would otherwise have been possible. Although the additions and omissions, as well as the general balance of the course, are eminently defensible, the structural emphasis made some teachers and geographers distinctly uncomfortable.

---

[23]　*Response Paper*, p. 57.
[24]　Ibid., p. 43.
[25]　Joseph Schwab, *The Education Record*, p. 197.

The HSGP knew, of course, that most teachers of secondary school geography courses did not and do not have considerable geographic backgrounds. In one sense, then, the system of materials organization most difficult for many teachers has been adopted. The HSGP has posed itself the challenge of producing scholarly and sophisticated materials to be used by often inadequately trained teachers of geography.

By now the reader must be asking, "Just what is *a* structure of geography?" Edwin Thomas contributed a structural formulation to an HSGP conference. Thomas said:

In general, the system follows this structure. First, we have the basic notion of a geographic fact. Geographic facts, once defined, may be expanded into the concept of the *spatial distribution*. The notion of the spatial distribution may be developed, in turn, into the concepts of *spatial interaction* and *areal association*. Then the concepts of the *region* may be synthesized from the notions of the spatial distribution, spatial interaction or areal association, depending upon the type of region one wishes to treat, i.e., its degree of complexity or sophistication.

The *concept* of scale may be treated as another basic concept which enters the system at an elementary level and then continues to operate throughout it, modifying particular geographic facts, areal associations, spatial interactions and regions.[26]

Thomas' structure of geography is more elaborately delineated and carefully defined than is indicated by the brief excerpt presented here. A very clear discussion of geographic facts, spatial distribution, areal association, spatial interaction, and region is presented by the HSGP in the *Teacher's Guide for Introductory Materials* (Boulder, Colo.: HSGP, 1965). In the Guide examples of the application of each concept are given and an effort is made to illustrate the cumulative or sequential aspect of this geographic structure.

The Joint Committee decided that the best way to encompass what Pattison called geography's four traditions and its postulated structure in a course of study, was by constructing a number of problem-oriented units which would vary in complexity and scope. These units would be given continuity by their exploration of the various phases of a single complex

---

[26] Edwin N. Thomas, "Some Comments About a Structure of Geography with Particular Reference to Geographic Facts, Spatial Distribution, and Areal Association," *Selected Experiences*, p. 45.

For an alternative structure of geography see Peter Greco, "Geography," *Social Science Education Consortium* (Boulder, Colo.: SSEC Publication # 102, 1966).

phenomenon. The idea of a settlement theme was accepted because of its utility in allowing treatment of each of the main emphases of the four traditions.

In all, six units are to be produced, the first of which is the subject for our review. The unit titles appear below:

I. "Geography of Cities"
II. "Manufacturing and Agriculture"
III. "Cultural Geography"
IV. "Political Geography"
V. "Habitat and Resources"
VI. "Japan"

The decision of the HSGP to adopt a unit plan was typical of a discipline oriented curriculum project. "The curriculum is ... organized into units," observes Goodlad commenting on the tendencies of the new projects, "each unit progressing in difficulty and both reviewing and extending one or more concepts introduced earlier in the student's experience. Very often, the subject matter is similar to that of conventional programs. But the treatment called for is different." [27] In Unit I, "Geography of Cities," it is indeed true that "the treatment called for is different." [28]

MATERIALS

Unit I, "Geography of Cities," is presented to students via a Student Resources Booklet, a package of maps, charts, and data sheets, a Student Manual, and miscellaneous material to be provided by the teacher. "Geography of Cities" is presented to teachers via a Teacher's Guide. The Guide discusses each activity in the unit, suggests reference readings, and presents a general overview of the unit's scope.

The overview is explicit and concise. The strategy and tactics of "Geography of Cities" is explained under the headings: Integral Activities, Time in 50 Minute Class Periods, Media and Procedures, Major Ideas and Skills, Possible Home Assignments, and Related Optional Activities.

It is to be hoped that future curriculum projects will use a similar format for outlining their substantive and logistical properties. Perhaps the reader will better appreciate the value to teachers of precise statements of

---

[27] John I. Goodlad, *School, Curriculum, and the Individual* (Waltham, Mass.: Blaisdell Publishing Co., 1966), p. 165.

[28] The authors of *The New Social Studies: Analysis of Theory and Materials* are grateful to William D. Pattison, Nicholas Helburn, and Dana Kurfman for their generous provision of HSGP materials.

unit content if we quote the Overview's description of the very first (of the eight) "Geography of Cities" activities.

Integral (required) Activity—City Location and Growth

Time in 50 Minute Class Periods—3

Media and Procedures.—Students select settlement sites using hypothetical diagrams. They then prepare diagrams for a current subdivison site as well as for one in the future. Next they use drainage maps of the American Midwest and predict where settlements might develop. Predictions are checked with reality.

Major Ideas and Skills.—Site features and locational factors influence city growth. Locational advantages or disadvantages are relative to the times and do change. Skills in making and justifying decisions.

Possible Home Assignments.—Preparation of Site Diagrams. Readings: "Present Day Site Selection" and "Frontier Lawyer."
Related Optional Activities.—"A Tale of Three Cities" or Bruges (Readings).

The unit objectives for all eight activities of "Geography of Cities" as presented in the Teacher's Guide are:

At the conclusion of the unit the student should be able to:
1. Anticipate and account for the probable location and growth of urban places in terms of transportation, the overall pattern of settlement, and the physical environment.
2. Account for and anticipate patterns of urban land uses in terms of transportation and the physical habitat.
3. Anticipate patterns of socioeconomic characteristics in urban settings.
4. Illustrate how people have both modified their physical environment and adapted to it.
5. Discuss settlements of different sizes in terms of their trade areas and their pattern of relationships with other settlements.
6. Use models to account for and anticipate settlement and land-use patterns.
7. Analyze a model and its limitations in terms of assumptions and implications.
8. Use data from a variety of sources to make hypotheses and test them.

The HSGP authors suggest that the teacher begin the unit by projecting a site diagram transparency on a screen using an overhead projector (the transparency is contained in the package). The students have a printed version of the diagram in their Student Manuals. The site diagram presents four possible locations for a settlement in a coastal area. The students choose one of the four locations and defend their choice.

After the students have crystallized their thinking through the discussion they are formed into groups which consider the next four site diagrams in the Manual. When the groups have made their choices, the teacher compares the selections of each group, allowing the students to explain the factors they considered in arriving at a decision. In the course of these explanations, the teacher attempts to make explicit the implicit assumptions of the students regarding sites and settlers. The Teacher's Guide contains a discussion of the relevant considerations which ought to be recognized as important by the students as they analyze the diagrams. In the course of the class session the teacher manages to impart this information if the students haven't enunciated it.

If the teacher wishes to pursue this introduction to locational analysis, two optional assignments are offered. The Student Resources Booklet's first reading is "Present-Day Site Selection." This reading presents in two pages factors likely to be considered by a developer in the selection of a tract of land on which he will build houses. The developer's need to accurately predict the expectations of potential buyers is convincingly explained. The students, of course, had been anticipating the expectations of settlers when they attempted to pick the settlement locations on the site diagrams.

A second reading, "Frontier Lawyer," is also available in the Student Resources Booklet. "Frontier Lawyer" is the title given an apocryphal letter supposedly written by a young lawyer named Thad Stevens. The letter, dated 1805, describes Stevens' reaction to the Ohio Valley frontier. A series of Thad Stevens' letters appeared in earlier HSGP unit versions. The letters served as vehicles for relating locational analysis to the historical development of urban centers in the United States. Thus, hypotheses generated by site selection exercises were validated by recourse to reality. The Thad Stevens letter in Unit I, like its predecessors, suffers from its obviously contrived quality. The reading is, we repeat, optional.

The second activity of the "Geography of Cities" unit is "New Orleans." Materials for this unit which are provided in the HSGP package include: a wall map of New Orleans, 20 sets of 7 stereograms, 20 stereo viewers, 2 sets of 20 topographic maps of portions of New Orleans, 20 sheets of topographic map symbols, 20 pamphlets on topographic maps, and 20 sheets of census data. Stereograms are made from aerial photographs which include an overlap so that terrain included in one shot is also presented in the next photograph. In this manner, stereograms, in serial order, recapitulate the flight path of the photographer's plane. The stereoscope is the viewer or binocular lense through which the stereogram is surveyed. Control of the distance between identical referents in the stereogram makes possible control of the impression of height when the referent is viewed through the stereoscope. With some practice in using the stereoscope the students can study New Orleans in three dimensions.

The students do not do any reading in their Student Booklets for the "New Orleans" activity, but they do use worksheets in the Student Manuals. After the teacher has given them an introduction to the large topographic map of the New Orleans region, students receive the stereograms and viewers and answer questions such as: "What land uses can you find?" and "Select three of the land uses that you have identified. Why do you think they are located where they are?" The Teacher's Guide contains possible answers.

The students check their answers to the questions with the answers suggested by an accurate interpretation of the topographic map. Each pair of students receives the topographic map symbols sheet to aid in the comparison of stereograms and map. In some cases the stereograms show sections not depicted on the topographic map. The Student Manual anticipates the students' discovery of this lapse and aids them in explaining it by advising them that the aerial photographs on which the stereograms are based were taken in 1964, while the map predates 1964. The Student Manual also directs the students to use the map to answer the question, "What evidence can you find to show that the physical features of the land have influenced man-made features?"

The next set of questions in the Student Manual refers to a set of the stereograms which portray the Greater New Orleans Bridge and vicinity. Essentially, the students are supposed to account for the location of the bridge. The teacher, aided by the information in the Teacher's Guide, presents cues which lead the students to the conclusion that the location of the bridge was dictated by the position of the central business district. To justify this conclusion, the students singly or in pairs, attempt to delineate the boundaries of the CBD.

The last section of the "New Orleans" activity is an imaginative exercise which achieves its impact by contradicting certain common stereotypes. Teachers with some showmanship will probably want to arrange this activity so that students look at the first two stereograms, which depict two New Orleans neighborhoods, before they begin inspection of the third stereogram which presents the third neighborhood. The students, after they view the stereograms, are asked to state what they would expect to find if they were able to walk through these neighborhoods. On the basis of the size of each house's lot, the proximity to the railroad, the abundance or lack of shade trees and so forth, the students are encouraged by the teacher to speculate on certain attributes of the first two inspected neighborhoods, such as median property value, median family income, median school years completed, and percent Negro.

The Teacher's Guide tells us that neighborhood 1 will probably be identified as a relatively poor, Negro section by the students, while neighborhood 2 will probably be labeled as middle-class white. The student hypotheses are valid. If the students are now given the stereogram for the third neighborhood, they will see that it resembles neighborhood 2. The students can now be given the census data sheets. These sheets will confirm the suspected similarity in terms of property value, family income, and school years completed between neighborhoods 2 and 3.

The teacher at this point informs the students that the third neighborhood is a Negro neighborhood. The students can verify this assertion by looking at the appropriate tracts of the census data (they didn't have the tract references previously). The students can also verify their hypotheses regarding the other neighborhoods by checking the census sheets.

If the teacher wishes, some closure for this "New Orleans" activity can be obtained by a discussion which would involve student responses to such questions as "What kinds of information can you get from aerial photographs?" and "What did you learn from studying about New Orleans that might apply to other cities?" In this activity the concepts of scale, spatial distribution, density, pattern, and areal association are introduced. The students are also given an opportunity to practice the skills involved in map reading and aerial photo interpretation.

The third activity of the "Geography of Cities" unit is "Models of City Form." Like the second section of the unit, this third activity requires about four class periods. Almost all of the information which the students will receive in the course of the activity is in the Student Resources Booklet; several transparencies provide additional data. The teacher is advised to read the Student Resources Booklet, "Models of City Form" section before reading the corresponding section in the Teacher's Guide.

Early in the student reading for Activity 3, the concept of model is introduced. The authors go to considerable lengths to rigorously define this concept. They characterize models as "a simpler representation of the real thing," as "tools," and as "working hypotheses." The activity authors warn the students that, "any model fails to explain reality to the extent that all the possible factors are not included."

The first model presented in the reading is composed of proportionately larger circles which surround an innermost dot which represents the central business district. The Teacher's Guide identifies this model as an adaptation of Ernest W. Burgess' concentric ring model of city growth, proposed in 1923. The Student Resources Booklet increases the sophistication of its version of Burgess' theory by suggesting that transportation arteries might cause city expansion to parallel access routes rather than occur evenly from the center outward. Four population density maps of Chicago and its environs (1875, 1900, 1930 and 1955) are introduced in the Student Resources Booklet to strengthen this suggestion. If the arterial effect is incorporated into the concentric ring model a many armed star is produced.

At this point the notion of density is expounded. The teacher is reminded in the Guide that for some students the idea of density may be new. An exercise in determining the pattern of student occupancy of a floor of the school is suggested as an introductory device. The concept of residential density can be taught to students, advises the Teacher's Guide, by first defining for them in meaningful terms the extent of an acre, (about as many square feet as a football field) and then by explaining to them that demographers or other researchers use formulas involving houses, garages, and so forth to decide if any given acre is primarily residential. The residential density of a city is obtained by dividing the population by the number of acres devoted to residential purposes.

Thus acquainted with residential density, the students find in their booklets a persons per residential acre map of Chicagoland. This map vividly contradicts the concentric ring model of city growth because it indicates the relatively high population density in Chicago along the entire lake front. Furthermore, more zones of high population density exist to the west and south of Chicago's CBD than to the north.

The Student Resources Booklet explains the lake front population on the basis of aesthetic and transportation factors, and the general staggering of the population to the south of the CBD on the basis of southern suburban industrial plants or "outliers." It also exposes the students to the idea of age distribution by area. Population pyramids graphically present the fact that suburban areas contain a proportionately greater number of children, given the total suburb by suburb population, than do the Chicago lake front zones.

The students learn from their booklet that such population statistics are compiled by obtaining census figures for a few districts in each Chicago or suburban area and then extrapolating from the data. The technique involved in sampling is explained but, for some reason, the words sample and sampling never appear.

One sample area west of Chicago's CBD is spotlighted. This area has an age distribution typical of suburbs (relatively many children), but an inner city location. The students are asked to explain this anomaly. The Teacher's Guide advises the teacher that the cited phenomena is a symptom of Chicago's pattern of residential segregation. Segregation is the fourth factor (along with the attractiveness of the lake front, transportation routes, and location of industry) which accounts for the failure of the concentric ring model to fit Chicago's physical and population expansion patterns.

At this point in their reading the students are gently admonished that, "Once we have found a model that explains, there is a tendency to cling

to it. Often people try to ignore information that does not fit the model."
A sector model of city form is presented and buttressed by maps of Chicago
depicting median family income, median school years completed, and percentage of male workers in white collar occupations. The students can see by
comparing these three maps that a sector model explains facets of Chicago's
form which cannot be accounted for by using a concentric ring model. The
Teacher's Guide contains the information that the sector model was
proposed by Homer Hoyt in 1936.

The "Models of City Form" activity ends asking the student, "Can you
figure out a model that combines both sectors and rings?" The Teacher's
Guide contains a composite model which, the teacher is advised, still does
not explain everything, but which is more valid than the concentric ring
or sector model.

In the "Models of City Form" activity the HSGP staff is obviously
attempting to expose the high school student to some of the academic
geographer's habits of thought. Skill in the use of abstractions and practice
in hypothesis formation and validation are the outstanding legacies of the
activity. The circumspection with which the HSGP staff approaches the
use of models and their recurrent cautionary remarks should prove reassuring to geographers and geography teachers as yet ill at ease with
geography's ascent into the rarified atmosphere of social and behavioral
science.

The next section of the unit is its most ambitious one. "Portsville" is a
base for studying urban geography by way of the examination of a city in
three different periods of its growth. The "Portsville" activity requires
eight to ten class periods. Each student receives maps and each class is
given four sets of Modulex Lego building pieces, the nature and use of
which will become clearer in time.

The activity's authors claim that the name, Portsville, is used because
the students will be building their own cities, not copying the growth of
Seattle. The *roman a clef* is easily exposed and towards the end of the
section Portsville's identity is admitted. The pseudonym was apparently
adopted to emphasize the fact that the Seattle of the past need not have
become the Seattle of the present.

"The Story of Portsville" begins with a reading on site selection. This
is a historical narrative describing the factors that early Seattle settlers
considered in making their original site selection in 1851, and the factors
which later caused them to relocate. After the students have read the
selection, the teacher is urged to ask questions to ascertain the students'
understanding of the material. "Which of the following were disadvantages
of the first site?" A number of correct responses with elaboration are given
in the guidelines. "Which of the numbered places on the map seem to you

to be desirable as permanent sites? Which are not desirable? Be able to state your reasons." The map appears in the students' reading booklet.

The second reading, "Portsville from 1850 to 1880," recalls in a lively journalistic style, Seattle's boom and bust days. "Maynard got drunk that night, but by morning he was hot on the trail of some new business venture." After this reading, the students are asked more questions. Then the class is divided into four groups and each group is given its Modulex Lego kit. The groups also have a Portsville map model, an 1850–1880 date card, a dark and a light green perforated sheet, and scissors. The kit contains plastic discs each of which represents a city block area. These discs correspond in size to the scale of the map and a transparent overlay. The map is fastened to a map board which also has fasteners for the perforated overlay which is the base for the discs. Black plastic strips which stand for railroads are also included.

The rectangles are different colors, each color representing a form of land use:

manufacturing—yellow
commercial—red
public buildings—white
residential:
high income—reddish-brown
single family—buff
multiple unit—chocolate brown

Parks and cemeteries are depicted by cutting the dark green sheet into appropriately sized strips. Landfill is represented by strips of the light green sheet.

The task of each group is to build Portsville as it might have developed from 1850 to 1880. As each group builds its ideal Portsville, the teacher queries it making it justify its decisions in terms of the feasibilities of the time. After each group has completed its *nouveau* Portsville of 1800, the four models are compared. According to the teachers' guidelines, "The point of the comparison is to help show students that there are many different ways in which a settlement might develop in a single geographical setting."

In Part Three of the activity the students read "Portsville from 1880 to 1890." They discuss the reading and once again divide into four groups to construct their cerebral Portsville as they would wish it at the end of 1890. The same comparison follows the completion of this task.

Part Four of the activity is "Portsville from 1890 to 1900." The students again discuss the reading and then—back to the drawing board. A fifth section is offered, "Portsville after 1900," but if the class is tiring of the activity, the teacher is encouraged to end it after the fourth reading. The Portsville game is one of the activities depicted in the HSGP demonstration film available from the HSGP in Boulder.

Since the "Portsville" game is a rather elaborate one, it seems appropriate to consider the role of educational games in an instructional program. In the "Portsville" game, as in other HSGP simulations such as the Metfab game, the students are role playing. In "Portsville" they role play city planners, an activity anticipated by one of the first unit readings, "Present-Day Site Selection." Furthermore, they work in groups on a task for which they have guidelines, but no script. Thus, the "Portsville" game is an example of simulation. Unlike most simulation exercises the HSGP games do not pit one team or individual against another team or individual; in fact, the teacher is urged to quash signs of competition in terms of planning the "best" Portsville. In this regard, the HSGP games bear greater resemblance to policy simulations than they do to most educational simulations.

The following chart may help to clarify the nature and uses of simulation.

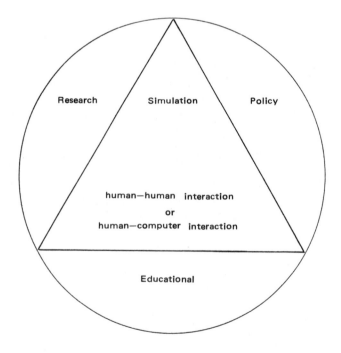

The weightlessness experiments of the National Aeronautics and Space Administration are examples of research simulation. The pacification games created for the Defense Department as a means of testing programs for combatting insurgency in Viet Nam are examples of policy simulation. Most games are easily computerized, making possible the development of more complex, hence more realistic situations and environments.

The HSGP has stated that as a result of participating in simulation exercises students may learn:

. . . their behavior can have effects on their environment; sufficient and relevant information is one prerequisite to wise decision-making; rational decisions are not always rewarded in real life.[29]

The HSGP's claims as to the benefits accruing from simulation are fairly modest. Unfortunately, not all curriculum developers have been so restrained. Perhaps the most objective analysis of simulation was produced by a cooperative research project.

In general, the claims and expectations we had for simulation have not been borne out . . . . Nevertheless, the somewhat pessimistic conclusions from the data should not obscure two important findings, namely, that behavioral measures of interest reveal simulation to be more involving and more interesting than case studies and that simulation offers much more student-to-student feedback than case discussion sections.[30]

The fifth integral or required activity is "Shopping Trips and Trade Areas," which is designed to last three to five class periods. The Teacher's Guide observes that student mastery of this activity is particularly important because the next two activities are dependent upon it.

The activity starts with a motivational exercise which the teacher may omit if he wishes. In this exercise the students work with a map of their own neighborhood (which they obtain or create) to establish customer constituencies of places like hamburger stands, movie theatres, and the school. The notion of trade areas and the differing shapes of the trade areas of the different enterprises is thus discovered.

In the first required exercise the students see a projected transparency image which depicts the shopping areas surrounding towns of different size. Next, the students refer to the Student Manual which contains maps of trade areas in Canada. The effect of cultural norms on commerce is

---

29   High School Geography Project, *Newsletter*, no. 15 (May, 1968), p. 3.
30   Lee F. Anderson et al., *A Comparison of Simulation, Case Studies, and Problem Papers in Teaching Decision-Making*, Cooperative Research Project No. 1568 (Evanston, Illinois: Northwestern University, 1964), p. 65.

demonstrated by a section comparing the shopping patterns of Mennonites with the shopping patterns of their neighbors.

The following three exercises in the "Shopping Trips and Trade Areas" activity as presented in the Student Manual and described in the Teacher's Guide call for the interpretation and explanation as to the cause of commercial behavior represented cartographically. The Teacher's Guide states that these exercises are intended to sponsor student discovery of central place theory. The Guide reminds teachers that the theory is attributed to Walter Christaller and involves the concepts of population threshold, hierarchy of settlements, function and nesting. These concepts are further developed in the last two activities of the "Geography of Cities" unit.

In Activity 6, "A Model of Settlement systems," the students develop a model which explains the regularities in the placing and spacing of cities and towns. According to the Teacher's Guide, the teacher starts the students off by asking them if they could draw a shape which would represent the most efficient pattern for adjacent trade areas. To help them the teacher focuses attention on the properties such trade areas would have to possess.

Either working independently or with the teacher the students apply the knowledge they have already gained (such as the fact that a circle representing a single trade area with a dot at its center representing a town would be the most efficient shape for a *single* trade area), and through manipulation of cut out or projected transparency circular shapes find the design which involves the least circular overlap—the hexagon.

With this design or model of the most efficient adjacent trade areas in hand, the students are asked by the teacher a number of questions about specific goods and services. The answers to these questions introduce the concepts of hierarchy and nesting. The students return if they wish to the "Shopping Trips and Trade Areas" maps in the Student Manual for additional information.

The students attempt to test the validity of the hexagon model by applying it to a trade area presented to them by way of a map in the Student Manual. The map is a representation of market towns in a Chinese province. A hexagonal design drawn to the same scale as the province map is on the facing page, thus juxtaposing the map and model. A reading, "Market Day at Gao," in the Student Resources Book accompanies the province map.

The Teacher's Guide suggests a number of questions for the teacher to ask the students, the last of which is "How does the pattern of roads and paths resemble the shape which was developed for the ideal trade area?" The Student Manual invites the students to make lists of the similarities and differences between the map and the model.

In Activity 7, "Time, Place, and the Model," the students are confronted with trade areas which, unlike the Chinese province, do not conform to their hexagonal model. Through discussions guided and enriched by the teacher the students learn the reasons for these deviations from their idealized design. They learn the concept of dominance by considering trade centers as focal points not only of commercial activity, but also of social, political, and religious activities. They consider the influence of transportation on trade areas through comparison of maps depicting towns in southwest Wisconsin in 1900 and in 1960. The maps, again printed on facing pages in the Student Manual, can be interpreted as revealing the influence of the automobile as an instrument of easy access to cities on lower hierarchy trade areas between such cities. Finally, the students see a map (in the Student Manual) which shows trade areas in a mountainous section of the previously studied Chinese province. The terrain has apparently forced alteration of some of the patterns which the students might, by now, assume to be typical.

If the teacher wishes, the students can be asked to write essays explaining settlement system changes over time. An attempt to explain the factors which altered the face of southwest Wisconsin as portrayed by the facing maps in the Student Manual might provide the focus for this essay. A "Time, Place, and the Model" reading in the Student Resources Booklet provides census data and trade area maps of the Upper Midwest. The use of a map presenting isopleths is also explained. The students, thus, can imitate professional geographers.

The optional activities and readings which are included in Unit 1, "Geography of Cities," are as carefully constructed as the required activities (in earlier versions of the *Geography in an Urban Age* course they were required activities). Because of considerations of space we cannot analyze them for the reader; we do feel that the elegance of these additional materials would probably make them difficult for most teachers to resist.

IMPRESSIONS

This review of the first unit of the settlement course of the HSGP makes clear the earlier HSGP assumptions regarding inductive teaching, use of models, and structure of the discipline. One of the first reservations to occur to any reader considering using Unit I might involve a reaction to the amount of paraphernalia included in Unit I and the suspected difficulties of equipment handling thus imposed. Actually, little machinery is used; what's more most teachers are already adept in the use of overhead projectors and maps, overlays and drawing materials. The model kits are easy to use because they have been refined through field testing and have clear directions; in fact, the Portsville kit resembles several familiar children's games. Although the unit booklets and activity materials require more management than a single text classroom, teachers experienced in a multi-text or classroom reference materials approach will find that the settlement theme format produces no undue strain.

A more serious reservation which we might anticipate, would question the HSGP's reliance on models or hypothetical examples. These abstractions have troubled geographic educators. "When geographers are more concerned to use theory to deduce what should be found in particular places than they are to determine what actually is found in these places," argues Preston James, "there is then some danger that geographic study might become detached from its own universe—the face of the earth." [31]

It should be noted however that, as previously reported, teachers found that students enjoyed the "pleasures of predictive power." If students are encouraged to inquire, some means of reducing the initial input of facts and interpretations must be found in order to prevent the questioning from becoming too diffuse. The hypothetical model, because it is a model, i.e., because it exhibits fewer variables than reality, tends to focus and make manageable class discussions which otherwise might deteriorate into amorphous conversation. Furthermore, the HSGP asserts, "The total body of geographic knowledge (in the world) is more than anyone can master. Only by teaching principles, ways of explaining whole *sets* of facts, and whole *classes* of patterns and processes can we hope to gain perspective on what is known." [32]

What will be the advantages of the new course? The units, in aggregate, indicate the many concerns of modern geography, update the scholarship commonly available to students, and provide intrinsic motivation through internal logic and sophisticated instructional methodology. Graduates of the course may, indeed, conceptualize a structure of geography which they will be able to bring to bear on novel situations.

What are the disadvantages of the course? The faults are mainly errors of omission rather than commission. Beyond the first two units the course is appropriate only for able students. Although geographic educators resent having their discipline relegated to slow learners, the HSGP's lucidity in terms of geographic structure and facility in terms of verbal and visual instructional techniques fairly begs to be utilized in the creation of a course for lower ability students.

The HSGP has accepted school systems as they are; in the future more thought might be devoted to non age-grade level courses and to the

---

[31] Preston James, "Introductory Geography: Regional," *The Journal of Geography,* February, 1967, p. 53.

[32] HSGP, *Newsletter,* no. 15 (May, 1968), p. 3.

exploration of additional possibilities for individualizing instruction. Many authors in the field write of maps as being analytic tools and, at the same time, fruits of inquiry. It is never made clear whether students are to treat maps as a means of conducting research or as a means of exhibiting conclusions to prove research competency. In Aristotelian terms, geographers do not usually admit the necessity of differentiating among theoretic, practical and productive orientations to their discipline.[33]

The geographers have attempted to articulate the HSGP course with the Earth Science Curriculum Project (ESCP) offering. The ESCP course might be offered in the last year of elementary school or the first or second year of junior high (assuming a 6–3–3 arrangement) although in some instances it might be a freshman senior high course (assuming an 8–4 pattern). The HSGP course could, therefore, be offered immediately after or simultaneously with the ESCP course. A simultaneous offering would be made possible by inclusion of ESCP in a high school program in the natural science sequence.[34]

The geography project has not, as yet, given serious attention to the possibility of articulating geography with other subjects (besides ESCP) taught at the same time. The desirability of attempting such articulation is suggested by recent research. One study found that at the junior high school level gifted students, "would choose interdisciplinary seminars such as one which might relate the natural sciences to the social sciences." [35] The same study discovered that, "Almost unanimously, the students expressed various needs to create tangible products." [36] Students might be well served by a year of disciplinary courses with interdisciplinary properties, if a formal seminar exploring the common threads of such courses was included. The cartographic and model making proclivities of the geography courses might further strengthen this possible "core" offering.

Although the desire of geographers to have the new course units used exclusively in a geography course is understandable, it is conceivable that one or more of the units could be utilized in extant social studies courses. The "Political Processes" unit, for example, could be profitably incorpo-

---

[33] Geography can be conceived of as theoretic when new geographic relationships are sought; as practical when geographic knowledge is used to influence public policy decisions, and as productive when geographic data is presented via cartography, etc., to consumers. For additional information regarding the relevance of this distinction, *see* Joseph J. Schwab, "Structure of the Disciplines: Meaning and Significances, "in *The Structure of Knowledge and the Curriculum*, G. W. Ford and Lawrence Pugno, eds. (Chicago: Rand McNally & Co., 1964).

[34] Earth Science Curriculum Project, *Newsletter*, no. 13 (February, 1967), p. 11.

[35] Joseph P. Rice and George Banks, "Opinions of Gifted Students Regarding Secondary School Program," *Exceptional Children*, 34, no. 4 (December, 1967): 270.

[36] Ibid., p. 271.

rated into a United States History and Government program. All of the other units share this versatility.

Why should students seek to master "the geographer's way"? [37]

From time to time rather diffuse sets of objectives have been postulated for *Geography in an Urban Age*. Since the HSGP through Robert McNee is indebted to Jerome Bruner, we feel justified in paraphrasing the HSGP and Bruner in order to condense the projected course's teacher and student objectives into our version of Bruner's four main desiderata.[38] Our analysis leads us to believe that the learner goals of the HSGP may be summarized as follows:

1. Children may learn much of the information traditionally included in geography courses and may remember it longer because of its contextual rationality.
2. Children may gain in critical thinking skills (intellectual potency) because of their practice in formulating and testing hypotheses.
3. Children may sufficiently master the syntactic and substantive tools of the discipline to apply them in presently unforeseen circumstances (heurism).
4. Children may gain from the course a sense of scope and order which will prove deeply satisfying (extrinsic to intrinsic rewards).

The last derived objective of the HSGP course is at once its most audacious and most commendable. With penetrating insight into the human condition, Gilbert White writes:

Perhaps most of all, men in the western world are troubled by the individual's search for identity, by the struggle young people are having to see themselves as constructive parts of an intricate and massive set of interlocking systems.

However confusing its political and intellectual currents, the world nevertheless has sufficient unity and regularity for a young person to acquire a framework which explains some of the diversity and shows the points at which knowledge of process is wanting. This is a kind of discovery of the earth that can have the student deeply excited by the problems upon whose solutions the outcome of the human adventure depends.[39]

---

[37] This phrase should be credited to William D. Pattison. It will be further elaborated in his forthcoming book, *The Geographer's Way*.

[38] Jerome S. Bruner, *On Knowing: Essays: for the Left Hand* (New York: Atheneum Publishers, 1966), p. 83.

[39] Gilbert White, "Rediscovering the Earth," pp. 7–8.

CHAPTER V

Sociology

5   EVERETT K. WILSON

Inductive Methods in Teaching Sociology*

Most of my clan are university-trained as sociologists, not as teachers. But promptly on receipt of the degree, we proceed to spend most of our lives doing that for which we've *not* been formally trained—that, indeed, for which we may be unfit. We teach. And the simplest solution to this, the severest penalty entailed by Adam's fall, is to play back a recording of graduate school notes and nuggets from professional journals. Whether—or to what extent—this ever pays off, we never know. For evaluation of product and quality control in the booming educational industry is, to put it charitably, but slightly developed. Perhaps fortunately, we don't know what we're doing.

I've had the good fortune these past two years to be taught by teachers: Jim Eckenrod, Bill Hering, and Tom Switzer. Among other things I've picked up terms like the "inquiry method," the "discovery method," and "learning by induction." In my naïveté I'd always assumed that learning meant inquiring and that, with a little bit of luck, inquiry led to discovery. So, also, I'd assumed that in between the query and discovery the student would confront data, the analysis of which would lead to learning.

But there is a vast gap between preaching and practice, between learning theory and classroom operations. Like others, I've been addicted to a dull pattern of expository teaching, hung around a framework of topics, not

* From American Sociological Association, *Sociological Resources for the Social Studies Newsletter*, no. 5 (Summer, 1968), by permission of the author.

Adapted from a paper presented at the meetings of the National Council for the Social Studies, Seattle, 1967.

a set of urgent questions. This pipeline pattern of transmission is doubtless due to many things. One factor, certainly, is the lack of appropriate material in sociology—or the imagination to design material that links significant questions with appropriate data.

But the prospects now, I think, are brighter. Over the next few years a NSF (National Science Foundation) funded project of the American Sociological Association will exploit the talents of more than one hundred high school teachers and sociologists. They are producing an exciting range of materials, demonstrations, exercises, experiments, cross-cultural materials —all with an emphasis on inductive teaching-learning. From its inception, SRSS (Sociological Resources for the Social Studies) has emphasized inductive procedures. What's implied by the stress on inductive procedures? Reasoning from the particular to the general means, in concrete terms, (1) starting with questions, including, above all, the student's questions, (2) thinking through to plausible answers, and (3) assembling and analyzing the data that enable a choice among the plausible answers, the hypotheses initially proffered.

To plump for inductive procedures is not to rule out deductive aspects of inquiry—the line of reasoning that moves from theory to the concrete situation, terminating in testable hypotheses. But it *is* meant to guard against the authoritative transmission of the sociological gospel from some pedagogical Sinai. And it is meant to discourage the cobwebby discussion of ill-formulated problems, or the simple trading of personal views in artless disregard of the data that would test them.

I should like to consider briefly this business of induction, pausing first to defer to deductive processes of learning. Then I shall turn to three concomitants of inductive procedures that seem especially to promote learning.

I

The distinction between inductive and deductive thinking is, in a way, spurious. In the classroom, in everyday life, in scientific inquiry—both processes are at work. We move from the general to the particular as well as, inductively, from the particular case to a generalization, but this process is seldom a neatly ordered sequence of steps. Instead a generative mind moves back and forth between the two levels—confronting the theoretical with the empirical, and vice versa. The ultimate goal, never reached, is the parsimony of poetry and mathematics in making illuminating statements about man's life among men, the domain of the social studies.

So while this paper is addressed to inductive teaching of sociology, I do not want to betray the need for (and the beauty of) deductive reasoning. It is as much a part of our pattern of problem-solving as the other. For example, we have certain general propositions about the democratic process: (1) Free expression provides a pool of ideas leading to better solutions than were decisions authoritatively handed down from on high, by tyrant or oligarch. (2) Democratic process is hospitable to change and self-correction as other decision-making processes are not. (3) Democratic process is efficient: for while it may seem slow and blundering, in the long haul we inch toward decisions more satisfactory and enduring than those imposed dictatorially. (4) Widespread participation in decision-making generates a commitment to those decisions. While these general propositions may be more implicit than explicit, we do deduce from them the appropriate behavior in a specific instance, e.g., a committee meeting: free expression, encouragement of widespread participation, decision by majority vote—a decision to be revised when most people change their minds on the issue. This is the garden variety of deductive thinking. Because there are such general patterns—the Mosaic code, professional ethics, general convictions about free enterprise, or socialism, or communism—daily life itself is endowed with a coherent pattern. Indeed, if we did not think—perhaps feel—deductively, life would be chaotic. From the general we deduce the particular, lending a consistency to man's affairs.

In science we do the same thing. It is a gross distortion to think of science as though it were a matter of garnering discrete grains of sand (facts, data) which, without mortar or matrix, build into some shapely intellectual structure. Significant scientific contributions are possible as we accumulate a body of reliable knowledge—general propositions—from which new and interesting consequences can be deduced. And *useful* consequences. In sociology, for example, probability theory enables us to deduce from its general propositions and assumptions the answer to this important question: How confident can I be that what I say about the part is in fact true of the whole?

And so this introductory demurrer. Deduction and induction are twin aspects of the inquiring mind. And as we are conscious of their interplay, we will help our students enter the exciting world of inquiry equipped with roving, playful minds, dually oriented.

Let us grant, then, that learning, problem-solving, entails both inductive and deductive processess. But for the present, let us dissect—perhaps bisect—what is in reality a complex whole. We will focus on inductive aspects of learning, considering (1) what it is, what does, and what it can't do, and (2) what evidence we have, in reason or experience, that convinces us of its usefulness in our teaching.

II

To think inductively is to move from concrete to abstract, from particulars to the general. We ask: What is? and seek the data that provide an answer. It is not to take a position and then select supporting evidence. Nor is it to take a proposition, axiomatically, and from it deduce its logical consequences. We may ask, for example, what do people of different faiths believe about the existence of God, the divinity of Jesus, the virgin birth, and life beyond death? And we discover that (in northern California) members of Protestant sects, southern Baptists and Missouri Lutherans are more committed to these beliefs than are Catholics.[1] These data tell us *what* is, not *why* it is that way. Indeed, inductive processes typically raise more questions than they answer. We need to discriminate between the use of induction to describe what is, and the futile attempt to use induction to explain why it is that way. This last always requires us to bring deduction to bear as we invoke generalizations from past experience to impute meaning and motive to man's behavior.

While induction cannot demonstrate the truth of a proposition, it is no small gain to be able to use data induced to make a statement in probability terms. Likewise, to turn up a negative case enlarges our knowledge, not only by puncturing the general proposition, but by constraining us to reformulate the statement, to take account of the instance that doesn't fit. Thus induction helps us to narrow the range of ignorance and to move progressively closer to adequate statements about social reality.

Induction, then, is as indispensable as it is inevitable in the problem-solving process. But it also has certain pedagogical values. For it entails certain teaching patterns that enhance learning. Let me note three such pedagogical concomitants of inductive procedures: *participation, relevance,* and *commitment.*

Participation

The argument, here, is that conventional expository teaching makes a cerebral blotter of the student, and that such passivity is a poor condition for learning. When, on the other hand, students are actively engaged—as they must be in inductive procedures—in gathering and analyzing the data needed to answer their questions, then learning is promoted.

Reason and experience support this view. Nearly 50 years ago Dewey argued that the customary classroom discipline impeded learning, for it restricted that bodily activity, movement, and manipulation without which

---

[1] Based on a study of Charles Y. Glock and Rodney Stark, "Is There an American Protestantism?" *Trans-action*, vol. 3, no. 1 (November/December, 1965).

the perception of meaning must be incomplete.[2] Two years earlier A. I. Gates has found that "learning scores jumped 100 percent when four-fifths of the subject's time was devoted to recitation rather than to passive reading."[3] After reviewing a large number of learning studies, Haggard and Rose concluded with this law of active participation: "... when an individual assumes an active role in a learning situation (a) he tends to acquire the response-to-be-learned more rapidly, and (b) these response-patterns tend to be more stably formed than when he remains passive."[4] Gordon Allport reports asking 250 college students to recall their experiences in the eighth grade, writing down three vivid memories about their school work. "Three quarters of the memories were for situations in which the subject himself was actively participating, even though the percentage of time actually spent in the average eighth grade room must be small."[5] "Facts of this sort," Allport says, "prove to us that people have to be active in order to learn, in order to store up efficient memories, to build voluntary control, to be cured when they are ill, restored when they are faint."[6]

And so to pose significant questions, to pursue and analyze the data that yield tentative answers—to engage actively in such a process may be supposed a more effective mode of teaching than the customary teacher-exposition.

Relevance

For students to share actively in the process of problem-solving is not enough. Beyond the matter of teasing illuminating generalizations from particular data, there is another dimension of induction. This is the movement from personal to general relevance. What are the wider implications of individual experience?

In a good learning situation we can expect the student (and the teacher) to ask: "So what?" The query is not a skeptical impertinence. To fail to answer it is to overlook the moral component of inquiry. For there must be a judgment, at least implicit, about the *worth* of the proposed inquiry—a judgment about the better and the worse. We're asking students to invest themselves in a task. If it's an important job, there will be trying moments, for problem-solving is arduous. Is it more or less interesting,

[2] John Dewey, *Democracy and Education* (New York: Crowell Collier and Macmillan, Inc., 1916).

[3] A. I. Gates, "Recitation as a Factor in Memorizing," *Archives of Psychology*, vol. 6, no. 40 (1917), cited in Gordon W. Allport, "The Psychology of Participation," *The Psychological Review*, vol. 53, no. 3 (May, 1945).

[4] E. A. Haggard and R. J. Rose, "Some Effects of Mental Set and Active Participation in the Conditioning of the Autokinetic Phenomenon," *Journal of Experimental Psychology*, 34 (1944): 45–49.

[5] Allport, op. cit., p. 20.

[6] Ibid., p. 121.

more or less relevant, more or less meaningful than other questions we might pursue? Are we justified in imposing the problem on our students?

The issue is one of thrusting something on somebody. We think it justified to protect ourselves against bodily intrusions. We write anti-billboard laws lest our eyes be offended. We try to protect ourselves against noise (ear pollution). We protect our noses and lungs against air pollution and we refuse to eat what we deem unpalatable, not to say poisonous. Shall we teach our students to be less precious about what's thrust into their minds?

Perhaps any inquiry requires an *apologia pro sua vita*. But induction, with its detailed grubbery, especially reminds us that inquiry has two faces, one bearing on the true, the other on the good. As to the true, we move from *perception* to *conception*. As to the good, we justify the project by moving from the personally, immediately relevant to matters of general concern.

Because of its subject matter, sociology may have a special advantage. For it is a humane discipline, studying that humanity which can emerge only from man's life among men. Cross-cutting the range of human relationships, it illuminates that most important part of nature we call *human* nature. But on the other hand it may be very vulnerable. For students may think they are to deal with matters that are familiar, personal and therefore obviously relevant. Yet they are asked to deal distantly and objectively with novel social dimensions lacking immediate personal bearing.

If we are to capitalize on sociology's humane side and protect its vulnerable flanks, we must attend to the moral aspect of induction. Sociological problems must be *worth* pursuing. This means that they must be linked with matters personally relevant.

Personal relevance is a problem not only because the social deals with dimensions not found in the individual—vital rates, social distance, social integration—but because teachers and sociologists may not speak the language of youth. (This may be particularly crucial for sociology where an emphasis on what *is* runs afoul the highly moral concerns of youth for what *ought* to be.) The roots of this separation of elders from youth lie in the nature of our society. Quite unwittingly we have developed a policy of apartheid for the young. Committed increasingly to the company of their peers, young people are separated from family, work, serious civic participation, or religious concerns. Through past decades, changes in the social order have increasingly set the young apart, a group of privileged pariahs. They stand outside the major institutional spheres that preoccupy the elders. Theirs not to reason why, theirs simply to comply.[7]

---

[7] This argument is developed in my essay, "Our Privileged Pariahs," *The Antioch Review*, Fall, 1966.

If this is so, the matter of personal relevance becomes extraordinarily important. It implies an interplay between the personal and the impersonal, between things immediate and matters more remote. We need to know where the student itches, so that we may start there with a scratching as gratifying as we can manage. It means that we begin with a personal problem or problems common to young people, or that young people can realistically anticipate. We need then to move to the more general level of social problems, both to heighten awareness of general issues of civic concern, and to help the student discriminate between a social issue and a sociological problem. For as promptly as may be, we want to move toward our central concern, sociological analysis.

Teaching sociologists are divided on this issue. Probably most of them see personal and civic questions as quite secondary, if relevant at all. My own inclination is to persuade the high school student of the necessary alliance between the man of action and the man of knowledge—especially since these are invariably two facets of the same person. And I suspect that personal and civic issues offer good motivational leverage for getting into disciplined inquiry. In any case, I think we cannot blink the "So what?" issue. And to answer "So what?" means we have to follow an inductive process along the moral dimension: from personal things that count, to social matters of civic and then intellectual concern.

Commitment

I argue, finally, that commitment to the task goes along with active participation in the attack on relevant questions—and that all three (active involvement, relevance, and commitment) are fostered by inductive procedures.

You will recall the surprising findings in a study of the Hawthorne plant of General Electric in Chicago.[8] The working day was shortened and production increased. It was lengthened: production increased. Rest periods were changed, more of them, fewer of them, made longer and shorter. Production rates went up. Level of lighting was varied. Production went up. A return to the original conditions with a regular working day, no refreshments, and no specified rest periods brought the same results. Why? Apparently because a sense of active involvement in a common enterprise was triggered by the experimenters. The result was what we now call the "Hawthorne Effect," more sense of involvement in a common enterprise, more engagement in the task.

---

[8]   Elton Mayo, *The Human Problems of an Industrial Civilization* (New York: Crowell Collier and Macmillan, Inc., 1933). *See also* F. J. Roethlisberger and W. J. Dickson, *Management and the Worker* (Cambridge, Mass.: Harvard University Press, 1939).

And in this connection, Gordon Allport has written:

... When the individual goes through motions that he does not find meaningful, when he does not really participate, then come rebellion against authority, complaints, griping, gossip, rumor, scape-goating, disaffection of all sorts. The job-satisfaction is low.

... a person ceases to be reactive and contrary in respect to a desirable course of conduct only when he himself has had a hand in declaring that course of conduct to be desirable.[9]

* * *

I've been suggesting that a stress on inductive learning (1) promotes participation, (2) constrains us to consider the relevance of problems posed, and (3) promotes a commitment to the task not so readily engendered by conventional teaching patterns. Participation, relevance, and task commitment, in turn speed learning and lengthen retention span. Or so my argument runs.

I am not contending that inductive procedures constitute *the* way of teaching. I'd suppose that a change of pace and method would be, in itself, a useful pedagogical device. Pursuit of a question by careful research methods is a teaching tool, a means to an end, and a tool to be used in combination with other tools.

There are less abstract issues to consider, the nuts and bolts matters that are perhaps closer to the classroom. For example, is induction too slow? Isn't straightforward exposition more efficient and economical in teaching? Or, what happens when the inductive process leads to wrong conclusions, perhaps due to bad methodology? Maybe their sample is bad, or perhaps they fail to control a crucial variable. What then? Does the inductive procedure have elements of surprise, excitement, intrigue that other patterns of teaching lack? Is there a useful distinction to be drawn between a purely inductive process and guided induction—between guided replication of an experiment, for example, and simply throwing a problem (or data) at the student?

These are some of the more concrete issues that warrant our attention. Perhaps what we need most of all is a test of alternate procedures, used by the same teacher on the same subject matter with comparable groups of students. This brings to mind one final comment. Teachers using inductive methods in teaching sociology will be both better equipped and more inclined to apply inductive tests to their own teaching.

---

9   Gordon Allport, op. cit., pp. 122–23.

Sociological Resources for the Social Studies

Sociology, like other social sciences, has its ardent supporters and detractors. Some teachers and administrators are convinced that sociology is too controversial to be taught in secondary schools. They claim that much sociological research is over-burdened by charts and statistics to be meaningful or of interest to high school students. Other detractors suggest that the sociologist is a detached scholar who understands clearly the nature of society's ills, but offers no personal commitment or clues to their solution.

On the other hand, an increasing number of professors in the field of social science education, and many social studies teachers, are convinced that more sociology ought to be taught on the high school level. They argue that sociology dealing with intergroup relations can be of great help to students in understanding contemporary societal issues. Toward this end, sociological concepts, like *status, class, social mobility* and others can be of great value. It is also argued that sociological modes of inquiry, including surveys, polls and factor analysis, can be of inestimable value in the study of history, both past and contemporary.

Some educators believe that sociology points too honestly to painful realities that are inherent in our way of life. When asked why he carried on his research, Max Weber replied, "I want to see how much I can stand!" [1] Most people cannot stand very much. Consequently, in the first national trials the SRSS (Sociological Resources for the Social Studies) materials were often considered to be too controversial.

There is the reaction from the community (voiced either by community leaders or by parents) which says "You are not gonna teach that stuff to our kids." Then there is the reaction of school personnel, usually based upon the anticipation of objections from the community.[2]

The realization that "sociology is intrinsically disruptive" has prompted Everett K. Wilson, former sociologist-in-chief of the project, to observe with an air of resignation that the discipline is "doomed to become a thin

---

[1] Max Weber, as quoted by Reinhard Bendix in *Max Weber: An Intellectual Portrait* (Garden City, N.Y.: Doubleday & Company, Inc., Anchor Books, 1962), p. 9.

[2] Robert C. Angell and F. Lincoln Grahlfs, "The First National Trials of SRSS Episodes," paper prepared for delivery at the Sixty-second Annual Meeting of the American Sociological Association, San Francisco, August 30, 1967, p. 7.

gruel, so concocted as to affirm the current verities and placate any distrustful authority." [3]

In the long run, however, the stark realism of sociology may contribute to its greater, if initially grudging, public acceptance. Since the social and urban problems of the 1960's demand our unflinching attention, the sociological perspective may be thrust upon us out of necessity. The heads of the sociology project welcome this development but they would undoubtedly argue the assumption that their subject has relevance only in times of national emergency.

ORIGIN AND RATIONALE

The origin of SRSS lies in the American Sociological Association's decision to form a Committee on the Social Studies Curriculum of American Secondary Schools in 1961. Under the chairmanship of Neal Gross, the committee realized that "neither the substance nor the methods of modern sociology were adequately represented in high school social studies curricula, not even in courses labeled 'sociology'." [4] It then entertained ideas as to how the sociological profession could cooperate with high school teachers to improve the situation. The result of these deliberations was a proposal to the course improvement section of the National Science Foundation, which led to the creation of SRSS. The organization, now active in the creation of curriculum materials, is headquartered at the First National Building in Ann Arbor, Michigan. Let us now examine the benefits that these materials might have for high school students.

In introducing SRSS's new sociology course, Everett Wilson claims that "sociology is admirably suited to enlarging one's view of human nature and the social world in which that nature is cultivated. . . . Since the self is preeminently social, it helps the student discover his identity and its social sources." [5]

There are number of ways in which the discipline might enhance one's understanding of self and society. First, it offers a fresh examination of everyday realities that are usually taken for granted. George Homans asserts that sociology can "make the commonplace strange." [6] And one of its major functions may well be the illumination of realities that hide behind run-of-the-mill facades. As new insights appear, the limitations of "common

---

[3] Everett K. Wilson, "The SRSS Course in Sociology for High School Students," paper prepared for delivery at the Sixty-second Annual Meeting of the American Sociological Association, San Francisco, August 30, 1967, pp. 1–2.

[4] American Sociological Association, *Sociological Resources for Secondary Schools Informational Materials*, p. 3.

[5] Everett K. Wilson, "SRSS Presents a New High School Sociology Course" in SRSS, *Newsletter*, Fall, 1967, p. 1.

[6] George Homans, *The Human Group*, Harcourt Brace & World, Inc.

sense" are often exposed. Hopefully, the student will develop a spirit of healthy scepticism and question dubious assumptions like the one below:

Better educated men showed more psychoneurotic symptoms than those with less education. The mental instability of the intellectual as compared to the more impassive psychology of the man-in-the-street has often been commented on.[7]

Secondly, sociology can alert the student to the societal regularities which constrain and shape the individual's life. C. Arnold Anderson indicates that social sciences should "demonstrate that human actions follow stable patterns, that they are predictable in the large, and that they can be objectively analyzed." [8] With such a perspective one may find new significance in internalized aspects of our way of life, like orientation to the clock and schedules.

Growing out of the perception of order can be an attention to isomorphisms or "similarities of form or process in apparently unlike events or situations." [9] One might be surprised, for example, at the similarity between a Southern white supremacist and a Northerner in advocating elite education.

Finally, if the student can visualize his surroundings as being part of a system, he may detect heretofore undiscovered connections between the discrete parts of society. A social system with its roles and relationships can be profitably studied in terms of manifest and latent functions and the unintended consequences of many human actions may be discovered.

By what kind of pedagogy do the project personnel hope to implement the above ideas? In general SRSS has decided to emphasize inductive teaching or the leading of the student from the specific to the general. The aim of all of the materials is to expose the student to empirical data which eventually lead them to theoretical formulations.

It should be pointed out, however, that the authors have avoided the pitfalls of treating induction as an educational panacea. Unlike many of the current projects, they have come to grips with the complex relationship between induction and deduction.

This is to emphasize the inductive aspects of learning. But the distinction between inductive and deductive thinking is in a way spurious. In the class-

---

[7] Paul Lazarsfeld, "The American Soldier," *Public Opinion Qaurterly*, Fall, 1949, pp. 379–80. In the article the author exposes many myths such as the one cited.

[8] C. Arnold Anderson, "A New Frame for the Social Studies," *The School Review*, Winter, 1964.

[9] Everett K. Wilson, "The Sociological Perspective: Some Basic Notions for the High School Student," talk given at meetings of the Minnesota Council for the Social Studies, October 21, 1966, p. 10.

room and elsewhere, in everyday life as well as in scientific inquiry, both processes are at work. We move from the general to the particular as well as, inductively from the particular case to a generalization. Both in science and in daily life this process is seldom a neatly ordered sequence of steps. Instead a generative mind moves back and forth—sometimes darts artfully between the two levels—confronting the theoretical with the empirical and vice versa.[10]

In reminding us of this complex relationship, the project reflects the influence of Robert Gagne, whose work in learning theory has generally not received the attention that it deserves.

Having settled on induction as a basic strategy, the guiding lights of SRSS attempted to clarify their views on related aspects of student motivation. They disagree on whether it is advantageous to start with the student's immediate and personal world. Nevertheless, virtually every sociologist consulted feels that the needs of young people must be taken into account at some developmental phase. And the project explores in detail the problem of the generation gap, adolescent societies, and juvenile delinquency. As we consider some of the trial materials in the next section of the chapter, it will become obvious that there is a conscientious attempt to meet the test of relevance.

MATERIALS

Although sociologists are no less attached to their discipline than scholars of other fields, they have adopted a limited and realistic strategy for dealing with the high schools. Realizing that the curriculum is already overcrowded, the project directors have directed only a portion of their resources toward the development of an eleventh or twelfth grade semester course. The brunt of their effort involves an "attempt to infiltrate the existing curriculum" [11] with short episodes and a series of paperback books which can be incorporated unobtrusively into existing course formats. An episode is a supplementary unit or more precisely "a set of instructional materials designed to provide the high school student a brief, but dramatic and enlightening firsthand encounter with sociological data." Several of these episodes will be reviewed in this chapter.

The paperback thrust of the project is bold in conception. The books are collections of outstanding articles by sociologists, that have been re-

---

10　Everett K. Wilson, "Notes for Building a High School Course in Sociology," *Indiana Social Studies Quarterly* (Muncie: Ball State University, Winter, 1967–68), p. 79.

11　William M. Hering, Jr., "Sociological Resources for Secondary Schools and the High School Curriculum," paper delivered to the NDEA Summer Institute for State Supervisors of Social Studies, Carnegie Institute of Technology, Pittsburgh, Pennsylvania, June 14, 1967, p. 4.

written in popular form. Helen Hughes, the Supervisor of Operation Paperback, explains the procedural aspect of this approach:

Briefly, our procedure is to select good sociological articles, usually from the professional journals, choosing them with the advice of experts in the field. Now it need hardly be said that these are not fit for high school reading and indeed often even the authors' colleagues are hard put to it to understand what has been written. We have a corps of professional writers who put the pieces into layman's language and make the presentation brighter and more inviting. However, we have learned that layman's language as the professional writer understands it, is not high school talk. Therefore, the next step is to have the pieces tested informally by several high school teachers who work with us. From their experiences with the rewritten articles, we learn if they are interesting and intelligible and if the vocabulary is appropriate.... In recasting articles written 25 or 35 years ago when much of the fundamental sociology was appearing, we ask our writers to bring facts and figures up to date, where possible, with material from the 1960 census, or we ask the original writer if he can provide us with more recent calculations to make his data current. But many sociological analyses are on the whole as good now as when they were first expounded.[12]

It is encouraging to note that at least one of the new projects is experimenting with this kind of translation. A similar procedure has been advocated by Joseph Schwab for the improvement of science teaching. In "The Teaching of Science as Enquiry" (an essay full of implications for the social studies) Professor Schwab presents a rationale for "idiomatic translation." [13] While there are, as he points out, occasions when such alterations will violate aesthetic considerations, we in the social studies would do well to test the strategy of rewriting in a wide variety of situations.

The first paperback is entitled *Cities and City Life*. Its table of contents gives the reader an idea of the wide range of studies that are utilized.

Cities and City Life consists of 20 articles. The Table of Contents is as follows:

1. The Urbanization of Mankind ...... from Kingsley Davis
2. Urbanism as a Way of Life .... from Louis Wirth
3. What Kind of City Form? .... from Kevin Lynch

---

[12] Helen MacGill Hughes, "Operation Paperback: Sociology in the High School Library," *Indiana Social Studies Quarterly* (Muncie: Ball State University, Winter 1967–68), p. 69.

[13] Joseph J. Schwab and Paul F. Brandwein, "The Teaching of Science as Enquiry,"in *The Teaching of Science* (Cambridge: Harvard University Press, 1964), pp. 79–81.

In developing its materials SRSS has been especially cognizant of the importance of field-testing [14] and of the teacher-variable. As a result of the first national trials, the project learned that the "most serious single weakness of all of the episodes is insufficient detail in the teacher's guides." [15] However, this information merely confirmed what the directors had gleaned from preliminary revisions of the episodes tested. In a directive dated April 17, 1967, Robert Angell, executive director of the project, reminded the writers of their responsibility to classroom practitioners:

First, we want to emphasize that the teacher-designers who have been working on the episode are *not* the audience to which the teacher's manual

---

[14] The *Readings in Sociology Series* is available from Allyn and Bacon, Inc.
[15] Angell and Grahlfs, op. cit., p. 14.

is addressed. It is addressed to persons who have never seen the episode before and may never have thought of the ideas contained in it. They will not have had the advantage that the teacher-designers have of being able to talk over the whole matter with a sociologist-designer. Moreover, most of the teachers will have had little work in sociology. Therefore, the teacher's manual must give the individual all possible help to teach the episode.[16]

This statement is a good indication of the project's practical bent. The leaders of the project are anxious that the knowledge of the sociologist be made useful to the secondary schools.

The episode on Stereotypes appears to be more psychological than sociological, but the student should realize that these areas overlap considerably. The unit asks the student to consider the notion that "what we experience from our senses is not an exact reproduction of the world as it really is." At the outset the strategy is largely inductive, and the class is involved in a replication of an experiment designed by Allport and Postman in 1940. The exercise elicits reactions to a picture showing a verbal interchange between a Negro and a white man in a crowded bus. The white man is represented with a razor in his hand. Without being told that the unit is to be about stereotypes or prejudice, the class is divided into groups of six or seven. One person in each group is given a 6 × 9 copy of the picture whose contents he conceals from the others. He then turns to the person next to him and out of earshot of the rest describes the details of the picture as accurately as possible. The procedure is repeated until the last person writes a verbatim report of what he has heard.

Almost without exception the written account will not do justice to the original. It is quite likely that the student will come to appreciate the selective nature of perception and the ways in which prejudice may guide that selection. While the original experiment often resulted in unfavorable depictions of the Negro, the writers wisely point out that some students of the sixties and seventies will bend over backward to be favorable to him. Despite the fact that some children will approach the procedure in the spirit of a parlor game and produce accounts so different from the original as to be ridiculous, the activity will probably be a provocative eye-opener for the class as a whole.

Immediately thereafter the unit presents an analysis of the term "category" and of reasons why categorization is a significant process. This section lays the groundwork for considering stereotypes as a variety of category.

So that the class will gain a working understanding of stereotypes, the teacher constructs with the students a profile chart which represents

---

[16] Robert C. Angell, *Directive on Teacher's Manual*, April 17, 1967, p. 1.

characteristics associated with the owners of a variety of car-makes. The information from which the chart is created is collected from the group about a week prior to the beginning of the stereotype unit. Originally, the project considered sampling attitudes about ethnic groups, but chose a more neutral topic. This decision was reached because the authors "did not wish to embarrass students who were members of groups unfavorably stereotyped by their classmates." We find this reasoning to be justifiable, but remind the reader of the problem in classroom honesty that has been raised. It is quite likely that in certain areas and schools, the ethnic approach would prove to be more fruitful. One might also note the potentiality for embarrassment in the Allport–Postman experiment.

After examining their own attitudes about car owners, the students are introduced to the ways that advertisers make use of stereotyped conceptions. Some may object to this seeming popularization of the psychology of advertising, but a day spent on the "hidden persuaders" will do no harm and may even prove to be motivational. It can also provide an opportunity to consider the accuracies and inaccuracies involved in stereotypes.

By now the students ought to be ready for a more disciplined involvement with the sociological perspective. The next assignment entails a detailed examination of Sherif's study of inter-group relations in a boys' summer camp. By leading the class through a seven-step version of "the scientific method," the authors hope to acclimate the student to the rigors of experimental procedure. Although some may consider the step ideas to be a naive conception of science, it is an excellent device for illuminating a piece of research for high school students.

As an exercise in closure, teachers are urged to show the film, *Eye of the Beholder*. Its story concerns differing perceptions of Michael Gerard, an artist, by five people with whom he has recently come in contact. As the teacher's guide explains:

Each (of the five) knows a little of the real Michael, each is ignorant of much of the real man, and each thinks some things that are untrue. We have learned very little about Michael, but we do know something about each of the beholders.[17]

The guide includes some advice on how to extract the maximum pedagogical value from the film. Possible stopping places are indicated, and provocative questions are supplied.

Many teachers will find that they have used many of the techniques set forth in this episode. Some of the ploys are beginning to achieve a

---

[17] SRSS, "Stereotypes," *Teacher's Manual*, p. 14.

hackneyed status. Nevertheless SRSS has provided a service by bringing the approaches within the confines of one volume.

The unit on "The Sociology of Religion" affords us an excellent opportunity to comment on one of the project's most important ideas, namely that students should have some introduction to quantitative procedures. Although such an aim is ambitious in light of the fact that many social studies teachers are not mathematically-minded, one is bound to conclude that for the most part statistical approaches are judiciously used.

For example, the booklet warns the student about attaching value judgments to arrangements of numerical information. This matter appears in the context of an attempt to relate non-religious differences to the conflict between religious groups.

Suppose that the members of a society are divided into five classes on the basis of their income; the prestige of, and the skills required in, their occupations; and other factors. Thus we might assign a score of 5 to the man who holds a highly skilled professional job, and a score of 1 to the man in an unskilled job with low and unsteady income. In the same manner, we could make a scale out of the educational factor, perhaps assigning a score of 5 to the person with some college training or a college degree, 4 to a person who has graduated from high school, and ranging down to 1 for the illiterate person without education. National origin might be noted . . . . When these three scales are combined, the highest possible numerical score is 15 and the lowest is 3. The point I am making here is that if most of the members of one religious group have relatively high scores . . . and most of the members of another religious group have low scores . . . there is a greater likelihood of religious conflict.[18]

The Student Manual also carefully points out that "these scores are not a matter of better or worse. ('Better and worse' are matters of your own judgment.) The scores are simply a way of showing how the members of a population can differ in various ways." [19] This statement is unlikely, however, to be very comforting to a student whose parents would get a low score under the system just described. If the authors really believe qualitative differences are not reflected, they might better put across this notion by assigning low numbers to high income and so on. To expect high school students not to feel negative about low income may be a bit unrealistic, regardless of the assurances offered. The point that judgments whether negative or positive are in the last analysis made by people is profitably mentioned nevertheless.

---

[18] SRSS, "The Sociology of Religion," *Student Manual*, pp. 14–15.
[19] Ibid., p. 14.

Other nuances are examined. In considering religious intermarriage, the students learn to convert data into percentiles. They then are shown the important distinction between group and individual rates:

The percentage of intermarriage for each religious group is higher if the total number of marriages is considered, but lower if the total number of individuals involved is considered.[20]

Some crucial work is also done on the idea of correlation, and care is taken not to equate correlation with causation. Only once do the authors seem to be overly esoteric. This is in their detailed consideration of the concept of probability. Even then, however, they concede that the ability of the class will be the determining factor.

The rest of the unit also deserves close attention. It begins much more deductively than the stereotypes episode and sets forth working definitions of *role* and *institution*.

The student has an opportunity to practice some demographic research techniques such as making a religious map of the community. Also recommended is the solicitation of information through personal interviews with ministers in the area. A great deal of attention is paid to proper interviewing technique.

It is fitting in light of the times that the reciprocal relationship between religion and society is probed. A case study of the Black Muslims is an excellent example suggested by the unit. A questionnaire may shed light on the relationship between religious belief and community action.

In a more recently tested episode, "Leadership in American Society: A Case Study of Negro Leadership," a timeless sociological topic is given a timely focus. After examining some popular approaches to the study of leadership, the authors conclude in the student manual that "we cannot learn about the nature of leadership by studying the *personalities* of those who are regarded as leaders or potential leaders." [21] They then offer another alternative: the situational idea. The sociological perspective, they assert, pays "special attention to the *group* aspects of leadership and the social situations that affect leadership." [22]

From the latter form of reference the student views Negro leaders of the past and present. As they study careers ranging from that of Booker T. Washington to that of Stokely Carmichael, classes are asked to account for the rise of each man to prominence in terms of the following situational components: long-range factors, short-range factors, leadership base, general

---

[20]   Ibid., p. 19.
[21]   *Student Manual*, p. 6.
[22]   Ibid.

group objectives, specific group objectives, leader, action strategy, and leadership behavior. A specific example is provided below:

A DIAGRAM OF MAJOR SITUATIONAL COMPONENTS OF LEADERSHIP BEHAVIOR
Sample 2: Nat Turner

Leadership Behavior: Directing the massacre of whites and gathering arms.

Action Strategy: Annihilate resistance and former oppressors.

Leader: Nat Turner

Specific Group Objectives: To capture the county seat and obtain the necessary supplies and weapons.

General Group Objectives: To achieve freedom or at least escape to the Great Dismal Swamp.

Leadership Base: Discontented slaves willing to take risks with a radical.

Short-range Situational Factors: Deteriorating conditions of slaves in the area of Southampton County, Virginia, and the religious development of Nat Turner.

Long-range Situational Factors: Dissatisfaction with the subordinate position of being slaves.

The diagram illustrates clearly the view that leadership is a phenomenon shaped by many constraints which to a large degree define the response of the individual concerned.

Most of the historical and bibliographical data upon which the student bases his analysis is interesting and well written. The teacher, however, should note the sources of this material. For example, the sketch of Nat Turner is provided by William Styron whose characterization has been subjected to a harsh attack by some Negro writers who have accused Styron of looking on the Turner rebellion from a white perspective.

The *pièce de résistance* of the episode is a case study of the Tallahassee Bus Protest. By use of the situational technique, the student has an opportunity to account for the shift of Negro leadership during that situation and thus to demonstrate his competence with another sociological device.

In the conclusion of the Student Manual, the authors claim that the student should develop an ability "to look below the surface" of an event. We concur and believe that the episode on leadership is a substantial contribution to the understanding of the Negro civil rights movement.

Another episode on "Social Mobility in the United States" tends to be a bit heavy on the statistical approach, but directs attention to the problem of stratification, a matter of crucial import in considering the origin of some recent civil disorder. The student is introduced to the theories of Marx, Weber, and Warner and then asked to consider why stratification is an endemic part of virtually all societies. The major contribution of this unit seems to be in pointing the attention of the students to the role of class and status, two concepts which are often ignored in civics textbooks.

Finally, "The Family in Three Settings" sheds light on a societal institution often taken for granted, but not fully understood. A sociological way of thinking is revealed when students try to imagine how the functions of the family would be carried out by a society in which such an institution did not exist.

Because the episodes are written by a variety of authors, they tend to be uneven in form and quality. While the unit on stereotypes is less original in conception, it has more internal structure with a series of activities reaching an over-arching culmination. Sometimes there is a disparate quality to assignments. Especially in the religion unit do we have the sense of one activity after the other with no meaningful sequence. In light of the strategy of infiltration, such weaknesses are not to be unexpected and constitute no major problem. Ideas have been collected and filed together, and the teacher presumably can use them in a variety of ways.

CONCLUSION

There can be no doubt that SRSS has made a noteworthy contribution to social studies education. Classroom teachers and administrators should welcome the fact that the directors have offered a number of routes for the incorporation of their discipline into existing curriculums. If the secondary schools are to make the most of this opportunity to understand society better, it is essential that they perceive sociology in a way that is relevant to today's complicated world and not as a hackneyed rehash of topics like marriage and the family.

A timely and thoughtful assessment of sociology's role has been offered by Peter Berger in his *Invitation to Sociology: A Humanistic Perspective*.[23] Although parts of his message are more applicable to higher education, this book should be read by all social studies teachers. Essentially, Berger calls for individuals to assert their influence in a world that often appears too much to cope with. Insisting that man too often practices "bad faith" (Sartre)—"attributing to . . . necessity what he in fact chooses to do" [24]—

[23]   Peter Berger, *Invitation to Sociology: A Humanistic Perspective* (Garden City, N.Y.: Doubleday & Company, Inc., Anchor Books, 1963).
[24]   Ibid., p. 144.

he argues that sociological knowledge can indicate the exact nature of the constraints upon us and thus make us freer men, schooled in an understanding of the system and thus better able to devise a way to beat it at its own game. The analysis includes an extremely lucid examination of myths and realities about the discipline.

Teachers might also consider the role that sociology can play in alerting their students to the importance of the problem of knowledge. In *The Image*,[25] by Kenneth Boulding, they will find a provocative treatment of knowledge-building processes, full of implications for the curriculum. For example, the book underscores the need to show that human endeavor is a result less of what reality is than what we *think* it is.

Sociology might also offset some of the cynicism that some individuals develop about our sorely beset society, when they discover the difficulties in its functioning. In this regard the knowledge of the evolution and operation of institutions would seem to be most vital. Here sociology can assist the social studies students in better understanding of institutional and societal conflicts.

---

[25] Kenneth Boulding, *The Image* (University of Michigan Press, Ann Arbor Books, 1966).

CHAPTER VI

Economics

7   ECONOMICS

Excerpts from Economic Education in the Schools, the Report of the National Task Force on Economic Education *

THE NEED FOR ECONOMIC EDUCATION

Economic understanding is essential if we are to meet our responsibilities as citizens and as participants in a basically private enterprise economy. Many of the most important issues in government policy are economic in nature, and we face economic problems at every turn in our day-to-day lives. Consider, for example, some of the economic issues confronting the nation and many of us as individuals in recent years: inflation, recession and unemployment, a lagging rate of economic growth, the impact of automation, the "farm problem," financing of schools and highways, medical care for the aged, foreign aid, government deficits, and taxes. Economic problems arise at every level—national, state, and local—and in both public and private affairs.

The economic role of government and the complexity of the economic

---

* Members of the Task Force: George Leland Bach, Chairman, Dean, Graduate School of Industrial Administration, Carnegie–Mellon University; Arno A. Bellack, Professor of Education, Teachers College, Columbia University; Lester V. Chandler, Chairman, Department of Economics, Princeton University; M. L. Frankel, Director, Joint Council on Economic Education; Robert Aaron Gordon, Chairman, Department of Economics, University of California, Berkeley; Ben W. Lewis, Chairman, Department of Economics, Oberlin College; Paul S. Samuelson, Professor of Economics, Massachusetts Institute of Technology; Floyd A. Bond, Executive Secretary, Dean, School of Business Administration, University of Michigan.

issues with which it deals have grown enormously in the past fifty years. For this there have been many reasons—the increase and urbanization of our population, the sheer growth of wealth and incomes, rapid scientific and technological change, two world wars, a great depression, continuing international tensions, and changing attitudes toward government. One may approve or deplore the power of government in economic affairs, but no one can deny its existence nor that the quality of government policies is a major force in determining the performance of our entire economic system.

In the final analysis, the effectiveness of government depends on the capacity and understanding of the people. For it is the people who, through their votes and other influences, determine within broad limits the scope and nature of government policies. If they are to exercise their great political power responsibly and effectively, more of our people must know more about our economy and must learn to think about economic issues objectively and rationally. The alternative is to make decisions on the basis of ignorance and prejudice. Nor is the case for economic understanding limited to preparation for effective voting. Leaders in every walk of life— business, labor, agriculture—need to understand the American economy, as do the people who work for the businesses and who are the members of the unions.

If our citizens of tomorrow are to achieve the desired minimum economic understanding, most of them must get it in the schools. It is no good to say that they can wait until college, for less than half of them go on to college, and most of those do not study economics when they get there. Thus, most of our youth must rely on the high schools for the economics they are to learn.

How Are the Schools Meeting Their Responsibility for Developing Economic Understanding?

The understanding of the American economy developed in most high schools today is not adequate for effective citizenship. While excellent teaching of economics occurs in some schools, very few high school students take a course in economics; textbooks and other teaching materials are all too often inadequate; and most teachers in the social studies have insufficient preparation in economics to teach the subject effectively. Despite a trend in recent years toward inclusion of more economics in the schools, the existing situation is far from satisfactory.

Economics in the Curriculum

Apparently only about five percent of all high school students ever take a separate course in economics. Perhaps half of all high school students do study "Problems of American Democracy," or a similarly oriented "problems" course, in which a substantial block of time is devoted to economic aspects of current broad social problems, such as natural resources, labor-management relations, and social security. Nearly all students take a course in American history, where some attention is given to the development of economic institutions and legislation. Scattered attention is given to economic institutions and problems at a variety of other points in the curriculum, notably in the social studies courses throughout the grades.

Even in the separate course in economics, however, the orientation is generally descriptive and all too often dry and sterile. Little attention is given to helping students learn to think for themselves about the big economic problems our nation faces today. Few analytical concepts are developed, and fewer are used. In the problems of American democracy and American history courses, even less attention is given to the development of independent analytical thinking by students on economic problems. The flavor of these courses is often chronological and descriptive, with teachers placing primary stress on those areas where their own training is strongest, usually in history. On economic issues it appears that teachers often insert their own value judgments and "answers" on economic issues as to what the student should believe, all too often without identifying them as such.

Teaching Materials

Teaching materials are improving, but they remain generally inadequate. A recent survey of the economics content of leading textbooks for courses in economics, problems of American democracy, and American history, made by three groups of respected American economists, indicates that high school students are being given a running glance at a wide array of economic topics, but that only in rare cases are the teaching materials focused on developing fundamental economic understanding.

The treatment in textbooks is mainly descriptive; economic analysis is almost entirely absent; the reasoning is often loose and superficial; value judgments of the authors, generally unidentified as such, abound. The committees reported that these books generally fail to develop an awareness of what the fundamental economic problems are, and of how rational, objective reasoning can contribute effectively to their solution. In the American history books, to which most high school students are exposed, the treatment of economics is primarily descriptive and fails to emphasize economic analysis of the major problems involved, since the emphasis of the books is historical.

Since most social studies teachers have had little, if any, formal training in economics, they cannot reasonably be expected to add to their textbooks an objective, analytical approach to the understanding of the modern American economy. The quality of textbooks and other teaching materials thus becomes all the more important.

In addition to textbooks, there is a mass of special pamphlets and materials available to social studies teachers in the high schools. These materials, flooding the schools, come from institutions and organizations of every description, many of them with propaganda intent. Some of these publications represent sound scholarship and a genuine desire to make available objective and useful information. Since most teachers are neither adequately prepared nor have the time to assess all of this printed matter, its usefulness in most high school teaching is dubious. The large volume of urgent requests from teachers and administrators for evaluation of such publications, and for lists of recommended books, pamphlets and audio-visual aids, reveals the desperate need for assistance felt by those responsible for teaching economics in the high schools.

The Teachers

Today we rely primarily on high school teachers in the social studies and American history to develop understanding of the American economy. While most of these teachers are conscientious and sincere, only a little more than half of them have ever had as much as a single college course in economics to prepare them for this important part of their teaching job. Most of these have apparently had only one or two college courses in economics. Virtually none have undergraduate majors in economics, even those teaching special courses in economics in the high schools.

Obviously, teachers who have inadequate preparation cannot be expected to do an adequate job in the classroom. This explains why economic analysis gets virtually no attention in most history courses, and is often poorly taught in problems of American democracy and civics courses. To make this point is not to malign the training, skill, and splendid work of many able and dedicated teachers in the high schools. It is merely to be realistic about the necessity of adequate training to do a proper job.

State teacher certification requirements are intended to provide minimum standards for teachers. Yet apparently only sixteen of the fifty states require even an elementary course in economics for certification to teach high school social studies. This situation is reflected in the curricula of the colleges that train teachers in the social studies. In a recent study of social studies teacher programs in 50 selected colleges and universities throughout the country, 38 were found to offer a major in social studies. Of these, only 25 required any economics for the major, with a median requirement of only one year of elementary economics for these teachers of tomorrow who will be largely responsible for teaching basic understanding of the American economy in our schools.

The dearth of teachers able to teach economics was dramatically illustrated recently when a large city decided to introduce economics into its high schools. The operation would have required 300 teachers, but only 17 could be found with adequate training for the task!

The Public's Attitude

Recently, there has been a strong growth of interest in the teaching of economics in the high schools. Only with such basic public support can real improvement in this area come about. Unfortunately, it is necessary to recognize that many individuals and groups see economics in the schools as a device for stressing their own viewpoints, as an opportunity to foist on the schools their own private views. Too many do not recognize the value of impartial analysis and discussion of varying viewpoints and interpretations of controversial issues. Too many insist, indeed, that controversial issues should be avoided in the classroom. Most important problems are controversial, and today large numbers of social studies teachers avoid controversial issues because they fear public criticism. This is not the way to train our youth to face the important problems that will confront them as citizens. It is not the way to the development of sound economic understanding. . . .

The Need for a Rational Approach to Economic Problems

Why Economic Understanding Is Important

As we have seen, modern man is faced with a host of economic problems. This is the basic reason why economic understanding is important. Such personal decisions as what occupation to enter, how to spend his income, or in what form to invest his savings, he must be prepared to make himself.

Others are public economic problems at the state and local level on which he must decide and vote as a citizen. Should he, for example, vote to raise taxes in his community to finance better schools, or to bring new industries into his region? Should the state's unemployment compensation law provide larger and longer benefits?

Still others face us at the national level, such as what the federal government should do to support high employment and rapid growth while at the same time preventing inflationary increases in prices? If a recession threatens, what steps can and should be taken? Indeed, why do we have recurring periods of boom and slack times?

Americans live and work in a particular kind of economic system.

Many people call it a "private enterprise" system. What are the essential characteristics of this system, and how does it differ from others? How do consumers make their wishes known so that the goods they want are produced in the right quantities? What role does competition play, and what sort of antimonopoly legislation do we need? Why does agriculture (the most competitive of all our industries) seem to be in continuous trouble, and hence, what should we do about the "farm problem"?

On the international level, should we have tariffs to protect domestic markets for American producers? How much foreign aid can, and should we afford for the underdeveloped nations?

All these questions—and many others—must be answered. We can answer them on the basis of ignorance and emotion, or we can act *rationally*; that is, on the basis of a reasonable understanding of how the economy operates, a clear recognition of the goals we want to achieve, an appraisal of the relevant facts, and a reasoned choice of that line of action which will best achieve our goals. Everyone must to some extent act as his own economist—in his private life and as a citizen—and both he and the community will be better served if he is well informed and can think clearly and objectively about economic questions.

What we want to emphasize is the need to develop in the student the ability to reason clearly and objectively about economic issues. The future citizen needs to acquire a modest amount of factual information about the economic world, but the primary obligation of the schools is to help him to develop his capacity to think clearly, objectively, and with a reasonable degree of sophistication about economic problems. Mere description of economic institutions is not what we mean by economic education . . . .

RECOMMENDATIONS

. . . [The preceding comments] outlined the minimum economic understanding essential for good citizenship and attainable by high school students. They emphasized that this requires not only a knowledge of important facts about the economy and its institutions, but also a rational, objective way of thinking about economic issues, and certain concepts and analytical tools to help in this thinking. We turn now to the question of how such an understanding can be achieved. This requires comments on the curriculum, approach and method, teachers, teaching materials, and controversial issues.

We offer a number of specific suggestions in this chapter, emphasizing, however, that they are meant to be suggestive and illustrative, not blueprints for universal adoption. We recognize, for example, that school authorities must weigh the curriculum changes that we suggest against many competing demands. Students vary widely in ability. Some schools have teachers well trained in economics; others do not. Moreover, those charged with responsibility for creating and using specific teaching methods and materials may often be able to improve upon those suggested below. We hope, however, that the general guidelines proposed here will be helpful to those charged with this important task.

The Curriculum

1. *We recommend that more time be devoted in high school curricula to the development of economic understanding.*—It is unrealistic to hope that most students will learn to think effectively about economic issues and to understand the functioning of the American economy without a substantial increase in the time devoted to this purpose in high school curricula. Economic understanding may be taught in separate courses in economics. It may be taught in other courses dealing with economic institutions and issues. How it is most effectively taught will, of course, depend on the students involved, the preparation of the teachers, the amount of time available, and other such conditions. But more time and serious attention... are required in most schools if anything approaching the minimal competence indicated there is to be attained by most students.

In the following sections we indicate our recommendations, depending upon the amount of student time that local school boards and administrators choose to devote to economics in their curricula.

Courses in Economics

2. *We recommend that wherever feasible students take a high school course in economics or its equivalent under another title (such as Problems of American Democracy); and that in all high schools of substantial size there be at least an elective senior-year course in economics.*—To attain the level of economic understanding suggested above will require at least a full semester course for high school students. For most students, even a full course may prove insufficient unless a preliminary groundwork has been laid in earlier courses, introducing both economic institutions and a logical, objective way of thinking about social problems. Thus, we believe that the equivalent of a one semester course is necessary, but not sufficient for most students, to assure the minimum level of economic understanding we recommend.

We recognize the many competing demands on the high school curriculum. Each school board, of course, must decide in view of its circumstances whether or not to *require* a separate course in economics of all its students. We see no practical alternative to assure that all high school graduates attain something like the level of understanding indicated above.[1] Where no such course is required, we do urge that it should, at a minimum, be available as an elective in all schools of substantial size.

While we recommend no particular course arrangement or teaching approach in such a course, we do urge that stress be placed on objective, careful reasoning about economic problems... on understanding the over-all functioning of the economy and on the major problem areas, institutions, and analytical concepts.... We warn against the superficial description that appears to characterize so many present high school courses, and against teaching that stresses memorization of trivial facts, dates, and unused lists of concepts. Such information is soon forgotten, and courses of this sort have little claim to the serious high school student's time.

Economics in Problems of American Democracy Courses

3. *We recommend that courses in problems of American democracy (now taken by perhaps half of all high school students) devote a substantial portion of their time to development of economic understanding....*—Such courses usually cover a variety of problems, or problem areas, like social security, international relations, big business, conservation of natural resources, public finance, and agriculture. Since the course employs the "problem approach," it can afford excellent training in economic reasoning. On each problem studied, teachers can show that rational decision-making must be based not on ignorance and prejudice but on a careful process of understanding the relevant facts, of analyzing the forces that produce the "problem," of clarifying goals, and of choosing carefully among the available alternatives. Some of the essential concepts and analytical tools ... can be developed in connection with each problem area.

For example, the "farm problem" leads readily to analysis of demand and supply as they interact in the market to establish prices, and to the role of markets in channeling productive resources to meet consumer demands. Government policies to deal with low farm incomes and farm surpluses pose the need to define the economic problem to be solved and the social goals to be achieved, then to list the main alternative courses of action, to evaluate the consequences of these courses, and finally, to choose

---

[1] For the minority of students going on to college and already sure they will take a college course in economics, it may be desirable to take instead further high school work in mathematics, advanced English composition, or some comparable foundation course. But even for these students some degree of repetitive learning between high school and college economics may be advantageous. Most subjects are not thoroughly learned the first time they are studied. Moreover, as more students come to college with a minimal understanding of economic institutions and processes the level and effectiveness of college courses in economics can be raised as has been the case in physics, chemistry, and mathematics in recent years.

the alternative which promises best to achieve the desired goals. Teaching materials for such an approach could include readings on the changing political and economic role of the farmer, data on farm incomes and living standards compared to other groups, information and conflicting views on the values of rural vs. urban living, and recent proposals for "solving" the farm problem through alternative governmental policies—in addition to the analytical materials on supply, demand, prices, and markets suggested above. Economic concepts and principles will have meaning for most students only as they are applied to concrete problems and situations.

Similarly, consideration of monopoly and big business can lead into analysis of the nature of a basically private enterprise economy; the role of competition in markets for products and for labor; the effects of monopoly power on output, prices, and incomes; and the problems of achieving simultaneously reasonable competition and low-cost mass production. The topic of comparative economic systems offers a challenging opportunity to emphasize that all types of economics must somehow deal with the three big economic problems (what, how much, and for whom), and then to compare and contrast their objectives and the methods, institutions, and incentives they to achieve them. . . .

Introduction of more economic analysis into problems of American democracy courses can help significantly to develop the economic understanding needed for good citizenship, if it is done with the objectives and flavor indicated above. We repeat that mere description of facts, institutions and situations accomplishes little of lasting value. Analytically oriented teaching materials, competent teaching, and specific focus on the goals of developing economic understanding and ability to reason independently, are all required if problems of American democracy courses are to contribute significantly to economic understanding.

Economics in History Courses

4. *We recommend that more economic analysis be included in history courses.*—Almost all students take an American history course in the eleventh grade or in a two-year sequence through the twelfth grade. This course presents excellent opportunities for deepening economic understanding and for adding a new dimension to history itself. It inevitably deals with many economic events—tariffs, banking controversies, inflation and deflation, the rise of large-scale business, growth of labor unions, the growing role of government in economic affairs, and many more. If such problems are considered analytically as well as merely descriptively and chronologically, great numbers of high school students will gain in both economic understanding and historical perspective.

American history courses often attempt to cover the entire sweep of

American political and social history including attention to developments in many facets of American life. Moreover, they customarily stress chronology rather than an analytical approach to particular elements of historical development, such as the specific economic problems indicated above. Lastly, historians themselves are understandably often concerned with teaching an historical discipline itself as a major goal in such a course.

Thus, to introduce emphasis on economic understanding along the line we suggest will require, for most history courses, significant changes in approach, materials, and teaching method. We nevertheless urge that this be done, since for many students this is the only formal exposure in the high school curriculum to economic institutions and problems. Special units of economics, in addition to the usual descriptive materials on economic events, could introduce students to the elements of economic reasoning. Such units could easily be developed by economists and historians working together, as we recommend below.

To illustrate, agricultural developments during the last century could readily be taught along the lines indicated above for the problems in American democracy course, by allocating some extra time and using appropriate supplementary readings. Another illustration is provided by the great depression of the 1930's. Most American history texts deal with this descriptively, with primary attention to political developments and the legislation of the New Deal, but little attention to the underlying economic forces involved, analysis of the social goals sought or effectiveness of such legislation.

To supplement this usual historical treatment, economic materials could readily be introduced showing the similarity of the basic economic developments of the 1930's to earlier depressions, and introducing a few of the simple economic concepts . . . —for example, gross national product, money and real income, aggregate demand (spending) and its major components. A simple analysis could be introduced stressing the shortage of aggregate demand in the depression, and the relation of monetary contraction between 1920 and 1933 to this demand shortage and to falling prices. Against this background, students could be led to consider government policies to stimulate recovery through monetary expansion and budgetary policy as well as through direct measures (like NRA and AAA). While the analysis would need to be very elementary, at least students could be led to see the elements of economic reasoning, . . . and could be introduced to a few of the central economic institutions and concepts. . . .

Numerous other possibilities for such units exist—for example, the post-Civil War inflation and monetary collapse, the Sherman Act and its relation to the monopoly problem, and the continuing tariff controversy.

It would be unrealistic to expect that the economic understanding needed for good citizenship can be achieved through American history courses alone. But such courses can make a worthwhile contribution, especially if they can build on earlier attention to economic institutions and if appropriate teaching materials are used to supplement the basic history texts.

Similar economic units could be introduced into world history courses, which typically concentrate on political and social developments. For example, comparative rates of growth in output and living standards of different nations provide a vital issue around which a unit designed to develop economic understanding can readily be built. Focus on natural resources, technology, education, labor force, form of economic organization, and other factors underlying economic growth could introduce these fundamental concepts. Data showing comparative growth rates for highly developed and underdeveloped nations could illustrate the importance of saving and capital accumulation and, at the same time, point up the different factors influencing these rates in different economies—for example, the private enterprise and the communist varieties. Consideration could also be given in this connection to the origins and development of capitalism, and the causes and significance of the industrial revolution.

Increased emphasis on development of economic understanding need not detract from the importance attached to other forces in historical development. Indeed, it can be used to enrich students' understanding of history. For this subject provides a broad framework for the understanding of social, political, and economic forces, within which increased stress on an analytical approach to economic developments can contribute to both historical and economic understanding.

Economics in Business Education

5. *We recommend that all business education curricula include a required course in economics.*—A large group of high school students take special studies intended to prepare them for careers in business. These curricula include bookkeeping, typing, office practice, and a variety of other courses focused on current business practice. Since few of these students go on to college, we especially urge that all such curricula include a course in economics, similar to the one outlined in recommendation No. 2 above.

Minimal training in economics for these students is justified on both citizenship and career training grounds. While the high school course in economics should be focused on business operations or personal finance, a reasonable acquaintance with basic economic institutions will prove valuable for any student entering a business firm. Moreover, many teachers in the business education curriculum have had at least one college course in economics, since this is required for teacher certification much more commonly than for teachers in the social studies.

Business education also provides other places for developing economic understanding. For example, bookkeeping courses can be given much more intellectual content by relating them to simple business accounting concepts, to the role of costs and profits in business firms, and to such concepts as gross national product and national income.

Other Opportunities

6. *We recommend that economic understanding be emphasized at several other points in the entire school curriculum.*—There are many opportunities for building economic understanding from the time the child enters first grade until he graduates from high school. Interesting experiments now under way suggest that such simple notions as division of labor, prices, exchange in markets, and even profit can be grasped by elementary school children if they are built into carefully planned teaching materials and methods. Inescapably, children are exposed to such ideas in their day-to-day lives. The elementary grades provide an opportunity to clarify them, and to relate them to daily problems of family living, especially in the social studies courses children take from the early grades. We commend these experiments and recommend adoption of these techniques in the earlier grades as this becomes feasible.

Geography courses, included in all curricula, provide excellent opportunities to relate the usual descriptive materials to the role of such factors as natural resources, climate, and transportation facilities to the basic economic processes of specialization and exchange. Discussion of differing rates of economic growth in relation to varying possession of natural resources can provide a lively focus for the importance of geography. So can analysis of the geographical bases for the location of different industries. Introduction of such economic issues can help to enliven courses that often become routine.

Mathematics courses offer special promise for introducing students to precise reasoning about economic problems. Although arithmetic and algebra courses typically include problems in personal finance and in business arithmetic, they could equally include use of other economic problems and concepts. For example, supply and demand curves could be employed to illustrate simple graphs. Simple relationships between income and consumption could illustrate the use of linear equations in elementary algebra. We urge teachers and textbook writers to include more such examples, and professional economists to help provide them.

Civics courses, usually taught in the ninth grade, touch at many points on economic issues and problems. Courses in home economics offer opportunities to discuss such things as the role of the consumer, personal saving, and social security in the American economy. Curriculum planners, textbook writers, and teachers in all these courses can do much to provide a foundation for the economic understanding that should be a direct focus of academic work for most students in the final years of high school work. We believe that introduction of more economic materials and concepts need not detract from the educational value of these other courses, but can instead enliven and enrich them.

APPROACHES TO TEACHING

7. *We recommend central emphasis on the rational way of thinking . . . as a prime objective of the teaching of economics.*—We are not competent to advise in detail how teachers in the schools might best develop in their widely differing students the economic understanding we suggest as needed for good citizenship. The most effective approaches and methods will vary depending on the course, teacher, and students involved. But we believe it is far more important for students to learn to think about economic situations objectively and rationally for themselves than to learn masses of institutional details, or memorize lists of unused economic concepts. . . . What they do study . . . should be studied analytically and in reasonable depth, rather than as superficial memory work. A rational way of thinking about economic problems is the first step toward economic understanding.

For students of all ability levels, it is important to establish courses of rigor and challenge comparable to those now offered in science and mathematics. There is research evidence to substantiate the claim that analysis is beneficial to everyone, not merely to those of high ability. It is true that students of high ability can be expected to learn more in less time. But this should not mean analysis for the bright and mere memorization for the less able, though for them a greater stress on facts and institutions will generally be realistic. . . .

We wish to reemphasize here that "objectivity" in economics does not mean merely giving equal time and attention to all competing biases. Rather it means thinking through the situation with clear recognition of the alternative assumptions being made in competing arguments. "Objectivity" implies rational analysis. It does not mean giving students the idea that any view or answer is as good as another.

Lastly, we urge that teachers emphasize getting students to *use* the economic concepts they are asked to learn. Supply and demand means little unless the student sees how he can use them in understanding why farm surpluses persist in the face of government price support policies, or in studying other such practical issues. Saving has meaning when he sees what it means for the family and the local business firm as well as for the economy as a whole. Gross national product is merely a set of technical words unless he sees how it helps him to measure the comparative performance of the American and Russian economies. These are only examples, but they suggest the importance of stressing student use of economic concepts in analyzing practical problems, and the importance of giving the concepts and institutions taught concrete meaning in relation to the student's own experience and interests.

CONTROVERSIAL ISSUES

8. *We recommend that examination of controversial issues be included, where appropriate, in teaching economics.*—Economic understanding and objective analysis cannot be developed in the schools if controversial issues are eliminated from consideration. The more important the economic issue, the more controversial is it likely to be. To avoid issues because they are controversial or to limit serious discussion of them will not make the problem go away or contribute to their rational solution. It will only invite decisions based on ignorance, prejudice, and passion.

The very nature of democracy implies serious discussion by the people. Limitations on discussion of important public problems are not merely infringements on the rights of teachers to teach. More important, they are infringements on the rights of students to learn, to think, and to arrive at their own conclusions. They are thus a threat to the quality of future citizens and to the success of democracy itself.

In approaching controversial issues, teachers should be responsible for leading students to use the analytical, objective approach described earlier —get the relevant facts; clarify objectives; identify, analyze, and compare the various alternative courses of action; and choose among the alternatives in light of the objectives sought. In this process students will inevitably be exposed to points of view not shared by some parents and other groups in the community. They will also subject to critical analysis some points of view to which their parents and others may be devoted. It is not to be expected that such searching analysis will be universally welcomed. But to deprive students of the opportunity to think through controversial issues for themselves is to deprive them of fundamental training for good citizenship and to deny the fundamental tenets of a free and democratic society. To insist upon and defend this right of the teacher and of the students is the duty of every citizen, as well as of teachers, administrators, and school boards, even when particular groups criticize the teacher involved. Ours is a strong society which need not fear open discussion of its economic institutions and processes.

TEACHERS

9. *To improve the ability of teachers, we recommend several steps.*—
Obviously, economic understanding cannot be imparted by teachers who
do not themselves understand economics. As we pointed out . . . apparently
almost half of all high school social studies teachers, and perhaps a quarter
of all those teaching actual courses in economics, have not had as much as
a single college course in economics. This is intolerable if we want their
students to develop real economic understanding. It would be equally futile
to expect teachers who had never had a college course in mathematics or
physics to teach mathematics or physics effectively.

Most teachers try sincerely to do a good job. They work hard to
obtain better materials for their courses and to improve their own abilities.
The need is to provide more effective ways to help present teachers improve
their own understanding, to provide better teaching aids and materials,
and to be sure that new teachers obtain the needed preparation in
economics during their college years. Thus:

a. *We recommend that teacher certification requirements in all states
require a minimum of one full year (6 unit) course in college economics for
all social studies and business education teachers.*—An elementary understanding of the way our economic system functions, and of economic
reasoning, is a minimum basis for reasonable teaching of economics in
history, problems of American democracy, and all other such social studies
and business courses in which economics has a logical place. At least
another year of college economics beyond the elementary course would be
highly desirable.

b. *We recommend that school boards and administrators consider
these certification standards as minimum requirements, and they take steps
to enforce higher standards wherever feasible.*—For instructors who teach
specific courses in economics we recommend, wherever feasible, at least a
college minor in economics (usually about 18 units), and preferably
a college major in the field. Short of a college minor, the high school
teacher of economics has formal training that puts him only a small margin
ahead of his best students. This is not the way to obtain teaching that
stretches the minds of high school youths and leads them to thorough understanding. While small school systems may be unable to afford such a
trained economist, every large school system should have at least one such
person on its social studies staff, both to teach its courses in economics and,
equally important, to help other teachers in selecting materials and teaching
approaches where economic issues are involved.

c. *To help present teachers improve their economic competence, we
recommend increased use of summer workshops, teacher participation in a*

nationwide television economics course planned for 1962–63, and return to college for additional work in economics.—School authorities should encourage and assist teachers to improve their economic understanding through all these channels, including, wherever feasible, provision of financial support for further training. Summer workshops for high school teachers are available in most states through the Joint Council on Economic Education. During the 1962–63 school year, a special television program on the American economy will be presented nationwide daily, to help all interested high school teachers obtain a reasonable grasp of the functioning of the economy. It will also offer suggestions as to how economic understanding can be woven into history and problems of American democracy courses, as well as taught in courses in economics. This Learning Resources Institute television course, co-sponsored by the American Economic Association and the Joint Council on Economic Education and under the guidance of a group of distinguished economists and educators, will emphasize the approach to economic understanding outlined ... [previously] and will involve many of the nation's outstanding economists and educators as teachers.

d. *We recommend that colleges preparing teachers improve the economics courses offered for this purpose, and establish other opportunities for high school teachers to increase their economic understanding.*—Colleges can help by designing improved courses in basic economics specifically for high school teachers. ... In many institutions, this will require a substantial change in the emphasis and direction of basic courses in economics. These colleges can also help by designing extension courses for teachers along similar lines. Furthermore, we recommend that more colleges and universities offer summer workshops in economics for high school teachers. All too often, leading university economists pay little attention to this pressing problem of secondary school teaching. Finally, we recommend the establishment of university centers for economic education such as those at Iowa, Illinois, and Purdue, which focus on research and aid to the teaching of economics in the schools.

TEACHING MATERIALS

10. *We emphasize the need for more effective high school teaching materials and recommend that steps be taken by private publishers, foundations, and others to increase the supply of such materials.*—Better teaching materials are essential if the minimal level of economic understanding described above is to be achieved by most students in the high schools.

As we pointed out ... better texts are beginning to appear, but too frequently the textbooks on economics used in the schools are prosaic and uninteresting. They are devoted largely to facts and descriptions unrelated to major current public problems, lacking in careful analysis, and full of policy prescriptions based largely on the unsupported views of the authors. Materials on economics in problems of American democracy and history texts suffer from the same failings, when, indeed, any pretense of dealing with economic issues is included. The supplementary materials that pour in on social studies teachers from many different groups like business, labor, and farm organizations range from the objective and informative to sheer propaganda. Far too much of such materials falls close to the latter extreme. Most high school teachers have neither the time nor the training to sift through all this to choose what would be effective in the classroom. Thus, major steps are needed to provide better teaching materials. Better high school texts on economics and means to help teachers select from among the flood of supplementary materials available are required for all except the most sophisticated instructors.

Good teaching materials should be made generally available at modest cost if they are to be widely used. They are needed perhaps even more for problems of American democracy and history courses than for courses in economics, for almost none of the present materials for those courses appear to be aimed at developing the kind of economic understanding we urge for effective citizenship. Such materials need to be prepared as practical units for insertion into problems of American democracy and American and world history courses without the complete restructuring of such courses, for they have other important objectives as well. Joint work by economists, historians, sociologists, and political scientists will be required in producing the needed materials. As a specific example, we suggest that the Joint Council on Economic Education and the Service Center for Teachers of History cooperate in developing guides to teachers wishing to incorporate more economic analysis into history courses.

Some steps in this direction have already been taken. A group of teachers and economists has sifted through the great mass of materials on "economics" already available with a view to selecting, recommending, and making available to teachers and students those that are most objective and most useful in promoting the desired economic understanding. The Joint Council on Economic Education is assisting in the preparation of new materials to the same end. More competent professional economists are becoming interested in preparing materials for the secondary schools, and some publishers are considering publication of textbooks and supplementary materials better suited to this purpose. We commend these efforts, and urge support by businesses, private citizens, professional economists, foundations, and government agencies for steps to provide teachers and students with the very best materials for developing economic understanding. We hope that the suggestions ... above may prove helpful to those interested in preparing new materials for high school courses and to teachers in deciding what materials can contribute most.

THE RESPONSIBILITY OF ECONOMISTS

11. *We recommend that professional economists play a more active part in helping to raise the level of economics in the schools.*—Leading economists have generally paid little attention to the teaching of economics below the college level. We consider this unfortunate. Professional economists can help significantly by assisting local teachers and school authorities in revising courses and curricula, by aiding in the preparation of more effective teaching materials, by supporting college courses for high school teachers designed to develop economic understanding of the sort described above, and by participating more actively in summer workshops and other special aids to high school teachers, arranged by the Joint Council on Economic Education or other responsible agencies. We urge our fellow economists to participate more actively in all of these ways to help improve the teaching of economics in the schools. To fail to do so is to shirk an important professional responsibility.

PUBLIC SUPPORT

12. *We urge widespread public support, both private and governmental, for the improvement of economics in the schools.*—Only if the leaders of public opinion, and the public itself, support higher standards for economic understanding in the schools will significant improvement occur. Community leaders need to give active support to teachers, administrators and school boards seeking to raise standards—and to push school officials where this is needed. In doing so, they must recognize that economic understanding rests on a good grasp of economic institutions and an orderly way of thinking about economic issues, not on acceptance of some particular group interest or some "brand" of economics.

Many of the suggestions made above will cost money, though some can be achieved within present school budgets. Most of the cost of better education must ultimately be borne by the taxpayers and others who now support the schools. In lifting standards of economic understanding during the years immediately ahead, however, we urge special support, both governmental and private, for measures like those recommended above to speed this improvement.

Economic Education Materials

It is extremely difficult to acquire a comprehensive and intelligible view of economic education in American secondary schools. Unlike the situation in sociology, anthropology, and other social sciences, there is no curriculum project that is referred to as "the economics project." In fact the number of economic undertakings from state to state is so large that the Joint Council on Economic Education has a formidable job in its effort to bring order out of chaos. M. L. Frankel, president of that organization, may have been amused when he received our request for a representative sample of materials. His letter contained what we later discovered to be a substantial understatement: "The number of our materials is so large at the present time that it really is impossible to send kits of these on approval." [1] However, despite the plethora of available resources, we feel that an effort to highlight some aspects of economic education is entirely in order.

Actually few subjects are as crucial to the general level of social literacy in a free enterprise nation. But it is generally agreed that while America can boast the strongest economic system in the world, the public is sadly lacking in a sophisticated understanding of it. The responsibility for this ignorance, of course, is often laid at the door of the American high school, whose teachers, it is claimed, are not well prepared to teach economics as a discipline. Although we wryly take note of George Bach's observation that "there seems to be no significant difference eight years later between those high school social studies teachers who took elementary economics in college and those who took none," [2] most efforts to improve the general level of economic understanding in the nation need to be examined carefully and judiciously. The past few years especially have seen a concerted drive on the part of the business community and the social studies establishment to prepare young people and adults for the economic world in which they live.

The purpose of this chapter will be limited in that the focus will be as much expository as critical. We will briefly describe some aims and functions of the Joint Council on Economic Education, evaluate the D. C. Heath case studies in American business history, and describe some supplementary

---

[1] Letter from M. L. Frankel to William B. Gillies, III, January 15, 1968.

[2] G. L. Bach, "The State of Education in Economics" in *New Developments in the Teaching of Economics*, Keith G. Lumsden, ed. (Englewood Cliffs, N.J.: Prentice-Hall, Inc., 1967), p. 16.

materials created by the Council for the Advancement of Secondary Education, and the Industrial Relations Center at the University of Chicago.

JOINT COUNCIL ON ECONOMIC EDUCATION

In 1948, after many years of war and depression, a three week conference was held at Riverdale, New York, to underscore the importance of economic literacy in the United States. The meeting resulted in the formation of a "national nonprofit educational organization to further the teaching of economics in the nation's schools." [3] In addition to placing key emphasis on the ability of teachers to use tools of economic analysis, the Joint Council has operated on the assumption that there is "no 'package' or single text prescribing the right answers to economic problems." [4] Consequently, it has urged a long and hard look at all curricular ventures in economics. So that its overall task could be more efficiently fulfilled the National Council cooperates with state organizations such as the Illinois Council on Economic Education, directed by Dr. Theral T. Herrick.

According to a recent newsletter, the Illinois Council aims to "emphasize economic analysis and principles" in "personal decision-making" and in "solving public policy questions." [5] At the same time the organization, like parent body, acts as an agency for coordinating economic education in the state, providing pre- and in-service training for teachers, and distributing new and old materials for classroom use. The Illinois Council also assists in the implementation of the DEEP project (Developmental Economic Education Programs), which is an intensive effort to involve high schools throughout the nation in a comprehensive teacher-training and materials development thrust. In 1966 DEEP involved 4,400,000 students, 175,000 teachers, and 6,800 schools throughout the country. [6]

One of the most noteworthy contributions of the Joint Council has been its development of criteria for evaluating materials for economic education. They are as follows:

1. Were the materials genuinely concerned with economic matters?
2. Were they analytical in nature?

---

[3]   Haig Babian, *The Councils on Economic Education ... and How They Work* (New York: Joint Council on Economic Education, 1964), p. 4.

[4]   Ibid., p. 11.

[5]   Illinois Council on Economic Education, *Econ.-Ed. News*, p. 2.

[6]   *Developmental Economic Education Program: What It Is and What It Does* (New York: Joint Council on Economic Education).

3. Were they appropriate for high school use? [7]

The Reports of Materials Evaluation Committees continues, describing these standards in greater detail:

Attention was focused on economics as a social science and on society's efforts to "economize". Economic understanding was equated with a knowledge of the structure and operation of the economy, not with the skills required in the everyday business of "making a living". [8]

The intention to avoid blanket endorsements of single projects was also again clearly presented. Particularly strong is the Joint Council's aversion to materials which grind a political axe and are slanted in a way detrimental to the free play of ideas in the classroom.

These criteria are helpful to the non-specialist. For example, the C.A.S.E. Economic Literacy Series of the Council for the Advancement of Secondary Education [9] could be intelligently evaluated by a prospective user considering at least in part the above standards. These small units of economic analysis, designed for interpolation into American history and Problems of Democracy courses, are in the form of six booklets prepared by economists who have had experience in secondary schools. Some of the titles are: *American Capitalism; Money and Banking; The USA in the World Economy.* In presenting a social science in a way that is comprehensible to the average student, these materials are a valuable supplement to a standard social studies curriculum. Careful use of charts and diagrams and the employment of an unfettered prose style present well the elementary mathematical and conceptual sides of economics.

D. C. HEATH & COMPANY: CASE STUDIES IN BUSINESS HISTORY AND ECONOMIC CONCEPTS

This project, which originally grew out of a cooperation between Harvard University and the Newton Public Schools, has tried to find a solution to a central classroom problem, namely that economics *per se* often proves boring to the student. It was the feeling of many who spearheaded the Harvard–Newton endeavor, as well as its culmination in commercial publication, that the case study method (involving in part the more familiar historical narrative) might prove to be a more practical medium for introducing the high school student to basic economic understandings. In

---

[7] *Study Materials for Economic Education in the Schools: Reports of Materials Evaluation Committee,* Supplementary Paper No. 12, Committee for Economic Development, p. 54.

[8] Ibid.

[9] In collaboration with the McGraw–Hill Book Company.

the words of Arthur Johnson of the Harvard School of Business: "business history provided the concrete type of material that not only illuminated history but also could be used to develop elementary economic terminology and concepts." [10]

As yet the project has not formulated a rationale explaining its curriculum theory or psychology of pedagogy. Although some attention is given to the problems of induction and intrinsic motivation, the major goal involves putting materials into the hands of the student. In the Introduction to the Student accompanying each case study booklet, the pupil is told of two major goals: "increased facility in use of terms [such as subsidy, union shop, and vertical integration]" and "ability to identify issues and alternatives" in American economic and business history. However, the closest the introduction comes to offering a theory of instruction is in its explanation of its basically inductive method:

Indeed, your ability to form useful generalizations from specific situations is one of the primary goals of the case study method. In each case study you have been provided with sufficient information to see the problem that individuals faced at the time. The goal is not for you to learn the material so much as it is for you to learn to use it in analyzing the behavior of the participants and the implications of their decisions for society.[11]

We do not mean to imply, however, that the problem of methodology has been ignored. In summer institutes designed to involve the public schools in the case study approach much time was spent analyzing and practicing inductive teaching techniques. The substance of these deliberations does not disclose a consistent rationale.

Some social studies experts may wonder about the failure to include an exhaustive philosophical and psychological base, but the absence of same need not deter prospective classroom users of the Heath materials. There is growing doubt in some quarters as to just how important esoteric rationales really are and realization in others that such creations too often serve as convenient targets for the educational establishment. Moreover, the case studies offered by the project are well done and remain consistent to the manageable aims set forth by the authors.

As historical vignettes the episodes are of high quality. Ample and interesting research has gone into recreations of the Jamestown Colony, the Massachusetts Bay settlements, the Ford Motor Company, and other economic ventures. The writing teams approached their topics judiciously.

---

[10] Letter from Arthur M. Johnson to William B. Gillies, III, April 11, 1968.
[11] Ralph Hidy and Paul Cawein, eds., *Case Studies in Business History and Economic Concepts: Individual Enterprise and National Growth* (Boston: D. C. Heath & Company, 1967), p. ix.

For example, the case on the beginnings of the factory system avoids the pitfalls of retroactive modernism and refuses to credit New England laborers of the 1830's and 1840's with the founding of today's union movement. In fact so strong is the project's determination to stick to the evidence that one teacher who worked on the Standard Oil case felt that the final account went overboard in its avoidance of a muckraking approach! Detailed biographical information makes men like Henry Ford, Samuel Slater, and Richard Sears come across as believable and alive human beings. Even the supporting cast such as Charles Sorenson, boss of Ford's Rouge River plant, is painted in vivid hues:

Sorenson, like Ford, was a "production" man, not a "desk" man, and he believed in tough discipline. More than anyone else, except possibly Ford, he was responsible for running the Rouge like an army. The men could not whistle, sing or talk. They could not sit down at any time. Lateness or slacking off was severely punished. A man who spent seventeen years on the production line was dismissed one day because a few seconds before the quitting bell rang he took a piece of waste and wiped the grease from his arms. There was no appeal from such dismissals. The Rouge was impersonal and cold.[12]

Before publication all of the cases were subjected to much criticism and rewriting. Such care has produced a readable style which incorporates naturally economic terminology into the flow of a historical narrative.

Perhaps most significant are the ethical and societal questions which the cases raise. The students must ask themselves whether John Smith was justified in setting up a virtual dictatorship in the Jamestown Colony. They must consider how the Puritans related the earning of money to the worship of God. And they must explore carefully the pros and cons of government regulation of business in many different contexts and situations.

There is ample room for flexibility in the teachers' use of the materials. Although the following two quotations are found in separate case studies, an interesting class discussion could evolve after the students see the comments juxtaposed:

The man who has the largest capacity for work and thought is the man who is bound to succeed.[13]
Most people believe that because a man has made a large fortune his views on any subject are valuable. For my part, I have always believed that most large fortunes are made by men of mediocre ability who tumbled into a lucky opportunity and could not help but get rich and in most cases others

---

[12]   Ibid., p. 49.
[13]   Ibid., p. 32.

given the same opportunity would have done far better with it. Hard work and attention to business are necessary, but rarely result in the achieving of a large fortune. Do not be fooled into believing that because a man is rich, he is necessarily smart. There is ample proof to the contrary.[14]

Used judiciously, the Heath materials will do much to brighten the traditional United States history course.

BASIC ECONOMICS SERIES: INDUSTRIAL RELATIONS CENTER, UNIVERSITY OF CHICAGO

In the early 1950's the Industrial Relations Center at the University of Chicago began a Basic Economics series for adults employed in industry. The program is built around eight booklets which lend themselves to two hours of class sessions apiece. To some extent these materials have been used as a supplement to secondary school social studies classes. And it is from that perspective that this review of the materials will proceed.

The titles of the booklets are as follows: *A Look at Our Economy, Competitive Prices in Action, Capital: Key to Progress, Profits: Sparkplug of the Economy, America and the World Economy,* and *Understanding Money and Banking.* A surface glance at the format of these presentations may turn the social studies sophisticate away from the serious consideration that their actual content merits. Some of the lettering and illustrations come close to being overly simplistic. For example, there is a stick figure with a coin for a head bearing the title "Mr. Profit." The reader also encounters an illustration depicting animals labeled "facts," "theories," "values," etc., confronting a rifle-toting civilian. The caption reads "We must hunt for the answers." Such surface difficulties are not serious, however, and a closer inspection reveals material that is very useful.

Each booklet emphasizes "economics as a social science" [15] and presents that aspect of the discipline very well. The process by which money is created through bank deposits is clearly explained, as is the difference between such related concepts as balance of trade and balance of payments. Emotional topics like deficit spending are given rational treatment. And the authors do not hesitate to take on a glittering generality. The claim that "if goods don't cross borders, armies will" [16] is questioned by referring to the "Cold War" between the U.S.A. and the U.S.S.R.

---

14   Ibid., p. 81.
15   Richard T. Thornbury, Orace E. Johnson, under the direction of Robert K. Burns, *A Look at our Economy* (Chicago: Industrial Relations Center, University of Chicago, 1965), p. 7.
16   Richard T. Thornbury, Orace E. Johnson, under the direction of Robert K. Burns, *America and the World Economy* (Chicago: Industrial Relations Center, University of Chicago, 1965), p. 5.

Occasionally, the booklets include a welcome humanistic touch. In explaining differing conceptions that nations have of the individual, the authors compare a letter of Abraham Lincoln to that of Kaiser Wilhelm. The effect is devastating.

DEAR MADAM:

I have been shown in the files of the War Department a statement of the Adjutant General of Massachusetts that you are the mother of five sons who have died gloriously on the field of battle. I feel how weak and fruitless must be any words of mine which should attempt to beguile you from the grief of a loss so overwhelming. But I cannot refrain from tendering to you the consolation that may be found in the thanks of the Republic they died to save. I pray that our Heavenly Father may assuage the anguish of your bereavement, and leave you only a cherished memory of the loved and lost, and the solemn pride that must be yours who laid so costly a sacrifice upon the altar of freedom.

Yours very sincerely and respectfully,

ABRAHAM LINCOLN

His Majesty the Kaiser hears that you have sacrificed nine sons in defense of the Fatherland in the present war. His Majesty is immensely gratified at the fact, and in recognition is pleased to send you his photograph, with frame and autographed signature.[17]

It is our opinion that these booklets are potentially a useful supplement to classes of average and lower ability.

CONCLUDING REMARKS

Since the number of economic materials available is overwhelming, we have merely commented on some resources with which we have been familiar. It is our feeling that the projects reviewed are a fair cross section or indication of recent developments. Beyond this brief overview there remain some important matters for all social studies educators to consider.

Given the demands of our society and the curriculum of colleges and graduate schools, what kind of economics should be taught in the high schools? Presumably, some sort of compromise between economics as a social science and economics as a consumer skill must be effected. But such a guideline is far too vague, and other questions must follow. Should the

---

[17] Thornbury, Johnson, and Burns, op. cit., p. 26.

emphasis be on macro as opposed to micro economics? If one is chosen, what kind of attention to the other will prove illuminating for the high school student? To what extent is the unit approach to economics outdated? Is the semester or year course more valid? And finally, what are the relative merits of the historical and the disciplinary approach? As answers to these and other questions are found, our capacity to evaluate intelligently the countless curriculum materials in this area will be substantially improved.

CHAPTER VII

History

9   THE AUTHORS

On the Teaching of History

It is rather paradoxical that at a time when more people write history and read history than ever before, the discipline of history is subjected to carping criticism. More and more people turn to history to escape the cruel dilemmas and frustration of their own time, but are disappointed when they discover that people in the past were not more successful in solving their problems than they are.

Most of this disappointment could be somewhat alleviated by a better understanding of the nature of history. History is interested in everything that men have accomplished, failed to accomplish, thought and said. It is not a study of the past, but in reality, only a study of that past which left some traces for the historians to see and evaluate. A historian, when reconstructing some segment of the past, is potentially as successful as the amount and quality of the historical debris left by that paricular event or period. Jacob Burckhardt was correct when he said, that "History is a contemplation based upon sources."

With this in mind, the reader of history may begin to look to history not for answers or "lessons," but for an enrichment of his understanding of human behavior. He could learn how men interrelated in times of tranquillity and peace, how leaders led their people to glory or to defeat and how laborious and perilous is mankind's quest for material and spiritual progress. He would understand that history is basically concerned with how changes occurred and how political, social, economic, and religious institutions, systems and ideas were changed and transformed. No other academic discipline is concerned with viewing the story of the human race in the total perspective of constant, sequential change and transformation. It may be argued that this is a waste of time, that history teaches little or nothing of value, that as Henry Ford once said, "history is bunk." There is strong and overwhelming evidence that people, all people, mighty and common folk want to know about the past. They want to know because in the realization of their own finiteness and mortality, the establishment of a link with the past is a hope and a consolation.

Hollywood movie makers know that the general public, young and old, will flock to see movies like *Gone with the Wind* or *War and Peace*. They know that they have a ready market for movies and television programs dealing with the West, the cowboys and the Indians and the Daniel Boone type frontiersmen.

Individual men and women jealously guard their own personal histories, however sordid and however tragic. No reasonably sane person would be willing to obliterate the past from his memory. On the contrary, people who because of a fall or an automobile accident, suffer from temporary amnesia, make superhuman efforts to recapture clues to their past. They want to know where they have lived, who their relatives are—in a word, where they belong.

And yet, the study of history presents difficult and seemingly unsurmountable problems. While the public in general, and school children in particular, may be interested in specific events of the past, the study of history, as an uninterrupted chronological narrative is often boring and uninteresting. History becomes the story of "dry facts" and dates, taught superficially on the basis of inane textbooks.

What is more, the "facts" of history and the dates usually pertain to what is called political history, which as Voltaire observed, is interested only in kings and in wars and which has little interest in what people did or thought. Such history is usually, in reality, a story of the continuous power struggle among rising and dying nations and empires, only occasionally brightened by the appearance of such interesting human beings and geniuses as Alexander the Great, Ghengis Khan or Napoleon. And even when such men who could inspire the imagination of the learner, appear on the pages of history, they are given short shrift by the teacher, either because the teacher himself knows or cares little about them or because he feels compelled to hurry or to "cover" the syllabus or the course of study assigned to him. Artistic and intellectual achievements of the past are usually left out and little or no attention is paid to economic or sociological developments.

There are, of course, perfectly sound reasons why history as taught in schools, or even as written by historians, tends to center primarily on periods of strife and conflict. We teach the Crusades or World War I, or the Civil War, or the Spanish American War, not only because these periods form some natural stopping points (or periods) in the flow of the historical narrative, but because conflicts, revolutions and wars leave us the historical debris, in the form of letters, speeches, diaries, newspaper articles. This accumulation of data makes it possible for us to teach about that particular conflict or war. Periods of tranquillity, the germination of great ideas, the day-to-day struggle of millions of individual people to simply exist, leave very few traces except archeological remains like potsherds, urns, kitchen utensils and weapons. It was by an extraordinary stroke of luck that the hot ashes and the lava of an exploding Vesuvius allowed us to excavate the city of Pompeii and to get an intimate glimpse into the daily life of the Romans. We know a great deal about Reformation because the appearance of Martin Luther brought about a long and often bloody struggle which left us rich historical materials, but we know little, precious little, of what millions of people really believed in, religiously speaking, in many parts of the world during many and long centuries.

A more recent difficulty with which history teachers have been compelled to struggle, is the charge that history is irrelevant to contemporary life. Since education is perceived to lead toward some specific goals, it is widely suggested that the study of history is indeed an exercise in futility, because it provides no guidance or assistance toward the solution of contemporary, individual or societal problems and conflicts. Many, including Professor Edgar Wesley, the original theoretician of the modern social studies, have recently demanded that history be de-emphasized in school curricula in favor of social and behavioral sciences.[1] It is their conviction that the social sciences would be more effective in the training of skills of inquiry, in developing the ability for critical thinking and in training students to cope intelligently with their lives. It is argued that acquisition of skills to inquire and to think critically, and not the learning of historical content, ought to become the main objective of social studies. It is futile to study the ever-increasing accumulation of historical research. What is important is to give the child the skills and the mental tools to learn and inquire by himself. Obviously, the learning of inquiry and of critical skills is not the end in itself. The expositors of this theory are not usually explicit about this, but it is logical to assume that they hope or assume that two other steps will follow the acquisition of skills. First, that the students will be self-motivated to use their newly acquired abilities to think rationally and reflectively in order to inquire into new and more complex issues and problems faced by the society in which they live. Second, that the results of these investigations will cause the inquiring students to reject propaganda and indoctrination, to prefer a democratic way of life to the totalitarian

---

[1] *See* Edgar Bruce Wesley, "Let's Abolish History Courses," *Phi Delta Kappan*, September, 1967.

one, to believe in the dignity of all men, to reject ethnocentric approaches to world cultures and to work for the continual betterment of the world. Stressing this last point, Professor Jerome Bruner [2] states his preference for the behavioral sciences over history, because in his view, history studies the "achieved," while the behavioral sciences are concerned with the "possible."

It would seem to be reasonable to ask those who place the acquisition of skills of inquiry and the ability to think critically of the most valued objectives in the teaching of history whether the two implied assumptions are valid. First, do we have any evidence to suggest that if and when the principal emphasis on education would be placed on the teaching of skills of inquiry and analysis, that students would pursue new inquiries as a self-motivating experience? Classroom and research evidence suggests that only a small minority of children would do so.

The second assumption that students, when taught to think critically and analyze complex issues by a diligent search for logical alternate solutions, would become sound thinking and active members of the national and world community and would believe in and work for a democratic society, ought to be subjected to serious scrutiny. There was nothing wrong with Lenin, Stalin or Ho Chi Minh's skill of inquiry or ability to think critically, and Mao Tse-tung was no loose thinker. For that matter, Mussolini, a Socialist journalist, before his March on Rome, was quite capable of a critical analysis of issues. And yet, all these men used their skills of inquiry and their great ability to analyze the thinking of their countrymen to extinguish freedom and enslave the minds of men. So it would seem that the possession of mental skills alone is no assurance that these skills would be used either for the enrichment of the individual or for the enhancement of the society.

It is also said that instruction in the behavioral sciences will gradually replace the teaching of history for two additional reasons. History, it is said, deals only with the record of the last five thousand years, while the social sciences deal with millions of years of man's evolution. More importantly, while the social sciences attempt to find some general insights into human behavior, history stresses the particular and the singular in the past human behavior.

As to the first argument, one can only suggest that without belittling the importance of the understanding of the origins of human species, the study of those "mere" five thousand years of recorded history are of crucial importance for our young generations if they are to live intelligent and

---

[2] Jerome Bruner, "Education or Social Invention," *Saturday Review*, February 19, 1966, p. 103.

useful lives and if they are expected to make an effort to prevent the destruction of the human race in an atomic holocaust.

Many contemporary problems cannot be even well understood without a reasonable knowledge of their historical background. The knowledge of Negro history in this country, from slavery until today, including some of the peculiar and singular events like the Turner rebellion and the murder of Dr. Martin Luther King, are essential if our society, and especially our young people are to form some intelligent positions on the racial question.

Can our young generation be expected to cope with the problems of peace and coexistence with China, or to make a contribution to the eventual solution to the conflicts between Arabs and Israelis, Indians and Pakistanis, the Cypriote Greeks and the Turks, without the study of the historical backgrounds of these conflicts?

The faith placed by many critics of history in the social sciences, sounds a bit naive and misguided and it must make many scholars in the various social sciences feel quite uncomfortable. The plain truth is that neither history, nor the social sciences, are in a position to provide ready, definitive answers or solutions to the major problems plaguing our nation or the world community.

Political scientists were unable to contribute a great deal to the better understanding of the Vietnam war and even less to its termination. The frequent public confrontations by leading political scientists in the country, offering widely divergent analyses of the origins and nature of the Vietnam conflict, eloquently arguing for different courses of action and offering contradictory prognosis of future developments, were hardly circulated to support the argument (which to our knowledge has never been made by responsible political scientists), that political science would help children in schools to understand or to deal with contemporary issues more effectively than history.

Economists have hardly been more successful in their interminable and often harsh arguments over the gold drain, the monetary crisis, taxation and inflation. Are we to teach in schools the John Galbraith brand of economics, or that advocated with equal brilliance and cogency by Milton Friedman?

It is reasonable to assume that social scientists are pursuing a futile fantasy if they assume that they can organize their respective disciplines in tight and empirically tested structures. They will undoubtedly be even more disappointed if they expect to come up with laws and predictions similar to those evolved in the natural sciences. Human beings just do not behave like robins or atoms—they are, as we well know, quite unpredictable. No amount of sample polling and testing, scientific interviews, or statistical correlations, will make it possible for a sociologist to predict the conditions under which a race riot will occur. Many variables, like the weather of the mood of the people, or a particular unexpected event which may trigger a riot are completely unpredictable. Nobody knows and economists can't predict the next stock market crash. There are hundreds of controlling variables, many which defy quantitative measurement or prediction. No matter how mathematically-orientated political scientists become, they cannot predict what will happen in China after the death of Mao Tse-tung.

"In human affairs," Barrington Moore, Jr., wrote, "the mere fact of uniformity or regularity, expressible in the form of a scientific law, may often be quite trivial." Many generalizations in the social sciences are simply not very significant. Moore concludes: "Social scientists condemn themselves to unnecessary frustrations by trying to erect an intellectual structure that will permit predictions in the manner of natural sciences." [3]

How to study history is as important as what to study in history. In an important occasional paper entitled, "The Growth of Mind," Jerome Bruner suggests that there is nothing more important in the teaching of a particular discipline than to teach the student the particular ways, mores, attitudes, languages or jargon, or even the jokes of that discipline. In other words, the best, or at least one of the best ways for the teaching of history is to teach the ways in which historians go about their work. "At the very first breath," Bruner writes, "the young learner should, we think, be given the choice to solve problems, to conjecture, to quarrel, as these are done at the heart of the discipline." [4]

If this is to be done in history, there is an obvious prior obligation to establish some basic rationale for the study of history. It is perfectly valid to argue that while history does not really teach us its lessons in the ordinary meaning of the words "teach" and "lessons," the study of history is an absolute prerequisite for an intelligent study of any important contemporary issue. It would be foolish indeed to attempt a serious inquiry into the problem of race relations without the study of slavery, abolitionism, the Negro hopes and frustrations during the Civil War, and the complicated and bloody story of Reconstruction and its tragic aftermath. Similarly, no serious student would attempt to understand the present conflict in the Middle East without a thorough analysis of the historical relationship of Arabs and Jews and of the Arab states and Israel. The knowledge of past blunders and follies of mankind in its attempts to organize a peaceful and livable society may not prevent similar mistakes in the present or the future,

---

[3] Barrington Moore, Jr., *Political Power and Social Theory* (New York: Harper & Row, Publishers, Torchbooks, 1962), p. 159.

[4] Jerome Bruner, "The Growth of Mind," Occasional Paper No. 8 (Cambridge, Mass.: Educational Development Center, Inc., 1966), p. 11.

but it may well make the odds a bit more favorable. History, if taught with scholarship and imagination, can give the student a link with past human experience, to help him feel that his own life span may have a meaning of its own in relation to the generations past and to his contemporary experience.

A case ought to be made without reservation or apology for the study of history for its intrinsic interest to satisfy the intense curiosity of intelligent human beings in the past. This curiosity, so clearly visible on the faces of men, women and children who walk the streets of the restored colonial villages of Williamsburg and Sturrbridge, or who contemplate the beauty of the great pyramids in Egypt or the grandeur of the Notre Dame Cathedral, or who thrill at the glory that was Rome when viewing the ruins of the Coliseum, or the remains of Pompeii. The magic look into the past does provide those fortunate to peer into it with an unforgettable thrill of discovery at least as intense and at least as satisfying as the thrill of discovery over an organizing principle or a great generalization.

The pursuit of history is not only intellectually justifiable, but it is a satisfying and most agreeable occupation. There is a curious satisfaction to learn about the vagaries and contradictions of human behavior and to search for the secrets of human failures and successes. Few disciplines can be as instructive as history in the all-important process of decision-making.

Professor G. R. Elton put it this way:

The study of history is an intellectual pursuit, an activity of the reasoning mind, and, as one should expect, its main service lies in its essence. Like all sciences, history, to be worthy to itself and beyond itself, must concentrate on one thing, the search for truth. Its real value as a social activity lies in the training it provides, the standard it sets, in the singularly human concern.[5]

In this great endeavor, history must be looked upon not as an accumulation of facts to be studied and taught as an unrelated mass of information, but as a particular way to organize knowledge of past human experience. Historians do enjoy certain advantages in this enterprise. They can appeal to a wide variety of human intelligences and interests, they need a minimum special technical expertise knowledge and they can (and if they are wise, they do) entertain their reading public. In fact, when they fail to entertain, their work is unread and soon forgotten.

Much of the debate on the place of generalizations in history seems to be misguided and based on an erroneous understanding of what history

---

[5] G. R. Elton, *The Practice of History* (New York: Thomas Y. Crowell Company, 1967), p. 49.

is. It almost seems that many who regularly denounce history as an accumulation of facts and dates, seem to think exclusively of history contained in high school and college history textbooks. A historian could not write a page, a chapter and surely not a volume without generalizing. Whatever he writes is based on his point of view of human beings to life which he brings into the history he writes. This point of view is nothing but a set of generalizations which the historian has formed from his life experiences, his education, his home life and his general cultural environment. Edward Gibbon looked and analyzed Imperial Rome and Byzantium against a set of his own generalizations. The same of course is true of Edmund Burke's writings on the French Revolution, Thomas Paine's impassioned pleas for the right of the American colonies to rebel or Charles Beard's inquiry into the making of the American Constitution. Soviet historians have a different set of generalizations which they apply to the study of history than those that guide the historians working in the universities in the People's Republic of China.

History represents the appraisals and reflections upon the past by historians working and writing at a given time. What they write, evaluate, reflect upon, represents as much the date and the circumstances of the historical happening as the date and the time when the account is written.

Any work of history abounds in generalizations or statements which "cover" or explain not one fact or one event, but a whole class of events. When a historian of the Middle Ages writes almost offhandedly, "It is hard for us—who are able to take a wide view of work which is being done in many parts of Europe—to remember how little the men of the tenth century knew of what was going on around them," or "No political boundaries survived in their entirety the death of a ruler . . .,"[6] he is, of course, generalizing. It may even be that another historian, in scrutinizing this latter generalization, may find that somewhere in Europe or in Asia, political boundaries did remain intact after the death of a ruler. This discovery would still not invalidate the generalization because a historical generalization does usually allow for some exceptions.

The difficulty that the critics of history seem unable to overcome is their unwillingness to differentiate between a law and a generalization. Historians dealing with the vagaries of human behavior, with the uncountable variables which account for human decision-making, are not in a position to formulate laws in history as stable and as rigid as Newton's law of gravity. Historians can and do generalize that "bad money drives out good," that "nationalism when brought into conflict with religious

---

⁶ R. W. Southern, *The Making of the Middle Ages* (New Haven and London: Yale University Press, 1967), p. 16.

allegiance or with any ideological movement, seems to be victorious in the long run," that "all revolutions became tired with the passage of time." But these are exactly what the word "generalization" implies, a *general* description of similar events *and not a predictive law*. The writing and teaching of history involves the use of generalizations and of abstract concepts.

When freed from the rigid approach to predictions of future behavior, it is quite plausible to argue that history and historians can be useful for predicting the future. Human history does disclose patterns of human behavior and some human behavior is predictable. There is enough evidence in history to suggest with a degree of certainty, for instance, that no rigid economic and political system will survive intact for a long period of time, and intelligent statesmanship and diplomacy could very well build on this reasonable assumption. It is likewise quite clear from the record of history that wars, even when decisively won, do not lead to permanent solutions of the crisis or crises that were their cause, or that it is more often than not relatively easier to go to war than to achieve a satisfactory and lasting peace settlement.

We must teach our students that they ought to question any and all versions of history presented to them as *the true* account of past events. Responsible historians are agreed that *their* history and all history ought to be and will be subjected to a questioning scrutiny by their colleagues and by the public at large. Professor Wesley is on very doubtful ground when he asserts that, "Only the historian thinks that pure, undiluted, unmixed and uncontaminated history exists and requires rigorous teaching and study. This tantrum-like demand, is of course, unrealistic, unenlightened, and unpsychological. History needs no separate existence for teaching or learning; it is a service study, not a self-serving discipline." [7] History is a discipline, an ancient and honorable discipline, but no recognized historian considers his discipline "pure" or "undiluted" or "unmixed." The very notion of "pure" history makes little sense to a historian. He knows that there is little that is pure or uncomplicated about the history of man. In this sense, Wesley is storming at an open door. Historians know better than others how *little* can be known about the past with certainty. But they at least have to prove what they know on the basis of evidence. Written history is laborious, uncertain and often not fully reliable. But, in this uncertainty and in this unreliability, it faithfully reflects the actions and the fate of human beings it describes.

Similarly, Professor Wesley's suggestions for teaching history, not as courses, but as a resource, are quite reasonable. Wesley's plea to history

---

[7]   Edgar Wesley, op. cit., p. 8.

teachers to "focus attention upon documents, old and new, public and private" is sound and ought to be heeded. We have always assumed, and we know from hundreds of visits to classrooms, that many history teachers do, as Professor Wesley demands, teach history "by means of topics, persons, periods and problems." Those who teach history by the chapters of the textbook, do not teach history. They merely indoctrinate, probably without much success, the particular, usually secondhand version of history, as summarized by the textbook writer.

History can, and has been used, for good or evil purposes. Wise leaders of nations have used history to inspire and rally the people to great creative efforts and to the defense of great ideals. But, just as often, evil men, demagogues, have used history to mislead their peoples, to engage in brutal aggressions and to submit to cruel and oppressive regimes. It makes good sense to argue that the fact that history is such a potentially dangerous weapon, makes it imperative to teach young people to understand the nature of history and to learn how to intelligently read historical writings.

The teaching of history presents many serious and complex questions. Much is expected of history as a subject of instruction, but the expectations are seldom realized. Let us state at the outset that the fault for relatively meager results in the teaching of history is not the fault of the discipline of history, but in the way it is being taught. Another source of difficulty is that not only the general public, but also the teachers of history are often confused about the nature of their discipline. All across the land men and women teach the history from textbooks, without realizing that there is no such thing as *the* history—there is no such thing as a body of tested and agreed upon descriptions and interpretations of past events. Had they understood the obvious fact that history is what historians write about the past and that there is no *one* history but in essence as many histories as there were and are historians, the teaching of history would be an exciting inquiry into the past instead of the cramming of unrelated "facts." We have said that historians can analyze and interpret only sources available to them. Obviously, their analysis and their interpretations will differ according to their own beliefs, skills, views and biases.

Knowing this, no teacher of history would be satisfied with teaching only on the basis of textbooks which are compilations of data and *conclusions* about the past by the authors of the textbook. He would at least supplement the textbooks with other interpretations and descriptions of the past of other historians and even more importantly, he would strive to create the conditions for his students to conduct their own inquiries. Such a teacher would, of course, not look upon the history he teaches as a mass of unrelated facts about events and people and he would not concentrate on "covering" content material. He would rather concentrate on an in-depth investigation of how at a given period of time, people ordered their lives, chose alternatives and made decisions in periods of crisis.

History is the only subject matter which is taught under the compulsion of state laws in almost all states in our country. Why do the state legislatures pass such laws? The answer has to do with one of the major expectations that society has for history instruction. From ancient times till today, leaders of nations and states were and are convinced that the study of history is an excellent means for instilling patriotism. There is widespread conviction that learning of a nation's history instills love of country. To be sure that this objective is achieved, history textbooks virtually all over the world are written extolling the nation's past, its glory, its honorable dealings with other nations, and omit, minimize or distort the record of the country's blunders, misdeeds and aggressions. This is particularly true in countries like France, Germany, Italy, Russia, China and India, where schools are operated by a central Ministry of Education and where textbooks are written on order and under the strict supervision of that department of government. The results are often astonishing and depressing.

We have, a few years ago, examined history textbooks in East and West Germany, in Israel, and in the United Arab Republic. The textbooks in the two parts of Germany gave completely different and contradictory accounts of the causes of World War II, of the course of the War and of the post-war settlement. In reading in the Israeli and Egyptian textbooks, the description of the war which followed the establishment of the State of Israel in 1948 and of the events which preceded the 1956 Suez Canal crisis, We had to remind ourselves repeatedly that we were reading about the same event in history. Nothing would be as instructive for our teachers as the reading of a few foreign history textbooks. They would forever be cured of the illusion that there is such a thing as *the* history of the past.

History textbooks in countries like England and the United States, where there is no central governmental control over education and where textbooks are published by private publishing companies, are less prone to include outright propaganda or blatant distortions. But these books too are neither completely honest or comprehensive. Their authors too, perceive that in order to instill patriotism, the story of the country's past must be presented in the best light possible.

American textbooks omit completely or gloss over the sorry, shameful record of American extermination of the great majority of Indians and the subjugation of the remaining tribesmen on pitiful reservations. The savagery of the Indian attacks on settlements in the West is fully depicted, but nary a word is said in the textbooks about the broken treaties solemnly made with the Indian tribes, the brutal attacks on Indian settlements, and the savagery of the expulsions of Indians from their ancient homegrounds and the decimating forced marches to new and distant lands. Our children learn little or nothing about the dignity, the high standard of community life and the deep religious beliefs of many Indians. They are given no chance to understand what Alexis de Tocqueville understood in 1834, that the Indians looked upon the whites as inferior barbarians whom they had no wish to imitate. De Tocqueville predicted that the red man will be exterminated.

Little needs to be said about the treatment of Negroes in our history textbooks. A reading of U. S. history textbooks discloses that a vast majority still contain no reference to over 5,000 soldiers who fought valiantly in the Revolutionary Army. Most still do not contain an outright condemnation of slavery as degrading to human beings and contradictory to the very ideals on which America was founded. The textbooks still speak with disdain, if not outright condemnation of the abolitionists, and most leave out any mention of the black abolitionist movement. The magnificent record of the 180,000 Negro soldiers in the Union Army, who according to Lincoln's testimony, helped mightily in the victory over the South, is still the best kept secret in the textbooks.

The story of the Period of Reconstruction in history textbooks is still the most distorted and the most offensive. A recent careful study of *The Negro in Modern American History Textbooks,* made by Irving Sloan for the American Federation of Teachers, AFL-CIO, reported that most of the current editions of textbooks are moving in the direction of better balance in their presentation of the role of Negroes in American history. But the study noted that, "the exceptions are shocking. For example, the treatment of the rise of the Ku Klux Klan as a response to the Reconstruction governments in almost all the texts, implies a moral justification, suggesting that the 'moderate whites' had no choice. Rarely is there an expression of disapproval of the activities of the Klan." [8]

The outright distortions concerning Indians and Negroes and general reluctance of textbook writers to deal honestly and forthrightly with the past and present failures in American foreign policy and with the unsolved domestic problems, make it difficult to instill in our students an understanding, a love and respect for the history of America and for the American Creed and the American Dream. When students discover that they have been misled on some aspects of American history, they tend to be cynical and disbelieving about all that they have been taught in American history.

---

[8] Irving Sloan, *The Negro in Modern American History Textbooks,* pamphlet sponsored by the American Federation of Teachers, AFL–CIO, Washington, D.C., 1967, p. 6.

And yet, a strong case can and should be made for teaching national history. There is no reason to assume that American history, taught with skill and imagination, and without glossing over or leaving out the shadows, cannot lead to giving our students a sense of pride in the American past and a faith in the enduring quality of American ideals. National history taught in books, legends, songs and poetry, has made it possible for Jews to survive exile and persecution in many countries, and knowledge and pride in national history and national heritage allowed the Poles and the Italians to survive centuries of foreign domination.

If and when these difficulties in teaching history are resolved, other difficulties and pitfalls still remain to be dealt with. While indoctrination will obviously not work as a means for instilling love of country, the obligation to teach national history still remains. John Dewey, who abhorred indoctrination in any form and who rejected the process of transfer of information from teacher to student, nevertheless advocated the teaching of history to allow the children to "recapitulate the progress of the race." The child, Dewey maintained, "should go back of present conditions where everything seems to be given, almost without the exercise of intelligence ... (and) should get himself back in his imagination to the primitive conditions of man." "History," said Dewey, "requires the child to recapitulate in himself the occasions which have made the race think, and makes him appreciate in terms of his own experience, the sort of thinking that actually had to be done, with the motives for it on one side, and the results that were reached by it on the other side." [9]

Students of Dewey will readily appreciate that the key in this statement is the words, "in terms of his own experience." In teaching the story of the past, the teacher must build and make use of the child's own experiences and interests. This ought not to be difficult because as Dewey noted, "the child's interest in the way people live, and how and why they lived as they did, what kind of houses they had, what kind of clothes they wore and how they did business—that interest is endless and ceaseless. . . ." [10]

Dewey saw the importance of teaching the history of our country in making a connection with present social life, while the importance of the study of history of other nations (Dewey mentions particularly the history of Greece and Rome) is to get a remote view, "getting a view of a society and civilization whose strong points were very different from ours, and whose weak points were also very different from ours." [11] In the teaching of history, Dewey saw great importance in picturesque and dramatic

---

[9]   John Dewey, *Lectures in the Philosophy of Education*, Reginald D. Archambault, ed. (New York: Random House, Inc., 1966), p. 258.

[10]   Ibid., p. 260.

approach and in the stress on biographies of representative people.

Besides these general thoughts on the importance of history, Dewey did not consider the specific problems teachers of history have to overcome to make their instruction effective. These difficulties and problems ought to be faced and if possible, overcome.

One such difficulty concerns the nature of explanations of historical events, which is the essence of history instruction. On this issue, the teacher of history has a different problem than that with which the academic historian has to deal. The historian in explaining an event, tries to find a cause and effect relationship. A historian writing about the French Revolution, could point to the cause of the unrest and the growing dissatisfaction with the regime that brought about the upheaval. The phenomenon of the revolution itself is not new to the historian and neither are the essential facts about the revolution or its sequential development. Not so with the student. To him the very concept of revolution is new and strange and the teacher must do his best to give him a clearer understanding of what a revolution is. Once this is done, the student must acquire, hopefully by his own reading and an intelligent classroom dialogue, or a brief lecture some knowledge of the events that make up the French Revolution. It is only then that the teacher may pose the question of whether the Revolution could have been avoided and what were the essential causes of the Revolution. This is a long and involved process and the teacher's task is correspondingly difficult and responsible.

Impressed by the difficulty of this task, some educational psychologists have suggested that it may well be that children are indeed incapable of studying history. A British psychologist, E. A. Peel, who has studied the problem, concluded that history presents two major difficulties for the school pupil. First, in the study of history, the historian infers from the deeds and statements of men, their motives. We judge and evaluate Neville Chamberlain's motives for going to Munich and for accepting Hitler's assurances in good faith on the basis of his record as Member of Parliament, party leader and Prime Minister, and we infer a great deal from the statement he made in the London airport when he arrived from Munich, from his speech to Parliament justifying his action and from his letters and speeches made long after the event. Such inference, Peel argues, takes a great deal of sophistication which children lack. In addition, it may be added, that such reasoning takes a great deal of knowledge or intuitive knowledge that children do not have. History requires some sharp psychological insights which young learners cannot be expected to possess.

---

[11]   Ibid., p. 263

Secondly, learning about events which happened many hundreds of years ago, requires of the learner a sense of time or more accurately, a sense of the passage of time. It also requires the ability to bridge the gap of centuries and to comprehend a distant century on its own terms. Few adults are capable of such a leap across time and of children this ought not even to be expected. Peel maintains that research has proven that the time comprehension of children is very limited. "The total experienced time, he writes, including past, present and future, all of which are present in mind and affect action, changes from a span only of yesterday, today and tomorrow with 5–6 year olds, to a span of three seasons in case of 10–11 year olds, a span of three years in the case of the pre-adolescent and finally to a span of five years in the past and future in the case of the adolescent." [12] Peel has provided us with some important new insights into the psychological problems in history teaching. His findings, however, do not weaken the basic arguments for the teaching of history. What they do suggest is the need for more attention to the methods and approaches to the teaching of history.

History in essence is a series of dialogues—a dialogue between the historian and his evidence, an unspoken dialogue between the heroes of the story and a dialogue between the historian and his readers. So conceived, history cannot be taught effectively as a transmission of knowledge or information. The act of teaching history must also involve a dialogue between the teacher and his students and a never-ending genuine search by both the teachers and students for historical truth.

There is a remarkable affinity between the "historian's way," the way in which the historian does his research and searches for his understanding of the past and the way an effective history teacher does his job. Both search for their own way to organize and analyze the available data and both are ready to make hypotheses and discard them when the data does not seem to support them. The historian seeks out the view of other historians who have written on the subject, while the effective teacher of history is hospitable to the views and findings of his students. Few steps could be more useful for the improvement of history instruction in schools and in colleges than an active, continuous collaboration and exchange of views between the academic historians and the history teachers.

---

[12] E. A. Peel, "Some Problems in the Psychology of History Teaching," in *Studies of the Nature and Teaching of History*, W. H. Burston and D. Thomson, eds. (New York: Humanities Press, 1967).

The New Social Studies Reconsidered *

In 1966 I was working on the first draft of a little book called *The New Social Studies* which I was writing on a year's leave of absence from the Carnegie–Mellon University, a leave during which I visited social studies curriculum projects throughout the country and read the materials they had produced. That book was published in the spring of 1967. If I had a chance to write it again, I'd retain the same basic structure but I'd emphasize a number of issues quite differently and I'd make a far stronger plea for two things: for teacher involvement and for teacher militancy. Let me try to explain why. I have been changing my mind about a number of issues. Let me begin by discussing the tendency of the new social studies to focus primarily upon able students.

This year (1969) I am directing a project to develop a course in American history for junior high school slow learners. Eight graduate students do the hard work. Four of them taught the course in inner city schools last year, and all eight now teach the revised version in or near Pittsburgh as we prepare it for publication.

I have taught full or part time in secondary schools for ten years. All of my graduate student-colleagues are experienced teachers. But none of us has ever encountered students who are so difficult to teach as these slow learners; never before have we felt initially the force of such open hostility; never have recognized so clearly how irrelevant much of our training and our preconceptions were to the task before us. Most of our eighth grade students read at a fourth or fifth grade level. They are 14 or 15 years old, too young to drop out legally and too old to accept passively the nonsense which some teachers subject them to. They think they are dumb, at least in respect to the demands made by the established order. They don't want to learn, at least not to learn what schools customarily teach. They don't know how to learn, at least, how to learn from books. Their value systems— if poorly integrated sets of hostilities can be termed a system—alienate them from our society, at least, from the schools, the police, the social workers, and the ghetto which are America to them. The fact that they know little about our nation's past seems of little importance in comparison to these other characteristics.

* Excerpted and adapted from a speech by Edwin Fenton, Professor of History and Director of the Education Center at Carnegie–Mellon University, given at the Annual Meeting of the New York State Council for the Social Studies at Grossingers, April 9, 1968.

The new social studies has neglected the slow learning child and, for that matter, many low average students. Organized primarily by college professors with Ph.D.'s in history or one of the social sciences, most of the social studies projects set out to teach vital parts of traditional academic disciplines to children with characteristics as close to those of college students as possible. In part, project directors were simply following the lead of the scientists and mathematicians. In part, lack of classroom experience as typical teachers explains the direction of their efforts. More important, however, was their stubborn isolation in academic departments immune from colleges of education where a virulent philosophy called life adjustment had cut off disciplined and respectable thought, or so they had been told.

Most of us now know better. I have discovered that one after another of my most illuminating insights has been plagiarized from me and published by an educationist some 20 or 30 years ago. But we still must marry the best insights from the social science disciplines with the best insights from the discipline of education. And, at least in American society, handholding, conversation, and even a love affair fill the months between meeting and mating. It's time for social scientists and educators to begin touching hands.

Learning the latest interpretation of Jacksonian Democracy makes no sense as the major focus of a history course for slow learning eighth graders. You wouldn't have a window left in the school. Nor can emphasis on sophisticated inquiry procedures designed primarily to teach the conceptual structure of a discipline so that students can hypothesize independently, receive predominant attention. Chaos would erupt in every classroom. Nor can we defend the practice of concentrating so heavily on teaching reading through social studies that we neglect almost everything else. Social studies teachers don't know how to teach reading, and in addition, there are other more vital things to do.

The experience of the Carnegie–Mellon group indicates that teachers should emphasize four sets of objectives in addition to knowledge and to inquiry skills with slow learning students. First, they should help these students to develop good self concepts in order to convince them that they aren't hopelessly dumb, that they can graduate from high school, that they can get a job, and that they do belong—to a community, to a nation, to mankind. Second, they should help students to develop better attitudes to learning: to be willing to bring paper and pencil to class, to be willing to listen when others speak, to be willing to participate in class discussions, to be willing to do supplementary work voluntarily. Third, they should help students to clarify their opinions about the nature of a good man, a good life, and a good society. Without clarified and integrated value systems, many of these children will erupt onto the streets at the first opportunity in a blind and desperate search for loot, for vengeance, and for identity. Finally, teachers of slow learners should emphasize learning skills. Reading is among the important ones, but these children should also learn to interpret graphical materials, to listen to recordings, to look at pictures, and to view the films and television programs from which they will receive most of their education once they slam the school door behind them for the last time. Most of the social studies projects ignore many of these objectives, treat them as incidental learning, or give them a low place on the learning hierarchy. Instead, we should let student characteristics determine objectives, material, and teaching strategies, a conclusion which educators have known for decades.

The social studies projects are providing new opportunities to make learning relevant, but new materials cannot replace the teacher. Teachers must decide that the contemporary civil rights movement is more important to our children than the names, dates, and national origins of sixteenth and seventeenth century explorers. Teachers must choose to use one of Richard Brown's units and to integrate it with the other work of a course. Teachers must choose Donald Oliver's pamphlets and stretch themselves to learn new ways to teach them. Teachers must choose the supplementary materials which our Carnegie project gives them a chance to exploit. And if teachers do not make choices, little worthwhile is likely to happen to the children they instruct.

Teachers must also learn to use a variety of inquiry approaches. In the little book published in 1967, I stressed an analytical mode of inquiry for the social studies. It was essentially a historian's way of thinking about how to interpret the past, and it is primarily useful to teach the cognitive skills on which all thinking depends. But is not a very useful mode of inquiry for clarifying values or for thinking through solutions to contemporary problems. Let me describe more appropriate teaching techniques for these objectives.

Our Curriculum Center has just produced a film based on an inquiry process designed to clarify values ("Clarifying Values: Mr. Hopkins' Will; A Tape Recording," a 22-minute kinescope; part of a series of six entitled *Using Media for Inquiry in Secondary School Social Studies*. Holt, Rinehart and Winston, Inc., 383 Madison Avenue, New York 10017). The basic ideas of the teaching technique originated with the Harvard Social Studies Center to which so many of us owe a great debt. The lesson begins with a recording of an imaginary conversation between a millionaire named Mr. Hopkins and his lawyer who has been told to draw up a will leaving Mr. Hopkins' $ 15 million fortune to found a college for poor white boys. The lawyer objects on the grounds that the will excludes Negroes. Mr.

Hopkins claims that he made his money and has a right to leave it to whatever cause he wishes. Moreover, he points out, his fortune will contribute to equality because it will be used to educate poor boys who would otherwise be unable to go to college. "But why exclude Negroes?" the lawyer asks, and the discussion goes on.

Once the recording has finished, the teacher asks the students to state the positions of both Mr. Hopkins and his lawyer. The issue quickly becomes clear: How can anyone justify leaving money to a school which discriminates against Negroes? Then the teacher starts to ask questions about analogous cases. Would Mr. Hopkins be justified in leaving his fortune to a social club —say of immigrants from one Sicilian village— which barred everybody else from membership? What if he left it to a church which discriminated? Suppose a man wanted to leave his money to a women's college which discriminated against men. Can he justify his bequest? Suppose he wanted to leave it to a scholarship fund exclusively for Negroes? In the film, one boy who had participated thoughtfully in the discussion suddenly had an insight. "Setting up a scholarship fund exclusively for Negroes is discrimination," he said, "but it is discrimination in order to bring about equality, and that's a funny idea."

This inquiry technique helps students to clarify their values. The objective is not consensus about what Mr. Hopkins can justify; the objective is to have each child think the issues through in order to arrive at a defensible position for himself, either the same position as he held at the beginning of the discussion—but with evidence to support it—or a new position adopted because his original stand failed to meet the test of evidence. These are the sorts of teaching techniques which we have too long neglected, and I emphasize the words "teaching techniques." The materials for this discussion consist of a recording which plays less than five minutes. The remainder of what happens depends primarily on the ability of the teacher to develop analogous situations and to encourage honest and open discussion of a subject which involves emotionally charged issues.

Any imaginative teacher can think of a number of other situations where value clarification taught in this manner is appropriate. Can you justify the Civil War draft riots with analogies to a dozen contemporary outbreaks? Can you justify a heavy graduated income tax in order to build new highways, improve slum housing, revolutionize our educational system, or kill more people in Vietnam? All we need do is to develop the skill and the courage of our convictions.

Still another mode of inquiry can be used to investigate solutions to contemporary social, economic, and political problems. I ran across one account of an appropriate technique a decade ago when I had an opportunity to teach economics at Carnegie–Mellon University. We used George Leland Bach's college text, *Economics: An Introduction to Analysis and Policy* (Prentice–Hall, Inc., now in a fifth edition, 1966). There Bach outlined four steps in an inquiry procedure for thinking about alternative public policies. In essence, they were:

1. First, define the problem, a process which includes understanding a situation thoroughly and clarifying objectives to be achieved.
2. Second, map out the major alternative ways to achieve the desired objectives.
3. Third, trace through the alternative policies outlined in step two to determine the effects each policy is likely to have.
4. Fourth, check your solution for flaws in your analysis.

Despite the venerable age of modes of inquiry such as this one, few of the contemporary social studies projects have employed them in a disciplined fashion. Yet the sorts of problems to which these techniques are germane are legion.

I have been discussing three modes of inquiry for the social studies. How are teachers to learn them? Clearly, we must have better pre-service education and more in-service work. How many teachers whom you know can describe—never mind use in the classroom—these three approaches to teaching? How many college professors who direct NDEA institutes know how to use them? The universities, the government, school systems, and individual elementary and secondary schools must invest additional resources in teacher preparation and teacher retraining. Without this additional investment, all our beautiful new buildings and imaginative materials may make little difference in the behavior of students. In addition to demanding higher salaries, teachers ought to demand more money for materials and better in-service work. Such demands should help to enlist the support of parents and administrators. All of us—teachers, curriculum specialists, teacher trainers, school administrators, parents, and students—must work closely together for common goals.

Increased teacher responsibility for curricular decisions does not imply an attack on the work of curriculum projects, state guidelines, or locally written courses of study. Many of the current social studies projects have produced elaborate teachers' manuals, sometimes more extensive than the student materials themselves. These manuals contain carefully constructed suggestions about teaching procedures designed to show instructors how to attain specified objectives with the materials provided. Teachers would be foolish indeed to ignore this careful work. But at the same time, they should feel free to teach for alternative objectives given the composition of a particular class, and this decision would imply a shift in teaching strategies. The trick is to blend careful inspection of the work of curriculum experts with sound judgment of the needs of individual students.

This entire line of argument rests on the assumption that teachers want more responsibility, are willing and able to use additional responsibility, and are prepared to become informed educational decision-makers. A number of teachers I know well in Pittsburgh and elsewhere in the nation share this attitude. They want more responsibility for basic curriculum decisions; they want money to purchase supplementary materials for use in their own classes; they want a greater voice in long range planning of projects like Pittsburgh's proposed five Great High Schools which are destined to replace our present obsolete and inadequate buildings and become the center of widespread services, educational and social, for the entire city; they want a better mechanism by which their complaints about incompetent or sadistic principals can be heard without threat of reprisals; they want to help organize faculty meetings and in-service days so that more time will be devoted to education and less to administrative detail; and they want to join administrators in a search for ways to make teaching a genuine profession free of milk money, hall patrol, collecting tickets at ball games, and the host of clerical duties which plague every classroom teacher.

I know other teachers—far too many—who care little about such matters. They want higher pay; they miss classes as many days each year as sick-leave provisions allow; they teach routinely; and they spend their evenings with NBC rather than Jerome Bruner. It's time for the rest of us to join conscientious administrators and aroused parents in an attempt to induce these time servers to change their attitudes or to get jobs in professions where they will do less harm to children. We make a tragic mistake when we permit tenure to sanction incompetence and laziness.

Which brings me to the subject of teacher militancy. I do not favor militancy for all objectives or in all situations. After all, Hitler's Storm Troopers were militant. But as a teacher searching for a voice in the issues that matter in the schools—curriculum, teaching methods, the dignity of the profession, and the shaping of American society—I have become staunchly militant. Only the individual teacher in the classroom knows his individual students well enough to prescribe instructional materials for them. Let's let everyone hear this message. Only the individual teacher in the classroom can choose a particular teaching technique at a particular moment for the needs of an individual child. Let's get this message across. We teachers must also speak out clearly on national issues, by flying to Memphis as New York City teachers did to protest injustice to trash collectors, by inundating Washington with letters to our Congressmen, by telling our fellow citizens "like it is" and encouraging them to change, and by demanding salaries that permit us to study instead of to drive busses in the summer. Children may well learn more about making a decent society by watching what their teachers do than by listening to what they say. At this moment we must speak most clearly about two issues. The first, justice to America's minorities in a land where many of the children we teach laugh in derision at texts which ignore or falsify the bitter facts of their own lives. The second, the tragedy of Vietnam where it costs us, I've heard, a half million dollars to kill a Vietcong while children in urban and rural slums alike starve spiritually, physically, and mentally for lack of the schools, the houses, the jobs for their fathers, and the rodent control this money could buy. So let's make sure that everyone hears this message, loud and clear.

11   THE AUTHORS

The Carnegie–Mellon University Social Studies Materials

There is an urgent need for a judicious analysis of the New Social Studies of Edwin Fenton. His successful, if perhaps unintended, popularization of the word "induction" has led some social studies practitioners to reduce his comprehensive and complex program to a single motif or a catchword of limited value. However, the imposition of rigid categories on Fenton's approach detracts from the important dialogue which he has initiated about the role of history and the social sciences in the secondary schools. The purpose, then, of this chapter is to examine the *many* facets of an ambitious and provocative project.

In order to view Fenton's ideas in historical perspective, the reader should recall the post-Sputnik reassessment of secondary education and the enlistment of college and university scholars to help upgrade the high school curriculum. Professor Fenton is one of the academic specialists who has become interested in the problem of social studies in the secondary schools. Having received his doctorate at Harvard, he is now a member of the history department of Carnegie–Mellon University, where he directed with John M. Good one of the curriculum projects financed by the Office of Education under the Project Social Studies Program.

Currently, he is the general editor of a social studies curriculum published by Holt, Rinehart, & Winston.[1] Fenton has written two books: *Teaching the New Social Studies in Secondary Schools: An Inductive Approach* (Holt, Rinehart, & Winston, 1966) and *The New Social Studies* (Holt, Rinehart, & Winston, 1967). An assortment of articles has appeared in *Social Education*, the journal of the National Council for the Social Studies. These publications enable one to identify some of his major assumptions and theoretical underpinnings.

RATIONALE

The Holt Curriculum represents an effort to forge a viable partnership between history and the social sciences. A glance at the course titles gives one a feeling for the counterpoint between the historical and scientific approaches. Sometimes the insights of the social sciences are an overt concern as in "Comparative Economic Systems." However, in the history offerings they are incorporated more subtly, as in a study of "changing American social structure."

Professor Fenton's decision to link history and the social sciences has received considerable attention from friend and foe alike. Some experts see his attempt as an act of desperation by a "card-carrying" historian who is determined to keep his subject from being replaced or contaminated by newer disciplines. As one writer puts it: "historians desire to use materials from the social sciences just as long as they select what is to be used and history continues to be the core of the program.[2] While it is important to realize that Fenton has a commitment to history and believes that "a person should know about the heritage of Western society," [3] we believe that his use of social science insights and concepts stems from a reasoned consideration of the roles such disciplines can play in enriching social studies instruction.

One of these, of course, is the guidance in content selection that an established body of knowledge naturally provides. Another relates to the problem of relevance. Since history may not always seem meaningful to young people in a world of rapid change and mass media, it is quite likely that Fenton and his colleagues feel that insights from the social sciences provide a current perspective from which to examine unique events of the past.

Professor Fenton also may implicitly view history as what Philip

---

[1] This project will be subsequently referred to as the Holt Curriculum.

[2] Albert S. Anthony, "The Role of Objectives in the New History," *Social Education*, November, 1967, p. 576.

[3] Edwin Fenton, *The New Social Studies* (New York: Holt, Rinehart, & Winston, Inc., 1967), p. 22.

Phenix refers to as a "synoptic" discipline, which can draw from the best that the social sciences and the humanities have to offer. Admitting, for example, that psychology and other disciplines can make an important contribution to historical explanation, Phenix reminds us that their role is limited:

Valuable as the generalizations of the social sciences are in framing historical hypotheses, they are not sufficient to account for the unique particulars of history. Here is where the arts become relevant, particularly drama, which is a fictional presentation of persons making decisions affecting their destiny. The novelist's or playwright's convincing portrayal of life in fictional form can provide helpful suggestions to the historian as he seeks to present his convincing portrayal of life answerable to the conditions and evidences of reality.[4]

Fenton speaks to this assertion by incorporating literature into his social studies program. His demonstration of how thirteenth-century France can be understood with the help of a medieval romance should be read by all social studies teachers.[5]

Like many innovators in the field, Professor Fenton has also acknowledged his debt to some of the ideas articulated by Jerome Bruner in *The Process of Education* (Vintage Books, 1960). Although he would not concur *completely* with Bruner's claim that we will move "away from the study of history," he has been impressed by the inductive aspects of the Harvard psychologist's pedagogy, his notions about a spiral curriculum, and his inquiries about the structure of disciplines.

Pursuing the problem of knowledge at greater length, Fenton has become familiar with Joseph Schwab's work on structure. Influenced by Professor Schwab's notion of "imposed conceptions" which "define the investigated subject matter and control its inquiries," [6] he has been seeking a concept of structure which would benefit history and the social sciences. He has as yet reached no final conclusions, but has identified three major structural components: generalizations, concepts, and analytical questions. Since the latter of these is central to active inquiry and the process of developing and validating hypotheses, he feels that it will probably be the most valuable for the social studies. His penetrating critique of the banality of most generalizations is valuable and timely, but the stress on analytical questions may not be totally illuminating. Although we can agree that

---

[4] Philip Phenix, *Realms of Meaning* (New York: McGraw–Hill Book Company, 1964), p. 241–42.

[5] Edwin Fenton, *Teaching the New Social Studies: An Inductive Approach* (New York: Holt, Rinehart, & Winston, Inc., 1966), p. 240–53.

[6] Joseph J. Schwab, "The Concept of the Structure of a Discipline," *The Educational Record*, 43 (July, 1962): 199, 203.

CHART OF THE HOLT SOCIAL STUDIES CURRICULUM
(a suggested sequence)

First Semester

Second Semester

Grade 9
"Comparative Political Systems"
A comparison of a primitive political system with the governments of the United States and the Soviet Union examining the nature of leadership, the institutional setting, decision-making, the role of the individual citizen, and ideology.

Grade 9
"Comparative Economic Systems"
A comparison of a traditional economy with systems where most decisions are made in the market (United States) and where most decisions are made by command (Soviet Union), focusing upon three basic questions—what is to be produced, how is it to be produced, and for whom is it to be produced.

Grade 10
"The Shaping of Western Society"

A study of change over periods of time in four areas of Western society—the economic system, politics, the social organization, and patterns of thought.

Grade 10
"Tradition and Change in Four Societies"
An examination of four countries—South Africa, China, India, and Brazil—analyzing in each case the traditional society, the impact of Western ideas and institutions, and one major contemporary problem, such as economic growth.

Grade 11 "American History"
A study centering on four major themes—the development of the American economic system, the growth of the American political system, the changing American social structure, and the reflection of these developments in the American intellectual tradition.

Grade 12
"Introduction to the Behavioral Sciences"
A study of two issues: the methods of inquiry of the behavioral sciences (psychology, sociology, and anthropology), and selected generalizations about the behavior of men as individuals and in groups.

Grade 12
"Humanities in Three Cities"

A study of the conceptions of the good man, the good life, and the good society revealed in literary and artistic works produced in ancient Athens, Renaissance Florence, and modern New York City.

such an emphasis is not a "mere quibble," [7] we have known for a long time the strategic value of asking the right questions.

Another motif of Fenton's new social studies involves its use of the inductive mode of teaching. However, one must be precise in applying the term "induction" to the Holt Curriculum. To be accurate one should realize that Fenton and his colleagues are interested in developing "inquiry skills" of which induction is only one. They have developed a continuum which envisions a gradual progression from discovery to expository learning. Somewhere in the middle lies the technique of "directed discussion" a word which replaces "induction" in Fenton's latest book. While it sometimes refers to a systematic examination of value-laden issues, it most often entails leading the student to a predetermined set of conclusions by presenting him with appropriate cues in the form of key questions. At times this approach differs little from traditional methods in terms of *what* is learned. The student still may be hunting for Easter eggs which his instructor has found and re-hidden. The oft-heard complaint that Fenton is belittling the importance of content cannot be supported. Moreover, he admits quite openly that "directed discussion teaches students impressive amounts of sheer data." [8] And in discussing a lesson on the concept "frame of reference" he puts the matter still another way:

Our students would know the meaning of the term "frame of reference" less clearly if they had been told what it was and asked to recite a definition. *Nor could they have "discovered" the meaning of this term without guidance from the teacher, since they would have no idea about what to "discover" from a list of eighteen creatures.* [italics mine] [9]

Classroom teachers should find his representation of methods useful in attempts to vary their format, but he has yet to spell out in exhaustive fashion the relationship between induction and deduction.

The above method is utilized to accomplish one overall objective: "to help each student develop to the limit of his ability into an independent thinker and a responsible citizen of a democratic society." [10] Since Fenton realizes that such an over-arching goal is too vague to give detailed guidance to the teacher, he divides it into four major areas: attitudes, values, knowledge, and inquiry skills.

However, even then the statement of aims will not necessarily en-

---

[7]   *Teacher's Guide for Comparative Political Systems*, Public Domain Edition, p.v.

[8]   Edwin Fenton, *The New Social Studies* (New York: Holt, Rinehart, and Winston, Inc., 1967), p. 48.

[9]   Edwin Fenton, *Developing a New Curriculum: A Rationale for the Holt Social Studies Curriculum* (New York: Holt, Rinehart, and Winston, Inc., 1967). p. 18.

[10]   Ibid., p. 2.

lighten the curriculum consumer. There are times when one or more of the four parts seems more important than the others, and the relationship of one aim to another is not always clear. For example, in the category of values it is hoped that the student will evolve "a coherent value system to act as an anchor in a storm-tossed world." [11] Does Fenton then suggest that a value system will enable a student to think independently, or does he feel that independent thinking is the means to the end of a value system? Or does he have in mind elements of both possibilities? Whatever the case, clarification is needed.

Nevertheless, there is no need to belabor this point. Statements of objectives in the social studies are rarely totally satisfactory, and the Holt rationale is specific enough to allow for a meaningful analysis of the project's materials.

THE MATERIALS

The final product is a sequential and cumulative offering for the four years of high school. We conclude that for the most part the curriculum remains true to its premises.

The authors rely heavily on readings in secondary and primary sources to develop the student's skill in generating analytical questions. These episodes or case studies illuminate the organizing elements (concepts, values, and skills) that hold the courses together. On the whole, however, only lip service is paid to the expository side of the methods continuum. The teacher will have to take considerable initiative in deciding on lectures and the like.

In order to make the analysis more specific we are going to proceed with a detailed examination of the introductory course in *Comparative Political Systems*. Following that will be commentary related to selected aspects of other semesters.

It is interesting that the political science section employs a comparative approach. Only recently Frederick O. Gearing has argued cogently that man can improve his perception of the world by means of a variety of comparisons. He explains that "a student cannot adequately see the flow of political influence through impersonal mass media and legislatures until he has also watched influence flow through a community-wide network established by some configuration of kinship relations." [12] He might be pleased with the Holt course which introduces the student to the uses of power in the modern world by considering the workings of primitive, democratic, and totalitarian societies.

---

[11] Ibid., p. 15.
[12] Frederick O. Gearing, "Why Indians?" *Social Education*, February, 1968, p. 131.

Five concepts comprise the major organizing elements for this investigation.

1. Political Leadership: the group of people who make, interpret, and enforce the rules by which a political system operates.
2. Political Decision-Making: the process by which these rules are made, interpreted, and enforced.
3. Political Institutions: accepted organizations for or ways of handling political decision-making.
4. Political Ideology: the body of beliefs, attitudes, values, and goals underlying political decisions.
5. Citizenship: the role played by the individual in the system.

An overview of how these concepts can operate is provided in Unit One's case studies of a World War II prison camp and an American Indian group. Stoerpenberg Prison and the Cheyenne represent microcosms of the larger world. In the accompanying Teacher's Guide, the instructor learns that "the attributes of leaders in Stoerpenberg resemble traits generally admired in American society and that the political institutions were simplified versions of American ones." [13]

Although the immersion in the processes of these societies may involve too much time and occasionally transform interest into excitation, the source materials are excellent motivational devices. Especially effective is "The Tribal Ostracism and Reinstatement of Sticks Everything Under His Belt." The story line is not as engaging as the title, but the description of tribal policy formation is convincing enough. Throughout the unit the student is exposed to the intricate interplay between formal and informal influences in political life.

Unit Two takes up the problem of ideology and shows how the value system of a group can affect its political practices. Initially this section deals with some fairly standard themes such as federalism, checks and balances, and the rights of the individual. However, an examination of the pros and cons of wiretapping provides a break in the routine and reminds one of the approach to controversy advocated by Oliver and Shaver. Then the student contemplates a comparison between the United States and the Soviet Union.

The authors deserve considerable credit for avoiding a cliché-ridden approach to the study of the USSR. Refusing to blur important differences between the two world powers and pointing judiciously to interesting similarities, they present an interesting picture of government in the Soviet Union today.

---

[13] Mindella Schultz, *Teachers Guide for Comparative Political Systems: An Inquiry Approach* (New York: Holt, Rinehart, and Winston, Inc., 1967), p. 3.

Leadership should interest youth in this era of the Black P Stone Nation and other gang associations, and high school classes are not likely to be disappointed by the third unit's account of "Moochie, the Magnificent." While they may register initial annoyance at the prospect of another prison-camp adventure, there is an irresistible pathos in the rise and fall of the leadership of an American G.I. That personal charisma is a transient attribute, often a function of time and place, is a point that is well made in this wartime adventure. The scene then shifts to the States, where Congressional politics are seen through the eyes of veteran compaigner, Jerry Voorhis. An equally human portrayal of a Soviet party secretary describes the "delicate balance to be maintained between persuasion and coercion" [14] necessary even in a totalitarian state.

The unit on decision-making, after surviving a version of the somewhat overworked Cuban Missile Crisis, gives the student a realistic picture of the lawmaking process. Instead of the traditional committee by committee account, a more convincing configuration of lobbying and informal politics is presented. The student may also be surprised to note the manager of Gosplan, the Soviet planning committee may encounter similar obstacles to obtain needed legislation.

The remaining units are very *au courant* ranging from an oblique consideration of the credibility to a "Violent Harvest" in Cicero, Illinois. For one who feels that draft-resistance is a hackneyed topic, the strange career of Tommy Rodd will contain fresh insight and a poignant reminder of an issue that must be faced by society.

It is possible that the course contains an overdose of readings featuring catchy titles. However, the danger that the student will remember the names and nothing else is mitigated by the quality of the sources. Writers like Stewart Alsop, Harrison Salisbury, and David Halberstam give the students an opportunity to read material that captures the spirit of political life and overcomes the surface blandness of the course's title and concepts.

Certain aspects of the Teacher's Guide are a bit simplistic. Questions such as "Are your notes helpful in guiding you toward possible generalizations?" and objectives such as "To be willing to complete work as assigned" seem to be putting the students on. But these are minor objections to an otherwise challenging course.

"The Shaping of Western Society" begins with a six-day "quickie" introduction to the study of history. The rationale behind this do-it-yourself kit is that the student will learn the skills of a trained historian and practice them in subsequent encounters with ancient Greece, the

---

[14] Mindella Schultz, *Comparative Political Systems—An Inquiry Approach* (New York: Holt, Rinehart and Winston, 1967), p. 104.

Renaissance, and other periods. Some scholars, however, have doubts about the assumption that high school students should "learn the role of the historian." In an article in *Social Education,* Richard Farrell and James Van Ness question seriously the feasibility of such a notion:

This suggestion has a rather comic aspect; the students are to become what their teachers are not. Teachers of American history in the secondary schools are students of history—many are very perceptive students of history—but they are not trained historians. They do not have time to develop the skills of a trained historian .... To become a trained historian requires intensive and extensive work. The idea that it is easy to be a historian needs to be kept out of the secondary school history curriculum.[15]

Others wonder more about the desirability of the plan. Reminding us that disciplined inquiry "represents a relatively limited slice of human experience," Fred Newmann asks whether children should concern themselves with the questions raised by academic specialists. He claims that current curriculums tend to ignore nonrational and imaginative thought by their offering of "the model of the scholar pursuing truth in his study." [16] While one may take issue with these arguments, they are worthy of consideration, because reformers in the social studies are too often mesmerized by the inquiry modes of the academic disciplines.

We agree that a student cannot become an instant historian, but see value in a brief introduction to the craft. Such a unit becomes a handy reference point to which the student can be referred at appropriate times throughout the course. The initial exposure serves as an overview of an initiation into the historical fraternity that will last throughout the course. If carefully employed, this approach might well develop deliberative and retrospective qualities in the student. But if abused, it will become very artificial. Even the most gifted high school pupil will tire of being "his own historian" too often.

Pursuant to Newmann's warning, which was not, incidentally, directed specifically to Fenton, one discovers that the Holt Curriculum has left room for possible creative activity. In the Humanities course the students are asked to produce a photographic essay or to keep an intellectual diary.

It might be mentioned at this time that the Holt Curriculum keeps the interests of high school students in mind. Although we must confess that it is often difficult to determine accurately the "needs" of youth, the charge that Fenton uses irrelevant materials seems largely unjust. Even

---

[15]   Richard Farrell and James Van Ness: "A Thematic Approach to American History," *Social Education,* December, 1967, p. 689.

[16]   Fred Newmann, "Questioning the Place of Social Science Disciplines in Education," *Social Education,* November, 1967, p. 595–96.

the traditional history material is brought to bear on timely topics and problems. A study of the diffusion of western ideas and a case study of migration are examples of this tendency. Only occasionally does Fenton overstate his case, as in the dubious claim that a study of William Bradford will make the Pilgrims become "understandable human beings." [17]

FEASIBILITY

Before the classroom teacher embarks on a trial of the Holt materials, he should be aware of the far-reaching objectives of the project and of the issues these objectives raise. For example, let us reconsider the author's belief that the student should develop a *coherent* value system.

Much writing on values tends to stress the need for consistency as the individual builds his worldview. That is to say, there should be no contradiction between the various beliefs and attitudes that are held. But a cautionary note seems necessary here. There may be times when consistency is not at all desirable. Insistence upon it may hamper a person in unique situations when he is called upon to renounce values which would ordinarily be dependable in action. One thinks of Herbert Hoover who had a very consistent value system, but let it restrict his vision in a time of unusual emergency. All of this is to raise a question that teachers might think about: Under what circumstances should one consider departing from his established value system?

One must also be aware of difficulties involved in asking young people to develop a coherent value system, something which many adults do not have after many years of living. Even granting that the student can perform the task, a teacher is not likely to measure successfully the role that classroom experience plays in such an achievement. Fenton's assertion that the conclusions of teachers about student values are the result of a "somewhat subjective" process is a bit understated.[18] The real test comes when the student is confronted with the demands and responsibilities of active citizenship.

In dealing with inquiry skills as distinct values, the authors have had much more success in evaluation. They have collected statistically significant results which demonstrate that students taking their experimental courses increase their ability to inquire, as measured by the Carnegie Social Studies Inquiry Test.[19] Whether this test, however, has predictive validity for per-

---

[17]   Edwin Fenton, *The New Social Studies,* p. 21.
[18]   Edwin Fenton, *The New Social Studies,* p. 24.
[19]   John M. Good, John U. Farley, and Edwin Fenton, "Developing Inquiry Skills with an Experimental Social Studies Curriculum," dittoed statement.

formance in the world of restless men is a matter which has not yet been settled.

One very attractive feature of the Fenton materials lies in the fact that they can be interpolated into more traditional high school offerings in a variety of ways. Teachers reason, with some justification, that with the Holt and other projects available, they need only pick and choose at their convenience to produce an interestingly varied and eclectic social studies experience. There are times, though, when such an eclectic approach is no guarantee of success. The teacher may assemble a hodge-podge of experiences with little or no logical sequence. Beginning teachers encounter considerable difficulty in starting a traditional history course with inductive materials borrowed from the Fenton collection. For example, materials involving differing accounts of the Hungarian Revolution often confuse and disrupt a class that is used to a deductive strategy. A framework has to be created, and the teacher must have the confidence of the class. Then, the *occasional* use of specific materials from various projects will make sense in relation to the myriad of variables comprising the classroom situation.

One of these variables is the ability-level of one's students. And the Holt Curriculum takes this problem into account more than some critics have been willing to admit. While originally the authors designed their course for above average children, a new version has been prepared to take care of lower ability groups. It is interesting to note too that very minor adjustments in esoteric material can often make it suitable for all varieties of students. Edgar Bernstein, director of the Chicago Social Studies Project, tells how the *Iliad* and the *Odyssey* can be made palatable to poorly-motivated students by the substitution of modern names and places for the classical ones.

There is little doubt that Professor Fenton and his colleagues have created a quality program in history and the social sciences. Since its emphasis is basically inductive, those who intend to use it must be aware of the promise and pitfalls of a demanding pedagogical approach. Often, for example, the line between student initiative and teacher direction is very difficult to draw. It is also important to remember that the student may benefit from frequent exposures to deductive exercises. To quote John Holt:

It has seemed to me for a long time that, though children are very good at inductive reasoning, at making generalizations from specific cases, they were poor at deductive reasoning, since even the best students could rarely give examples of any generalizations they happened to know.[20]

---

[20] John Holt, *How Children Fail* (New York: Pitman Publishing Corp.).

The worth of the Holt Curriculum will be enhanced as classroom teachers and curriculum specialists conscientiously confront it with a variety of theoretical constructs and environmental situations and then articulate their findings to the profession as a whole. Both groups have much to work with: a comprehensive package of materials, audio-visual aids, and teacher's guides, as well as a detailed rationale. From examination and reexamination of the Holt Curriculum, we are bound to emerge with fresh insight about social studies in the secondary schools.

12   THE AUTHORS

Reflections on the Teaching of Negro History

The teaching of Afro-American history has become a front-page topic in newspapers, on radio and on television. The reasons for the phenomenon are complex and deserve to be explored.

The teaching of Afro-American history is now the battle cry of Negro student militants in the schools in Greater Chicago and across the country. It heads the list of demands that are presented to school authorities.

What are the reasons for this phenomenon? It primarily has to do with the expected effects of the study of Afro-American history. These expectations include a number of things. I shall list them not necessarily in the order of their importance:

1. To acquaint the students with the contributions of Negroes in America.
2. To give the black students a feeling of group identity and group pride. Afro-American history, it is said, will help Negro children to gain a self-concept and have pride in their heritage.
3. To correct the distortions contained in the U.S. history textbooks and history syllabi which have been in use in schools for many years.

It is already quite clear that in reference to the first objective, the need to acquaint the students with the contributions of Negroes to the building of America, there are a number of pitfalls which must be considered. Some Negro spokesmen make no secret of their lack of interest in providing these courses on Afro-American history to white students.

The usual answer on this point is, "You whites have distorted American history for years—it is now *your* job and *your* concern to right the wrong." The objective is clearly to teach the history of Negroes in America in order to make the black students proud of their contributions and their history. This is a legitimate objective, but caution seems to be indicated that a sense of balance be maintained that old distortions not be replaced by new distortions.

In some syllabi on Afro-American history that I have examined, Crispus Attucks, the runaway slave who was killed in the so-called Boston massacre, is portrayed as a hero of the American Revolution, equal or greater than Thomas Paine and Sam Adams. This makes little sense, since there are in the history of blacks in this country enough truly genuine heroes.

Our thoughtful Negro friends would undoubtedly explain some exaggerations by saying that the Negro child, who suffers from an inferiority complex, drummed into him by his white environment, needs that compensatory feeling of superiority. This may or may not be true. But as a historian and as a teacher, the occasional disregard for historical truth, as derived from available evidence, causes me discomfort and unease.

The second objective is indeed very important. It is said that courses in Afro-American history are intended to give the black student a sense of pride in the history of his people and to strengthen his identification with his community. History has been used and is still used for similar purposes by Jewish, Mormon and Polish minorities in America.

In the case of the Negro community in America, it is indeed necessary to take special steps to counter the effect of decades of teaching and preaching about the so called innate inferiority of the black race. For that reason, Negro spokesmen may well argue that if past injustices and past and present caricatures and distortions are to be compensated for, courses in Afro-American history ought to be made compulsory in all schools.

The third objective aims to do away with the imbalance, the omissions and the sheer injustice done to Negroes in our U. S. history textbooks and courses. We ought to teach Afro-American history not only because we want to teach about the story of millions of our black citizens in the course of American history, but also because the infusion of this history would make for more balanced and more sound, and yes, more truthful history of the American people. The omission of the part played by Negroes in many periods of our history, or the outright distortion of the role of the Negro minority, not only did violence to the history of the blacks in this country, but also gave a false picture of many historical events in the general history of our country. It is difficult not to sympathize with a

young Negro student leader in Chicago, Victor Adams, who recently said that the demand for courses in Afro-American history and culture is a "search for an image. Now we have nobody to identify with—nobody to whom we can say, 'Doggone, I would like to be like him'."
(*Chicago Sun-Times*, October 13, 1968).

Thus, it clearly follows that what is needed, either in addition to the courses on Afro-American history, or in lieu of them, is a thorough revision and updating of our presently used textbooks, curricula, guides and materials used in U.S. history courses in our elementary and secondary schools.

Before we proceed to examine the revisions needed in the teaching of U.S. history, a word must be said on another connected issue. Some Negro leaders and their student spokesmen in schools are demanding that only black teachers be allowed to teach courses in Afro-American history. This reasoning seems to be based on the assumption that only Negro teachers can truly understand the sufferings and deprivations of the black minority in this country and only they can teach Negro history effectively. In all frankness, this seems to be a poor argument. Carried to its logical conclusion, one can argue that only Englishmen ought to teach English history, only professors from Ghana or Nigeria can teach courses in the history of Africa and only Jews can be allowed to teach the history of the Hebrew people. This, of course, makes little sense.

We must, without hesitation, uphold the only position which is consistent with democratic principles and academic freedom, that all courses and all subject matters can be taught by all teachers who are academically and professionally qualified. We expose ourselves to great perils if we equivocate on this issue. Most, if not all of us, have been fighting for years for racial desegregation of schools.

It is unfortunately true that there are many white and black teachers who teach Afro-American history because they were asked to do so, but who lack the necessary qualifications to do the job. Little or no provision has been made for these teachers to take the necessary courses or at least go through a period of training in a workshop or a seminar. There are, of course, a number of teachers who by their own effort, teach Afro-American history with great effectiveness.

The complexity of this issue is clearly illustrated by the controversy which developed around the publication of William Styron's Pulitzer Prize-winning book, *The Confessions of Nat Turner*. Ten black writers published a book entitled, *William Styron's Nat Turner*, in which they assailed Styron for depicting Nat Turner as influenced more by his white than his black environment, as an impotent queer and as a fool and a coward.

They picture Turner as a "virile, commanding, courageous figure," who did not have, as Styron implies, ambivalent feelings about killing whites. They further contended that Nat Turner had not a shred of belief in the basic humanity of the whites and that, in fact, he was a dedicated hater of the whites.

Reviewing the book of the black writers, Professor Martin Duberman, the author of *In White America*, wrote,

If this is what blacks mean by "rediscovering black history and finding historical figures with whom black youths can identify," then the prospects are grim, for in the case of Turner at least, the figure they present for emulation is frighteningly one-dimensional, even pathological. It is a question, moreover, whether the new emphasis on black heroes really will demythologize our past . . . more or whether it will replace one set of myths with another . . . .

Blacks are entitled to their version of Turner, Attucks and others, but let them not pretend that those versions are incontestably validated by the historical evidence.[1]

There are a number of issues connected with the teaching of Afro-American history.

In speaking on this emotion-laden subject, it may be best to start with what appears to be the crux of the issue, and the crux of the issue is the fact that the study of American history in our schools has been and still is incomplete and often distorted as far as the role played by Negroes in the history of our nation. More often than not, the American Negro has been given the silent treatment by historians, history textbooks, and the writers of syllabi for history courses. Even the awareness of this fact is a new phenomenon. If anyone had known that American history, as written and taught by omitting the history of a sizeable portion of our population was incomplete, he kept it a well-guarded secret.

It is only in the last fifteen years that voices have been raised demanding the study of Negro history. Hundreds of articles have also been written, pointing out the omissions and distortions in history textbooks as far as the history of American Negroes is concerned. Many volumes, some good, mostly bad, have been put out by over-eager publishers on some aspects of Negro history.

The Negro historian, John Hope Franklin, believes the new U.S. history must be ready to make some basic new assumptions. The most important one, Professor Franklin wrote, "is the assumption that American

---

[1] *New York Times Book Review*, August 11, 1968, p. 26.

history is not the success story of white Anglo-American Protestants, who, as the story goes, made this country strong and great against all odds. Rather, the history of the United States is the story of a joint enterprise, with various groups and individuals playing certain roles, either taken by them or assigned to them. The roles they played, however exalted or however humble, have been important in the making of America." [2]

Few things infuriate Negro writers and scholars more than the ever popular concept of America as the melting pot. History textbooks and history teachers picture the United States as the haven of refuge for millions of Englishmen, Poles, Germans, Irish, Jews and others who left wretched conditions in the "old country" to find in America a land of freedom, equality and opportunity. The "old country" is, of course, Europe. In a number of years, the immigrants shed their old country characteristics and became Americans. There is really nothing wrong with this picture. It is basically true for all the white children who sit in our classrooms, but it is not true for the Negro children. They know that their great grandparents, their parents and they themselves have not succeeded in melting into the American environment. They have remained black, and therefore, different. For the Negro children and for the over 20 million Negro Americans the "melting pot" concept is a myth and an insult. Another aspect of the "melting pot" concept presents equally important difficulties to Negro students. The concept rests very heavily on the faith in the equality of opportunity for all those who have come as immigrants to the United States of America. It stresses that the destitute and often bewildered newcomers rather quickly improved their standard of life and their social position by hard work, frugality and initiative. This was undoubtedly true of millions of white immigrants, but the Negro students, especially those of high school age, know that their parents and grandparents and great grandparents often worked very hard, but did not enjoy an equal opportunity to improve their lot.

What Negro scholars and leaders are telling us, is that the story about the "melting pot" idea which does not apply to Negroes, is not an isolated case. They argue that generally, American history as taught in upper grades of elementary schools and in high schools, either ignores or distorts the history of Negroes, thus in effect distorting the entire history of the American nation.

Why is this so?

This question is not easy to answer. An honest answer may well have to do with psychological factors and even be in need of a psychiatric

---

[2]   John Hope Franklin, "The New American History," *Negro Digest*, February, 1967, p. 11.

analysis. Since I claim no expertise in these fields, I shall merely mention those factors without attempting to establish their reliability. It has been suggested that the omission of the Negro from our history books and text-books results from the collective sense of guilt felt by the white community for its treatment of the Negroes. White Americans, it is suggested, are not proud of the long history of violence in their relations with the Negro minority.

Whether this is true or not, Americans have been aware and are aware of the truth of a prophetic statement made in 1835 by Alexis de Tocqueville who wrote, "The most formidable of all the ills that threaten the future of the Union arises from the presence of a black population upon its territory."

Noting the corrosive influence of slavery on the white masters and the blacks, Thomas Jefferson wrote in his *Notes on Virginia* that slavery "was a perpetual exercise of the most boisterous passions, the most unremitting despotism on the one part; and degrading submission on the other. . . ."

The conviction that the two races are fundamentally incompatible and that any personal mixing of blacks and whites would lead to the weakening of the fiber and the traditions of the white race was a deeply ingrained and very early belief, mostly covertly, but sometimes overtly present, in the entire course of American history. Eli Ginzberg and Alfred Eichner wrote in their excellent book, *The Troublesome Presence: American Democracy and the Negro* that "Concern about mongrelization, about racial defilement in its most primitive form, lies at the root of the Negro issue."

It may not sound too important, but upon reflection it may be conceded that it is of utmost importance that the social studies teachers who teach Afro-American history be sensitive to the systematic, even if unplanned and often unconscious drive in our language imagery and the concepts by which we live, to equate black with, evil, danger and death.

The good guys wear white sombreros, the bad guys wear black hats and black handkerchiefs.

The angels are all in white, but death comes enveloped in a black cloak.

White is pure and innocent, as testified by the pure white gowns worn to weddings and confirmations . . ., but writers glibly speak of "black savagery and of black hearts."

Pure white is the "skin you love to touch," but if your daughter could not get into a sorority she wanted to join, she was "black-balled." And so on and on.

One can only imagine what all this, repeated daily in conversation, in books and on television, does to the mind and the heart of a black child.

It is obvious now that even if we historians and history teachers were still determined to write and to teach as if the Negroes did not exist, this can no longer be done. One of the most important features of the civil rights revolution, is the determination of the Negroes to assert their group self-respect.

There is a fundamental question to be resolved on how the Negro history is to be taught. I assume that we can all agree on how it should not be taught. It should not be taught during a proclaimed Negro History Week, during which some lectures are given on important Negroes. The life story of Booker T. Washington, or the story of the remarkable baseball career of Jackie Robinson, or the success story of Nat King Cole, do not constitute or even resemble Negro history. It is, however, legitimate to ask whether Negro history should be taught as a separate course or be integrated in the American history curriculum. There seems to be a reasonably convincing case for the integration of Negro history in the mainstream of American history. An integrated study would eliminate embarrassment to some Negro students who feel singled out. As Americans it can be claimed their story should be taught as an integral part of American history.

Some Negro scholars suggest that teaching Negro history only as it pertains to general American history would omit much of importance and significance because the Negroes in this country have had a history of their own as a separate community. This is a legitimate point. What can be done is to add in U.S. history textbooks and syllabi some chapters dealing with the pertinent aspects of Negro communal life in the past in the last decades.

How must the American history courses, as currently taught, be revised? To begin with, the misery and the degradation of Negro slavery and the story of the long and uphill struggle of the Negro for full citizenship, ought to be told fairly without condescension and without any undue emphasis on the guilt of the white community. Generally, it would be most helpful if Negro history be taught, as Tacitus demanded, *"sine ira et studio,"* without passion or prejudice. The teacher ought not to wear his heart on his sleeve—the factual evidence will speak for itself. This, of course, does not mean that we ought to expect more detachment and more objectivity in Negro history than we expect in any other history. History writing and history teaching is not an objective enterprise. But professional historians do at least, make an attempt to weigh the evidence, all of the evidence and beware of a simple-minded indoctrination or propaganda. Such high standards ought to also prevail in the teaching of Afro-American history.

Limitations of space and time make it necessary that the illustrations for the integration of the history of the black people in the story of the United States of America, be few and limited in detail.

The colonists considered the Negroes physically and culturally inferior, and consequently, unfit to be free and equal members of their society. They felt no contradiction between fervent devotion to Christianity and their acceptance of slavery. The Northern colonies generally sanctioned slavery *de facto,* while in the South, slavery was sanctioned by law.

It would come as a surprise to most of our students if they were told during the study of Colonial America that in 1730, the population of the colonies stood at one and one half million whites and 400,000 Negro slaves, which means that in the colonies Negroes constituted 21 % of the population, that ¼ of New York's population was Negro and that in the Southern colonies, particularly in South and North Carolina, Negroes were in overwhelming majorities. No wonder that even as slaves, Negroes exercised a lasting influence on Southern speech, religion, music, art, and sexual mores.

Professor Carl Bridenbaugh, a most distinguished authority on the Southern colonies wrote in his *Myths and Realities: Societies of the Colonial South:*

In the final analysis, therefore, the oft repeated statement that the country Negro was contented is a myth; it is perhaps one of the great historical delusions; and of all human factors determining the nature of the Carolina Society, the silent influence of the Black African was the most subtle, the most forceful, the most pervading, and the most lasting.

When one talks of the "Mind of the South," one inevitably ought to refer to the mind of the white Southerners and of the Southern Negroes. This, of course, is done very seldom.

With the outbreak of the Revolutionary War, the colonists who based their case on the principle of natural rights of men, regarded Negroes as property and therefore not involved in the struggle for the independence of the colonies. There were important exceptions which ought to be noted. James Otis, in his pamphlet *Rights of the British Colonies,* maintained that Negroes had the right to freedom and Thomas Paine repeatedly thundered against the iniquity of slavery and the tyranny of slaveholders.

Thomas Jefferson owned slaves, but disliked the institution of slavery, and included in the original version of the Declaration of Independence a passage denouncing King George for promoting slavery by his support of the slave trade. The Southerners saw to it that this passage was later eliminated from the Declaration.

Negroes, both in the Northern and the Southern colonies, exhibited an early enthusiasm for freedom. In the Protest March in Boston in 1770, later known as the Boston Massacre, a Negro runaway slave, Crispus Attucks, participated. He was among the five killed after Captain Preston, over-reacted to the jeers and the heckling of the mob of about fifty Bostonians.

Negroes were excluded from the Massachusetts and Connecticut militias, but some Negroes did fight in the battles of Lexington and Concord and Bunker Hill.

Educators, especially elementary teachers, face a real problem on how to tell their students, as I believe they must, that George Washington, the Virginia plantation owner, had no objection to slavery and did not want any Negroes in his army. On July 9, 1775, he issued an order forbidding the enlistment of "any stroller, Negro or vagabond." The new Revolutionary Army was not to have any Negroes, free or slave.

But when in November, 1775, Lord Dunmore, British Governor of Virginia, declared all Negroes free and invited to join the British Army, and after thousands of Negroes flocked to the British ranks, Washington, on December 8, 1775, allowed the enlistment of free Negroes.

It is estimated that 5,000 Negroes fought on the side of the American Revolution and acquitted themselves well in the battles of Monmouth, Savanna, Saratoga and Yorktown.

While George Washington as we saw, had no objection to slavery, Thomas Jefferson fully realized the evil of slavery and looked forward to its eradication. He fought against importation of slaves and in 1784 proposed the abolition of slavery in all the territories. Disbelieving that Negroes could ever be integrated in the American society, Jefferson proposed, like Lincoln after him, that Negroes be resettled in some other country.

In 1787, Benjamin Franklin became President of the Pennsylvania Society for Promoting the Abolition of Slavery, and the Relief of Free Negroes Unlawfully Held in Bondage. On November 9, 1789 he wrote and signed an Address to the Public appealing for funds to promote abolitionist activities. A few weeks later he petitioned Congress in favor of abolition of slavery.

The Constitutional Convention of 1787 reached a compromise on the issue of slavery, by not giving outright legal sanction to slavery, but by accepting its de facto existence. The Constitution provided that Negroes would count for purposes of representation and taxation as three-fifths of a person. But, slave trade was to cease after twenty years. The Constitution also provided for the mandatory return of runaway slaves. Southerners insisted that the Constitution gave legal sanction to slavery and that abolitionist propaganda was illegal and unconstitutional.

Thus, slavery was sanctioned and it became a tragic and divisive issue in the nation until it was resolved by a clash of arms in 1861. Hopefully, there is no need to belabor the point that the cruel and degrading nature of Negro slavery ought to be faced honestly and squarely in the American history course. It does no good to try to lighten the impact of the sordid practices of slavery and its debasing effect on slaves and masters alike by irrelevant emphasis on the Negro slaves, singing, dancing, and their placid and cheerful nature. The use of human beings as chattel, the selling away of mothers from their children, the use of the whip and the branding iron on the defenseless captive slaves cannot be and should not be explained away or equivocated with. Facing it squarely will only add luster to men like Lincoln and the enlightened part of the North's population which concluded that the blight of slavery was incompatible with the basic values on which this country was founded. The importance of the issue of slavery in the decades between the adoption of the Constitution and the Civil War can hardly be exaggerated. Even when obscured by other issues, it loomed like a large submerged iceberg—a constant danger to navigation.

The analysis of the causes of the Civil War in our textbooks and curricula is distorted and more often than not completely off base. For some reason, probably because we are as yet quite unwilling to face up to the enormity of the crime and evil of slavery, there is a persistent attempt to perpetuate the myth that slavery was not the root and the single most important cause of the Civil War. It is suggested that the Civil War was caused by the issue of secession, conflict over states rights, economic rivalry between the North and the South, etc.

The issues mentioned were important, but the fact is, as Lincoln told the Negro delegates who came to see him in the White House, that without the Negro and Negro slavery, there would have been no Civil War.

The question of the inevitability of the Civil War and the secondary place that abolition of slavery played in it has been heatedly debated by historians for many years. Those who insist on belittling the importance of slavery as a cause of the Civil War and the centrality of the issue of Negro freedom and equality both in the Civil War and in the period of Reconstruction, ought to be called upon to give some plausible explanation to the fact that those who wrote about the war from the perspective of personal participation and involvement, did not seem to have much difficulty in defining the basic issue between the North and the South.

Ulysses S. Grant, Commander-in-Chief of the Union Army, wrote in his *Memoirs* that slavery was the cause of the war and Jefferson Davis, the President of the Confederacy, wrote in his history of the Civil War, entitled *The Rise and Fall of the Confederate Government,* that the armed conflict ensued because of Lincoln's conviction that the Union could not permanently endure "half slave and half free."

Slavery and only slavery was the theme of the last attempt to avert a civil war. That attempt was made at the Peace Conference which convened in Washington in February, 1861.

Samuel E. Morison, in a pointed rebuke to those who would deny that the Civil War was a war on human bondage and on the denial of human rights, wrote:

I wish that some of our evasive historians, our mufflers of great, passionate issues, who are trying to persuade the American public that Negro slavery had nothing to do with the Civil War, would read the debates in this [February, 1861] Peace Convention. There is no suggestion in any of the Southern delegates' speeches of any grievance against the North, or against [Lincoln's] Republican party, other than hostility to slavery. Tariff, internal improvements, all those trumped-up issues which were the grist of the Confederate propaganda then, and since, were never even mentioned . . . .[3]

The existence of slavery which was detested as a moral and political evil by the great majority of the people in the North and defended as a "sacred institution" indispensable to the Southern way of life, obviously was the single most important cause of the Civil War.

A course in American history which would do justice to the story of the Negro struggle for equality ought to do away with the persistent myth of Lincoln's lukewarm attitude to slavery and his equivocation on the issue of Negro rights. For a variety of reasons, some historians and most textbooks insist in the perpetuation of this harmful myth. It is harmful because it detracts from the stature of Abraham Lincoln and even more importantly, it belittles a heroic effort to right the injustice against the Negroes. It has now come to pass that some Negro leaders and historians are trying to spread the myth that Abraham Lincoln was a racist and a white supremacist. As Al Smith used to say, let's look at the record.

Abraham Lincoln detested slavery from his youth and desired its prompt abolition. In the early 1830's, Lincoln as a young lawyer, devoted a great deal of his time to destroying the legal basis of the Negro indenture system which amounted to a *de facto* slavery in Illinois. In 1839, Lincoln in the case of Cromwell vs. Bailey, won a decision in the Illinois Supreme Court on behalf of an indentured slave, Nancy. The court ruled in a historic decision that in Illinois the presumption was that a Negro was free

---

[3] Samuel Eliot Morison, *Vistas of History* (New York: Alfred A. Knopf, Inc., 1964), p. 142.

and not subject to sale. In 1836, Lincoln, a representative in the Illinois House of Representatives, inserted a protest in the *Journal of the House* in which he castigated pro-slavery resolutions passed by the Illinois General Assembly. In 1846, when in the House of Representatives, Lincoln fought to abolish slavery in the District of Columbia. In a letter to George Robertsen of Kentucky, dated August 15, 1855, he wrote:

The condition of the Negro slave in America, scarcely less terrible to the contemplation of a free mind, is now fixed and hopeless of change for the better, as that of the lost souls of the finally impenitent.

During the Lincoln-Douglas Debates in 1858, Lincoln resolutely rejected the principle of white supremacy advocated by Stephen Douglas. Douglas said in Jonesboro: "I hold that this government was made on the white basis, by white men for the benefit of white men and none others.... The signers of the Declaration (of Independence) had no reference to the Negro when they declared all men to be created equal." In his answer, Lincoln stated that the Declaration of Independence did pertain to the Negroes as far as their right to life, liberty, and the pursuit of happiness is concerned. Already at the opening of the Debates, Lincoln condemned slavery in unequivocal terms. In Chicago he declared: "I have always hated slavery, I think, as much as any abolitionist."

It makes no sense to expect that Lincoln would have talked about Negro rights like Whitney Young or Dr. Martin Luther King. Misguided people always cite Lincoln's statement made in 1858 in which he said that he was not in favor of social or political equality for Negroes. In 1858 this was a wild idea. In 1858 the only issue was the existence or the abolition of slavery. In 1858 nobody even thought of the political equality of Negroes.

Lincoln was much impressed with the courage and valor of the 180,000 Negro soldiers who served in the Union Army. For some reason this chapter of history which should show the Negroes as making an important contribution to the saving of the Union is almost uniformly ignored by many historians and history textbook writers. College and high school students know all about the letter to Horace Greeley in which Lincoln, who by that time had already prepared the Emancipation Proclamation, stated that if he could save the Union without freeing any slaves he would do it, but they seldom are told of his letter to James G. Congling written three days later on August 26, 1863. In that letter the President wrote:

You say that you will not fight for the Negroes. Some of them seem willing to fight for you; but no matter.... Peace does not appear so distant as it did .... And there will be some black men who can remember that with silent tongue, and clenched teeth, and steady eye, and well-poised bayonet, they have helped mankind on to this great consummation, while I fear there will be some white ones unable to forget that with malignant heart and deceitful speech they have striven to hinder it.[4]

As the war drew to a close, Lincoln devoted a great deal of time to thinking about the future of the Negroes in this country. He considered it a moral obligation on the part of the white people and the Federal Government to secure fully the security and the human rights of the Negroes and to give them gradually the right of franchise. In January, 1864 (there is no precise day mentioned), Lincoln wrote to General James S. Wadsworth a remarkable letter which might be read with profit by high school and college students. The entire text of the letter reads as follows:

How to better the conditions of the colored race has long been a study which has attracted my serious and careful attention; hence I think I am clear and decided as to what course I shall pursue in the premises, regarding it a religious duty, as the nation's guardian of these people, who have so heroically vindicated their manhood on the battlefield, where, in assisting to save the life of the Republic, they have demonstrated in blood their right to the ballot, which is but the humane protection of the flag they have so fearlessly defended.
The restoration of the Rebel States to the Union must rest upon the principle of civil and political equality of both races; and it must be sealed by a general amnesty.[5]

How can we continue to talk about our support for Negro rights and equality and still continue to teach the history of Reconstruction in a way which is an insult to our Negro pupils and to their parents and which, more importantly, is a biased and distorted story of that period in our history.

The history of Reconstruction, as taught in most of our schools, virtually cries out for reassessment and revision. The subject is too complex to be analyzed in a relatively short paper. I can merely state a few suppositions.

The story of Reconstruction as presented in many classrooms is a black-and-white picture which lacks judiciousness, balance, and depth. The story, like the typical television Western, or like the distorted and biased

---

[4] Henry J. Raymond, ed., *The Life and Public Services of Abraham Lincoln* (New York: Derby and Miller, Publishers, 1864), p. 443.
[5] Quoted in Grady McWhiney, *Reconstruction and the Freedmen* (Chicago: Rand McNally & Company, 1963), p. 8.

book, *Gone with the Wind,* and the film based on the book, has heroes and villains: villains commit their villainies for a time, but at last the heroes prevail. The villains are the "vindictive" and "selfish" Radical Republicans like Stevens and Sumner, who with the help of the "barbarous," "illiterate" Negroes and the "rapacious" and "unscrupulous" carpet-baggers and scalawags, imposed on the South "Devil" and "corrupt" governments. The hero is usually President Andrew Johnson, whose attempt to follow the merciful and magnanimous policies toward the South enunciated by Abraham Lincoln, was frustrated and sabotaged by the "unscrupulous," "ambitious" and "vengeful" Radicals. The South, beaten and oppressed and despairing of getting justice and compassion at the hands of Congress, had no choice but to turn to massive resistance to the military Reconstruction governments. Occasionally, the southern whites were compelled to use extra-legal means of keeping the Negroes and their Republican allies from the polls by employing the scare tactics of the Ku Klux Klan and the Knights of the White Camelia. Finally, the efforts of the Southerners, aided by friendly elements in the North, succeeded in throwing off the yoke of the Reconstruction governments which were dominated by ex-slave Negroes. The Union was restored and freedom and tranquillity returned to the South.

What is wrong with this tale? First, it paints the picture of the Reconstruction in black and white colors when the predominant color should have been gray. The tale assumes that all Radicals, or as James Randall called them, "the Vindictives," were all devils, while in fact they were a varied group of diverse individuals. Similarly, the hero, Andrew Johnson, emerges from a close examination not as a knight in shining armor, but as a dour, dedicated, inflexible and ineffective President. In short, neither the tortuous story of Reconstruction, nor the much varied groups of its heroes, lend themselves to narration as a simple tale of heroes and villains. It requires thorough research, balanced and judicious weighing of the evidence—of all the evidence available.

W. E. B. Du Bois, the Negro historian, was unfortunately basically right when he wrote in his book, *Black Reconstruction:*

... One fact and one alone explains the attitude of most recent writers toward Reconstruction; they cannot conceive of Negroes as men; in their minds the word Negro connotes "inferiority" and "stupidity" lightened only by unreasoning gaiety and humor . . . .

We only have time to discuss one more aspect of American history that impinges directly on the history of the Negro minority. It is no accident that the emergence of America as a great world power before and after the

Spanish American War, coincided with the passage of much of the Jim Crow legislation in the South and with the consignment of Negroes to second class citizenship in the North.

It is surprising and even shocking to contemplate that both the supporters and the opponents of American imperialism and expansion, based their arguments on racist considerations.

Henry Cabot Lodge, the expansionist, argued that the United States ought to bring the benefits of its democratic practices and Christian ideals to the unfortunate, inferior little brown brothers, while William Jennings Bryan, the anti-imperialist, warned that the infusion of the inferior Malays, Filipinos and yellow races into the territory and body politic of America, would result in the lowering of standards in the United States and the weakening of the white race.

Faced with the necessity of ruling over non-white peoples abroad, the American North stood by, if not approving, at least accepting, as C. Vann Woodward pointed out, the avalanche of the Jim Crow segregation legislation which in a short time virtually eliminated Negroes from the political life in the South and made social and educational segregation a part of the Southern way of life. The Yale sociologist, William Graham Sumner, actually revived the Lincoln-Douglas Debates. He wrote: "Nothing is more certain than that inequality is a law of life .... No two persons were ever born equal. Thus, if you asked Thomas Jefferson when he was writing the first paragraph of the Declaration of Independence, whether in 'all men' he meant to include Negroes, he would have said that he was not talking about Negroes." [6]

Northern historians who still influence our textbooks and our history instruction, men like Burgess, Dunning and Bowers, wrote their histories of Reconstruction from the Southern point of view in a firm belief that this rewriting of history would strengthen the unity of the nation. That this unity was based on the second or third class citizenship status of millions of Negroes, did not seem to cause much concern, but was accepted as the natural consequence of their supposed innate inferiority.

No wonder that Southern senators, like the arch-racist, Ben Tillman, of South Carolina, half-mockingly and half-seriously, thanked their Northern colleagues for accepting their view on the inferior races. In a Senate speech, Tillman said:

No Republican leader, not even Governor Roosevelt, will now dare to wave the bloody shirt and preach a crusade against the South's treatment of the

---

[6] Rayford W. Logan, *The Negro in American Life and Thought, The Nadir, 1877–1901* (New York: Dial Press, Inc., 1954), pp. 125–26.

Negro. The North has a bloody shirt of its own. Many thousands of them have been made into shrouds for murdered Filipinos, done to death because they were fighting for liberty.[7]

The editor of the *Atlantic Monthly* wrote that "if the stronger and cleverer race is free to impose its will upon 'new-caught, sullen peoples' on the other side of the globe, why not in South Carolina and Mississippi."

High school students ought to learn about the connection between the passage of the Jim Crow legislation in the South and the period of American expansion and imperialism, and history textbooks and syllabi must give an adequate account of the Negro civil rights movement and do justice to such men as Frederick Douglass, Booker T. Washington, W. E. B. Du Bois, and Dr. Martin Luther King. The point must be made that the incessant demands by Negroes for equal rights have contributed to whatever progress in the area of civil rights has been achieved.

In conclusion, it is regrettable, but understandable, that the teaching of Negro history has become a political issue or even a political football. But we, as educators ought not to lose our cool. We ought to reject any attempt to make the courses on Afro-American history, either historical puffery or vehicles for racial propaganda. What we must do is to right a wrong done by the distorted teaching of the history of this nation as far as the story of the Negro minority is concerned.

We must resolve to present the history of our nation with integrity and balance. The studied omission of the role of the Negroes in the long and difficult struggle for a better and greater America, came about because of a national tendency to gloss over or soften the story of the grievous wrong done to the black people. The injustice, it must be stressed, was done not only to the Negro people, but to America, because the basic desire of the American people to live up to the lofty ideals of the Declaration of Independence, became blurred and distorted. There is no need to fear that a white student, who will learn of the evils of slavery and of segregation, would think less of America. On the contrary, when taught America full face, with some warts showing, he will come to love his country which is struggling fiercely for its own soul.

There is no question that to teach the old history would be so much easier and so much more comfortable. But, this would be an offense to our integrity as teachers and scholars, an offense to historical truth and a source of division and friction which this sorely beset nation cannot afford to tolerate.

---

[7] C. Vann Woodward, *The Strange Career of Jim Crow* (New York: Oxford University Press, 1955), p. 54.

PART III

Integrative Approaches

CHAPTER VIII

The Jurisprudential

Approach

13   FRED M. NEWMANN

The Analysis of Public Controversy:
New Focus for Social Studies *

As the post-sputnik awakening to ills of education in the United States at
last begins to touch subjects relegated to lower status than mathematics,
natural sciences and languages, we notice a burst of activity in the revision
of social studies curriculum. More than twenty major projects now
operate under the auspices of universities, foundations, professional organizations of scholars, and the United States Office of Education. We
welcome the increased attention now being given to social studies as we
exercise the obligation to evaluate the soundness and usefulness of
emerging approaches to curriculum revision.

A typical approach is the search for structure in each of the separate
social science disciplines.[1] The search for structure seems to have been

---

* From *Revolution and Reaction:* Cranbrook Curriculum Conference, 1965.
School Review, Vol. 73, No. 4, 1965, The University of Chicago Press. Copyright
1965 by the University of Chicago.

[1] Of fifteen projects sponsored by the U.S. Office of Education, five focus upon
a single discipline: two projects in economics, one in anthropology, one in history,
one in criminal law. The private corporation, Educational Services, Inc., has
separate projects in anthropology and history. The American Economic Association, American Sociological Association, and the National Council for Geographic
Education are among the professional organizations involved in efforts to improve
instruction in their fields at the public school level.

Several projects have a more generalist or interdisciplinary orientation. They
attempt to glean from the social sciences as a whole, crucial concepts, theories and
generalizations and to weave them into a general social studies program. Seven
projects sponsored by the USOE fall into this category.

stimulated in part by recent curriculum efforts in physics, biology and mathematics. In these fields, university scholars and outstanding school teachers jointly developed a set of instructional materials and teaching procedures designed to communicate what the scholars considered the most salient knowledge and methodology their field could offer. Jerome Bruner, in his *Process of Education,* has made more explicit the basis of a discipline-centered approach to curriculum revision. By concentrating on the notion of structure of a scholarly discipline and by speculating on relevant issues in learning theory (e.g., "readiness" and "motivation"), Bruner formulates a curriculum revision task of essentially two initial steps: (1) the definition and discovery of the structure of a discipline by the scholars themselves; and (2) the translation of this structure into language and relationships meaningful to the student.

In discussing new trends in social studies, it may be useful to distinguish between two levels of educational innovation: one could focus either on a particular curriculum proposal or on a general model for the *formation* of curriculum proposals. In a definite sense, one's model of curriculum reform may be a function of one's bias toward certain kinds of curriculum. By construing Bruner's model of reform as the two-step process mentioned above, one can then deduce a general profile of the curriculum that would result from such a revision process: i.e., the curriculum would consist of separate courses modeled after courses in academic disciplines such as history, anthropology, economics, etc. By way of contrast consider a model of social studies reform that might call for (1) a national conference of practicing social service and youth workers to draft a series of papers on emotional and educational needs of youth; and (2) an organization of competent social studies teachers whose task it is to devise and coordinate implementation of recommendations of the conference. Again, the action model reflects the content orientation of those who propose the model (in this case, there would probably be less emphasis on traditional intellectual fields, more on emotional, vocational or general role adjustment). In order to thoroughly evaluate proposals for educational change, we need to examine both the action (reform) model and the curricular outcomes that the model may be designed to produce. This discussion will begin with a concern for reform models, but it will use evaluative criteria that can be applied both to reform models and particular curriculum proposals.

THE SEARCH FOR STRUCTURE AS A MODEL FOR CURRICULUM REFORM

Structure as an Analytical Concept

In searching for structure in a social science discipline, what should we look for? To what does the concept refer? Bruner proposes, "Grasping the structure of a subject is understanding it in a way that permits many other things to be related to it meaningfully. To learn structure, in short, is to learn how things are related" (1960, p. 7). Elaborating on this he distinguishes between *specific skills* and *fundamental ideas* through which the structure of a discipline makes itself manifest. That is, in order to "grasp" relationships inherent in structure, one must first be able to use specific skills transferably: "Having learned how to hammer nails, we are better able later to learn how to hammer tacks or chip wood" (1960, p. 17). Second, the student should be able to understand the subject's "fundamental ideas," defined as those ideas that have "wide as well as powerful applicability." Problems of clarity and definition arise. The grasping of fundamental ideas seems to be an intellectual enterprise not mutually exclusive to the development of specific skills. We could argue that the transfer of hammering skill heavily depends upon perceived relationships of similarity between nails, tacks and chips—i.e., a fundamental idea or category must develop, embracing many phenomena as appropriate objects for the hammering skill.

One might identify as fundamental ideas not only categorical constructs (as above "things to be hammered"), but also explanatory generalizations or hypotheses that disciplines have verified. "A nation must trade in order to live" is fundamental for Bruner in the sense that it makes a series of American colonial experiences easier to understand (commerce in molasses, sugar cane, rum and slaves).

One might also include as fundamental ideas broad principles of methodology and inquiry (e.g., probabilistic models or rules of logic) that allow a discipline to get on with the job of creating new knowledge, creating new fundamental ideas. If we accept the relatively "unstructured" concept of structure proposed by Bruner, we must be prepared to search for a combination of skills, categories, generalizations and procedures that scholars within a discipline agree upon as offering optimal possibilities for the grasping of relatedness.

For the moment let us assume that reputable scholars in a discipline have reached consensus and produced a list of skills and fundamental ideas crucial to their field. We might also assume that the list alone would be inadequate and insufficient as an expression of the structure of the discipline. The scholars must also arrange and articulate the listed items in such a way as to demonstrate (1) basic relationships among the items and (2) an over-all pattern of relationships characteristic of the discipline as a whole. In visualizing the process of scholarly investigation and inter-action aimed at discovering a discipline's structure, the following question comes to mind: Can a discipline have a structure independent of scholars' ability to articulate it?

An affirmative answer carries with it an implication that some sort of intellectual natural law transcends scholarly endeavor, unaffected by the studies of human beings; that preexisting structures lie waiting to be discovered. On the other hand, a negative reply suggests that the utility of structure as a concept depends mostly upon a prediction that scholars will in fact be able to articulate the structure of their field. If the existence of structure is mainly a function of the scholars' ability to construct it, then there is no logical basis for assuming that any given discipline has a structure. Until more systematic consideration is given to structure as an analytic concept, used as Bruner suggests, these definitional, operational and epistemological questions will continue to beset us.

Structure as a Psychological Need

The recommendation to search for the structure of a discipline and then to teach it to children might be justified by appealing to structure conceived as a psychological need. Psychologists have observed a variety of behaviors interpreted as organizing, structuring activities. Evidence suggests that, *in greater and lesser degrees*, human organisms perceive and behave in such a way as to maximize a psychological sense of order and clarity; to minimize randomness and ambiguity. Patterns and processes of cognitive structuring have been studied from several vantage points: the psychotherapeutic work of Kelly (1955); studies of categorizing by Bruner et. al (1956); studies of cognitive dissonance by Festinger (1957); the analysis of belief systems by Rokeach (1960), and others. Experiments demonstrating a human propensity to organize and clarify have been lumped together as a body of evidence indicative of a virtually instinctive drive to structure experience (Royce, 1946). Wide individual differences have been observed in the ways by which humans structure experience and the degrees to which they strive for structure. The identification of differences has led to the postulation of structuring as a personality trait that may take pathological form; for example, in the extreme authoritarian personality. An occupational manifestation of a need for structure is the academic enterprise—an entire profession devoted to the discovery of evidence, laws, categories and methods of inquiry to build comprehensive sets of relationships, to minimize randomness and ambiguity in man's interpretation of the universe.

It is not the purpose of this paper to assess the validity of the need for structure, conceived as a motivational variable. The intent is merely to acknowledge various bases for the claim that the need operates as a significant cognitive mechanism. Those who hold this position may recommend that in order to meet the psychological facts of life, curriculum must be designed to cultivate in students a sense of structure. However, curriculum recommendations cannot be entirely justified by reference to hypo-thesized psychological phenomena. In discussing structure as an educational objective we shall attend to problems of justification.

Structure as an Educational Objective

Apart from the question of psychological need, we notice a common assumption among teachers and scholars that the most appropriate and desirable form of intellectual activity involves the study and discovery of relationships, or the "search for structure." But should one accept this premise simply because it is held by the academic world? When faced with the duty of justifying educational recommendations for a system of general public education, one must look beyond the value realm of the academic profession. Why should a general lay population be taught to perform intel-lectual operations of a nature preferred uniquely by the academic profes-sion? That is, why should all children be taught to ask and answer the kinds of questions that interest historians, political scientists, economists, etc.? When confronted with this challenge, academicians might appeal to a cluster of more fundamental values. They might argue along different lines, some of which may be characterized as follows:

1. The variety of approaches represented by the many disciplines offers the student a great deal of flexibility and choice in the selection of intellectual strategies. If people are aware of alternative ways of viewing the world, this will help generally to preserve intellectual diversity—the hallmark of freedom.

2. Construing the world in a "structured" manner meets a basic psychological need and will, therefore, contribute toward the individual's emotional well being.

3. The ability to perceive relationships will be materially useful to the individual, i.e., the possession of basic knowledge offered by the social sciences will be monetarily rewarded in certain occupations (e.g., teaching, social service, politics, economic consulting).

4. The uniqueness of man lies in his intellectual ability to abstract, to perceive and create relationships; it would be harmful to defy the laws of nature by failing to develop this ability to its utmost.

5. The comfort, progress and survival of man depends upon the untiring pursuit of knowledge; there is a social obligation to transmit to future generations the ability and curiosity to carry on the studies of the disciplines.

While these statements may misrepresent sophisticated lines of justification, they do illustrate justifications of structure that rest upon additional values. Appealing to structure as a self-evident ideal is, within the framework of American public education, an insufficient ground on which to justify educational policy.

When the search for structure is legitimized by proposing it as a means to more fundamental ends (as in the five positions above), then we must ask the further question: Will curriculum development based on the principle of structure necessarily fulfill the ends it seeks?

Assume that each of the social science disciplines has formulated its structure and developed teaching materials accordingly. To what extent would this accomplishment logically guarantee steps toward the fulfillment of the five underlying values listed above (human freedom, emotional well being, material reward, harmony with nature, the survival of man)? It is conceivable that disciplines could evolve rigid structures that would compartmentalize and constrain human choice instead of liberating it or making it more flexible. It is also possible that a collection of discrete and unconnected courses in each of the disciplines would bombard the student with a confused, atomized, unrelated curriculum that could bring psychological damage, rather than health. Furthermore, we may find that individuals accustomed to structuring the world according to academic styles will not be materially rewarded, but on the contrary, punished in some occupations or endeavors. In short, we have no assurance that the more fundamental goals will be served if the cardinal principle of curriculum development is the transmission of academic structures.

On the basis of common sense and some research we must conclude that achievement of the fundamental goals is a function not of the concept of structure *per se*, nor of specific social structures, but of a variety of variables that affect educational processes: the *nature* of the individual structures communicated, the nature of teacher-student interaction, the quality of instructional materials, the overall curriculum design, and the broad institutional milieu in which learning is acquired and applied.

Having suggested some of the difficulties in justifying the search for structure *in general* as an educational objective, let us now examine the particular challenge that the concept presents to scholars concerned with social science structures. In a given discipline, will scholars be able to reach consensus in articulating their structure? Introductory social science courses at the college level represent considerable diversity in approaches to a given discipline. *Within* fields (e.g., psychology or history) we find a tendency toward specialization that reduces communication and collaboration among practitioners who presumably have much in common. The "evils" of specialization that hinder interdisciplinary approaches to education increasingly emerge to block intradisciplinary consensus. A possible result of intellectual pluralism within a field may be the creation of several alternative structures to represent a discipline. If scholars cannot develop a single structure for their subject, then public school teachers may have to select from several possible curricula per discipline.[2]

We must assume that as the pursuit of knowledge continues, disciplines will adopt new methodology and new concepts. Revisionism and innovation will most likely affect basic structures. If the teaching of social science structures is accepted as the major principle for curriculum revision, and if public education is to avoid obsolescence, then it will be necessary for each discipline periodically to examine its structure and to make appropriate revisions. If scholars effectively discharged this responsibility, it would stimulate an invigorating, continuing search for structure that would probably benefit public close up education *and* the disciplines themselves. But within the context of (a) prevailing educational roles and institutions in this society, and (b) accelerating conceptual divergence within each of the social sciences, the search for structure as a model for curriculum reform encounters a host of operational difficulties.

The discussion of structure as a concept, as a psychological need and as an educational objective has touched on analytical, definitional, logical, epistemological and operational problems. To support criticism raised thus far, one must make more explicit some basic criteria by which he evaluates models for social studies reform. The following section is presented, not to establish an exhaustive evaluative formula, but only to outline three criteria that seem especially relevant in dealing with the search-for-structure approach.

Three Criteria for Models of Social Study Revision

I would assume that models of educational innovation should take into account the nature of the educational system in which the innovation will be applied. The American system can be characterized as a publicly financed enterprise in which laymen (i.e., not scholars and professional educators) theoretically have ultimate control over objectives, institutional organization and the content of the programs. Though specific objectives of public schools vary from district to district, national consensus exists with regard to fundamental goals. One way of phrasing the primary goal is "the attainment and preservation of individual human dignity and self

---

[2] This is not to imply that it would be wrong or undesirable for teachers to make such choices. Additional curriculum materials are most welcome. We might ask, however, whether a broad subject area should rightfully be called a discipline if it breeds many possible stuctures.

realization for all." Since the public educational system is committed to serve virtually all individuals and since, in reality, individuals live within society (which may include a cluster of many societies), then curriculum must emphasize training for individual dignity within a societal framework. Traditionally and quite logically the subject, social studies, has focused most explicitly on relationships among individuals in society and relationships between societies.

Not only through social studies does youth acquire learning relevant to the attainment of human dignity. Numerous other school subjects contribute to the general objective, as do crucial socializing influencing outside of the school (e.g., family, church, peer group, occupations, etc.). However, social studies, as a curricular category, is uniquely oriented toward a vital facet of the broader task. That facet is the relationship between the attainment of human dignity and issues of concern to the "public" society. I call this curriculum area "citizenship education," and propose as a first criterion that each model for curriculum revision in social studies should develop an *explicit concept of citizenship education*.

One's concept of citizenship education would most probably grow out of elements of general social theory, i.e., descriptive generalizations and empirical predictions regarding the nature of the society into which the training will be introduced. We find, however, that when presented with recommendations for citizenship training we are not usually able inductively to construct the social theory that, as a rationale, gives birth to the recommendations. For example, familiar recipes for citizenship training emphasize active participation by the student in public affairs. The prototype of the active political citizen might spring from a preference for or commitment to any number of theoretical contexts: Athenian and/or Jacksonian democracy, the "Protestant ethic," a Jeffersonian distrust of centralized power, social Darwinism, or others. However, when the underlying theoretical framework remains ambiguous, it is impossible to justify the curriculum's selection of content, and impossible to systematically revise it. In order for social studies curriculum to be properly justified, it must be developed out of an identifiable social theory. *The theory must be explicitly presented or reliably induced from the proposed concept of citizenship education*. This is the second criterion.

Related to the request for a theoretical position on the individual and society, a third criterion requires models of social studies reform to provide *analysis of their own implications for the general process of educational change*. An ardent enthusiast of programmed instruction and teaching machines might suggest a model of social studies instruction that could lead to drastic changes in institutional structure, professional training, and socialization. If his model fails to confront problems arising out of its implementation, then the model could be so provincial and self-contained as to be eventually self-defeating. Suppose a doctor discovers a cure for cancer in specific organs, learns that the drug causes a number of deadly diseases in other organs, but refuses to concern himself with the other organs and maladies. The discovery is useless unless the doctor's research is continually sensitive to the needs and dynamics of the entire organism. The teaching machine enthusiast may consider himself only a technician and reply that his proposals need not concern themselves with issues and problems that might be handled more appropriately by educational philosophers, sociologists or administrators. Such a response signifies to this author an abdication of intellectual responsibility that can result at most in backwards, after-the-fact, unrealistic, and inefficient approaches to educational innovations. It would seem more reasonable for innovators themselves, in constructing and justifying their proposals, to anticipate and deal with strains and adjustments that their models imply for broader educational process in this society.

Having cited three major criteria for social studies models, let us examine the search for structure in the social sciences as it relates to these criteria. This is not to recommend that social studies models meet *only* these criteria. These seem fundamental—necessary but not sufficient—but they could be supplemented by additional considerations such as logical consistency, feasibility, susceptability to evaluation, etc.

There has been some effort to outline structure of separate disciplines (e.g., the two collections: *The Social Studies* and *The Social Sciences, 1962*) but there has been no published attempt to justify the "search" as a primary model for social studies reform. Because of a lack of scholarship on this matter, one runs the risk of setting up and destroying straw men. Nevertheless, much has been said by scholars and curriculum planners and their remarks reveal a typical frame of reference from which the search for structure derives as an educational recommendation. That frame of reference might be characterized, and hopefully not over-simplified, as follows:

The ultimate objective of education should be the cultivation of intellectual excellence. To define intellectual excellence we need only observe activities and products of those men, past and present, seriously engaged in the pursuit of knowledge. From the work of scholars we should formulate models of intellectual excellence and translate them into instruction that will maximize the intellectual development of youth.

This position seems to originate in an implied reverence for the formal activity called "the pursuit of knowledge," a commitment to emulate the intellectual operations of men recognized as great thinkers and men involved in the academic profession (broadly conceived). If the position is founded only upon *a priori* faith, it fails to meet our criteria, for it does not explicitly confront the problem of citizenship education, nor does it emerge from an identifiable social theory. It is based only upon (1) a normative dictum that the function of education should be to continue the search for truth, and (2) a stipulation that the best models of training for this search can be found in the work of those formally engaged in the search. Stated this way, the position reflects a parochial value judgment that commits all youth to the asking and answering of questions according to norms and styles preferred by scholars. This is not to accuse the academician of being unable to justify his educational prescriptions on the basis of broader social concerns. He may carry his position further:

The free pursuit of knowledge and unlimited critical inquiry is necessary for the attainment of human dignity and the progress of civilization. It is the essence of freedom and requisite for the good life.

As pointed out earlier, this strategy of argument signifies a reliance upon a different sort of justification. Here the pursuit of intellectual excellence is construed not as an end in itself, but as a means to other ends. The additional "ends" involve concepts that need further elaboration (e.g., free pursuit, critical inquiry, human dignity, progress, civilization, good life). If such elaboration were provided, then the justification would gradually be transformed from *a priori* faith in the pursuit of knowledge to a complex theory of the inquiring man in society. Our criteria would welcome such a transformation, but rarely do we find it developed by those who argue for a social science, discipline-centered approach to curriculum reform.

The search for structure model carries with it implications for the functions of the school teacher and the nature of classroom interaction. Let us assume that the "true" structures are to be found in the heads of university academicians, and that the task of curriculum reform involves translating these structures into materials and teacher training that will effectively transmit the structures into the heads of students. The model presents an image of the teacher as a transmitter, or possibly a hypodermic needle which injects serum taken from cells of the university into the bloodstream of the student. The teacher has no part in composing the message or the serum. He does, however, perform an important function in devising clever methods of transmission and injection.

This is not to accuse the Brunerian school of construing the teacher as an information-giver or drillmaster. On the contrary, Bruner's stress on "discovery" clearly attempts to refute the rote-memory, schoolmarm model. However, one must be cautious not to equate emphasis on the process of discovery with absolute intellectual autonomy. What are students supposed to discover as they study the disciplines? My impression is that they would discover that by using intellectual approaches recommended by scholars at the university, they (the students) will reach many of the conclusions that university scholars have reached by using those approaches. Are we to conceive of the discovery process as a treasure hunt in which the teacher provides motivation and excitement for students to engage in the hunt? We may find students excited, interested, curious as they experience the hunt, but final evaluation of the process might well depend upon the usefulness of the treasure. If the treasure is the structure of a particular academic discipline, we may find that a sizeable proportion of students consider the treasure useless or uninspiring—in which case the teacher's role as motivator or communicator will become more difficult.

The discipline-centered model of social studies seems unconcerned with the preservation of the teacher's intellectual autonomy. Yet the domain of social studies offers, perhaps, the greatest of opportunities for the creation and trial of new structures not only by those who operate within the recognized discipline frameworks, but by any individual who reflects seriously upon society. If curriculum is conceived as a canned product, and the teacher as a handmaid to the university scholar, this imposes significant barriers to attracting better teaching talent into the classroom. By an implicit neglect of this issue, the discipline-centered model fails to offer analysis of its own effects on educational institutions and process.

The Analysis of Public Controversy: An Alternative Approach

An elaborate, definitive rationale for a social studies curriculum is provided by Oliver and Shaver (in press). The rationale, in discussing approaches to social studies curriculum, defines a concept of citizenship education in the context of and consistent with a broader social theory. We may summarize their approach in terms of criteria suggested above.

Citizenship Education

The model citizen is one who, in the manner of an intelligent journalist, engages in dialogue with others in an attempt to reach positions on controversial public issues. The function of dialogue is to provide clarification, allow for the justification of one's position, and to gain cognizance of positions and justifications other than one's own. To operate successfully in the dialogue, the citizen must use various forms of inquiry, analytical and argumentative skills; he **must have a fund of** information to support claims and definitions; and he must use a repertoire of analogies to support or refute judgments. In proposing such a notion of rational discourse as the core of citizenship training, two qualifications are important: (1) The defining of characteristics of an intelligent or rational discussion is a topic of research and development unto itself, so this curriculum should be seen as only one approach to or model of rational discourse. (2) Emphasis on rational dialogue does not exclude the use of violence as a policy by which to settle controversy. It is up to the citizen to decide, *through* rational dialogue, the most appropriate form of action.

In reflecting upon this concept of citizenship education we should recognize those traditional and familiar educational objectives that do not constitute the nucleus here. The proposed training is not intended necessarily to develop (1) motives toward and competence in political action; (2) intellectual competence in each of the social sciences; (3) basic literacy skills; or (4) a greater appreciation of the American past. It is likely that some of these outcomes may result as by-products of the curriculum, but they are not central to our concept of citizenship education. The central focus is on intelligent rational dialogue as a medium for the clarification, justification and resolution of social disputes.

Social Theory

The Oliver-Shaver rationale portrays public controversies in the United States as manifestations of latent dilemmas ingrained in a cluster of values that has been called the American Creed. When proclaimed abstractly, the Creed (for example as described by Myrdal, 1944) attracts a high degree of affective consensus. Almost everyone will declare his commitment and allegiance to general values such as: individual autonomy, community welfare, equal opportunity, liberty of property, national security, majority rule, minority rights. However, consensus that exists on a general level becomes threatened when, with regard to a specific public issue, two or more of the values come into conflict. A restaurant owner, invoking the value of liberty of property, may refuse service to a Negro as the Negro, appealing to the value of equal opportunity, insists upon service. Construing social conflict this way compels one to analyze the most explosive public issues in terms of underlying value conflicts. Then the burden of the intelligent dialogue is to clarify the nature of the value conflict, to test (by the use of analogies) the degree to which disputants would stand by or modify general value commitments, and to explore the forms of justification mustered in support of each position.

To support the emphasis on the clarification of value conflict, a theory of American social development is outlined. The theory postulates a view of American society as a pluralistic community bound together by an intense commitment to a liberal and constitutional tradition. It notices in history a series of perilous strains on the political-legal system, strains that reflect conflicting value commitments and dilemmas of ethical choice that continue to generate controversy. Yet societal cohesion has been maintained (in spite of upheavals like the Civil War and the Depression) largely because of the effective promulgation of a national mythology or folklore that develops in youth, before they reach secondary school, a strong commitment to general values in the Creed. During the critical analysis of a social issue, some of the assumed greatness in the national mythology may be challenged (e.g., through a Beardian interpretation of the founding fathers, or a frank presentation of Japanese relocation in World War II). However, the curriculum accepts the American Creed as a legitimate value framework, so it will continue to reinforce commitments to general values.

The curriculum reveals a twofold commitment of its own; first to the Creed, and second, to the use of rational discourse in implementing the Creed. As mentioned above, this particular model bears its own bias regarding the nature of an "intelligent" dialogue dealing with public controversy. Since there is no intentional attempt to teach correct positions on given issues, the curriculum is in a sense "open-minded." Yet no program that definitely teaches something can be absolutely open-minded, for the decision to teach something in particular is in effect a decision to predetermine what the student will learn. We candidly recognize our faith that the best way to approach the resolution of social controversy is through rational discussion. In this sense we do "indoctrinate" the student to use a particular analytical approach to reach his own positions on social issues.

Interdisciplinary Approach to Public Controversy

To construct a model for the analysis of public controversy, one must go beyond the confines of any particular discipline, and notice that social controversies might be construed in several ways:

A.   They may be categorized as instances of persistent universal problems, designated by such topics as (1) the use and control of violence; (2) the attainment and maintenance of a certain standard of living; (3) the establishment and distribution of privileges; (4) the balance between public conformity and public dissent; (5) the preservation of private autonomy.

B.   Disputes may also be construed in terms of conflicting legal-ethical categories; for example, personal liberty vs. community security, constitutional, vs. unconstitutional, due process of law vs. trial by ordeal, or retribution vs. rehabilitation.

C.   Controversies may be seen as illustrative evidence for various themes and concepts drawn from social science theory; for example: repressive measures used by societies against deviants who threaten the social order; the problem of maintaining workable pluralism among differing ethnic or religious groups who cling to former identities; or the psychological bases of demagoguery.

In a given argument over a question of social policy, disagreement occurs on different levels. A discussion over the outlawing of racial discrimination in places of public accommodation might range over any of the following issues: the legal powers of Congress as outlined in the Constitution and interpreted by the Supreme Court; the intentions of the framers of the Constitution, as discovered by historians; predictions of the effects of such legislation on the behavior of different groups of people; the definition of key terms such as equal opportunity, liberty of property, and interstate commerce; ethical dilemmas created by the need to choose one value as having precedence over another; competing political theories regarding the delegation and reliability of testable statements. Such varying levels of disagreement raise a spectrum of questions that touch all of the social sciences and other academic areas as well (e.g., natural science, philosophy, law).

Can separate disciplines which operate within relatively provincial frames of reference be applied together in the study of social issues in general? This curriculum assumes that the social sciences and other academic fields have much to offer the analysis of public controversy in the way of concepts, constructs, generalizations and methods of inquiry. While the selection of content from many disciplines poses an enormous problem we feel it is not insurmountable. The Harvard Social Studies Project staff consists of faculty members and graduate students equipped with broad backgrounds in the social sciences. We began by identifying and making distinctions between the kinds of controversy that we consider germane to the most serious public issues that the United States and the world at large will face in the lifetime of our students. We then selected a series of cases to illustrate the overall scope of the curriculum.

The case studies describe situations and dilemmas in concrete and dramatic style. Cases take many forms: autobiographical and biographical accounts, journalistic narratives, excerpts from fiction and literature, court opinions, historical vignettes, etc. The purpose of a case is to communicate the concrete, raw data of a situation, to pose a problem in terms relevant to the student, with a minimum of analytic or interpretive material. Rather than being explicitly defined and developed within the cases, social science concepts will be introduced via dialogue with the teacher. By establishing the concrete contexts for controversies, without explicitly teaching the interpretations and theories of social science, the case materials allow teachers flexibility in deciding what concepts and themes to develop in the dialogue.

In keeping with a certain need for cognitive structure, the three-year curriculum is organized according to various themes and topics. The organization plan represents no more than consensus by the staff that a particular pattern or sequence would constitute a meaningful way to present what might otherwise be seen as a series of unrelated stories. Some material is chosen because it provides a background or framework in which to examine an issue; other material is included because it may illustrate the utility of various social science concepts. The major criterion for the selection of content from social sciences is whether or not the staff agrees that a particular theory, generalization, concept, set of data, or process of inquiry would be useful in the analysis of a given social issue or set of issues. Social science contributions are introduced not necessarily in the context of the discipline's larger structure, but in the context of the public dispute being analyzed. This principle of content selection is clearly eclectic and carries no commitment to the teaching of any discipline *in toto*. At the same time, the Project recognizes and exercises an academic obligation to avoid perverting or distorting offerings of the disciplines. Scholars in each of the pertinent fields examine case materials and teaching plans. They offer suggestions and corrections that are taken into account in constructing and revising the materials.

The Need for General Education

An interdisciplinary approach to the analysis of public controversy reflects a basic preference for general education as the most desirable objective for new projects in curriculum development. Without presenting an elaborate rationale for general education, we might point to a few crucial points in such a rationale.

Armed with some assumptions about the nature of that society which accomplishes the maximum degree of human dignity, and on the basis of numerous historical and cross-cultural observations, one might suggest that one of the greatest threats to human dignity would be a world overrun by what Joseph Royce (1964) calls the encapsulated man. The encapsulated man is the professional or layman who, when asked to comment on a topic or problem, replies, "I'm sorry, that's not in my field." He is epistemologically rigid, because he may use only one of four possible methods of "knowing" (as categorized by Royce): rationalism, intuitionism, empiricism, authoritarianism. Having learned only highly specific skills, he is occupationally paralyzed, for his training will become obsolete almost before he can apply it. He construes experience within narrow limits, unable to change, unable to communicate or effectively relate to others. We would predict that in the face of expanding technology, population explosion, urbanization, industrialization, nuclear international conflict, the revolution of "rising expectations," and the accelerating specialization of knowledge, a world composed of clusters of encapsulated man would be incapable of overcoming the many obstacles to human dignity.

It would seem that in order to cope with accelerating social change of the impact implied above, public education is obliged to cultivate at least two important qualities in the children it educates: (a) intellectual flexibility; and (b) a sense of relatedness. There are clearly a host of other important educational objectives; e.g., occupational competence, values and attitudes, but these two seem essential as protection against cultural encapsulation.

Education's contribution to the encapsulated man derives largely from curricular specialization that at the college level either allows or commands the student to select one major subject relatively early in his career and to spend most of his time studying within that single field. Without belaboring the controversy carried on in university faculty curriculum committees and without detailed reference to the work of Hutchins, Whitehead and others, we must assume that if elementary and secondary education were to perpetuate the degree of specialization currently rampant at the university level, this would stifle the development of both intellectual flexibility and a sense of relatedness.

The familiar alternative to specialization is to postpone the student's choice of a major field until he has studied a number of fields in an introductory fashion—and to require continued study in subjects outside of the major. Let us imagine curriculum in elementary and secondary schools fashioned after this university model of "liberal education." The social studies curriculum would consist of a collection of discrete courses in history, economics, political science, sociology, anthropology, psychology, etc. If students were required to have an acquaintance with all fields, this might appear to lower the likelihood of academic encapsulation. However, on closer examination, this model of "general education"—essentially an introductory visit to each of the disciplines—carries little assurance that encapsulation will be avoided. In the absence of a formal curricular attempt to relate the disciplines to each other, it is possible that students would adopt a posthole or compartmentalized method of construing reality. Each field may be perceived as a sovereign intellectual domain, having total jurisdiction over specific topics. To discuss any given problem, situation, issue, or question, it may be necessary first to categorize the item as falling within the domain of only one field, and second to study it only within the conceptual limits that the field has to offer. It is not unreasonable to predict this sort of outcome from a curriculum which encourages the teaching of the various disciplines in isolation from each other. This sort of "general education" would seem to breed *in*flexibility and a sense of *un*relatedness.

If general education seeks to avoid encapsulation through the development of flexibility and relatedness, then it may be useful to apply varying approaches represented in the social sciences to a common enterprise. Focusing on a common enterprise (e.g., the analysis of public controversy) would seem to open channels for investigation of relationships of the disciplines to each other. Interdisciplinary relationships could be developed and analyzed in terms of their mutual connection to a single topic. In order to grasp a sense of relatedness through an undertaking of this sort, scholars and students would be required to develop and exercise the flexibility and imagination necessary to transcend the parochial concerns of each field. This sort of curricular model seems more appropriately designed to meet the burdens and challenges of general education.

Implications for Institutional Change

It should be clear from above emphases on interdisciplinary curriculum, general education, and classroom dialogue, that widespread implementation of the analysis-of-public-controversy model would require fundamental changes in educational institutions and attitudes. For example, the model portrays the teacher as an inquiring, intelligent generalist who values the way students construe reality and who adopts a posture of inquiry that students consider honest, legitimate and helpful. The teacher, no longer psychologically dependent upon a particular subject that served as his college major, exercises intellectual autonomy in constructing and revising his own curriculum—even though it may appear unrelated to the study of history or geography.

To fill classrooms with teachers like this and to make their instruction effective, perhaps we need revolutions in each of the following areas: teacher training preparation and dissemination of instructional materials; parents' conceptions of valid curriculum; college admission policies; educational finance; teacher hiring policies; state curriculum policies; and even curriculum in higher education. The Oliver-Shaver rationale anticipates these problems. But, when a curriculum's implementation seems to require the conquest of obstacles like these, then the curriculum model is often dismissed as overly idealistic and visionary. Whether the model is operationally feasible on a national scale is a different issue from whether or not the model has been systematically formulated. In fact it would be difficult to make an intelligent judgment on the former question until the latter consideration has been fulfilled. In the present case the model was designed not only to meet a need for curriculum development in the social studies, but also, and most importantly, to establish a context for the conduct of educational research. While the model addresses itself to both research and development, it seems to have met the major criteria suggested above.

CONCLUSION

If curriculum for each of the social sciences is developed in isolation from the others, then "social studies" has no real value as an instructional category. Presumably, however, the category signifies a legitimate concern for commonalities of social sciences into a form of citizenship education consistent with the educational objectives and needs of the society. This is not to degrade or dilute the significance of the scholarly fields themselves, but only to suggest that in terms of broader educational and social theory, the emulation of traditional academic paradigms should serve only a limited function. We would prefer to conceive of social reform as the formulation of new theories and curriculum that incorporate and coordinate pluralism of social science as it may relate to man's effort to achieve human dignity.

14   THE AUTHORS

Harvard Social Studies Project Materials

The jurisprudential approach to the social studies was developed by Professors Donald Oliver of Harvard, James Shaver of the University of Utah, and by Fred Newmann of Harvard. The teaching materials, based on this approach, were prepared by the Harvard Social Studies Project, under the direction of Oliver and Newmann.

The essence of the new approach to the social studies curriculum is a new concept of citizenship education. The Oliver-Shaver theoretical underpinning rests on the assumption that there is in the American pluralistic, diverse society, a broad consensus on a number of basic values which are sometimes referred to as in the American Creed. There is broad agreement, they suggest, on such general values as human dignity, freedom of speech, sanctity of private property, majority rule, the rights of the minority, individual autonomy, and others. Much of our history is a story of conflicts between one of these general values and the specific public value espoused by some segment of society. Even more often, there is a conflict among the general values as to their hierarchical precedence. The value of general welfare and internal peace demands, some maintain, strict controls on the sale of guns, but the many rifle and gun clubs in the country maintain that such legislation infringes on their right to possess arms and their basic property rights. Proponents of equal housing legislation argue for the general basic value in the American Creed of equal opportunity, while opponents maintain that open occupancy laws violate their right (value) in the creed of individual freedom in disposing of their private property as they see fit. Thus, the conflict in values.

Oliver and Shaver argue that the rational clarification of these value conflicts is the proper emphasis in the teaching of social studies. This rational discourse is looked upon as the core of citizenship training, and the critical dialogue between the teacher and the student and among the students is looked upon as a substantive and central curricular objective. "The central focus," wrote Fred Newmann, "is an intelligent rational dialogue as a medium for the clarification, justification, and resolution of social disputes." For some reason, Professor Newmann felt the need to stress that the jurisprudential approach is not necessarily intended to develop motives and competence in dealing with political issues, or develop competence in the social sciences, or provide the students a greater appreciation of the American past. These things may result from the new curriculum, but "they are not central to our concept of citizenship education." [1]

This disclaimer is a bit puzzling because it seems to shortchange the benefits and the advantages of the new approach. It need not, however, be taken too seriously. In practice, the materials produced by the Harvard Project and the techniques evolved suggest much broader aims than merely the evolvement of a process of a free-ranging critical inquiry into value conflicts.

In the context of the Oliver-Shaver theory, each public controversy of some significance, in addition to historical, legal, social, and economic issues, does involve an ethical dilemma. A law on wiretapping involves important legal, constitutional questions, but in essence it is also a moral conflict involving the need of society to protect itself against crime and criminals and the right of the individual to protect his privacy. It is in this ethical dilemma that the jurisprudential approach wishes to involve the teacher and the student.

Oliver and Shaver experience some difficulty on the issue of whether to teach about values or inculcate values. They concede that there may be some difficulty with an unlimited freedom of inquiry and the *a priori* com-

---

[1] Fred M. Newmann, "The Analysis of Public Controversy: New Focus on Social Studies, *School Review*, Winter 1965, p. 423.

mitment to the basic values in the American Creed. In a somewhat Delphic statement, Professor Shaver once exclaimed, "I am not suggesting that we should inculcate values; I am not suggesting we should not, either." [2] What he meant by this, he later explained, is that the students ought to be helped through a free unlimited inquiry in developing concepts to identify and define their own values, but that there must be a commitment and a prior acceptance of rational inquiry as the best mode for conflict-resolution, or at least conflict-clarification, in a democratic society. In their book, *Teaching Public Issues in the High School,* Oliver and Shaver expressed their unequivocal commitment to human dignity and rational consent as basic principles of the American Government.[3] In another place, Shaver stated, "As social studies curriculum people, we should not blush to impress on students the importance of these societal values, perhaps stressing human dignity as the basic commitment—with other central values, such as freedom of speech, defining the characteristics of dignity." [4]

We shall see that this unresolved theoretical difficulty, if not an outright contradiction, has had in practice little, if any, negative effect on the materials produced in the Harvard Social Studies Project.

What do the directors of the Project have to say about the teaching techniques which are to be followed?

The teaching strategies used in the Harvard Project involve an inquiry or a dialogue on a variety of questions dealing with particular public policy issues for the aspects of history, law, and ethics. The approach emphasizes two or more difficult points of view on a particular controversial public policy issue. In getting the students to engage in an individual and collective inquiry into the issue, the teacher acts as catalyst, motivator, resource, and as discussion leader: "Our focus," Oliver and Shaver wrote, "is on the dialogue, either between teacher and students or among students." [5]

The teacher's role in this dialogue is similar to that of Socrates in Plato's dialogues. He must assist in the clarification of issues, ask for substantiation of a particular point of view, and help the students to understand the complex strategies employed by the protagonist, of their point of view.

The dialogue emphasizes conflicting values, which when embraced by the students, may often cause them to shift their positions. For that matter

---

[2] Irving Morrissett, ed., *Concepts and Structure in the New Social Science Curricula*, Report, Social Science Consortium (West Lafayette, Ind.: Social Science Education Consortium, Inc., 1966), p. 124.

[3] Donald W. Oliver and James P. Shaver, *Teaching Public Issues in the High School* (Boston: Houghton Mifflin Company, 1966), p. 70.

[4] Report, Social Science Education Consortium, p. 125.

[5] Donald W. Oliver and James P. Shaver, op. cit., p. 115.

the teacher, too, in the course of the inquiry and the dialogue, may change his views on the case under discussion.

Primary emphasis is placed in the jurisprudential approach on the conflict of equally tenable values. This is the heart of citizenship education conceived by Oliver, Shaver, and Newmann. The clarification of value conflicts and not the teaching of the structure of the discipline or the teaching of concepts and generalizations from the social sciences, is at the heart of the public controversy approach. The process involves both *evaluating*, meaning matching facts or actions against some set of criteria, and *making value judgments*, meaning deciding what these criteria ought to be. "Given this central position of value judgment," Oliver wrote, "empiricism's lack of capacity to posit values suggests that, while the concept of the structure of a discipline may well be an appropriate basis for determining what should be taught in a social science course, it is not adequate as the basis 'for the social studies curriculum.' " [6]

It is clear from the above that, unlike a number of other social studies projects, the Harvard University Social Studies Project has a coherent, well-worked-out, theoretical framework. What now remains to be seen is the extent to which the materials produced by the project fulfill the premises and the expectations of the framework. A few general observations can be made.

1. On the whole the materials are quite faithful to the assumptions and the objectives as stipulated by the authors of the jurisprudential approach to the social studies curriculum.
2. In spite of the harsh injunction of Oliver and Shaver in their book, *Teaching Public Issues in the High School*, against a history-oriented curriculum, and in spite of their expressed position that public controversy issues would use historical content only to give the problem a historical setting, the teaching units produced lean very heavily on them and may be termed imaginative presentations of conventional historical material. Thus, Oliver and Newmann (the units are produced under the direction of Professors Oliver and Newmann) are much kinder to history in practice than they are in their theoretical explication of their theories.
3. All the issues are contemporary, but they are presented against the back drop of history with the frequent use of historical flashbacks. This sometimes produces awkward problems of organization and confusion in sequence, but these difficulties are not of great import.
4. There has been intensive and careful testing of the units in a variety of schools. This testing resulted in extensive revisions and editorial rewriting. Significantly, the revisions resulted from a free-flowing feedback from teachers who used the units and their students.

---

[6]   Report, Social Science Education Consortium, p. 123.

The *Guide to Teaching,* authored by Donald Oliver, Fred Newmann and Mary Jo Bane, states that the separate unit books which were published by the Xerox Corporation for the Harvard Project, "indicate a heavy concentration on historical topics—The American Revolution, the growth of business and industry, the rise of organized labor, Christianity, Puritanism, immigration." The Guide suggests that the booklets ought to be used as "supplementary experiments for U.S. History or even as replacement for textbook treatment of certain topics." [7] This statement is significant because, unlike the position taken by Oliver and Shaver in their *Teaching Public Issues in the High School,* the jurisprudential approach is suggested not as a substitute for history courses, but is looked upon as supplementary or complementary to conventional history courses. This is to be welcomed, because the use of the jurisprudential approach alone would give the students a distorted picture of U.S. history. The history of this country is, of course, much more than a succession of great public controversies. Furthermore, the exclusive use of the jurisprudential approach and materials would be deadly boring to the students.

The case study materials used in the unit books of the Harvard Social Studies Project include:

1. *Story and Vignette.* These stories are fictional accounts of events, either based on authentic historical occurrence, or completely fictitious.
2. *Journalistic Historical Narratives.* These are accounts of incidents and events written in the style of a contemporary newspaper story.
3. *Research Data.* Data from surveys, polls, and statistical research.
4. *Documents.* Speeches, diaries, opinions, etc.
5. *Texts.* Introductions and overviews of the public controversy under study.
6. *Interpretive Essays.* These essays interpret and evaluate a specific position on a public policy issue.

In explicating further on the objectives of teaching techniques to be used in the study of the unit books, Oliver and Newmann make these significant additional points.

They are basically optimistic about the value of discussion in clarifying and inquiring into complex public policy issues and value conflicts, provided that a discussion is not looked upon as combat, but an opportunity for the participants to develop and clarify their views. A discussion conducted in this calm, rational atmosphere will make it possible for students to modify, to qualify, or even change their positions. The authors vigorously reject the often-held view that "one's opinion is as good as

---

[7] Donald W. Oliver, Fred M. Newmann and Mary Jo Bane, *Guide to Teaching* (Middletown, Conn.: Xerox Publishing Company, 1967), p. 3.

another's." They argue that some opinions are sound, based on rational inquiry and others are not, and they all can and ought to be challenged. Finally, Oliver and Newmann take a dim view of the notion that most issues can be settled by the acquisition of a great deal of factual information. Not so, they say. There never is enough factual information for a sound decision. "Discussion," they wrote, "can make our 'uninformed' decisions more rational. Finally, assuming that it would be possible to settle factual issues through the accumulation of evidence, there still remain ultimate questions of value and meaning." [8]

Mild reservation to this position would include an expression of doubt as to the obviously over-optimistic reliance on the prospects of resolving problems by a rational discussion. In fact, many of the complex public issues are not susceptible to a rational discourse. Take, for instance, the legalization of abortion. No amount of rational, logical debate could have much influence on some who *a priori* believe that abortion is a religious sin. In addition, we would be misleading our students and giving them an unrealistic preparation for many future life situations were we not to make clear to them that many, if not most, public controversies are not resolved by a rational debate, that accidents, and irrational and unexpected developments are very frequently decisive factors.

Finally, it is an experience quite familiar to many teachers that calm, tepid, dispassionate discussions bring about deadly boredom and that an aggressive, combative discussion is often good for the souls and the spirits of the students and exhilarating for the teacher. In essence, what seems to be best, is a discussion which is calm and dispassionate, but enlivened with occasional flare-ups of temper and conviction.

In the unit on "The American Revolution" (63 pages), the historical event is used to make it possible for the students to analyze the question of the legitimacy of governments in our contemporary world and develop criteria to help students to understand and to support, or to refuse support, for the revolutionary movements, for anti-government demonstrations and for the "wars of national liberation." *The Guide to Teaching* states: "This unit book on 'The American Revolution' is aimed at developing criteria to help students decide whether to support the revolutionaries or the existing government in particular situations." [9]

This is indeed a tall order and a far-reaching objective. Let's see how the authors go about attaining it.

Three pages are devoted to short, factual paragraphs on such descriptive topics as: The Navigation Act of 1651; The Staple Act of 1663; French and Indian Wars; The Sugar Act; The Stamp Act; The Boston Tea Party;

---

[8] Donald W. Oliver et al., *Guide to Teaching*, p. 7.
[9] Donald W. Oliver et al., *Guide to Teaching*, p. 15.

The Intolerable Acts; The Continental Congress; Lexington and Concord; The Committee on Independence; and others.

The case of George Watkins is a fictional account of an American colonist who through a debate with a Tory, a Dr. Soame Johnson, clarifies his own thinking on the right of the colonies to independence. Watkins then rides to a meeting to hear Sam Adams, whose arguments for freedom and liberty he found quite impressive. The account is well written, although it is not exceptionally exciting.

The case is followed by a list of ten values about government which the students are asked to check. The explanatory statement suggests that Watkins and Dr. Johnson held different values, but that Watkins had an additional dilemma because he held conflicting values.

Among the values listed are:

It would be wrong to change the system of government we have inherited. It has the benefits of long experience.
A leader is not responsible to the people, but only to God, from whom he receives authority.
Each man should have a say in determining his own fate. Thus, the government should be run by representatives chosen by a majority of the people.
A country belongs to those men who own property in it, and they should govern.

The struggle between the Patriots and the Tories is presented as a conflict of values about the government and the rights and duties of subjects.

The checklist of values is followed by a descriptive story on The Stamp Act and the reactions of the colonists to it.

The bulk of the unit is devoted to three differing accounts of the Battle of Lexington and Concord. The three accounts are of a colonist, a British colonel and an American Tory. The emphasis in these fictional accounts seems to be that the same event can be seen in an entirely different light, depending on the observer's personal views and conditions.

The stories are well written, interesting, and while fictional, provide a great deal of factual information about the conditions that preceded the battle, the state of mind of the colonists, the views of the British officers and the rationale of the Tories who remained loyal to the Crown.

The unit book ends with an account of the civil rights demonstration in Selma, Alabama, in 1965, in which demonstrators challenged city and other ordinances to press their march. In an essay story, the authors present the Selma event as a conflict of values between the stated aims of the demonstrators to attain equal rights for Negroes and the duty of the Selma county and state officials to uphold existing laws and assure peace and order.

The students are asked to see the similarities and the differences in the Colonial British Conflict in the American Revolution and the march in Selma, Alabama. Students are asked to discuss this analogy and to write essays about the comparison.

The unit book on "The American Revolution" is well prepared, well written and well researched. Students can study it with profit, especially if it is used as an important supplement to a well presented historical narrative. The presentation of the controversy between the Patriots and the Tories as a value conflict is valuable and ought to allow the students to understand and clarify their own values. The impression is created that the population was divided between Patriots and Loyalists. This, of course, is not true. About 10 percent were Tories, 40 percent were Patriots, and 50 percent were neutral, according to Samuel E. Morison and other historians who wrote on the American Revolution.

It is doubtful, however, whether the unit achieved its stated objective of developing criteria "to help students to decide whether to support the revolutionaries or the existing governments in particular situations." Such criteria have not been developed in the unit and this far-reaching claim ought not to have been made. It seems reasonable to suggest that the unique, particular, and complex characteristics of each revolutionary situation, make the development of such criteria impossible and even undesirable. The insistence on a straightforward analogy to a contemporary event seems strained and oversimplified. This does not detract from the value of the unit or the benefits to be derived from the jurisprudential approach. Using the unit book will, of necessity, emphasize some aspects of the American Revolution and omit others which many scholars of the Revolutionary Period consider very important. But this is bound to happen under any selection scheme that one could devise. The chief advantage is in the insight that, in an important sense, the American Revolution was a value conflict concerning the origin and role of the government and the duties and rights of the governed. The comparison to Selma, while far from analogous, provides an illustration of the historical continuity of similar value conflicts.

As one approach to the teaching of the American Revolution, the Oliver-Newmann unit book is helpful and effective.

The unit on "Religious Freedom" takes as its point of departure Article I of the Constitution, "Congress shall make no law respecting an establishment of religion, or prohibiting the free exercise thereof." The value conflicts arising from a clash between the minority religious groups to propagate and practice their beliefs and the existing laws protecting or enhancing general welfare, are dramatically and effectively highlighted.

The story of the Christian who went afoul of Roman laws and Roman traditions is related in a manner which attempts to present the Roman point of view with some degree of objectivity. This attitude is usually missing in most textbooks.

In two stories, one on the case of a young Amish girl in Kansas, whose parents did not wish to send her to school and were taken to court for violating the compulsory school attendance law, and in another, dealing with a Jehovah's Witness, who was taken to court for playing a record on the street attacking the Catholic Church, the authors present an illustration of a conflict among the basic values of our society and how they are resolved. The Supreme Court decisions in the cases of Jesse Cantwell, the Jehovah's Witness, and in the suit of Madalyn Murray against religious prayers in public schools, are summarized accurately and in an interesting manner.

The unit book on "Religious Freedom" is an excellent illustration on how the teaching of the Constitution can be improved. This instruction which is required in most states, is usually confined to the teaching of the text of the Constitution. The students learn about the structure of our government as spelled out in articles and sections of the basic document. They seldom learn both the structure and the process. They get no idea of how generations of Americans have actually interpreted and often sharply modified or adapted the provisions of the Constitution. The Oliver-Newmann unit book on Article I accomplishes this purpose.

The unit on "Negro Views of America," which the authors state is "intended as an introduction to America's race problem," presents the views of many individual Negro Americans living in distressed circumstances at different times and places in U.S. history." [10]

The authors define the crucial questions to be raised in the unit as: "In what ways can conditions in a person's environment affect his personality and his image of himself? Can government involve itself in human relations to guarantee each individual a sense of worth and self-pride? Should government do this?"

This complex question, complexly posed, is probably more suited to a discussion in a college political science or sociology seminar for graduate students. It could hardly be discussed, unless simplified and broken up into several components, in an average history classroom.

The second set of questions is less academic: "How can we explain differences between whites and non whites with regard to such things as

---

[10] Donald W. Oliver and Fred M. Newmann, *Negro Views of America* (Middletown, Conn.: Xerox Corporation, 1968).

income, education, employment, and crime? Should groups that are 'disadvantaged' in these respects be expected to pull themselves up on their own, or should the more fortunate in the society give them the goods and services they need?"

Unintentionally, the second part of this question is unfair and loaded. No Negro leaders have ever suggested that the more affluent should "give" the Negroes goods and services. The demand is for equal opportunities to obtain these goods and services.

The third and fourth questions read: "When, if ever, is it appropriate to use race as a basis for making private and public decisions? Members of a minority group may adapt themselves to a system of racial inequality or they may protest against the system. What are the possible advantages and disadvantages of each approach for the minority group and for the nation as a whole?"

Disregarding the ponderous, complicated manner in which these questions are phrased, they are essentially important and legitimate queries and sound lines of inquiry. The basic reservation that can be lodged against the way in which the authors answer these questions is the failure to provide the student with a well written sequential historical account. This failure was not decisive in the unit on "Religious Freedom," but a case ought to be made for the proposition that a meaningful inquiry into the present racial situation in America must be preceded by a systematic study of the history of Negroes in the United States and the sequence of developments in the relationships between the white majority and the black minority. The preferred method of sociological research in plucking out events, facts, and ideas from the past, without regard to their chronology and interrelationship, is not conducive, it seems to me, to an effective study of the contemporary race problem.

The "objective" presentation of two descriptions of slavery, one describing its evil and cruelty and another giving a favorable evaluation of slavery, is probably the worst possible way to start an inquiry into the Negro views on America, because as a matter of fact black moderates and nationalists do not have it in their hearts to forgive their white American brethren for the persistent effort to minimize the evil of the crime of slavery. It would seem little to expect that scholars and educators would adapt a stance that slavery, whether cruel or benevolent, was an evil institution, depriving human beings of their dignity as persons and utterly in violation of the ideals on which this Republic was founded.

The unit book describes, with great effectiveness, the struggle for a measure of self-respect by a young man in Harlem and the obstacles placed in the path of Negroes who desire to purchase a decent home. There is also important and well-presented statistical data on rates of unemployment among Negroes, education, income, and school integration.

Under the topic, "Three Theories of Racial Differences," the authors present three theories bearing on the achievement differences between blacks and whites. The "genetic theory" which postulates that Negroes are biologically, innately inferior to the whites, is given as much prominence and presented as objectively as the theory accounting for lower Negro achievements by the effects of discrimination and cultural deprivation. For some reason, the authors fail to relate the "objective" fact that the overwhelming majority of the world's anthropologists, biologists, and psychologists reject the *scientific* validity of the so-called generic theory and have branded its few advocates as racist jugglers of scientific data.

The unit on "Negro Views of America" has its merits. The case studies on Frederick Douglass and the life in Harlem and on Black Power are well worth reading and teaching, but without the historical background and perspective, it is virtually suspended in the air. The task of teaching about the contemporary race issue provides a classic example for the contention that same contemporary problems cannot and ought not to be taught without a systematic study of their historical origin.

Negro and white students ought not to be taught about slavery without an understanding in depth of some African history, of the origins and the inhumanity of the slave trade, and the history of Negro slave insurrections.

The frustration and despair of the Negroes can be understood only in the background of Negro participation in the American Revolution, the long struggle for the abolition of slavery, the role of Negro regiments in the Civil War, and the long, dark and bloody, and often distorted story of Reconstruction. It makes little sense to explain to the students the views and position of Stokely Carmichael and the black nationalists (as Oliver and Newmann have done) without acquainting them with the prior conflict between Booker T. Washington and W. E. B. Du Bois. It is this great controversy that gave spiritual and conceptual nourishment to the black nationalists. The obvious connection and interaction between American imperialism and Jim Crow legislation, and the exclusion of Negroes from the political life in the South, aided and abetted by the North, are essential and indispensable elements in any discussion on "Negro Views of America."

This criticism of the unit on Negroes in the Oliver-Newmann series is used here primarily as an illustration of a point of view, biased as it may be, that some public controversy issues require by their very nature a thorough, systematic, and yes, chronological historical background and explication. However, many other unit books, in addition to those mentioned in this essay, deserve to be used as widely as possible as supplementary materials in social studies classrooms.

The unit, "The Immigrant's Experience," fills out a void in the history textbooks. Most authors of textbooks have paid little attention to the impact, the complex problems, and the influence on our contemporary society of the several massive waves of immigration into this country. The authors of the unit discuss the immigration policy from 1924 to 1965 and present, through excerpts from pertinent literature and case studies, the hardships of the immigrants and the process of their adjustment to life in America.

One would have wished for some cases of success stories, like Samuel Gompers or Andrew Carnegie, but in general, the unit is successful in raising the question of America as a melting pot or a pluralistic society.

Several other units which were examined, "The Railroad Era," "Municipal Politics," and "The Rise of Organized Labor," are well written and effectively presented.

The pamphlets in the Public Issues Series deserve wide use in social studies classrooms.

CHAPTER IX

From Subject to Citizen

15 JAMES D. KOERNER

*EDC: General Motors of
Curriculum Reform* *

Until a few years ago, curriculum reform in the United States rested
in the hands of thousands of individual practitioners. There were no formal
channels, certainly no national channels, through which new ideas could
be brought to the classroom. Authority and influence in education were
scattered among teacher-training institutions, state departments of education, accrediting associations, and school administrators. Nobody was concerned about curricular improvement in the nation as a whole.

In the early 1950's, a growing concern about public education began
to bring changes in the distribution of power in education. Beginning with
the National Science Foundation in 1950, new institutions and agencies
were created in which university scholars and other "outsiders" were
brought into touch with the problems of the public schools. Soon a number
of organizations concerned with curriculum development throughout the
country were in operation. The most significant was an institution in
Cambridge called Educational Services, Inc. (ESI).

ESI was established in 1958 to administer a new high school physics
course developed under the leadership of Professor Jerrold Zacharias of
MIT. It grew rapidly and expanded into other subjects. Now, following its
recent merger with another group called the Institute for Educational
Innovation (IEI), the organization that was called ESI and is now Educa-

tion Development Center, Inc. (EDC), may well become the most influential curricular reform group in the country.

The merger of ESI and IEI may prove a great deal about the feasibility of making large-scale changes in American education. But it could also prove to be a resounding misalliance. EDC is one of twenty "regional laboratories" authorized in the 1965 Elementary and Secondary Education Act and now being established around the country. But it is quite different from any of the others in that ESI, the principal partner in the merger, is itself wholly unlike anything in our educational past.

ESI represents the first attempt in American education to bring large numbers of outstanding professors from the arts and sciences together with large numbers of experienced teachers from the schools, and to give them money enough so that they can address themselves over a lengthy period to the creation, to the trying out, and then to the re-creation of new courses of study in basic subjects—courses that are complete and original curriculum packages of textbooks, films, monographs, tests, and inexpensive apparatus. For many years before ESI came into being, other voices had been crying in the wilderness about the need to reform the public school curriculum and to give the best scholars from the universities, who knew the most about the subjects involved, a major role in curriculum development; but few people did more than talk about it, and still fewer thought about it on the required scale.

The old-line curriculum specialists are still legion, of course, but no longer dominant; they no longer run self-contained monopolies. Since ESI, systematic "research and development" of national significance has come into education. It has been done on an unprecedented scale and has involved many kinds of people never before engaged in such work. Nor has there ever been an agency of comparable size devoting full time to the development of educational materials.

As is always the case with agents of change, ESI can easily be criticized for things it has done or failed to do. But the change is what matters—the dimensions and quality of change—and in these respects ESI has been one of the most important organizations in American education. It has, moreover, had many secondary influences. Through the people associated with it, ESI has had a substantial effect on federal legislation, on "public television" and the Carnegie Commission, on medical education, on the creation of other reform groups, and on many projects in which ESI has acted as unpaid broker.

Soon after ESI came into being as the administrative umbrella for the Physical Science Study Committee (PSSC), which drew up the new physics course, it was clear that other subjects needed curriculum reform as badly as physics. ESI set up shop in a converted supermarket in

Cambridge and soon began to collect other projects. PSSC led to a concern for elementary school science and, in 1960, a project in this critical area was launched, is still running. These two projects soon led to one in college physics, and that to one in engineering education. Soon there was an extensive African Education Program—a project that grew out of the dismay Zacharias felt upon attending a conference in Israel on science in underdeveloped countries and finding most of the delegates talking about nuclear reactors and giant hydroelectric plants instead of about the inescapable prerequisite of a developed educational system.

In 1962, ESI expanded its activities beyond the sciences and put together a large curriculum project in that no-man's-land of American education, the social studies. Still other projects at all educational levels came along rapidly until today there are no fewer than 27 projects running. They include 10 projects in ESI's remarkable film studio, the best of its kind in the country. ESI's staff has over 400 persons and this year's expenditures are over $ 10,000,000. Thus ESI, going into the EDC merger, was by far the largest organization in the country devoting itself entirely to research and development in curriculum, and is still quite unique in the kinds and combinations of people, representing a variety of occupations and professions by no means restricted to education, who work with it. Looking at all this growth, some of which was deliberately sought by ESI and some of which came in the form of outside requests, one might easily see it as a classic example of educational empire-building. Perhaps it is, but, of education's many empires, this has surely been one of the most interesting and productive.

Behind ESI and its projects has always been the energizing force of Zacharias, not a withdrawn sort of fellow. As much as an institution is ever, in Emerson's phrase, "the lengthened shadow of one man," ESI is such an institution. Without Zacharias's deep concern, his enormous drive, his ego, his entrepreneurial talent, even his bullying, there would have been no PSSC, no ESI, no EDC, and possibly no regional labs at all. One should not underestimate the services of the many other distinguished people who helped mold ESI, such as Francis L. Friedman. Before his untimely death in 1962, he was the real genius, the intellectual anchorman—dedicated and uncompromising on any question of quality—behind much of the ESI material, especially the PSSC textbook. But the fact remains that throughout ESI's development, Zacharias has been the indispensable man, and ESI in many ways is a demonstration of how much influence one individual can exert on the Gargantua that is American education.

Certain basic ideas run through ESI projects. The most important one is the "discovery method," upon which a major stress is put in all ESI materials. By that or its sundry other names, the discovery method is the closest ESI has ever come to having a party line. Zacharias holds firmly to the view that scientists "always work from specific examples, however simple or complex, to the awesome generality." He further believes that there is only so much physics that "can come through the eyes and ears— the rest must come through the hand." Both ideas pervade ESI projects. The first idea was at the heart of Jerome Bruner's book, *The Process of Education*,[1] which came out of the famous Woods Hole Conference in 1959, itself dominated by ESI people. Reduced to an oversimplification, the ESI approach to pedagogy has been to create classroom and laboratory conditions under which students can uncover principles for themselves rather than accept what is "given" them by teachers. For example, instead of merely accepting physics as handed down by teachers—what Zacharias calls "physics theology"—they are led to test established doctrine, probe behind it, rediscover it. ESI's constant aim is to construct a curriculum that will lead students to ask fundamental questions and find answers from their own observations—in other words, lead them to recapitulate the process by which knowledge is gained in the first place.

The second principle that makes up what might be called the ESI system is merely an application of old-fashioned progressivism that never got carried out very well before: that people learn by doing. Thus the early versions of PSSC required students to make their own lab apparatus from cheap materials, and to learn some physics in the process. They made a 50,000-volt generator, for example, from a $ 1 electric motor, a few cake tins, a rubber belt, and a small glass tube. They made a telescope from surplus lenses mounted in drapery rings on pieces of wood doweling. They made a ripple tank from ordinary window framing, a pane of glass, coat hangers, and ping-pong balls, and with it they studied spherical pulses and period waves, reflection, refraction, diffraction, and interference patterns, and the principles behind the behavior of lenses and telescopes. In the interests of saving teachers' time, later versions of PSSC supplied kits for the making of lab apparatus, but the principle of learning by doing remains the same throughout ESI programs—doing things, that is, that are truly integral to the course and essential to full understanding.

Nobody realizes better than Zacharias and Bruner that the discovery method has become a cult, as has much of the talk about "the structure of the discipline" and the possibility of teaching anybody anything at any age. Like all cults, this one has distorted and exaggerated the original ideas, but the ideas remain central to most ESI projects.

These projects have not always been smashing successes by any reckoning. The social studies project got off to a slow and rocky start,

---

[1] [Jerome Bruner, *The Process of Education* (Cambridge: Harvard University Press, 1960).]

partly because of some personality clashes but mostly because the process of reaching a consensus about what should or could be done in this field, if it is a field, is much more painful than in science and math, and actual materials are much more difficult to produce. Nor has an ESI project to help Southern Negro colleges been very fruitful, nor one to bring ESI materials into teacher-training programs.

Nor has ESI been free of criticism, some of it highly acerbic. People point out, for example, that physics enrollments have fallen in the high schools since the introduction of PSSC, which was intended to raise enrollments, and insist that there is a causal relationship between the two events. They argue that PSSC is too tough, too esoteric, too specialized for anybody who does not intend to be a physicist, though splendid for those few who do (about 125,000 students were studying physics in the 1966-67 school year). They argue that it and other ESI projects are preoccupied with the bright students and unconcerned with the mass. They argue that ESI is too remote from schools, too unaware of what the real problems are. One man close to ESI even speaks of the "tremendous arrogance and snobbery" of Harvard and MIT professors telling the schools what to do and how to do it. Still others say that the "little curricular jewels" that emerge so nicely polished from the ESI workshop get shattered in the classroom because teachers are not adequately trained to handle them or because they are inappropriate for a given class. PSSC, as one man who worked in it says, "has never really had a fair trial in the high schools—it often gets raped by teachers."

For the most part, the educational "establishment," not surprisingly, has been able to contain its enthusiasm for ESI. School administrators sometimes feel pressures from their school boards or communities to use ESI programs and interpret this pressure as criticism of themselves. Curriculum specialists in schools do not take cosily to outside reform groups that threaten to make their jobs obsolete. Many classroom teachers look on radically new curriculum materials as implying that what they have been doing for years in their own classrooms is wrong and needs changing. And professors of education as a group have been something less than enchanted with ESI's habit of bypassing them in favor of collaboration with school teachers and academic scholars.

Criticism of ESI and its curriculum materials is not easy to evaluate. ESI supporters, of whom there are many, feel that most of the problems encountered by schools using ESI materials stem more from the schools than from ESI. These materials are tried out in schools, changed and refined, over a long period. Teachers themselves are involved in all phases of ESI projects. PSSC, say people like Nathaniel Frank, an MIT physicist and an old ESI hand, "is not aimed only at the bright students, any more than are the elementary school science materials or the social studies materials, but is appropriate for the average as well when the course is in the hands of a well trained teacher." Zacharias feels that the schools often create their own problems by being too ambitious and trying to cover the whole PSSC textbook in one year instead of being intelligently selective. He admits that ESI has not been closely connected with as many schools or with as great a variety as it might, but also points out that a pioneering venture of this sort, scarcely a decade old, can't do everything at once.

As for ESI materials threatening to monopolize the field, Zacharias recalls that one of the main reasons for the establishment of regional labs, in which he played an important role, was to insure a variety of up-to-date and imaginative courses and materials. He would like to see several complete physics courses. each sharply different from PSSC. competing in the schools. He applauds the fact that PSSC has been at least in part the impetus for another multimillion-dollar high school reform group, Project Physics, at Harvard. Project Physics puts greater stress than PSSC on historical and philosophical aspects of science and on its social implications. It is aimed at the wide middle band of students who do not take PSSC or any other kind of physics now (80 per cent of each year's senior class take no physics at all). "But it is not," says Zacharias, "different *enough* from PSSC."

Whatever the merits of the criticisms of ESI, the merger with IEI will reduce the number of critics. The new organization, being the regional lab for New England, will maintain close and continuous relations with many types of schools and school systems, and these relationships will be a leavening of ESI's customary mode of operation. Before the merger, IEI was a small, inchoate organization in which the professional educator had a dominant voice; it was formed in 1966 from an even more informal group and, like many similar developing agencies around the country, was in the process of trying to meet the requirements of the Office of Education for full recognition and financing as a regional lab. But many people, including U.S. Commissioner of Education, Harold Howe II, and ESI's president, Arthur Singer, felt that ESI should be the nucleus of any regional lab in New England. It was, in fact, ESI that Zacharias and others on the President's Science Advisory Committee had in mind as far back as 1961 as the possible prototype for additional research and development agencies they thought were needed in education. Such agencies were more formally proposed in 1964 by the President's Task Force on Education, most of whose members also had ESI in mind, and were then legislated into being by Title IV of the 1965 Elementary and Secondary Education Act.

Unhappily, however, the regional labs, as they are now working out, show little awareness of the intentions of Zacharias, Singer, Keppel,

Gardner, and others who promoted them. It is both instructive and disheartening to compare the rather grand vision that such people originally had of the regionals with the kind of agencies they are turning out to be. Gardner once spoke of these labs as "combining the resources of MIT, IBM, and the New York State Board of Regents." Francis Keppel spoke of them in an equally ambitious way at Congressional hearings before the passage of the 1965 Education Act. Zacharias remembers, "My original hope was that six or a dozen groups could be set up around the country with something of the size, scope, and style—by style I mean mostly, the mixture of people involved from industry, the arts, the universities, the schools, etc.—that has characterized ESI. I hoped these groups, no matter what problems they decided to tackle, would all have one thing in common: a willingness to talk back to the established system of education."

Whatever the intentions of the Task Force and of Congress, the prospectuses and newsletters of the new regional labs strongly suggest that ESI has not been the model for any of them and that the chances are dim indeed of their "talking back" to the established system. Most of these labs are clearly under the control of professional educators and do not represent anything like the diversity of high-level talent, either on the staffs or the boards of trustees, that was expected. Conspicuously absent from them are scientists, humanists, scholars, and academicians generally. Absent also are other people who were supposed to be actively involved in this brave new enterprise: artists, writers, composers, conductors, industrialists, inventors, and anybody else from any background who might be able to contribute to educational reform.

The rub is not only reform and the small chance of getting it in the present circumstances, but the imminent waste of an unprecedented opportunity in educational research and development. No one can expect these labs as now constituted to lead the way toward significant change or, to use one of their own favorite nouns, "innovation" in American education. An assortment of professional educators and administrators—who share a common background as well as a certain interest in the status quo and who make no use of the scientific-intellectual-artistic community, not to say the community at large—cannot come up with anything but routine answer to educational problems. One informed lab-watcher comments: "The research projects now being done by the labs in subjects like 'student-learning styles' and 'problem-solving processes' sound like old-line doctoral dissertations or, at any rate, like 10,000 other studies that have been done in schools of education."

ESI's stake in the regionals is obvious enough. ESI no longer exists as an autonomous agency; it is now and integral part of a regional lab and its future is closely tied to that of all the regionals. It has plenty to worry about. "The other labs," as one ESI man said with some bitterness, "are turning into just another boondoggle—they are nothing but schools of education with lots of money and no students."

In a word, ESI may have been education's Manhattan Project, or perhaps its *Nautilus*. But unlike science and the Navy, which were never the same after the atomic bomb and the nuclear submarine, education has many atavistic habits and may easily revert to earlier and more primitive forms. It is this reversion that the regional labs were supposed to prevent by following ESI's lead or, at the least, by developing a vigorous new approach of their own to educational reform; but if they fail to do so, they may bring the curricular reform movement into disrepute. They may also invite some snappy Congressional budget-cutting in the future and may discover what instant poverty feels like. If they go down, they could well take EDC with them.

EDC itself was not exactly a love match between ESI and IEI, though affection may grow in the future. It was more a marriage of convenience. Both sides were worried that two such organizations could not survive separately in New England competing for funds and support from the same sources. Also there was the matchmaking pressure from the Office of Education. But there were many misgivings among the trustees and staff members of both groups. ESI was fearful of losing its unique identity as well as perhaps losing some of the intellectual zest and *esprit de corps* that had always characterized it. It was fearful of domination by educational administrators and bureaucrats.

IEI, in turn, was fearful of domination by Zacharias and others of the Harvard-MIT group who have played a large role in ESI. And it was afraid that the ESI approach to educational problems would not blend well with the one likely to prevail at IEI. There was also the fact, as one observer put it, that "over the years, 'Zach' had made a number of scurrilous comments about professional educators which did not make the merger more attractive to them."

Both sides recognized, nevertheless, that a merger offered great promise. As a separate agency, IEI would have needed many years and millions of dollars to match the experience and resources of ESI, if it would ever have done so. And ESI, for its part, had reached the point where it needed wider contacts with schools and school systems. It had not given much consideration to, as James Killian puts it, "the school as a total process and had not always been sure about how ESI programs fitted into the whole program of the school." ESI especially needed more contacts with people able to bring about changes in schools. It had found that curriculum reform was only part of a complex pattern by which change is made in education and that a more active involvement of the professional establishment would be needed if ESI were to have its maximum effect.

ESI was conscious of having capitulated over the years to the established system on a number of matters in which it felt the system was wrong. PSSC scientists, for example, had been convinced early in the project that a combined physics-chemistry course extending over two years was the best thing, but they had to abandon the idea, partly because they could not in those days get the chemists interested, but mostly because schools could not or would not reorganize to accommodate such a course. They had wanted to create an essay-type exam for the PSSC course, allowing students to demonstrate how much they knew and could do, but, in the face of the established system of college admissions, had to turn to the Educational Testing Service to create the customary multiple-choice exam, allowing students to indicate mostly what they don't know. These and many similar problems might be solved in a better way in the future through greater involvement of the establishment with ESI.

The merger might also make possible some progress on a very difficult front, that of teacher education. The Achilles' heel of curriculum reform groups, no less ESI's than others', has been their failure to effect corresponding reforms in the training of teachers. They have had to be content with in-service institutes of greatly varying quality and effectiveness that in many cases have fallen far short of even immediate needs. Even more regrettable is the fact that colleges and universities that train teachers have not actively sought out ESI and other groups to see what use they might make of these materials in their own training programs.

Although EDC's role in New England is still shaping up, Arthur Singer, now president of EDC, hopes and expects that the two components will complement and reinforce rather than quarrel with each other. He also feels sure that the intellectual ferment of ESI will infect the whole of the new organization. He has the challenging job of making this come true through the exercise of what might be called the politics of symbiosis—an undeveloped art in education. But he should get help from the EDC board of trustees which is drawn equally from both predecessor groups and promises to be strong and active.

Among the initial projects to be undertaken will be large-scale cooperative ventures with schools and systems of a kind that will be new to ESI—such as the schools of Bridgeport, Connecticut, of inner Boston, of rural Maine. EDC expects to put a major emphasis on education of the deprived, on community involvement, and on out-of-school environment, though it is not at all certain as to how it will proceed against such problems. All this is a sharp contrast with ESI's past activities, so sharp that one experienced ESI man says, "It will be tragic if EDC becomes just another social welfare center, for it would probably be a poor one, and if the things for which ESI has always stood—intellectual excellence, innovative drive, first-class curriculum materials—are sacrificed to whatever fads may prevail among educational administrators or whatever gets the most dough out of the Office of Education."

But to Fletcher Watson, a central figure in Harvard's Project Physics, "the real danger of the merger is that the school people involved will be dominated by ESI and will not be able to give a fair consideration to other curriculum reform groups and to non-ESI materials." To Jerome Bruner, who has been active in many ESI projects, especially the one in social studies, the real danger "is that the ESI, dependent on the good will of the IEI people, will simply become part of the establishment. Reform groups must above all resist the temptations of establishmentarian blandness." To Theodore Sizer, dean of Harvard's Graduate School of Education and a trustee of EDC, the real danger "is in ESI's becoming institutionalized and freezing into a bureaucratic mold. Curriculum reform groups ought to be tent cities where the best people, the brilliant people, are brought together temporarily to do an important job and then return to their main careers. As soon as you institutionalize it, you run the danger of making it a walled town that is not nearly so attractive to outstanding people of the kind ESI has been able to call upon in the past."

The doubts, however, can easily be overstated. The main fact is that most people from both ESI and IEI are looking forward to a long and happy marriage, and not without reason. EDC is the only regional lab to begin life with a large, splendidly equipped organization in full operation and with a decade of experience in persuading distinguished people of all sorts to work together on curriculum reform. If EDC can exploit these great and unique resources and succeed in bringing radically improved curricula into schools and into teacher training on a wide and varied scale—if it can ultimately bring a measure of real reform to entire school systems and, conceivably, even states—it will have become one of the most important and powerful bodies in education. It will have disproved all doubts and will indeed deserve well of the republic.

EDC Social Studies Materials

BACKGROUND

The Education Development Center, Inc. (EDC), was formed by the merger of the Institute for Educational Innovation (IEI), one of twenty federally supported regional laboratories, and Educational Services Inc. (ESI), a private non-profit corporation which had come into existence in 1958 to administer the Physical Sciences Study Committee (PSSC) program. ESI was originally financed by the National Science Foundation, the Ford Foundation, the Alfred P. Sloan Foundation and other contributors. Now based in Newton, Massachusetts, the merger offspring, EDC, functions as a regional laboratory for the New England area and produces school curricular packages for national and international use.[1]

The social studies program of EDC stems from a chain of events which began in 1961. In that year a conference was held at Dedham, Massachusetts, attended by African and western scholars. An overseas program, partly inspired by the old ESI, was discussed and field services in science, math, and languages were planned. Social science and humanities courses were also considered, but the lack of theoretical groundwork proved an insurmountable obstacle. This situation led the American Council of Learned Societies (ACLS) to join ESI in organizing an interdisciplinary conference entirely devoted to study of the feasibility of creating a social science and humanities curriculum.

Jerrold Zacharias of PSSC fame, and Frederick Burkhardt of ACLS, were the actual proponents of the interdisciplinary conference and became co-chairmen of the Steering Committee which assumed proprietary responsibilities. Other members of the Steering Committee were:

Henry Bragdon, Phillips Exeter Academy
Robert Feldmesser, Brandeis University
John H. Fischer, Teachers College, Columbia
Francis Keppel, Harvard Graduate School of Education
Harry L. Levy, Hunter College
Elting Morison, Massachusetts Institute of Technology
Stephen White, ESI
James R. Killian, Jr., (ex officio) ESI
Carroll V. Newsom, (ex officio) ESI

---

[1] "Work in Progress, 1967," Education Development Center, Inc.

The Steering Committee was eventually successful in acquiring the co-operation of 45 scholars and schoolmen. This aggregation, with the addition of the Steering Committee and some observers, met from June 8 to June 24 in 1962 at Endicott House in Dedham. Each participant represented himself and, inferentially, his discipline, but not his parent organization or institution. The assemblage included partisans of history, classics, languages, the arts, law, education science, anthropology, sociology, psychology, political science, economics, geography, and philosophy. Surprisingly, no mathematicians were present. Perhaps the co-chairmen were dubious about the possibility of quantification in social science.

Upon arrival, the participants learned that the Steering Committee envisioned development of a K-12 [Kindergarten through twelfth grade] social science and humanities curriculum rather than construction of a course or two. The enormity of the task required grand designs. Among the questions which had to be answered were those concerning a disciplinary versus an interdisciplinary framework, an extant value versus an emergent value commitment, and a stage of learning versus a structure of the discipline pedagogy. During consideration of these issues the participants functioned not so much as ambassadors of separate sovereign domains adhering to state ideologies, as pragmatic legislators in a common congress forming shifting and evanescent coalitions.

Four ententes emerged in the course of the conference. These groups can be labeled history, behavioral science, social science, and humanities. Of course, interests and outlooks were not as clear-cut as the classification suggests. Throughout the conference, discussions regarding history seemed to alternate between focusing on history as conditioned by the elementary and secondary school social studies environment and history as a discipline in a higher education setting. Anthropology, social psychology, and sociology formed the basis of the behavioral science bloc. Geography, political science, and economics had an ambivalent status. At times, for example, the behavioral scientists seemed to proffer a tongue in cheek invitation to the geographers to join forces. Because of substantive differences this invitation was not accepted and geography, political science, and economics constituted a loose and somewhat schismatic system which might be characterized as social science. The humanities coalition consisted of the fine arts and art education, classics, and language and literature.

Just as the Physical Science Study Committee had eventually concluded that it had to work within the extant school subject-area framework, the social science and humanities experts felt obliged to accept the elementary and secondary school construct known as social studies as the appropriate vehicle for disseminating their innovation. Once social studies was selected as the medium through which intervention would be attempted, the actual state of that uniquely American invention became an immediate concern. Many of the participants had already formed at least a partial opinion of current social studies curricular designs—the nature of which is suggested by their interest in revision.

Spokesmen for behavioral and social science announced that the most glaring fault in the K-12 social studies curricula they had encountered was the inordinate attention paid to history. They proposed a de-emphasis of history and an increased concentration on behavioral and social science. Several of the behavioral scientists were contending that history could not even be considered a social science. They portrayed history as a discipline devoted to the unique an nonrecurring aspects of human behavior as opposed to their predilection for categorization and generalization. Furthermore, the behavioral scientists tended to regard school history as inextricably linked with the "indoctrination" or social training function of the social studies. They also denied the assertion that the methodology of historians and behavioral scientists was basically similar.

Elting Morison alleviated the tension by adopting a conciliatory approach. Instead of attempting a riposte the MIT [Massachusetts Institute of Technology] historian admitted the necessity of increasing the role of behavioral science in the social studies curriculum. Morison argued that survey courses in history probably did not produce the results sought by historians anyway so that no harm would accrue to that discipline if it reduced its curricular time allotment and concentrated on a few areas as in Charles Keller's postholing technique. In a later interview Morison elaborated on his position.

I think that if one *thought* (which I trust this whole ESI venture is designed to do) of ways of reorganizing the immense amount of valuable information that there is in the humanities, both literature and history, in new ways, you could greatly reduce the amount of information you have to teach, which would make it much more assimilable for students.[2]

Morison denied the contention that postholing would fail to give students "a feeling for the past." He claimed that if students acted as historians examining particular "episodes," increased sensitivity to a time continuum would be achieved.

History, according to Morison, dealt with particular situations in the

---

[2] "Men and Ideas," ESI's Social Studies and Humanities Program: A Conversation with Elting Morison, *ESI Quarterly Report*, Winter, 1962–63 (Watertown, Mass.: Educational Services, Inc., 1963, p. 39.

past. These situations were rich in data. The historian's job was to isolate that data which was relevant in terms of the point to be made and to communicate that point in an effective manner. The two great tasks of the historian were selection and expression. Social scientists, (Morison resists the term behavioral science) with their ability to synthesize mountains of data, could aid the historian in winnowing the relevant from the irrelevant. Artists and kindred humanists could assist the historian in his attempt to gain the favor of the Muses.

At first glance Morison's conception of history and the historian's role provides an easy entree for behavioral and social science and humanities into the social studies curriculum. The conclusion which the non-historian might derive from Morison's position is that behavioral and social science and the humanities must be taught independently of history.

Some questions remained unresolved. If history is a humanity and history is to be de-emphasized what is the fate of the humanities? The humanists were troubled by their unique alliance with history and by the necessity of functioning within a social studies context. Although the conference participants wished to escape from the constraints of the social studies tradition they could not entirely succeed in this endeavor. The humanists had to justify their claim to a share of the curriculum in terms of their relevancy to the goals of the other major powers. After all, history and social science, in the prevailing view of schoolmen, were the legitimate sources of data and concepts for the social studies.

It seems likely that influences even more subtle than those already mentioned operated to hinder the humanists. The social and behavioral scientists were attracted to a mode of instruction which would impart to students the pleasures of predictive power (see chapter 5 for the derivation of this phrase). In science certain objective standards of excellence exist. When the scientist can accurately predict phenomenological occurrences, he can claim validity for his syntactical and substantive concepts. Certain philosophers of science point out the necessity for qualifying this assertion somewhat,[3] but it is at least partially true that interest in regularities and the possibilities of prediction are distinctive characteristics of science. In the humanities no such opportunities to exercise predictive power exist.

The humanists, to be sure, wished to make instruction less dry and didactic. They demanded that the urge for expression precede practice in expression. They could not avoid, however, the necessity of imposing subjective standards for judging excellence in expression. One spokesman

---

[3] Homans observes that Darwin's theory of evolution does not possess predictive power and argues that, "What makes a science are its aims, not its results." George C. Homans, *The Nature of Social Science* (New York: Harcourt, Brace & World, Inc., 1967), p. 4.

advocated the installation of reproductions of formal art masterpieces in all classrooms to help children develop aesthetic sensitivity. In view of the advent of "op," "pop," and "now" art, this proposal would have been more interesting if criteria for differentiating masterpieces from trivia had been propounded.

It seems fair to say that the behavioral and social scientists assumed that certain types of activities, knowledge, and skills would produce certain attitudes. The humanists assumed that certain attitudes would produce certain activities, knowledge, and skills. In fact, the humanist position was somewhat analogous to traditional social studies doctrine. Desired values were to be attained by exhortation and appeal, by exposure to select meritorious exemplars. Perhaps the humanist orientation was deemed reasonable by the scientists because of the intellectual rigor demanded by its proponents. Many of the conferees pressed the classicists to compaign for the reintroduction of Greek into the school curriculum. The classicists reciprocated by suggesting a course based on the writings of Livy, Sallust, Caesar, Cicero, Virgil, Horace, and Tacitus to be read *in Latin*. The constraints imposed on the humanists—association with history, accommodation to the social studies, ambiguity in standards of excellence, and empathy with the most able students—were to have profound influence on the humanist contribution to the subsequent EDC K-12 social curriculum.

The participants in the Dedham Conference, like so many "new" social studies planners, were vitally interested in the spirit brought to instruction and the spirit acquired from instruction. Zacharias, for example, stated that, "The inescapable life conviction that I've had . . . is that it is silly to try to separate process, objectives, and methods. All of it must be mixed up together and worked out together." [4]

If children are to learn by doing, the question of what is within the capacity of children becomes most important. The consultants had to ask if elementary school children could emulate scientists. Robert J. Havighurst was asked to comment. Havighurst argued for the stage-development theory as buttressed by the work of Piaget and Inhelder. His presentation seemed to strengthen the expanding world (concentric circle) organization of the social studies.

Bruner attacked the expanding world format on two fronts. First he argued that the exotic and fantastic were as real for the child as the familiar. The child's interest, he claimed, could be piqued by things which were "imaginatively meaningful." After positing this hypothesis Bruner then went on to redefine the issue. He did not unequivocally deny the

---

[4] Jerrold R. Zacharias, "What's Ahead in Elementary Science," *The Instructor*, January, 1967.

validity of stage development theory. Instead he reasoned that a child's readiness to learn a higher order concept could be altered, accelerated in fact, by early practice with the antecedent lower process concepts.[5] Bruner's formulation was enthusiastically received.

At this point the conference divided itself into four working groups charged with drawing tentative designs for curriculum blocks. Three working designs emerged when the committee of the whole reconvened. The first one called for the creation of a K-6 curriculum heavily stressing behavioral science and historical postholing. The second plan proposed a 7–12 classics curriculum which would exist *outside of the social studies domain*. This sequence of courses would be electives. The third plan called for a 7-9 junior high curriculum which would be unified by a *Subject to Citizen* theme and largely indebted to history and social science. No senior high school plan immediately evolved.

After the conference adjourned the Steering Committee sought to raise funds to implement the designs. Initial grants were obtained from the Ford, Sloan, and New World Foundation, with later funding provided by the National Science Foundation, the Office of Education and others. Having successfully passed the collection plate, the Steering Committee appointed a Planning Committee:

Jerome S. Bruner, psychology
Gerald Else, classics
George C. Homans, sociology
Charles E. Brown, school superintendent
Douglas Oliver, anthropology
Franklin Patterson, political science
Everett Mendelsohn, history of science
Frederick Burkhardt, ACLS
Jerrold R. Zacharias, physics

Three teams were created to produce three curricula. All three teams were interdisciplinary, although some participants in the Dedham Conference had expressed doubt about the efficacy of the interdisciplinary approach. Adoption of this approach averted conflicts over which disciplines would receive the lion's share of curricular time.

The elementary school team was headed by Douglas Oliver. The basic framework for the six courses of study involved was formulated; history and behavioral science could be best served by the theme *Evolution of Man and Society*. The first grade course was based on study of the Netsilik

---

[5] David Driscoll, "Report of the Conference of Social Studies and Humanities Curriculum Program," Endicott House of MIT [Massachusetts Institute of Technology], Dedham, Mass., June 9 to June 23, 1962.

Eskimos of Pelly Bay, Canada. The simple society of these people attracted the designers. It was felt that by avoiding a more complex interrelated society the distractions and subleties which make it difficult for students to think in generalities could be averted. How could first graders encounter the Eskimos? Reading about them was out of the question. The team was drawn by the possibilities afforded by the use of films. Undoubtedly the success of PSSC films also influenced them. If we may abandon our chronology for a moment, we can advise the reader that the Netsilik Eskimo films which were eventually produced under the direction of Asen Balikci and Douglas Wilkinson with funds from the National Science Foundation are absolutely breathtaking. The film crew lived with the Eskimos and did, indeed, capture the essence of their culture. The films are silent which seems to facilitate the viewer's involvement. Perhaps the highest compliment which can be paid Balikci's product is to say that it is highly reminiscent of Robert Flaherty's 1922 masterpiece, *Nanook of the North*. Several promising precedents have thus been set and it is to be hoped that we will find, with increasing frequency, films which do not enrich a course of study, but which are its core.

The second grade course was to be based on study of Australian aborigines and African Bushmen. The children would begin making generalizations about primitive societies by comparing these two peoples with the Eskimos. A third grade course was entitled "Becoming Human" and dealt with free-ranging African baboon communities. The fourth grade course, "Husbandry and Its Beginnings," was originally conceived of as portraying a crucial step in the evolution of civilization. The fifth grade course was intended to provide insight into the beginning of city life via archaeological studies of a site such as Nippur in Iran. The sixth grade course was designed to serve both as a review of previously generated concepts and an introduction to Greek civilization. The anthropological orientation of the elementary program is apparent.

Several statements of curriculum objectives were produced. One which was particularly lucid and concise is reproduced here in its entirety:

To introduce children to the natural and cultural history of the human genus, from the time when it began to differentiate from other primates, until it reached the stage of *Homo sapiens* and the beginnings of what archaeologists now call "civilization."

To introduce children at the same time to one particular set of methods that contemporary Western man has developed to find out about the human past and the present human condition; that is, the methodology of the social sciences, especially anthropology, archaeology, economics, psychology, sociology and history.

To encourage children to study social science by giving them an opportunity to handle the raw data of social science, especially in the form of filmed sequences that bring into the classroom the lives of peoples all over the world, as well as sequences that show how social scientists work.[6]

The junior high school sequence under the direction of Dr. Franklin Patterson of the Lincoln Filene Center, planned six units to implement the *Subject to Citizen* theme. Three of the units were to be based on English and American history in the seventeenth century and three were to be based on English and American history in the eighteenth century. The junior high team referred to these six units as episodes. Each episode was to be studied via primary sources—documents, letters, diaries, and so on which would be reproduced for the students. Using these materials the students would function as neophyte historians.

The classics curriculum team, under the direction of Dr. Gerald Else, began assembling the materials for a unit on Rome as seen through the eyes of the great Latin authors previously mentioned. They focused on the fall of the Republic and the rise of the Principate.

The projected division of labor ran into trouble in 1963. In a terse statement contained in a general information sheet issued in January of 1964, readers were informed that, "Due to difficulties involved in obtaining support, it was decided that the program should be limited for the time being to the social studies, i.e., the social sciences and history,"[7] ESI (EDC) became sole proprietor of the program. The import of the message was easily grasped; the classics project was scrapped. In an effort to salvage some part of the classics contribution, the Roman Unit was added to the *Subject to Citizen* junior high design where it resided somewhat uneasily. The format of the junior high curriculum had, however, already begun to change. A transition block was anticipated which would bridge the gap between *Evolution of Man and Society* and *Subject to Citizen*. A seventh grade course, "Inventing the Western World," would articulate with the fifth and sixth grade offerings by providing case studies of the development of the West from Greece to colonial America. The case studies would emphasize the growth of culture and government in communities. The Roman unit was more comfortably ensconced in this new seventh grade framework. *The Subject to Citizen* label lost some of its descriptive accuracy and became the title of the eighth grade offering. *Man as a Political Being* became the total junior high package title.

   [6] Kevin Smith and Evans Clinchy, "The Social Studies Curriculum Program and Its Films," pamphlet, Education Development Center, Inc.

   [7] "Social Studies Curriculum Program," General Information Sheet, Educational Services, Inc., January 1, 1964.

By January of 1964 a quartet of leaders for a senior high school project had been recruited. Three of the planners were members of the Planning Committee—Morison, Bruner, and Homans; the fourth man was Morton White, professor of philosophy at Harvard. These leaders agreed that at least one of the proposed package's areas of concentration should be the nineteenth century.

Also in 1964 Jerome Bruner succeeded Douglas Oliver as director of the elementary school curriculum project. Under Bruner's direction the orientation of the *Evolution of Man and Society* sequence was somewhat altered. According to Bruner, three questions should recur throughout the curriculum: "What is human about human beings? How did they get that way? How can they be made more so?" [8] These questions led to consideration of "the five great humanizing forces": tool-making, language, social organization, management of man's prolonged childhood, and man's urge to explain.

Bruner managed to utilize the extant component of the elementary school program in implementing his schema. From Balikci's Eskimo film footage, for example, a new motion picture was created dealing with Eskimo childhood. The portions of the fifth grade block that dealt with myths were adapted to illustrate man's need to explain and the use of symbolic systems. "We want the students to understand myths," advised Bruner, "rather than to learn them." [9] As had been originally intended, conclusions would be generated by comparison and contrast of the various topical materials. Four vehicles of contrast were foreseen: "man *versus* primates, man *versus* prehistoric man, contemporary technological man *versus* 'primitive' man, and man *versus* child." [10] The title *Evolution of Man and Society* was dropped and was supplanted by *Man: A Course of Study*.

By 1965 the senior high school project's plans had crystallized. Morton White had assumed responsibility for direction of the work and the general thrust of the project had been determined. White and his colleagues made their interests clear. "Let us begin by saying unabashedly that in great measure we should try to communicate *knowledge*" [11] [emphasis in original]. The designers went on to explain that they meant knowledge in its broadest sense, aesthetic sensibility and moral virtue as well as data.

It is our aim to get the child to see history not only as the study of individual events following each other in time, but also as a discipline

---

[8]   "New Curriculum Models for History and the Social Sciences," The Social Studies Curriculum Program, Educational Services Inc., April, 1965, p. 2.

[9]   Ibid., p. 21.

[10]   Ibid., p. 23.

[11]   Ibid., p. 5.

which depends upon and illustrates certain generalizations about human behavior, and as a study which depends upon and illustrates certain general philosophical principles that govern research and discourse in history and the social and behavioral sciences. We conceive of the knowledge we wish to communicate, therefore, as occupying three distinct but connected levels, each more abstract than the other: (1) the level of historical fact, (2) the level of generalization in the social and behavioral sciences, and (3) the level of methodology or philosophy as that relates to historical investigation and discourse in the social and behavioral sciences.[12]

Three units are under construction which will probably compose the tenth grade course. George Brown and S. William Gouse of MIT are developing a unit called "The Steam Engine." The unit focuses on the history of the prime mover and will be divided into three periods: "(1) The control of natural energy sources, (2) the steam engine, and (3) the central station power plant and electrical power transmission." [13]

The second unit is "Manchester: Causes and Consequences of the Industrial Revolution." This unit studies the impact of technology on a specific area. Manchester is therefore presented as a case study. The curriculum makers have prognosticated three objectives for this unit. They wish the students to see the causes of the revolution that drastically altered society, to conceptualize the problems of the twentieth century as outgrowths of the developments of the nineteenth century, and to illustrate the variety of attitudes about man's social condition.

The third unit is "Darwin and Darwinism." The planners justify it saying, "Today, when science is coming to play a greater and greater part in our lives, it is highly desirable that our high school students come to see it as an intellectual advance and a social." [14] The readings are divided into three sections: Pre-Darwinian, Darwinian, and Post-Darwinian. The students will read primary sources to better understand the period in which Darwin worked, the nature of his theory, and its social and scientific consequences. Some team teaching involving biology and history specialists is suggested.

A fourth unit, also presumably destined for the tenth grade, was conceived in 1966. This unit will deal with the industrialization of Japan and will concentrate on nineteenth and twentieth century developments in that land. A number of units are being considered for the eleventh grade. These include units on Marxism, the development of American pragmatic liberal thought, the cultural aftermath of the French Revolu-

---

[12] Ibid., p. 7.
[13] Ibid., p. 17.
[14] Ibid., pp. 26, 27.

tion, Impressionism, and the novelist's attitude toward nineteenth century industrial society.[15]

Much work has been done on the *Man as a Political Being* junior high package. The unifying theme for the three year sequence will be provided by two political science concepts, political power and political culture. These concepts, according to the designers, suggest certain questions: "What is power in human society? Why is power a part of human society? What does power rely upon? What are the evils of power? How do people protect themselves against excesses of power? How does power operate to survive? What are the conditions under which power sickens and dies? [16]

Teachers may be encouraged by the assurance that, *Man as a Political Being* ... is *not* [emphasis in original] a set of courses designed for graduate study ... Our materials are concerned with data and processes through which children may work, assisted thereby toward concept development but not swamped by technical jargon." [17]

Attempts are made to articulate the junior high school package with the elementary school curriculum. The designers tell us that the instructor should raise questions such as: "Why are there different kinds of political cultures? How does the general culture affect the political culture and vice versa? How do political culture and technology affect each other? What part does language (including all forms of symbolic communication) play in political culture? How do people learn a political culture? What kind of political culture do we live in, how did we come to it, and what will it be in the future?" [18]

Man as a Political Being now consists of three courses, "Inventing the Western World," "From Subject to Citizen," and "The Civic Culture." The latter course is the newest and least developed of the junior high creations. It is the ninth grade offering which EDC hopes will replace traditional civics courses. "The real civic culture," the curriculum makers feel, "is not a simple idealized, all-out participant affair." [19] This course "should reassert in more direct fashion ... the central concept of political science, that of power. By concentrating on the experience of groups, immigrant and Negro, engaged in the struggle for political acculturation, students may see how deprivation or fear of deprivation, combined with an awareness of the possibility of remedy through political action, are powerful sources of political behavior." [20]

The first unit to reach the school trials stage in "The Civic Culture"

[15] "Work in Progress, 1967," pp. 11–13.
[16] "New Curriculum Models for History and the Social Sciences," pp. 29–30.
[17] Ibid., p. 39.
[18] Ibid., pp. 36–37.
[19] Ibid., p. 72.
[20] Ibid., p. 75.

is "The Negro in American Life." The sections of the junior high curriculum sequence now undergoing trials are: "The Death of the Roman Republic," "The Elizabethan Period," "The Glorious Revolution," "The American Revolution," and the aforementioned "Negro in American Life."

This brief overview of the origins and the orientation of the EDC social studies curriculum may give the reader some idea of the diversity and emphases of the three project packages. To treat in any detail every section of every project would be an overwhelming task. Since the authors of this volume have stressed secondary rather than elementary social studies, only the junior high or senior high packages can be considered. The junior high sequence is farther along than the senior high and therefore it will be our focus. The "From Subject to Citizen" course is the pivotal block according to its creators. The six units in this offering are: Unit I, "Elizabeth Society: 1588-1610," Unit II, "England in Crisis and Civil War: 1640-1649," Unit III, "The Glorious Revolution, 1688-1689," Unit IV, "Colonial America, 1630-1750," Unit V, "The Making of the American Revolution: 1765-1783," and Unit VI, "The American Constitution: 1778-1801." Unit I is our subject for review.

MATERIALS

The Elizabethan unit, "Queen Elizabeth: Conflict and Compromise," contains eight sub units:

1. "The Mystery of Roanoke: wherein the Queen's subjects plant a colony and search a new land."
2. "Politics and Religion: wherein the Queen chooses the middle way and pleases the majority of her subjects."
3. "High Dreams and Cold Cash: wherein the Queen with her subjects steers a cautious course toward riches and power."
4. "The Case of the Unnamed Heir: wherein the Queen acts but does not act."
5. "The 'Singed Beard' Seeks Revenge: wherein the Queen meets Spain with the 'heart and stomach of a king'."
6. "Patents, Parliaments and the Prerogative: wherein the Queen gets by giving."
7. "What is the Queen's Policy?: wherein King James is advised on his new kingdom."
8. "From Scotland Comes a King: wherein the Queen's reign is better understood."

The resource scholar for "Queen Elizabeth: Conflict and Compromise," was Dr. Louis B. Wright, Director of the Folger Shakespeare Library in Washington, D.C. Dr. Wright has written a booklet entitled *The Elizabethan Background of American History* which is included with the sub unit materials and which provides the teacher with additional information regarding Elizabethan England. Arleigh D. Richardson, III., who succeeded Franklin Patterson as director of the junior high curriculum project, certifies the accuracy and currency of the historical research upon which the sub unit is based. His pride is well founded.

"Queen Elizabeth: Conflict and Compromise" might reasonably require six weeks for presentation. The first sub unit, "The Mystery of Roanoke Island" is recommended for the initial two days. To begin this sub unit, the students read a twelve page pamphlet which includes primary and secondary sources pertinent to the Roanoke colony. The primary sections are excerpted (with some clarifying alterations) from Hakluyt's *Principal Navigations* and John White's *Journal* and are printed in a different type face than the other commentary. The difference in type faces is obvious to literati, but would not be obvious to eighth graders. Also presented in the pamphlet are reproductions of period maps and John Everett Millars' *Sir Walter Raleigh as a Boy.*

After reading the pamphlet which provides as much information regarding the fate of Roanoke as historians possess, the class looks at a series of reproductions of John White's Indian paintings, circa 1590. The Teacher's Guide suggests that the teacher form the students into small groups and ask them to make a case for the likely success or failure of the Roanoke colony based on interpretation of the art reproductions.

When the students have had time to reach a hypothesis they are given a sheet which asks "What Happened to the Colonists?" and which is divided into three parts labeled "Source of Clue," "Clues Supporting Your Theory," and "Your Theory." The students use this sheet to posit a historical argument regarding the fate of the Roanoke colonists.

This exercise is designed to introduce a number of concepts and skills to the students. The youngsters are supposed to distinguish between primary and secondary sources, to develop a sense of milieu, to face the problem of having to reach a conclusion with insufficient data; to begin to imitate historians, and begin to master forms of logical argument. The Teacher's Guide concludes. "The Mystery of Roanoke" is less significant for content than it is for an introduction to the methodology and approach of the whole unit." [22]

Perhaps the most important section of "Queen Elizabeth: Conflict

---

[21] "Queen Elizabeth: Conflict and Compromise," Explanation and Guide for the Teacher. Experimental Edition (Cambridge, Mass.: Educational Services, Inc., 1966). This analysis is based on an experimental version of "Queen Elizabeth: Conflict and Compromise" and may be in error if the final version of the sub unit is substantially revised. If *The New Social Studies: Analysis of Theory and Materials* is to be as *au courant* as the curricula it examines, experimental versions of forthcoming products must, occasionally, be used.

[22] Ibid., p. 26.

and Compromise" is the second one, "Politics and Religion." The Teacher's Guide provides background information regarding the basis of religious controversy in Elizabeth's era. The students read a pamphlet, "Politics and Religion," which depicts the Tudors and early Stuarts and cites the relationship which existed in European nation-states between church and state. Charts which stylistically represent the hierarchy of the Catholic and Anglican Churches are included. In a vivid manner the charts illustrate the political significance of English allegiance to Catholicism or Anglicanism. Also included is a geneology which somewhat unsuccessfully attempts to unravel the tangled familial relationships in the Tudor and Stuart clans. Students are asked to study the chart and then to circle all Protestants and underline all Catholics. Transparencies are also provided which feature portraits of the English monarchs of the period. The students can thus relate a name to a face. Although "Politics and Religion" is well written, the point is never succinctly made that it is conceivable that toleration of religious pluralism might have destroyed England as a nation. The neglect of this critical possibility makes the later description of Elizabeth's desire for Protestant uniformity and her willingness to compromise to achieve it somewhat incomprehensible.

After reading "Politics and Religion," the students read an interesting "dutch door" pamphlet called "What is Treason?" The dutch door description is appropriate because the pages of the pamphlet give the appearance of lacking their middle portion or waist—two separate sets of pages which do not cover the midsection of the interior covers of the pamphlet are used. The top pages provide legal definitions of treason, while the bottom pages present situations in which the definitions may or may not prove equitable according to the students' beliefs. One of the top pages contains the statement, "You are a traitor if you refuse to act as your government orders." The corresponding bottom statement advises, "The United States Army orders you, a soldier, to wipe out an unfortified enemy village, including 500 women and children because it is aiding the enemy and is in a strategic position. You refuse. Are you a traitor?" The exercise clearly demonstrates the difficulty of arriving at an unequivocal definition of treason and encourages the students to commit themselves to personally meaningful positions.

The next reading is entitled, Religious Issue # 1, "Campion: Traitor or Christian Martyr?" It details the career of the English Jesuit, Edmund Campion. Of particular interest are the excerpts from Campion's trial and the pamphlet illustrations which present reproductions of sixteenth century publications; also included are reproductions of engravings of executions by hanging, drawing and quartering. A transparency of London Bridge where severed heads were displayed is added. After the reading the students are given packets of cards containing pertinent questions and answers.

At this point, the Teacher's Guide suggests that a mock trial be held with students role playing Campion, the attorneys, witnesses, jury, judge, and Queen. Teachers are cautioned to remind their students that Campion's trial was not so structured. If greater involvement is sought, teachers are advised that one half of the class can be asked to write briefs defending Campion and one half can be asked to write briefs attacking him. Then, the sides can be switched. Students learn at the end of the trial that Campion was executed.

Religious Issue #2 is "John Penry: Traitor or Christian Martyr?" The students are told in this pamphlet about the Puritan position and the threat perceived in this position by the authorities. The class is informed in the text of Penry's execution. Additional reproductions of engravings are incorporated into the pamphlet and a chart compares the church hierarchy envisioned by the Puritans with the church hierarchies favored by Anglicans and Catholics. The Teacher's Guide wisely counsels against a second trial.

In Religious Issue #3, "Walter Strickland: Freedom of Parliamentary Debate," the students are acquainted with the precedent set by the arrest and subsequent release of a member of Parliament, who spoke out on forbidden religious matters. Two very striking reproductions of engravings are printed on facing pages; one depicts the interior of an Anglican church and the other presents the interior of a Dutch Calvinist Church—the juxtaposition of the church scenes graphically symbolizes the theological differences which existed between Anglicans and Puritans.

Students are asked to generalize Elizabeth's religious policy and a sheet querying "What Was the Queen's Policy on Religion?" is supplied. Several suggestions for topic questions to spur discussions are provided in the Teacher's Guide. For example, teachers are reminded that Strickland's case bears some resemblance to the case of the Georgia legislator who was twice denied his seat because of his opposition to the Vietnamese War. It is a disquieting truth that few textbook publishers would have had the courage to allow a remark on this striking parallel.

The organizing theme of "Queen Elizabeth: Conflict and Compromise" emerges in this sub unit. Elizabeth's compromises perpetuated her government and, unintentionally, encouraged enlargement of the scope of subject participation in the governmental process. This operating assumption apparently was the criterion for selection of most of the sub unit primary sources and historiography.

The third section of the unit is "High Dreams and Cold Cash." The pervading thought of this section is that a fortuitous wedding of profit and patriotism expanded England's influence, even though the Queen refused to officially countenance the more provocative activities of her pirate-patriots.

The students learn the incentives for the sixteenth century English voyages of exploration by playing an educational game called "Investments," Prospectuses are provided describing the projected ventures of Francis Drake and his circumnavigation of the globe, the Russia Company and the trading mission of Anthony Jenkinson, The Cathay Company and the passage-finding mission of Martin Frobisher, and John Hawkins' Syndicate and Hawkins' intended journey to the West Indies. Equipped with only as much information as the authentic investors possessed, the students, individually and in groups, are given sums of bogus money and told to decide how they wish to invest this money among the four possible opportunities. After choices have been made and justified, the students learn the results of the voyages and then compute their profits or losses.

In the concluding portion of "High Dreams and Cold Cash" the students read "How Shall the Queen Meet the Spanish Menace?" This synopsis compares the conflicting positions of Lord Burghley and Sir Francis Walsingham and asks why Elizabeth preserved both in office, heeding first one and then the other. The teacher is advised that a class debate is possible with students portraying the hawkish Walsingham or the dovish Burghley.

One of the best edited sections of "Queen Elizabeth: Conflict and Compromise" is the short booklet which deals with the captivity and death of Mary Stuart. "Mary of Scotland: Elizabeth's Dilemma," is a compilation of primary sources (including Elizabeth's letter to Mary's son after Mary's execution), lyrical secondary sources such as Stefan Zweig's *Mary of Scotland and the Isles,* and lean commentary. The role of compromise in Elizabeth's reign is again expounded; in this case the Queen's long postponement of a resolution of Mary's status and then her "well-publicized grief are viewed as modes of accommodation.

The longest section of "Queen Elizabeth: Conflict and Compromise" is the account of the battle with the Spanish Armada. This is reasonable since, historically speaking, any chronicle of Elizabethan England which omitted copious mention of that encounter would be absurd. The lengthy attention paid the 1588 action is, however, incongruous given the growth of a citizen culture via royal compromise theme repeatedly proclaimed for the unit. The Teacher's Guide somewhat lamely, in our opinion, pleads that study of the crises which led to the battle will "illustrate that the policy of compromise does not necessarily mean total negation of war, appeasement, or weakness." [23]

---

[23] Ibid., p. 47.

The historical materials here again are skillfully selected and edited. The students begin by reading, "Is War Inevitable?" which in a few pages presents the viewpoints of Philip II and Elizabeth, as well as the characteristic ambivalence of the Queen which the seadogs transformed into brilliance. The second reading in the sub unit is "The Strategy and Tactics" booklet. Using the engraving reproductions, diagrams, and data provided, the students role play English or Spanish allegiance and generate the appropriate battle plans.

If the youngsters are intrigued with this activity, optional readings are available to aid in the generation of strategy. These readings are thumbnail sketches of the opposing commanders with descriptions of equipment mobilized and past battles pertinent to the action anticipated. With all this sanguine expertise at their disposal the students, not unexpectedly, are granted the opportunity to play a war game. Unfortunately, the channel battle is difficult to simulate because the idiosyncratic elements resist reductionism. The reincarnated Medina Sidonias and Lord Howards are supposed to justify their proposed plans on the basis of the data given. A justification is not the same as victory and the game lacks a sense of closure.

After the game the students read "The Spanish Armada, Who Won?: Prologue," and "The Spanish Armada, Who Won?: Epilogue." These selections acquaint them with the problems faced by historians who must attempt to bring order and rationality out of chaos and confusion.

The sixth section, "Patents, Parliaments, and the Prerogative" seems more consistent with the unit organizing theme than does "The Singed Beard Seeks Revenge." In "Patents, Parliaments . . ." the students listen to a taped recording which is done in an "You Are There" style. The most significant actors in Parliament's historic dispute with the Queen over monopolies are heard in mock interviews. At the end of the recording, teachers are reminded that the question of monopolies is not defunct and modern examples might be considered.

Section 7, "What is the Queen's Policy?" is a short review presented in a rather ingenious manner. The students are asked to fill out a worksheet advising Elizabeth's successor, King James I, of things he should know about his new realm in order to successfully govern.

The last sub unit is "From Scotland Comes a King." A series of newsletters reciting significant events in James I's reign are given to the students. These newsletters serve as a basis of comparison between Elizabeth's pragmatism as exemplified by her acceptance of compromise with James' dogmatism and rigidity.

A number of class debates are proposed centering on questions of policy and historiography. The concluding activity might be the playing of two taped recordings. One portrays James' speech to the Judges in 1617 and the other reproduces Elizabeth's speech to her last Parliament. The subtle importance of style is thus nicely encapsulated.

Consistency

Unit I, "Queen Elizabeth: Conflict and Comparison," of the "From Subject to Citizen" EDC eighth grade course is, in our opinion, a scholarly and polished history curriculum package. The flaws it exhibits are ones of labeling. The six units in "From Subject to Citizen" supposedly contribute to American Citizenship training. The chasm between imperial England, colonial America and modern American public issues does not appear bridged. Unit I strives for relevancy by analogy: Elizabethan conceptions of treason are related to the contemporary question of the ultimate responsibility and accountability of a soldier in war; Strickland's precedent in freedom of legislative speech is compared with Julian Bond's exclusion from the Georgia legislature; and sixteenth century monopolies are compared with twentieth Century monolithic corporations. The cart appears to be before the horse. It would seem more logical to suppose that a citizenship training course should be devoted to study of modern policy problems with antiquarian analogies included for perspective.

"From Subject to Citizen" is indebted to Gabriel Almond's and Sidney Verba's, *The Civic Culture*.[24] In this ambitious work, Almond and Verba attempt to establish the congruency between political culture and political structure in five nations. In the course of this endeavor, the authors hypothesize the existence of subject and participant citizen cultures. In the subject political culture, the citizen possesses administrative competence; he can follow orders. In the participant political culture, the citizen can be oriented to an activist role in policy formulation, as well as a passive role in policy implementation.

The meaning of "From Subject to Citizen" becomes clearer, viewed in this context. The curriculum designers are interested in charting the development of policy competence in inhabitants of a civic culture who, previously, had only administrative competence. "But we are sticking to two hundred years," reveals Franklin Patterson, "in which some basic American political attitudes, behavior, and institutions took form." [25]

If we assume that knowledge of the development of a participant political culture will enable citizens to understand and perpetuate such a culture, we still must face the possibility that a good deal of Unit I of

---

[24] Gabriel A. Almond and Sidney Verba, *The Civic Culture* (Boston: Little, Brown and Company), 1963.

[25] Franklin Patterson, *Man and Politics*, Occasional Paper No. 4 (Cambridge, Mass.: Educational Services, Inc., 1965), p. 44.

"From Subject to Citizen" has little to do with the examination of compromise as a tool of democratic government or with the other insights purportedly elicited by the sub unit materials. It would appear that the curriculum designers have been trapped by their own pluralism. On the one hand they are attracted by the romantic and dramatic events of Elizabeth's reign; on the other hand they are concerned with *Man as a Political Being.*

It would be rather pedantic to suggest that the authors of "Queen Elizabeth: Conflict and Compromise" eliminate those readings which do not seem to contribute to the desired behavioral outcomes. Unit I's exposition of the character of Elizabethan society and its responses to challenges does not suffer from the artificiality which so often afflicts constitutional history and political courses. Teachers should work to stimulate student imaginations and allow for a maximum of incidental learning.

The second flaw in "Queen Elizabeth: Conflict and Compromise" is a dysfunction between pedagogic practices and sub unit readings. The recommendations in the Teacher's Guide (which, of course, teachers are free to ignore) do not seem to have grown out of the sub unit materials or objectives. The impression the reader receives while perusing the Teacher's Guide is that children are forever being divided into groups to debate or discuss questions of less than visceral interest. Furthermore, some beneficial results claimed as stemming from group experiences seem dubious. However, it is important to note the courage of the authors of the Teacher's Guide who never pull their punches when they recognize modern controversial parallels to Elizabethan developments.

The pedagogic difficulties seem to stem from the fact that, with the exception of several tape recorded sessions, the sub unit is basically a set of readings. By means of games, debates, discussions, and so forth, the pedagogic experts attempt to encourage careful reading of the materials and to vary classroom activities. Spread over a six week period, the amount of reading involved in the sub unit is relatively small—for able students. EDC has provided some intriguing theories formulated by David McNeill. In field-testing the Caesar unit, McNeill found that, "Without linguistic skills comparable to those they possess in handling spoken language, children could not fully exploit and become committed to the problems inherent in the written . . . material." [26]

When "Queen Elizabeth: Conflict and Compromise" is used with other than very able eighth graders, the teacher may find it useful to read the materials aloud. "What makes the difference, I think, is intonation," observes McNeill. "When I read a complex passage of prose aloud, I tend

---

[26] David McNeill quoted in Franklin Patterson, p. 37.

to distribute stress and pitch so as to rank order the logical propositions contained in the passage." [27]

As was mentioned in the background section of this chapter, the EDC has tended to favor college-bound students. This should not be taken as a permanent orientation, however, since the Bruner influence may be expected to hasten enlargement of curricular offerings. The Teacher's Guide maintains that, "Our material is not designed specially for the upper ability, college-bound group."[28] Notwithstanding this assertion, it seems probable that the greatest involvement in the materials will be encountered in upper-ability classes.

Able students will likely be charmed by the vividness of the primary sources—literary and graphic, and by the skillful illumination of the powerful personalities of the period which, through the ages, have fascinated poets, playwrights, and pupils alike.

What about the average student and the poor student? In the case of "Queen Elizabeth: Conflict and Compromise" we are fortunate in having a report from a city teacher not connected with any curriculum project who did teach an experimental version of the materials. Teachers of ghetto youth may be interested in this account of an attempt to use "Queen Elizabeth: Conflict and Compromise" with disadvantaged students. To be sure we are not offering this study as a definitive field test of the sub unit involved—nor are we attempting to generalize from one city school to all city schools. And it should again be mentioned that since an experimental version, rather than the final edition was utilized, the following report may be misleading if and when revisions will be made in the final version of the unit.

---

[27] Ibid., p. 36.
[28] *Queen Elizabeth: Conflict and Compromise, Explanation and Guide for the Teacher*, Experimental Editor, Education Development Center, Inc., 1966, p. 21.

*The Elizabethan Unit in an Inner-City School**

THE MYSTERY OF ROANOKE ISLAND: WHEREIN THE QUEEN'S SUBJECTS PLANT A COLONY AND SEARCH A NEW LAND

Content

This section of the Elizabethan Unit poses the question, "What happened to the colonists?" The students use various materials to develop their own theories as to the fate of the lost English colony. As background information, the unit authors have provided a map of the Virginia coastline and a narrative by Dr. Louis B. Wright. Some pictures of Indians made by John White in sixteenth century Virginia and three primary sources give the students evidence to use in supporting their generalizations about the disappearance of the colony. A dittoed worksheet completed by each student, including his theory, evidence to support it, and the sources of his data, summarizes the sub unit's work in one written page.

Objectives

The unit authors wish the students to have "an introduction to the methodology and approach of the whole unit." [1] This means the students are confronted with a problem which is open-ended. The students use pictures, maps, and journals to decide what happened to the colonists who traveled to Roanoke. They must come to a conclusion of their own as an historian might. They develop a theory using the evidence they have compiled. An evaluation of their work is made on the basis of how well they can support their theory with data.

Regulars: Day 1.—The teacher gave a brief explanation of the unit's content and objectives, putting the Elizabethan period in its historical perspective with the use of a time line. Then she read the introduction to Booklet One, "The Beginning of Our History," to the class.

To focus attention and create interest, the map was examined with this question being posed: "Why is this map printed sideways?" After brief

---

* From an M.A.T. Paper [Master of Arts in Teaching], *An Evaluaion of the Feasibility of Using an Education Development Center Curriculum Unit in a Chicago Inner-City School.*
[1] Queen Elizabeth: Conflict and Compromise, Explanation and Guide for the Teacher, Experimental Editor, Education Development Center, Inc., 1966, p. 14.

discussion, the teacher read Wright's narrative to the class and gave a short quiz. This exercise was not included in the unit suggestions, but the teacher felt the students needed to review the secondary source and to have some indication of how well they could handle the materials. Ten phrases, taken from the story just read, were written on the board, and the students were asked to pick the five which best explained the story's content. Papers were exchanged, and there followed a discussion of the choices. Each choice volunteered by a student had to be backed up with a reason, which the majority of the class could accept.

Essentials: Day 1.—The same lesson plan discussed above in the regular class was followed here and took twice as much time to complete in the essentials class. Everything went along well until the students turned to the narrative. They became interested in Millais' painting of "Sir Walter Raleigh as a Boy," insisting that they knew which youth was Raleigh. The teacher questioned their assertion, saying, "But you have been given no evidence to support your choice." To the teacher's surprise, the class came up with two supportive answers: Raleigh had to be the youth with the ruffled collar, because (1) he wears the same outfit on cigar boxes and (2) he is the more prominent of the two boys, being painted in the light, while the other is in the shade(!).

Essentials: Day 2.—The teacher read the narrative and then, while she listed the ten phrases on the board, the class read the second reading by Sir Francis Drake. After the quiz, the students discussed their choices for Wright's narrative, justifying each one they named. They were eager to know the teacher's choices and succeeded in persuading her that one of those they had unanimously included among their list of five phrases should have been one of the teacher's choices.

Regulars: Day 2.—The class read the Drake and White primary sources silently. A short discussion on the content of the two sources followed, in order for the teacher to be certain that the class had understood what it had read. According to a suggestion made in the Teacher's Manual, the teacher then divided the class into groups of five or six to study pictures painted by John White of the Indians living in coastal Virginia during the sixteenth century. Using an "evidence sheet" . . . each group found evidence to support the likelihood that the Roanoke colony would succeed or fail. Evidence of both possibilities might be found in one picture. All but one group had difficulty understanding what they were to do. After the teacher gave a suggestion (i.e., "How could the fish the Indians have caught here show that the colonists might succeed in the

New World?"), the students seemed to get the idea. Then another problem arose: the groups could not seem to relate the colonists to the pictures of Indians and kept trying to give evidence that the *Indians* would succeed or fail in the New World! In addition, the members of the groups had difficulty exchanging ideas. These students seemed to have little idea of how to relate to each other on an academic level. (They need to have practice in depending on each other for solving simple problems before complex ones can be attempted. This lack of communication must be worked on if the group is to become a positive part of the learning experience.) Also, the groups were too large to force participation by every member. But by the time the bell rang, each group had made a couple of suggestions and seemed eager to report on them the next day.

Essentials: Day 3.—The class reviewed the Drake reading and read John White's *Journal.* The unit authors' suggestion of breaking up into groups to examine White's paintings was not followed. The teacher felt that the assignment—to find evidence that the colony would succeed or fail—would be better grasped if each student filled out his own sheet of suggestions with the use of the transparencies of White's pictures shown on the overhead projector. As evidence was given by individuals the class took notes. Most of the suggestions were made by four or five members of the class, but questions were raised by everyone, and the level of interest was high.

Regulars: Day 3.—Using the transparencies of White's paintings each group leader gave a short report to the class of the evidence his group had found. Most of the suggestions were foods—as evidence of colonial success—and the Indians' weapons—as evidence of failure.

Then the teacher handed out "Your Theory" sheets, on which each student was to write his theory of what happened to the colonists, what evidence he had to support his theory, and where he got his data. The students were instructed that the papers would be graded on the basis of how well they backed up their theory with facts. The assignment needed to be explained numerous times, and, as the bell rang, the class still seemed dazed by what they were to do.

Essentials: Day 4.—After a brief review of the notes which the class had taken on Mr. White's Indian paintings, "Your Theory" sheets were distributed.... After an explanation of the assignment was given, each student proceeded to fill out his sheet, referring to the booklet readings and notes to explain the disappearance of the colony. The teacher was able to help each student with particular problems which arose, and, thus avoided, to a certain extent, the bewilderment of the regular class when they were given the assignment.

Regulars: Day 4.—Before the class began work on the "Your Theory" sheets, the teacher gave a short synopsis of the readings in Booklet I. The class was given the period to work on the sheets while the teacher answered individual questions. Many students, as in the essentials class, had difficulty understanding what was the difference between the data and the source of that data to be filled in separately on the sheets. Many gave more than one theory—often opposing ones—and gave one piece of evidence to support each theory.

Essentials: Day 5.—The class was the same as for the regulars except that these students seemed more at home with the materials, having been given some time on Day 4 to work on the assignment.

Essentials: Day 6.—Contrary to the unit authors' plan this class was given an extra day to discuss the "theories" they had written. Very few of the students had written concise ideas with evidence to back them up. Each paper, marked with comments by the teacher, was handed back, and every student was given a mimeographed sheet of two of the better theories written by members of the class. The class discussed why they felt the teacher had picked these two to show them and what made these two good examples of the assignment. Then, for the remainder of the period, each student corrected grammatical errors and spelling in the two theories, for each was dittoed exactly as it had been written. (The students like to see their own work or their classmates' in print and are able to recognize errors much faster. The teacher has found this to be a better method than just having each student correct his own mistakes—a process which usually means just recopying the selection with the teacher's corrections included.)

The students did poorly on the "Your Theory" sheets. The essentials' performance was lower than the regulars', although the essentials seemed confident with their answers and were given extra time for the work. The students' ability to understand how "theory," "data," and "source of data" are related and their awkwardness in coming to a decision as to what theory to take, resulted in a confused, yet wholehearted, attempt, which failed to reach the authors' goal that the students familiarize themselves with the historical approach to learning. After the first section, few students had learned the meaning of supporting a theory with evidence, much less become historians.

POLITICS AND RELIGION: WHEREIN THE QUEEN CHOOSES THE MIDDLE WAY
AND PLEASES THE MAJORITY OF HER SUBJECTS

Content

In this section the students look at three cases in which men opposed the Established Church for one reason or another. The Queen's "middle of the road" policy—her belief that peace could be maintained by pleasing the most people—meant that, in religious matters, she could not tolerate open dissenters who would threaten that peace. There are three cases dealt with in this section, each one presenting the students with a variety of materials to discover whether each man was a traitor to his country or a martyr to his religious conscience.

"Politics and Religion" by Mr. Wright and a genealogical chart provide the students with a background of relevant English history. Then, after a brief introduction to the meaning of "treason," the students read about each case. The materials for the cases include summaries of events leading up to each man's arrest and primary sources which bear on the question of guilt or innocence. In addition, comparative charts of the Anglican, Catholic, and Puritan church structures and visual aids, e.g., pictures of church architecture, help the students distinguish among the religions.

The students make briefs supporting either the defense or prosecution in one of the cases and put on a trial in the classroom, taking the parts of witnesses, attorneys, and the jury. At the end of this section the teacher gives an open book essay test where the students must review all the material and come to some conclusions about the Queen's religious policy.

Objectives

The authors wish the students to develop some ideas about the Queen's religious policy on the basis of evidence found in the three cases studied. The Queen was interested in a peaceful state, not with ruling men's souls. The three cases dealt with in this sub unit are designed to illustrate this policy and pose one major question to the students: "Were these men traitors or martyrs?"

To aid their comprehension of Elizabeth's motives the students participate in a number of activities with secondary objectives. They study the genealogical chart and Wright's summary to "gain a better understanding of Elizabeth's problems in relation to succession and religion." [2] The students match definitions of treason with situations of modern relevance to clarify the meaning of treason. The briefs the students write force them

---

[2]   Ibid., p. 16.

to take a position and support it with evidence, and the classroom trial dramatizes the major issues, illustrates the difficulty of making a clear-cut decision for or against the accused, and shows that the only way to win one's point is by presenting the best evidence. To sum up the religious issues, the students write an open book essay discussing the Queen's religious position with regard to her country. The students cite evidence to support their conclusions drawing from the narratives and primary sources found with each case.

Regulars: Day 5.—The teacher read "Politics and Religion" to the students as they noted the number of times English rulers changed religion. These notations and a discussion of the genealogical chart helped the students review the reading, see how often and quickly England shifted from one religion to another, and understand the relationship between religion and succession.

The class enjoyed the work, for they knew little about kings and queens and how they came to the throne. The teacher made remarks about Henry VIII's colorful life, "Bloody Mary's" reign, and so on, which increased the students' interest in the materials. The class took a quiz on the genealogical chart so the teacher could see how well they could use it. The students graded each other's papers, so they could see their mistakes immediately with the chart still in front of them. Most of the students did well on the quiz and after the bell many came to the teacher with questions about the chart.

Essentials: Day 7.—The class was the same as the Regulars Day 5. The class did just as well as the regulars on the in-class quiz on the genealogical chart, but more time was taken in explaining it beforehand.

Regulars: Day 6.—To introduce the students to the religious issue in the following pages the unit authors provide the student with general definitions of treason which he is to match with specific instances relevant today. This suggestion could not be followed altogether because the teacher could not do the assignment to her own satisfaction. Many of the definitions did not seem applicable to the particular situations, and the situations themselves were often ambiguous. It was not clear if each situation was to have a match or if some were to have many possible matching definitions and others none. So, instead of following the unit plan, the teacher began the class with a discussion of treason. The class took notes with books closed. A number of students volunteered answers to two questions: "What does the word mean?" "What constitutes a treasonous act?" The students realizing that their opinions on the second question differed, wished to know the "real" answer. The teacher said the answer depended on what country you were speaking of and proceeded to give an assignment to dramatize the lesson. Using the notes they had taken during the discussion and with the help of the various definitions in the book, each student was to make up his own definition of and penalty for treason, as if he were the leader of an imaginary country. Then, on the basis of *his* definition he was to decide if each of the particular instances in the book was treasonous. The assignment would be graded on how close the student's answers were related to his own definition.

The class had a feeling of participation in the lesson—more so than if they had matched someone else's definition with specific instances. The tendency was for the class to create short, simple definitions and to find that as they moved to each new situation they had to broaden and clarify their definitions. The teacher's purpose here was to make the students see that a generalization must be clearly stated in order for the necessary examples to be included and the unnecessary left out. (The essentials class was not given this assignment because of its marginal value. The teacher's primary purpose mentioned above could probably just as easily have been accomplished by a discussion, and the assignment as an introduction to the "Church and State" section need not be a full class period.)

Regulars: Day 7.—The class read the brief narrative on Edmund Campion and then the teacher summarized what they had read and read "Campion's Brag" to the class to be sure the students understood the major points and to help them wade through the language. Following these pages are separate bits of information on cards about Campion and the procedures used by Queen Elizabeth for dealing with religious questions. The students answered each question posed about Campion or the Queen on the basis of the information found below the question. The teacher gave this exercise to the students for the purpose of familiarizing them with evidence which would be used in their briefs. (A good deal of information was given to the class today and the narrative, cards, and Campion's confession needed to be understood as materials related to each other and studied for a purpose: to gather information about Campion in preparation for the class trial. The students so quickly lose their bearings and need constantly to be reminded of where they are and what they are doing. The more the students can work with the materials the better, and that is why the various exercises are given throughout the unit.)

Essentials: Day 8.—The class was the same as the regular class but more questions were asked about their comprehension of "Campion's Brag," and a good number of questions were raised about word meanings.

The class is most often able to understand this material only when the teacher asks questions and leads them through the lesson at every turn.

Regulars: Day 8.—The class reviewed their answers to the questions on the cards, discussing the information in light of its use as evidence for the defense or prosecution of Campion. For example, the teacher asked the students how Campion's words of loyalty to the Queen could be used by his defense attorney to refute the charge of treason. This discussion helped the students understand how they were to use this evidence to support a position in their briefs. In addition, the teacher wanted to point out the complexity of the Catholic/Protestant situation in Elizabethan England, e.g., that Queen Elizabeth neither always disliked nor always tolerated Catholic opinion. The strength of her enforcement of Protestantism as the only religion was relative to each situation and always based on her need as an administrator to maintain order in her realm.

Each student began writing his brief, picking either the defense or the prosecution of Campion to support. The assignment included the student's anticipation of arguments from the opposition, as well as his own defense of his position. The purpose of writing the brief was to familiarize the students with the materials, get them to take a position and support it with arguments, and learn to anticipate the arguments of the other side. The briefs were graded on the basis of how well the position was defended and how well the opposition's arguments were discussed. Those writing the best briefs were given first choice of a part in the class trial.

Essentials: Day 9.—The class proceeded in the same way as Regulars Day 8 but seemed to be confused about who were the Catholics, who were the Protestants, and what the Campion issue was all about. The teacher gave a short lecture on the differences between the two religions and reminded the class of the content of "Politics and Religion" which they had read earlier.

When grading the briefs the teacher found that in both classes there was a tendency to confuse fact and opinion. Students enjoyed giving their opinions about the case but rarely supported these opinions with data or asked questions of the opposition based on the materials in the booklet.

Regulars: Day 9.—The teacher handed back the briefs and announced the parts the students were to play at the trial. While the attorneys and their assistants worked together gathering evidence and choosing witnesses, the rest of the class worked on a mimeographed assignment prepared by the teachers. . . . The students were given a list of names of people involved in the Campion case, e.g., the Pope, Queen Elizabeth, the Earl of Arundel, and so on. They were to decide whether each person would testify for the defense or for the prosecution and why, using the blue booklets to find evidence for their answers. The assignment was designed to make the student question the roles played by individuals involved in the case and to influence Campion's defense or prosecution.

Essentials: Day 10.—The class worked on the same assignment given to the regulars for Day 9, after receiving their role assignments for the class trial. There was a good deal of excitement among the students in anticipation of the trial. This class performance on the briefs as mentioned earlier was disappointing. The main problem seemed to be the students' inability to distinguish fact from opinion. So, the teacher led a short discussion on the difference between opinion and fact and reviewed what was asked for in the previous day's assignment.

Regulars: Day 10.—The classroom was rearranged to look like a courtroom, and the trial of Edmund Campion began. Each attorney brought three witnesses to the stand and questioned them as the jury and opposing attorney took notes: The trial went poorly because the attorneys and witnesses did not have a firm grasp of their roles. In some cases the materials and characters had not been studied sufficiently; in other instances, the students just did not know how to use the materials they had studied. There were a good number of sources which could be used in the trial in a variety of ways. In addition, the very excitement of participating in a trial meant that many students were more interested in the mechanics of the proceedings and the dramatics of the performance than the trial's substance. The teacher helped create problems when she appointed a student to be the judge, thinking that he could handle the job because he seemed so eager to participate and had never entered into class activities before. He was just as baffled as the rest, and spent the entire period pounding the gavel and asking the teacher what he should say next.

The defense attorney, a heavy unattractive girl, who had never participated in class activities before, was the saving grace of the day's lesson. She had prepared good questions to ask her witnesses and had "boned up on her Perry Mason" to enable her to object to the prosecution's comments at the right moments. The judge was so impressed with her that he began to say, "Sustained," every time she stood up!

But other than the one student, the class as a whole had learned very little about giving and refuting evidence. Even so, this day was one of the most successful in terms of student interest, and many students asked if they could hold trials for Strickland and Penry too.

Essentials: Day 11.—The trial proceeded in the same way as with the regular class except that the teacher became the judge. Most of the questions which the attorneys asked the witnesses were the ones the teacher had given as examples. The attorneys often failed to ask the most sensible questions, and when they seemed to hit on a point which the jury considered important, they would drag that point into the ground. They often found it difficult to develop an argument by anticipating how a witness would respond at each step. Part of the problem lay with the witnesses, who often did not know who they were and therefore could not respond at all.

Regulars: Day 11, and Essentials: Day 12.—Both classes spent the period reading the materials on John Penry and answering questions on the content. . . . The teacher gave out the questions for review and to see how well the class could read new materials and answer questions about the major points mentioned without being coached by the teacher. The teacher made an effort to ask questions which could only be answered after the materials had been read in their entirety. Both classes did well on the assignment with no more than five failures in the two classes together.

Regulars: Day 12, and Essentials: Day 13.—Before moving on to the gathering of evidence about Penry, the teacher led a discussion on the meaning of evidence to be sure the class knew what the difference was between opinion and fact when trying to substantiate a theory or statement. For example, the teacher made the statement that "Willie Mays is the best baseball player," and asked the class how they would prove it. Suggestions such as batting average, salary, and press coverage were mentioned. When the teacher stated that "Willie is best because he is so good looking" the class realized immediately that this was not evidence because it said nothing about his ability as a baseball player. After a few more examples, the class turned to the assignment: "Give evidence supporting either statement (not both): (1) John Penry is guilty of treason and (2) John Penry is not quilty of treason." The assignment was essentially the same as the briefs on Campion, but was much more successful. Not only had the students had practice in writing briefs, but they had seen what a brief was in light of experiences to which they could relate.

Regulars: Day 13, and Essentials: Day 14.—Because the classes were becoming bored and frustrated with the amount of reading they were doing each day, the teacher suggested that they divide into two groups and read about Walter Strickland aloud to each other, taking turns. Then the teacher began a discussion with the question: "On the basis of what you already know, how do you think Strickland would be treated by the Queen?" After much debate the classes settled down to work, answering questions on the statements made by members of Parliament. The questions posed by the teacher were designed to get the students to see how the members of Parliament viewed their role in English government and why the Strickland case was handled differently from the cases of Penry and Campion.

Regulars: Day 14, and Essentials: Day 15.—As a way of summing up this section on "Church and State" the students in both classes wrote an open book essay discussing the Queen's religious policy. To aid the student in recalling the content of the section and in collecting relevant data, the teacher wrote a dittoed sheet of the major events and characters studied and suggested pages which might be helpful. The students had little trouble finding and supporting the idea that Elizabeth did not wish to pry into men's consciences in religious matters, but few asked why this was so and, therefore, missed the more general point that the Queen was more concerned with maintaining an orderly country than with promoting Protestantism for its own sake. Nevertheless, the essays in both classes showed some thought and made use of the evidence found in the booklets.

HIGH DREAMS AND COLD CASH: WHEREIN THE QUEEN WITH HER SUBJECTS STEERS A CAUTIOUS COURSE TOWARD RICHES AND POWER

Content

The materials in this section introduce the students to trade and expansion in England during Elizabeth's reign. There are two parts which deal with this question: one part focuses on the businessman who invest in England's economic ventures and the other part centers on the Queen's advisers who are concerned with England's trade and expansion abroad.

Each student, taking the role of a businessman, studies a sheet of "prospectuses" of four explorers and makes investments totalling £400 based on his knowledge of the proposed trips. The prospectuses are designed by the companies to give information about and promote interest in the voyages. The "Accounts of the Voyages" is 32 pages of written materials discussing each voyage and its outcome. Drake's sermon on side 1, band 1, of the record included in the unit, provides the students with an account of the drama surrounding Drake's voyage after an attempted mutiny. The students then turned to the problem of how the Queen was to deal with the Spanish menace. Explanations of two advisers—Lord Burghley and Sir Francis Walsingham—on their views concerning the Spanish threat provide the students with material for a debate on the possibility and desirability of war between England and Spain. Finally, King Philip II's, Queen Elizabeth's and Drake's positions on the antagonism developing between Spain and England give the students three points of view to be used in a classroom press conference where the three subjects are questioned as to the inevitability of war.

Objectives

This section entitled "High Dreams and Cold Cash" is designed to "introduce the students to the economic and political realities of trade and expansion in Elizabeth's time both from the point of view of a businessman and from that of adviser to the Queen." [3] The "investment game" using the dittomaster "Investments" and the four "prospectuses" gives the students an opportunity to step into the shoes of a businessman who had a certain amount of money (£400) to invest in any or all of four companies which were planning profitable voyages. To learn about the voyages and to complete their investment sheets the students read "The Accounts of the Voyages." Drake's sermon dramatizes the story of his voyage and provides the teacher with material for open-ended questions about his actions and capabilities as a captain: "Why did Drake insist that the gentlemen 'haul and draw' with the sailors? Would he have made the same statement to the London Court of nobles? Was Drake a wise or foolish leader of his men and why?"

The section on "How Shall the Queen Meet the Spanish Menace?" demonstrates the push and pull between liberal and conservative advisers, as well as the ultimate dependence they have upon the monarch's decision. The materials may be used as evidence to support each of two positions regarding the Spanish menace in a classroom debate.

"Is War Inevitable?" introduces the students to the relationship of subject to Queen during a time of crisis. In addition, this section hopefully will "develop in students a sophistication about why wars may not always be avoided, even when none of the parties wants to go to war." [4] The narratives on Philip, the Queen, and Drake are used in a classroom press conference where the students dramatize the views of these personages by asking questions. Notes taken at the conference provide the students with materials from which they write a news story or editorial from the point

---

3   Ibid., p. 22.
4   Ibid., p. 25.

of view of a subject of the Queen. As in the previous sections, . . . the underlying objective of the materials is to give the students the chance to use information from various sources and positions to come to some conclusions about the Queen—specifically, about her policies on matters of trade and expansion and the rift with Spain.

Regulars: Day 15.—The "Investments" sheets . . . and the prospectuses were handed out to the students to introduce them to a new section on economics and politics. These materials were designed to familiarize the students with the practices of businessmen who were involved in the trade and expansion of England. Each student was told he had £400 to invest in any or all of four companies which were undertaking voyages to expand British trading. The money was to be invested so that the investor would hopefully make the most profits. The students based their choices on the evidence found in each prospectus. Slips of paper stating the amount of money to be invested were placed in folders marked with the explorers' names. The students filled out the top half of the "Investments" sheets to keep as a record of their choices. A class summary of investments would be posted when all the investments had been made.

The regulars were involved in the task immediately and seemed to follow the assignment without difficulty. They responded well to the teacher's questions: "What would be an example of a piece of evidence which would influence your investment choices?"

Essentials: Day 16.—The same assignment was given and the same enthusiasm was prevalent although this class took longer to settle down to work. The students seemed to be confused about pounds and dollars and how they were to go about dividing the money up, but were more eager to use world wall maps than the regular class.

Regulars: Day 16.—The teacher gave a brief outline of the unit work to date and then the class divided up into groups of three, each group investing money in the company or companies of its choice. Each group was given £ 800 to invest and was required to explain its investments on the back of its "Investments" sheet.

Instead of putting four or five in a group as the unit authors suggested, the teacher felt that the smaller groups of three would work more effectively together. Earlier in the unit, the larger groups formed to discuss John White's Indian pictures. This plan did not succeed in promoting interaction. Instead each group relied on one or two to do the work. The groups of three formed were more successful, for not only was more expected of each member, but each member felt he could air his views more easily—there were fewer people with whom to compete.

The class had begun to lose interest in investing. One student exclaimed, "This ain't no fun, 'cause we don't really make no money." Nevertheless, they went through the motions without obvious signs of boredom.

Essentials: Day 17.—This class showed much more interest in the same assignment. Unlike the regular class, these students made good use of the wall maps, basing many of their investment choices on a comparison of the modern world maps with the explorers' drawings.

Regulars: Day 17, and Essentials: Day 18.—The classes spent some time reading about Sir Francis Drake. The teacher mentioned the significance of Drake's speech to his men, given after an attempted mutiny aboard ship. A number of questions about his speech were placed on the board before a recording of Drake's speech ... was played, and the students were asked to think about the questions as they listened. The teacher did not give the two classes dittoes of the speech, because she wanted the students to become aware of the difference in spoken English between the sixteenth century and the present day. After the record was played, the classes realized that the accent and use of words kept them from understanding what was being said; then, the teacher handed out dittoes and the speech was played again. This time the students in both classes followed along closely and were able to participate in the discussion which followed.

Regulars: Day 18.—The class spent the whole period tracing Drake's voyage around the world. Each student was given two maps—one of the eastern hemisphere and one of the western hemisphere—on which he located major places, e.g., the Spice Islands. ... The students in both classes had little knowledge of the world's geography and in most cases could not tell the difference between South America and Africa. Each student had an atlas and numerous wall maps to complete the assignment, but they found it difficult to relate one wall map to another. For example, one student asked where the wall map of Europe would be placed on the maps of the world. The students were not interested in using the narrative of Drake's voyage in the book to help complete the maps they had been given. The narrative was too complicated to use as a quick reference.

Essentials: Day 19.—Because the regular class had found the map work difficult, the teacher gave individual assignments to some students to find each of the several places included on the map. Each student showed the rest of the class where his geographical place was on a wall map of the world, and then the students completed the maps from the information they had collected. The assignment was completed by the end of the period and the students by using one wall map seemed less confused than the regular class.

Regulars: Day 19, and Essentials: Day 20.—The day was spent reading about Mr. Jenkinson's and Mr. Frobisher's voyages with a short discussion at the end of each class. The teacher asked a number of questions about the reading (e.g., "Why do you believe Frobisher's second and third voyages were unsuccessful?" and "How did religion influence Jenkinson's trip?") to see if the students could draw conclusions about the large amount of reading they had just finished. Discussions in the classes were similar. What the students could understand they could use, but more often than not the manner in which the selections were written impeded their ability to answer the questions.

Regulars: Day 20, and Essentials: Day 21.—The teacher gave out a worksheet to accompany the selections on John Hawkins' voyage to Guinea, Africa, and the West Indies. The task of reading the narratives silently was of more interest when the students could work with the story as they read it. It was important that the worksheet give problems which could not always be answered by just flipping pages. . . . (Those who read the materials did well and most of those who did not, failed.)

Regulars: Day 21, and Essentials: Day 22.—The teacher read "How Shall the Queen Meet the Spanish Menace?" and reviewed the part dealing with the opposing points of view of the Queen's chief advisers by making two lists on the blackboard—one for Lord Burghley's viewpoint and one for the opinions of Sir Walsingham. The students took notes on what was said in class, using the outline of the day's readings which the teacher had placed on the board.

Regulars: Day 22, and Essentials: Day 23.—The classes read silently "Is War Inevitable?" Each student was to pick one of the three articles on King Philip, Queen Elizabeth, and Sir Francis Drake, read it carefully, and prepare three questions which he would ask that person at a news conference the next day. The conference would be designed to question the three leaders about the possibility of war between England and Spain.

Students volunteered to play the parts of the three leaders. Because there were more interested people than parts available, one student suggested Lord Burghley and Sir Walsingham be questioned by the English reporters too. There was much excitement and the majority of the students in each class had prepared their questions before the period ended.

Regulars: Day 23.—The press conference began with the posing of a question to Sir Francis Drake by the teacher: "Mr. Drake, the Queen says she does not want war with Spain. You are her loyal subject. Why did you then steal from the Spanish ships?" The questioning continued around the room until every student had asked some member of the conference one question. Then the floor was open for questions. The reporters (all of the class not being questioned) had prepared good, provocative questions by and large, but the effectiveness of the conference was dependent on the knowledge of those who were being interviewed. Here, knowledge was uneven and those who had not learned their roles were chastised by the class who corrected their misinformation and pressed them when they were in doubt. Every student participated at one point or another during the period, and the class seemed to have a wonderful time.

The class had been instructed to take notes on the conference. These notes were to aid them in writing either an editorial or a news story discussing the conference. The assignment was due the next day.

Essentials: Day 24.—The news conference proceeded in the same fashion as in the regular class, with five speakers taking seats at the front of the room and the rest of the class posing questions as they took notes on the proceedings. The members of the panel were better prepared than those in the regular class, and there was heated debate over whether war was probable. The class also threw in a number of questions about King Philip's personal relationship to the Queen which added to the enjoyment of the conference, e.g., "King Philip, if you love Queen Elizabeth, why do you wish to upset her by persecuting the Dutch Protestants?"

The 40-minute period was not sufficient time to complete the conference, and the students asked that another day be reserved to complete the questions they wished to ask before they began their essays.

Essentials: Day 25.—During the first half of the period the class finished questioning the five panelists. Then the teacher gave a brief explanation of the difference between a news story and an editorial, and the class began work on their essays. (What essays the teacher received were written well on the whole, but more than half of the class did not hand in an assignment. Many of those who did not do the work were students who had never failed to hand in an assignment up until this time. When asked why they did not do it, they either shrugged their shoulders or said it was too difficult. The two reasons which the teacher feels were the causes were (1) that the students had not taken notes on the news conference while it was in progress and could not remember the proceedings well enough to write a report at home that night and (2) that they were not interested enough in the conference to draw conclusions on it, but rather only enjoyed the immediate excitement of role playing.)

THE CASE OF THE UNNAMED HEIR: WHEREIN THE QUEEN ACTS BUT DOES NOT ACT

Content

This section of the unit focuses on the dilemma of Queen Elizabeth as to what to do with Catholic Mary of Scotland, who was next in the line of succession to the English throne. The treatment of this problem is divided into three sections. The first is a historically accurate account of the execution of Mary, Queen of Scots. The second part is a narrative delineating the drama and characters which surround the series of events leading to Mary's execution. The third part includes descriptions of the plots and counterplots against Mary and Elizabeth.

Objectives

The purpose of this section is to clarify the problems of royal succession which had an effect on the political decisions of the Elizabethan period. These various materials illustrate the difficulties which Elizabeth had in making a political decision regarding succession and the ambiguity as to who was responsible for what followed Mary's death. The purpose of the report of the execution itself is to promote interest in the dilemma facing Elizabeth. The second section is concerned with "Who Shall Succeed?" and the final part raises the question "Who was responsible for Mary's death?" Descriptions of plots implicating both Mary and Elizabeth provide the sources which students use to help them decide on where the blame for Mary's death is to be laid.

Regulars: Day 24, and Essentials: Day 26.—The teacher read the introductory narrative about the actual execution of Mary, Queen of Scots. A discussion followed the reading in both classes. A number of questions were asked, e.g., "Why was Mary repulsed by Dr. Fletcher? What was the 'moment of human greatness amid the horror,' and why was it so called?" and the rest of the period in both classes was spent in lively discussion. At the end of each class the students were asked to decide who they felt was responsible for Mary's death. Everyone in the two classes claimed Elizabeth was the culprit.

Regulars: Day 25, and Essentials: Day 27.—The classes were asked to read Parts I and II of this section and write a paragraph answering the question, "Who do you feel was responsible for Mary's death?" The answer given must be backed up with evidence found in the materials covered in the pages studied for the past two days. The students were reminded of their response to the same question asked of them the previous day and were advised to take into account Part I as they wrote an answer.

The unit authors suggested that each class be divided into small groups which would make decisions as to who was responsible for Mary's death. The teacher did not follow this suggestion because from past experience she had realized that group work was not group work at all. Usually, one student took over the task set before all the members of the group. Also, in this case, there was a great deal of material which could be brought to bear on the question at hand, and it is difficult for these students to sift through complex sources, find the evidence they need to support their position, and present that evidence orally in a logical fashion. Unless there is a teacher at hand as a guide, the group work is useless.

The majority of the students finished the assignment without much difficulty, although many complained of not being able to understand some of the "Plots and Counterplots" in Part III. Also, many students wanted to know who *was* to blame and would not be satisfied with a noncommittal answer. Nevertheless, interest was maintained, and three of the better students in the class, upon suggestion from the teacher, decided to make up a list of Elizabeth's suitors and their qualifications for "marriageability." A separate column was to be included giving the reasons why Elizabeth married none of them. The list would be posted for all to see.

The "Singed Beard" Seeks Revenge: wherein the Queen meets Spain with the "heart and stomach of a king"

Content

The materials for this section focus on the war between Spain and England. The students begin by studying the plan outlined by King Philip to Medina Sidonia, Admiral of the Spanish Armada. Philip discusses both the invasion of England and the tactics to be employed. Based on Philip's original plan, there are a number of "Optional Readings" for students who wish to consider long-range factors when planning their own strategies—either English or Spanish. Among these optional materials are statistical charts and pictures of both navies, Spanish and English strategies suggested to the two rulers, and descriptions of the backgrounds and personalities of the Spanish naval captains. A descriptive map of Great Britain and a recorded debate between Philip and Elizabeth about the strength of their men and guns aid the students in planning their strategies. A large map of Great Britain and surrounding territories is used in the Spanish Armada game where the students play out their strategies.

For use in determining which side won the battles, the students are provided with an introduction, "The Spanish Armada, Who Won?," and a series of "Action Reports" of the sea battles between the two powers. The actual outcome of the war is summarized in the "Epilogue" with some suggestions as to how historians have gone about deciding who was the victor. A speech by Elizabeth to her people during the strife tells much about her policy as it does about the Armada conflict.

Objectives

The rather broad objectives of this section include "the political questions of monarch and subjects, of offense and defense, of diplomacy and technology, and of historiography." [5] Even though Elizabeth follows a policy of compromise, the unit authors wish to emphasize through study that this policy does not mean weakness or fear when one is threatened by another country. In addition, the authors hope that the student, when making decisions, will be encouraged to look beyond the courses of action he chooses to the possible results which might occur from that action. This kind of thinking would necessitate an "if-then" type of inquiry, designed to train the student to analyze the consequences of any action he might take.

Philip's plan must be followed when the student formulates his own strategy. If he picks the Spanish side, he will elaborate Philip's outline and give alterations to the original plan in case of unforeseen difficulties, e.g., a storm in the English Channel. If the student decides to side with the English, he must plan a defensive strategy based on his knowledge of Philip's orders. Philip's plan was included because (1) without it unrelated strategies were devised which were difficult to play out in the Armada game, and because (2) requiring the students to follow Philip's outline enabled them to experience the harsh limitations—and advantages—of a strong monarch commanding the operations.

The "Optional Readings," a strategy map, and record aid in the task of planning a strategy. With these aids the student can predict the major technological and geographical problems his side will face and plan his strategy accordingly.

The purpose of the Armada game is to give the students a chance to see their strategies at work. Two students—one for each side—move their ships around the map following their own plans. The rest of the class can challenge the moves of the players and, thus, draw on their own strategies.

The final section is a study of the usual combination of myth and fact

---

[5] Grambs, Fenton, and Fleischman, *Explanation and Guide*, p. 29.

which make up "historical" accounts of an event. The two action reports for each battle are designed to let the student devise his own theory as to the outcome as an historian would and see the inevitable prejudices to be found on both sides. The Queen's speech to her subjects at Tilbury merely draws attention to the policies of the Queen which led her country to war.

Regulars: Day 26, and Essentials: Day 28.—Both classes read Philip's letter to Medina Sidonia and "Tactics" silently, and discussion followed. The students were told to compile a folder of notes to help them plan a war strategy. To help them begin their notetaking—to help them see what was important to remember—the teacher wrote phrases on the board as questions about the readings were discussed. For instance, the teacher asked, "What suggestions does the king make as to ways of handling the mission?" The answers were jotted down by the students for later reference. Some are found below:

Aim guns low at the hull.
Attack at close quarters.
Keep the Armada together when fighting in the Channel.
Do not fight unless you are unable to complete your mission.

The teacher felt that just reading the plans and tactics of Philip was not enough. The students would have a difficult time drawing from the readings the points to be noted without actually noting them in writing. If they did find it easy to sift out the more important bits of information, they would be unlikely to recall them in the future. Too much information was included in these readings, and the sophisticated vocabulary and foreign topic left the student with no handle with which to grasp the significant points.

Regulars: Day 27, and Essentials: Day 29.—The students added to their notes a map of Great Britain . . . and a typed debate between Queen Elizabeth and Philip about the power of each side's ships. . . . After hearing the debate played on a record, the students were asked to predict the technological problems each side might face. The students enjoyed the record and came up with a long, imaginative list of strengths and weaknesses for each side.

Regulars: Days 28 and 29, and Essentials: Days 30 and 31.—The students in both classes spent two days preparing their strategies. Each strategy was to be written out in three parts: (1) The student was to pick a side; (2) he was to give the purpose of his side's mission; (3) he was to explain his plan of action (following Philip's basic outline), and include alternative plans in case of unforseen difficulties.

The teacher hoped that the students would read some of the "Optional Readings" to supplement their notes, but she found that most students did not want to tackle the written materials and rather turned only to the statistics on ships, men, and guns, and the pictures of the vessels.

Many students had difficulty knowing where to begin the task of writing a strategy. Unless told exactly what to do or questioned individually, the students rarely were able to create an organized strategy based on hypothetical problems.

Regulars: Day 30.—Due to an assembly day, a weekend and a school riot, the class was unable to play the Armada game until four days after they had completed their strategies. By then, much interest had been lost and it was both difficult to find two students willing to play and difficult to get the other students to question the players' moves intelligently. There was general boredom and confusion, even though a list of the rules for the game had been given each student beforehand and the teacher had explained the purpose of the game as best she could. The students seemed little interested in make-believe games, especially when there was no immediate reward for their participation.

Nevertheless, one day was spent playing the Armada game, and once the game was begun interest grew. Problems arose over what was to be considered a move; e.g., Could the whole fleet move, or only one ship? How far could a ship move on one turn? In addition, each player had done little reading on his country and could not, therefore, take advantage of additional information which might have helped his tactics and explained his moves. The teacher continually reminded students of basic information they had to have in order to play. For instance, the Spanish player had difficulty remembering what his mission was and never did reach the Duke of Parma and his armies.

The teacher felt that no one student knew the rules well enough to judge the game, so she took that role. She found it hard to decide under what circumstances a ship was sunk and what constituted a move, but the game moved along well. Although many students took an active interest, their interest was based on an excitement over trying to outmaneuver the enemy during the battle rather than trying to complete their mission in light of the information they had gathered about their opponent and about their own situation. The game could have been played with the same results without the two days having been spent on creating strategies.

Essentials: Day 32.—The essentials class was bothered by the same interruptions as the regulars and had much the same response to the Armada game when they finally began to play.

But more students participated in the game than in the regular class, and within ten minutes each side had at least three players. Much time was spent laboring over each move, and the game was not completed when the dismissal bell rang. The judge's decisions were challenged many times and the reading sources were often used in the discussion.

Interest was sustained through the entire period and a number of students requested that the game be continued the rest of the week. But in general, as in the regular class, the game had been "played out" and any additional time spent on it would only be repetitive and boring for most of both classes.

At the end of the day the teacher had a feeling of frustration concerning the day's activities. The students seemed to be going through the motions of doing what was required with little spontaneity or curiosity about the tasks set before them. The Armada game more than any other task seemed to be one which could promote interest because it centered on war and enabled the students to take the lead. Nevertheless, few students were interested and when they were, their questions rarely were formulated on the basis of the information they were to have gathered.

Regulars: Day 31, and Essentials: Day 33.—Both classes read "The Spanish Armada, Who Won?: Prologue" and discussed the first action reports describing a battle between the Spanish and English off Portland Bill, England. The Spanish and English accounts were outlined side by side and then the differences marked. The language used in the accounts had to be reworded in almost every sentence and the discussion was bogged down in dry explanations.

Regulars: Day 32, and Essentials: Day 34.—The classes spent the period discovering differences between each set of action reports and then for each deciding who won. Many of the differences in the action reports were too subtle or picayune for the students to grasp. The language was a continuous barrier. The majority of the students in both classes did not complete more than three of the battle comparisons.

Regulars: Day 33, and Essentials: Day 35.—The students read the "Epilogue" and listened to Queen Elizabeth's speech to her subjects during the Armada battle. Then they answered questions about these materials on a worksheet. Because the materials studied were not lengthy and were varied, interest was maintained and the worksheets completed. (Yet there was a general lessening of interest, and a number of students asked, hopefully, if this were the last booklet.)

Regulars: Day 34, and Essentials: Day 36.—The classes spent the period drawing pictures (1) of the clan formation of the Spanish ships during the battle, (2) the different size and shooting power of the two countries' ships, and (3) the boarding power of the two countries, using grappling tactics. The students could draw one picture showing all three things or three separate pictures. Each picture had to be labeled, and the papers would be graded on how clearly the pictures were explained through drawing neatness (which did not mean artistry) and the written explanations. Once the students saw how poorly the teacher drew and that artistry was not important, they settled down to work eagerly.

This task was not a suggestion of the unit authors, but the teacher felt the students needed a change from the normal routine followed throughout this course of study—namely, dealing with sophisticated reading materials.

The purpose of this task was to see if the students could transfer a written word, a definition, or an idea into picture form. For instance, some students had no idea of how to show the difference in size between the English and Spanish ships. Upon questioning them to find out if they first of all knew which ship was larger in every instance the students answered correctly. Then the teacher merely had to ask, "How would you show that in a picture?" and they were on their way. The students, when led by the teacher through what seemed to be obvious steps, work much better than if no verbal explanation of an assignment were given, however clear that written assignment may have been.

At this point in the course of study it must be mentioned that the teacher skipped the next two major sections moving to the last topic, "From Scotland Comes a King." The sections eliminated were: "Patents, Parliaments and Prerogatives: wherein the Queen gets by giving," and "What is the Queen's Policy?: wherein King James is advised on his new Kingdom."

These sections were eliminated for a number of reasons. The material itself did not seem to the teacher to add any new insights about the Queen. The classes were restless and responded negatively to the teacher's explanation of what followed the section on the Spanish Armada. Since Martin Luther King's death many students have insisted that the classes study Negro history, and students have already started bringing into class books on Africa. Many students who normally turn in their assignments, have half-heartedly done the work and some have quit participating altogether.

Students were becoming bored with the topic and frustrated with the prospect of having to plough through additional primary sources. The teacher felt the effectiveness of the unit up to this point would be negated if the course of study was to continue at any great length.

Therefore, the teacher decided to move on to the last section which deals with the problems faced by the new king, James I. A comparison of the policies and personalities of Elizabeth and James would be a good way of both leaving open the question of the future of England under new rulers and ending the unit on Elizabeth's reign.

FROM SCOTLAND COMES A KING: WHEREIN THE QUEEN'S REIGN IS BETTER UNDERSTOOD

Content

Included in this section are a briefing of King James on his new kingdom, an introductory narrative, a speech to the English judges, and eight newsletters telling of successes and failures of his reign. The introductory narrative was the only material used by the teacher.

Objectives

All the materials for this section focus on the question of how James would deal with the problems he would face as king and how his approach differed from Elizabeth's. The general narrative discussed James' move to the throne, his personality, and outlines some of the problems he was to face. The students were to use this narrative as the basis for the study of some of the issues and events which took place during his reign.

Regulars: Day 35, and Essentials: Day 37.—The two classes followed along as the teacher read the introductory narrative on James I aloud. Then a discussion followed, centering on three questions placed on the board: "(1) What do you think will be the greatest problems James will have to face? Why? (2) In what ways are James and Elizabeth alike? and do they differ? (3) Compare ways in which James and Elizabeth would go about solving the problems we discussed above."

The discussion in both classes went well, yet it was difficult to get all the students involved. A couple of students led the discussions in both classes.

Disinterest with the materials was setting in and the teacher decided that it was time to call a halt to the unit and hope that, the students' evaluations of the unit would not reflect their disenchantment.

PART IV

Implementation

CHAPTER X

The Regional Educational Laboratories and the Research and Development Centers

18   FRANCIS S. CHASE

Excerpts from "Educational Research and Development: Promise or Mirage?" *

Because education has lacked strong and closely linked communities for the production, transmission, and utilization of knowledge relevant to its functions and objectives, it has found it difficult to respond to the increased demands made upon it as a result of rapid transformations in culture and society. To remedy this lack—or to make a beginning in that direction—the Research and Development Center Program was established in 1963 under the Cooperative Research Act. According to a recent position paper of the Office of Education's Division of Educational Laboratories, this action was a response to three major concerns: (1) the small scale and fragmentary nature of previous educational research and devel-

---

*   Originally published in the *Journal of Research and Development in Education*, Autumn, 1968.

opment, (2) the gap between research and practice, and (3) the failure to attract to education the necessary research resources from behavioral sciences and other disciplines. Following the passage of the Elementary and Secondary Education Act of 1965, Regional Educational Laboratories were funded to provide another link in the knowledge-into-practice chain. Implicit in the decision to establish the new Centers in universities (and later the Regional Educational Laboratories) was the hope that the union of research and development might prove as productive in education as in other fields.

Basic Responsibilities of R & D Centers

A Research and Development Center may begin by scrutinizing needs identified by data from the census and other investigations. From the array of needs thus presented, the Center can then select for close examination those lying within its sphere of operation for which staff capability exists or can be developed. By some such process, the nine Centers have committed themselves to intervention focused on particular institutions or systems within the educational enterprise. In so doing they accept responsibilities for:

1. Continuing assessment of the situation or system which is the object of intervention in order (a) to identify functions to which operations are addressed (both nominally and actually); (b) to determine adequacy of performance relative to needs and resources; (c) to reveal operational problems, including those incident to intervention; and (d) to measure changes in the system.
2. A continuing search for knowledge relevant to the problems to be solved and a persisting attempt to draw inferences which may be treated as testable hypotheses and/or incorporated into the design of experimental models or systems.
3. Discriminating choice (and continuing reconsideration) of intervention strategies and the application of the strategies to decisions on (a) scope and sequence of activities, (b) persons and agencies to be involved in various phases and stages, and (c) tactics to be employed in initiating and reinforcing constructive change.
4. Identification and/or formulation of theoretical models or systems to perform stated functions; design of components or elements as required to move from conceptual to working models; and assembly of components into consistent systems to permit reciprocal action conducive to the functions to be performed.
5. Rigorous testing of the working model or system in laboratory situations to reveal malfunctioning, unsolved problems, and undesired side-effects; refinement and redesign as needed to correct defects and increase power and efficiency; and further testing under a variety of field situations to

gauge performance more precisely, to reveal modifications required by characteristics of the population served and other variations in situations.

6. Progressive precision in specification of intended effects and the resources and processes necessary to produce the desired effects; and careful analysis of the yields or benefits of the new or revised system under specified conditions, and of the measures and costs involved in maintaining the specified conditions.

SHARED FUNCTIONS

Some of the responsibilities enumerated, such as those in item six, may be shared with other institutions such as the Regional Educational Laboratories. Electronic, communications, data processing and other corporations which are producing educational media and materials may also play a part. There are other processes and tasks essential to educational research and development which lie at least partly outside the functions for which universities seem well adapted. Among these are:

7. Diffusion of tested innovations and systems through collaborative relationships with schools, colleges, and other agencies to promote installation, effective use, and continuing evaluation.

8. Continuous monitoring to ascertain full range of effects and discover inadequacies in design and other causes of unsatisfactory performance; and utilization of research, evaluation, and feedback from users and observers to modify, complement, and/or replace systems as new needs appear or as higher levels of performance are required.

9. Employment of appropriate research technologies at every stage to (a) fill gaps in knowledge, (b) reveal relationships among system components and other variables, and (c) evaluate the achievement of objectives and associated effects.

10. Development of communication systems and dissemination strategies which expose to the general public, and to audiences with specialized competencies for various types of operations, the bases for each of the crucial decisions and the consequences of the decisions.

Linkage with Educational Laboratories in some cases may relieve the university Centers of the major burdens for diffusion and continuous monitoring. In such cases it is important that the Centers concerned receive any feedback which has a bearing on theoretical formulations or research so that they may continue to fill gaps in the research and revise theories to provide better guidance for subsequent research and development. Responsibility for dissemination may be discharged in part by Laboratories and associated agencies; but a Center has a major responsibility for dissemination through publication and through the training of personnel for effective participation in programmatic research and development.

PERFORMANCE, PROSPECTS, AND PROBLEMS

The union of research and development in education holds promise for important contributions to (1) reconstruction of educational institutions, so that they become more responsive to social needs, (2) advancement of technologies of instruction, management, and problem-solving, and (3) progressive modification of materials and procedures to meet emerging or previously unmet needs. This promise is more likely to be realized through a linkage of a number of research, development, and operating agencies than through monolithic organizations. However, it is essential that concentrations of resources be brought to bear on sharply defined problems without losing sight of the broad context of educational operations.

University Centers for Educational Research and Development may prove valuable contributors to research and development by making the most of the university setting and such characteristics as: (1) the university's functioning as an educational (teaching) institution; (2) the presence of able scholars in biological, behavioral, and physical sciences, many of whom are conducting studies potentially relevant to education; (3) the increasing tendency to pursue problems *across* as well as within disciplinary boundaries; (4) the capacity to add to knowledge through the use of rigorous paradigms and, occasionally, to provide reconstructive or revolutionary knowledge by breaking away from paradigms as they prove inadequate; [1] and (5) the university's dual role as a critic of society and a producer of knowledge for its reconstruction.

There are a number of problems to be overcome if the developmental aspects are not to be neglected. Some of these problems are incident to fitting large research and development operations into a structure where collegial (faculty) controls are operative. A related problem is that traditional university criteria for appointment and promotion may not be easily applicable to developmental contributions. More crucial may be the tendency of universities to foster a low pressure idiosyncratic approach to problem-solving and a corresponding failure to generate a sense of urgency, which some observers believe important to effective research and development. Moreover, university traditions tend to favor letting new knowledge find its own applications after being communicated through publication and teaching. Finally, Research and Development Centers may alter the character of the host institutions. By careful planning, this last problem might be managed so as to make the university more adaptive and responsive, thus producing benefits for the university and society.

---

[1] *See* Thomas S. Kuhn, *The Structure of Scientific Revolutions* (Chicago: University of Chicago Press, 1962).

One thoughtful and informed advocate of educational research and development has suggested that the Centers ought to be judged on their contribution to three purposes:

1. To bring to bear on educational problems the insights, investigative techniques and constructive talents of a variety of supportive disciplines and related professions *as well as* those of the education profession itself.
2. To tackle problems which, because of their complexity or long-range nature, require persistent and sustained effort by teams of persons with varied inputs to make.
3. To improve continuity in the progression for exploratory research through applied research, design and development of practical prototype models, in order to accelerate or expedite improvement in educational practice.[2]

Conclusion

The evidence to date indicates that the nine Centers are making modest but significant additions to the body of knowledge available for construction of curricula, modification of learning environments, individualization of instruction, improvement of teaching-learning processes and institutional reconstruction. With each addition to knowledge, they are also exposing new gaps to be filled. In this way, and by demonstrating the relevance of research to educational reform, the Centers are giving impetus to supplementary research in their own and other universities. They also are providing model and prototypic systems or programs for further development by Regional Educational Laboratories. It is notable, for example, that several of the Laboratories are utilizing to good effect such systems as Individually Prescribed Instruction, Micro-Teaching, and Bilingual Instruction which were carried through the initial stages of development by university Research and Development Centers; and it is likewise worth noting that the most successful Center operations are based on antecedent research, both basic and problem-oriented. The Centers, therefore, perform important functions in the adaptation of knowledge to educational practice, primarily through programmatic or product-oriented research; and at the same time they help to stimulate disciplinary research relevant to education, further product development and testing by other agencies, and diffusion of new ideas and systems. Yet, it must be added that improvements in enabling legislation, funding, management, and processes of investigation, development, and diffusion are still needed to assure the conditions essential to sustained advance in educational practice.

---

[2] Steele Gow, "Criteria for Appraising Educational R & D Centers," paper prepared for American Association of School Administrators, Atlantic City, N.J. February 13, 1967.

Directory of Research and Development Centers

WISCONSIN RESEARCH AND DEVELOPMENT CENTER FOR COGNITIVE LEARNING
Headquarters: The University of Wisconsin, 1404 Regent St., Madison, Wisconsin 53706
Director: Herbert J. Klausmeier

This Center focuses on improving educational practices related to cognitive learning. The Center's major research and development effort focus on three programs: research in laboratories and schools on learning and instruction; development of instructional systems in reading, English, mathematics, science, and other subjects; development of an improved learning environment.

The strategy for research and development is comprehensive, including basic research to generate new theory about learning, the development of research-based products for school use, and the testing and refining of the products in school settings. The specific instructional components to be researched and developed originate through the cooperative efforts of school people, subject matter specialists, and behavioral scientists.

As new knowledge is generated, it is communicated to educators and developed into instructional systems soundly based on the best knowledge of subject matter and cognitive learning.

Sociologists, psychologists, curriculum specialists, and subject matter specialists make up the interdisciplinary staff of researchers at the Center.

RESEARCH AND DEVELOPMENT CENTER IN EDUCATIONAL STIMULATION
Headquarters: Fain Hall, University of Georgia, Athens, Ga. 30601
Directors: Warren G. Findley and Joseph A. Williams

This Research and Development Center at the University of Georgia is evaluating early and continuous stimulation of intellectual development for "persistent effects." A longitudinal study of early schooling, beginning at age 3 and extending through age 12, is being conducted with the cross section of a county's population representative of the national population. Curriculum materials and methods, assembled or developed by program staffs for seven subject areas, are being refined by a systems approach in the Center's study and in smaller rural and urban disadvantaged communities. The cooperation between home, school, and community is being studied, with evidence of positive or negative side effects on children's social and emotional development. The aim is increased student achievement and higher norms of learning, as well as a description of materials, methods, evaluation procedures, and school organization helpful to educational achievement.

LEARNING RESEARCH AND DEVELOPMENT CENTER

Headquarters: University of Pittsburgh, Pittsburgh, Pa. 15213
Director: Robert Glaser

The Learning Research and Development Center is engaged in the study of the problems of learning and instruction. Particular attention is paid to the educational and psychological environment required to help the individual realize his full potential. The Center's activities range from basic theoretical studies of materials and equipment for instruction to the development of education programs in school settings.

The Center has four major programs. In the Basic Learning Studies Program, research is conducted on learning that may be basic to the development of instructional materials and procedures. The Computer Assisted Instruction Studies Programs conducts research and development on computer-assisted instruction systems. A third program, Field Research, is oriented toward basic problems in educational and psychological measurement, including activities in curriculum evaluation and the assessment of the effects of socio-psychological variables on learning outcomes. The primary emphasis of the fourth program, Experimental School Development, is to develop, test, revise, and study new educational procedures, with particular focus on school situations which are highly responsive and adaptive to the requirements of the individual learner.

Overall, the Center's four program areas work toward an integrated research and development setting where each of the program areas can contribute to the work of the other.

CENTER FOR THE ADVANCED STUDY OF EDUCATIONAL ADMINISTRATION

Headquarters: University of Oregon, Eugene, Oregon 97403
Director: Max G. Abbott

The focus of the Center for the Advanced Study of Educational Administration is on the organization and administration of instructional change, especially for public elementary and secondary education in the United States.

The Center is developing organizational and administrative arrangements for the education that can accommodate rapidly changing instructional techniques, strategies, and goals. This objective is based on three major premises: (1) that increasingly sophisticated research on instructional processes, the psychology and social psychology of human learning, and curriculum design will produce revolutionary teaching procedures in the next 30 years; (2) that existing school organizational administrative practices may not be suited to the emerging instructional techniques; and (3) that the absence of appropriate organizational and administrative arrangements can seriously hamper the introduction of new instructional procedures or limit their utility once they are introduced.

RESEARCH AND DEVELOPMENT CENTER FOR TEACHER EDUCATION

Headquarters: The University of Texas, Austin, Texas 78712
Director: Robert F. Peck

The program of this Center has two major aims:
1. Basic research on the effects of various kinds of teacher education on actual teaching behavior; and research on the effects of such teaching behavior on child learning.

2. The development of a teacher education system with an array of small instructional components or "modules." In different combinations, such modules can be used in a flexible, often individualized manner for many kinds of teacher education. When any one module is ready for testing, it can be tried out in several institutions, both before and after adoption.

STANFORD CENTER FOR RESEARCH AND DEVELOPMENT IN TEACHING

Headquarters: Stanford University, 770 Welch Road, Palo Alto, California 94305
Director: Leland D. Medsker

The central purpose of this Center is to assist individuals and organizations responsible for American higher education to improve the quality, efficiency, and availability of education beyond high school. The goal requires research and development activities that take into account the diversity both of students and institutions that comprise higher education. The Center focuses on educational impact and student development (six projects), the viability of institutional structures and functions (twelve projects), an integrated developmental program (seven projects), and development of research instruments (one project). An extensive program dealing with problems of the university in an urban society is scheduled for early 1969.

CENTER FOR THE STUDY OF EVALUATION OF INSTRUCTIONAL PROGRAMS

Headquarters: University of California, Los Angeles, Calif. 90024
Directors: Merlin C. Wittrock and Erick L. Lindman

A major goal of this Center is to develop and field test evaluation systems useful to teachers, school administrators, and boards of education. This

Center's focus is on the study of evaluation of instructional programs, including the concept and theory of evaluation, the instruments and methods for evaluation, and the practice of evaluation at all educational levels. This evaluation is considered in simple and complex settings with a broad range of educational objectives and social consequences.

The Center has organized its research program around five kinds of variables important to evaluation. These include programs on the evaluation of classroom instruction, evaluation of the effects of individual contexts, the evaluation of the effects of organizational contexts, individual criteria, and organizational criteria.

CENTER FOR THE STUDY OF SOCIAL ORGANIZATION OF SCHOOLS AND THE LEARNING PROCESS

Headquarters: The Johns Hopkins University, Baltimore, Md. 21218
Director: Edward L. McDill

At the request of the United States Office of Education, the Center's efforts during the first year were concentrated on the general problem of school desegregation and its effects on students of varying racial and ethnic backgrounds. In its second year, the Center has organized its effort into four major research and development programs which conduct investigations on different aspects of the problem. These programs extend from the classroom to education at the national level, encompassing not only the practical effects of the social organization of schools on learning but also the mechanisms through which these effects take place. Studies are exploring various organizational and administrative arrangements and scheduling, the racial and socio-economic integration of schools, informal social structures among students and teachers, organizational patterns throughout school systems, and the relations between levels of education. Other work of the Center focuses on linguistic and cognitive development of students, particularly those aspects of the learning process which are likely to respond to differing educational and social contexts. The Center seeks to develop innovations in organization and curriculum, and to communicate its findings to pertinent institutions. Most of the Center's activities will result in policy implications and educational innovations to affect the learning of socially-disadvantaged children.

FRANCIS S. CHASE [*]

The Distinctive Roles of Educational Laboratories

Twenty Regional Educational Laboratories, authorized under Title IV of the Elementary and Secondary Education Act of 1965, have become operative since April, 1966. These new institutions are nonprofit corporations under governance of boards drawn from more or less definitive geographic areas; and are oriented toward conditions and problems which characterize education in their respective regions; but collectively they carry what is in effect a national mandate to raise the quality of educational performance as rapidly as possible through bringing the full power of modern knowledge and technology into the service of educational purposes.

A year ago most of the Laboratories were taking their first uncertain steps to the accompaniment of a barrage of suggestions and criticisms from well-wishers and doubters. Today most of them move with reassuring firmness of purpose toward the discharge of functions which are essential to the effectiveness of other agencies, but for which universities, colleges, schools and state departments of education are not well adapted. As a result the Laboratories are beginning to emerge as institutions performing distinctive functions in the field of education.

The several Laboratories differ widely in their choice of objectives and strategies and in the types of programs sponsored; but all are creating mechanisms and processes to make the fruits of theory, research, and invention readily available to educational practitioners. They are learning to specify with increased precision the kinds of changes to which their efforts are directed, the instrumentalities and the stages through which the ends are to be attained, and the approximate inputs of time, talent, and other resources required for goal achievement. Thus, they are beginning to close the gaps that have separated discovery of knowledge and invention of techniques from widespread use in education.

The Laboratories tend to look to universities and other research organizations for basic theory and research relevant to their purposes, and to various sources—including Research and Development Centers, curriculum projects, etc.,—for theoretical models or prototypes which they can test and adapt to educational uses under a variety of situations. In the latter

---

[*] CAREL *Speaker*, Central Atlantic Regional Educational Laboratory, No. 1, February, 1968.

stages of development, field testing, and demonstration, the Laboratories link up with state departments of education and with schools and community organizations through Title III projects and otherwise. Although they depend heavily on other agencies at both ends of the research-into-practice chain, the Laboratories are accepting a large measure of responsibility for linking the whole series of processes ranging from discovery and codification through field testing and adaptation to widespread installation and use.

Feedback from the development activities of the Laboratories may enable scholars in universities and elsewhere to become aware of theoretical inadequacies and the need for research to fill gaps in the knowledge which they are supplying. Demonstrations of how new knowledge and technologies can be incorporated into functioning systems may provide state educational agencies with specifications of the conditions essential to realize optimal educational effects, thus providing bases for more effective advisory and regulatory services. Through experimentation in modifying the behavior of teachers and other educational personnel, the Laboratories promise to make important contributions to both the early and continuing education of teachers; and through identification of the resources and measures necessary to achieve specific educational goals, they may offer sounder bases for the decisions of educational administrators and boards.

The operation of the Laboratories offers promise, therefore, of strengthening state departments of education, schools, colleges, and universities in the performance of their own primary functions by promoting mutually beneficial reciprocal interactions and by facilitating the flow and counterflow of information among discoverers, inventors, producers, appliers, and consumers of knowledge and technology applicable to education. Although the several Laboratories differ in the extent to which they exemplify the indicated developmental and facilitating roles, many of them already are offering convincing demonstrations of the possibilities; and others are moving rapidly to assume and discharge the functions implied.

In general, the approaches used by the Laboratories are consistent with the concept of schools and other educational organizations as open social systems, operating within the enveloping social systems of community, state, and nation, and interacting with complementary systems such as health, employment, religious, welfare, and youth organizations. The school itself is visualized as composed of sub-systems which interact with each other more or less harmoniously and effectively. The curriculum, for example, is viewed as a system or mechanism for regulating learning environments so as to facilitate the attainment of specified and agreed upon educational objectives.

A Variety of Approaches

Activities in which the Laboratories are engaged reflect a variety of approaches, including:

1. *A Systems Approach to Curriculum Building.*—The concept, as indicated above, is that the curriculum is a system for generating and reinforcing behaviors which eventuate in added skills, new perceptions, and increased capacity to direct future experience. The effort of the Laboratories is directed toward modifying such components of the curriculum system as instructional materials, teacher behaviors, sequence of activities, time allocations, social interactions, evaluation and reinforcement. The usual procedure is the identification of a need such as the development of problem-solving ability or the elimination of serious deficiencies in mathematics or reading as a basis for the setting of a series of tasks. The initial task may be defined as the development of a prototypic program which will enable all children, or all in a particular population, to acquire a reading vocabulary of a specified number of words or a specified performance level in mathematics within given time periods. (A saving of time and Laboratory resources is possible when a suitable model or prototype emerges from the work of other research and development agencies.) The next task may be the progressive modification and testing of the program under a variety of conditions. A third step may be working with state departments of education, local school systems, teacher training agencies, and producers of educational products to facilitate widespread use of the improved materials and techniques. A further step will be the continuing modification of materials and processes in the light of careful evaluation and feedback from users. The process used in some of the Laboratories resembles such national curriculum projects as SMSG, BSCS, and PSSC in the development of "packages" of instructional materials and in recognition of the necessity for teacher education; but may make more systematic provision for the continuing improvement and adaptation of all the components in the learning situation until objectives are achieved in a satisfactory manner.

2. *Diagnosis of Individual Needs as a Basis for Individualizing Instruction.*—The concept of "Individually Prescribed Instruction"—worked out at the University of Pittsburgh Learning Research and Development Center, under the direction of Robert Glaser—is receiving further development and refinement through tryouts in several school systems. Attention is being given to the improvement of evaluative instruments and procedures and to identification of effective approaches to the training of teachers, as well as to revealing what data are essential in prescribing for

learning needs and how much gain in pupil achievement may be expected under given conditions.

3. *The Progressive Modification of Teacher Behavior through Intensive Experiences in Laboratory and Clinical Situations.*—Several Laboratories are using the technique of micro-teaching as pioneered by Stanford University. Video tapes of teacher performance make it possible for the teacher to analyze his own behaviors and compare himself with master teachers. Another approach is the use of instruments such as the Flanders Interaction Analysis Scale. Many other avenues are being explored in an effort to find effective ways of helping teachers acquire and practice behaviors relevant to specified educational objectives and consonant with such roles as promoters of individual inquiry. A number of the Laboratories are attempting to train leaders who will assume responsibility for the training of others in specific techniques or to prepare them for the continuing education of teachers as needs for changed attitudes and new skills appear.

4. *The Use of Linguistic Analysis and Anthropological Theory to Adapt Curriculum and Instruction for Learners from Differentiated Cultures.*—Several Laboratories are employing linguists and anthropologists as consultants or regular staff members in adapting materials and methods of instruction in the language arts to those from non-English speaking families or cultures which deviate appreciably from the standard American middle-class culture. Among the groups to which attention is being given are Mexican-Americans and other Spanish speaking populations, those from Indian tribal cultures, Eskimos, impoverished rural migrants in urban ghettoes, and isolated hill folk.

5. *Widespread Community Involvement in Changing Factors Detrimental to Learning and Enhancing Positive Factors.*—An essentially sociological approach treats the school as a social institution which can be effective only as it is reinforced and complemented by other institutions which determine values and expectations for work, social conduct, and education. Instead of trying to protect the school from outside influences, effort is exerted to make the school a vital influence in the life of the neighborhood and the larger community, to involve parents and other citizens in decisions affecting education, and to help pupils integrate the experiences of home, street, and total culture through the school.

6. *Applying the Full Potentials of Communications Technology and Mobile Equipment to Improving the Quality of Education for Those*

Living in Impoverished Conditions with Meager Cultural Resources.— The establishment of resource centers or educational cooperatives where a rich variety of resources are brought together and made accessible to children from isolated rural communities or from city slums is one form of enrichment. Another is to take master teachers into each classroom through television, films, and video tapes. Other resources include mobile shops, traveling libraries, portable museums, and helping teachers.

7. *The Application of Sophisticated Information Processing Technologies to Educational Decisions and to Instruction.*—Experimentation is going forward in the use of computers to store, analyze, and retrieve data which will inform decisions on school location and construction, personnel policies, and instructional technologies. Decisions regarding programming for individual needs, differentiation for various purposes, and choice of instructional materials and methods are also being subjected to modern technologies of information processing. Education itself is being perceived in part as a process of information processing and the uses of computers to help learners become more adept in their own processing of data is being explored.

The approaches described are used more often in combination than singly. The systems approach to curriculum may, and often does, utilize anthropological and linguistic scholarship; individualized instruction may be advanced through use of modern media and technologies of communication; and the achievement of particular objectives may be sought through a combination of many, or all, of the seven approaches.

FIVE PROGRAM CATEGORIES

The five-fold category of programs set up by the Laboratory Branch of the Office of Education offers a contrasting and supplementary view of Laboratory activities:

1. Programs which emphasize the improvement of the curriculum by developing new materials and instructional methods for teaching all students.

These programs include:
programs of the Southwest Regional Educational Laboratory in Inglewood, California, (1) to develop research-based and classroom tested instructional materials and methods to teach children in kindergarten and the first three grades to read, to write, to speak, and to listen; and (2) to develop a new curriculum to teach children at the kindergarten through fourth-grade level strategies for solving verbal and non-verbal problems; a program of the Central Midwestern Regional Educational Laboratory in St. Louis, Missouri, to develop a comprehensive curriculum in mathe-

matics for grades K-12, based on previous work in the School Mathematics Study Group;

the program on Individually Prescribed Instructional Program carried on by Research for Better Schools, the Laboratory in Philadelphia, to field test and further develop a system of instruction for the elementary school which prescribes each child's daily learning experiences according to diagnoses of his individual needs;

a program of the Rocky Mountain Regional Educational Laboratory in Greeley, Colorado, to develop materials for the pre-vocational, vocational and training programs of secondary schools;

a program of the Central Atlantic Regional Education Laboratory in Washington, D.C., to specify objectives for arts and humanities instruction in the elementary schools and design curriculum activities to reach those objectives.

2. Programs which emphasize the improvement of education offered to particular student populations, by developing new materials and techniques.

These programs include:

programs of the Southwest Educational Development Laboratory in Austin, Texas, (1) to create a curriculum in language and reading to equip elementary Mexican-American, French-American, and Negro children with communication skills in standard English, and (2) to create a model elementary school for migrant students;

a program of the Southwestern Cooperative Educational Laboratory in Albuquerque, New Mexico, to develop materials to improve the skills necessary for Indian and Mexican-American children to learn to read;

a program of the Southeastern Educational Laboratory in Hapeville, Georgia, to demonstrate ways of teaching basic skills to and enhancing the motivation and self-concept of deprived Negro youngsters;

a program of the South Central Regional Educational Laboratory in Little Rock, Arkansas, to develop materials, combinations of compensatory practices, and evaluation instruments appropriate for teaching Negro, Indian, and other culturally disadvantaged children.

a program of the Center for Urban Education in New York to develop, field test, and adapt curriculum materials in reading, mathematics, sciences, social studies, and linguistics to schools in the urban ghetto;

a program of Appalachia Educational Laboratory in Charleston, West Virginia, to compensate for the shortage of guidance and counseling personnel by developing self-administering instructional kits for rural youth to enable them to learn about the world of work and to make informed vocational decisions.

3. Programs which emphasize the development of the skills of teach-

ers and other educational personnel to enable them to utilize new materials, new methods, and new behaviors.

These programs include:

a program of the Far West Laboratory for Educational Research and Development in San Francisco, California, to develop "micro-teaching" packages to train experienced teachers in the use of specialized teaching skills like questioning techniques, use of verbal reinforcement, and classroom management;

a program of the Northwest Regional Educational Laboratory to train teachers and administrators to develop students' skills of inquiry, and to become skilled analysts of classroom interaction;

a program of the Michigan-Ohio Regional Educational Laboratory in Detroit, Michigan, to combine techniques that have been used singly for training teachers and to assess the effectiveness of this combination under different conditions in schools;

a program of the Mid-Continent Educational Laboratory in Kansas City, Missouri, to develop means of training teachers to foster self-directed learning in their students;

a program of the Regional Educational Laboratory for the Carolinas and St. Paul, Minnesota, to develop a model of teacher training which ties pre-service and in-service preparation more closely together;

a program of the Regional Educational Laboratory for the Carolinas and Virginia, in Durham, North Carolina, to utilize ETV broadcasts to train teachers in a large geographic area to teach new mathematics curricula;

a program of the Eastern Regional Institute for Education in Syracuse, New York, to train teachers in 20 elementary schools to utilize *Science, a Process Approach*, a curriculum developed by the American Association for the Advancement of Science, and to explore how the curriculum, the training program, and the varying conditions of the school all affects students' learning.

4. Programs which emphasize the development and application of technology to facilitate the management of classroom instruction, the process of instruction, and the management of school systems.

These programs include:

programs of the Southwest Educational Development Laboratory and the Northwest Regional Educational Laboratory to familiarize teachers and administrators with and to train them in the applications of computer technology in education;

a program of the Central Midwestern Regional Educational Laboratory to demonstrate and field-test a system of computer-assisted instruction in arithmetic developed by Patrick Suppes at Stanford, California;

programs of the Southwest Regional Educational Laboratory (1) to design a computer-based budget-planning system for school administrators, and (2) to design a classroom management system that enables the teacher to monitor student progress, diagnose individual learning difficulties, and select remedial materials;

a program of the Northwest Regional Educational Laboratory to train secondary students in computer technology through the development of curriculum in programming and systems analysis, and to familiarize all students with general uses of computers and their social implications.

5. Programs which emphasize the development of new forms of school organization, including new roles for educational personnel, and programs to develop new forms of relationships between schools and communities.

These programs include:

a program of the Cooperative Educational Research Laboratory in Northfield, Illinois, to develop specifications for and train personnel to assume new school positions specifically designed to speed the installation of new educational practices;

a program of the Southwest Educational Development Laboratory to involve the parents of disadvantaged children in the formal educational process to increase their understanding of the school program and foster their children's motivation to achieve;

a program of the Appalachia Educational Laboratory to utilize modern technology and mobile equipment to develop in isolated rural schools the capability of receiving and utilizing modern instructional materials and methods;

a program of the Educational Development Center in Newton, Massachusetts, to create an innovation team supported by a resource center which works in a community and its schools to improve curriculum and instruction.

Research and Development

Closer examination of the programs with respect to target groups reveals strong emphasis on the education of disadvantaged populations. At least nine Laboratories focus on the culturally deprived or differentiated in reading and language arts; seven programs in mathematics and science, and a number in other subjects have similar foci. Five Laboratories beam their teacher education efforts to this type of target, and three of these, plus three others, are studying learning behaviors of disadvantaged children. Moreover, seven Laboratories are developing programs in educational planning, with special attention to the needs of those to whom existing schools seem poorly adapted. Improving the educational achievement of those handicapped in learning because of meager environments or other circumstances, therefore, is a major concern of many Laboratories and an important goal of most. With regard to curriculum and instruction, emphasis falls heavily on reading, language arts, mathematics and science. All Laboratories are giving attention to teacher education either as a means of achieving other goals or as an objective in its own right.

It may be noted that none of these approaches or programs is exclusive to the Laboratories and that in fact all had been advocated and to some extent developed, before the Educational Laboratories were established. What then, is the contribution of the Laboratories? It seems to me to be based on (1) the *systematic* development of these ideas and technologies; (2) their progressive adaptation to each other as components of systems for the attainment of educational objectives; (3) careful calculations and tests of the educational gains from installation of the new components and systems and the cost of the gains; and (4) prompt communication to other educational agencies of the information essential to effective use. These functions, to be sure, are shared with other agencies, but the Laboratories appear especially adapted to providing the necessary linking mechanisms and to undertaking those processes to which other agencies find it difficult to give consistent and sustained attention.

Rapid changes in knowledge and technology make continuous research and development at least as important to effective functioning in education as in other major enterprises in the contemporary world. The lack of institutions with primary responsibility for product-oriented or problem-oriented research accounts at least in part of the erratic nature of educational innovation. All too often heralded innovations have meant the introduction of partially worked out and inadequately tested theories or technologies without adequate provision either for continuing development or for the modification of other elements with which the new components must interact. The result frequently has been arrested development and consequent discard before the potential of the innovations is fully explored.

The Laboratories already are addressing themselves to the need for research-based development in education in ways that hold much promise for the future. If they continue to seek fruitful collaboration with university research and development and with state and local agencies, they not only will contribute to improved products and processes in education, but they will also help to incorporate of principle of continuous adaptation to remedy deficiencies and meet new needs.

Contributions of the R & D Centers
and the Educational Laboratories
to Social Studies Education

Although the Educational Research and Development Centers and the Regional Educational Laboratories are not producers of renowned or widely available curriculum materials, knowledge of their efforts in social studies curricula may prove useful for teachers. Both the R & D Centers and the Regional Labs are considering the education of disadvantaged youth and are likely sources of materials which will be stimulating for Negro, Indian, and other minority group students.

The efforts of the nine R & D Centers and the twenty Labs are coordinated by the Bureau of Research of the Office of Education. Supposedly a division of labor exists whereby the Labs develop and disseminate the educational research findings and techniques achieved in the R & D Centers and elsewhere. As can be seen from the example of EDC, this dichotomization of emphasis is sometimes blurred. This managerial imperfection is probably very beneficial in increasing the vitality of the laboratories.

THE RESEARCH AND DEVELOPMENT CENTERS

Three of the Research and Development Centers are engaged in activities directly related to social studies. Only the work of these three will be cited although several other centers may, indirectly, influence social studies through their exploration of promising innovations such as Individually Prescribed Instruction.

At the Johns Hopkins R & D Center, Saranes S. Boocock is Director of Project Simulation, Games and Control Beliefs. At least three games for social studies classes will be produced. A career game and a legislative game will embody in simulation two of the recurrent themes in social studies class: guidance and citizenship training. A third game simulating a community disaster is an especially interesting attempt at teaching students the interdependence of the members of modern society. These three games, like the Portsville game of the High School Geography Project, are examples of educational simulation. A fourth game of Boocock's is a research model for the American Sociological Association and is an example of the use of simulation for the generation of new hypotheses.

The Stanford Center for Research and Development in Teaching has a project directed towards social studies teacher training. First, the project team, led by Richard E. Gross, will develop scales for classifying and rating intern teacher classroom behavior. In other words, beginning teacher tactics will be operationally described and codified. Then video tapes will be made of teachers demonstrating behaviors thought to be efficacious. When finally assembled, the tapes will comprise a means of training social studies teachers in the exercise of those behaviors thought most desirable. Experienced teachers and department chairmen may find the teacher rating scales and video tapes of this project useful for in-service training.

One of the most interesting and timely ventures is being undertaken by the University of Georgia Research and Development Center in Educational Stimulation. In light of the current absorption in disciplinary structure, the Center has a Project, Structure as a Stimulant, directed by Warren G. Findley which involves, according to Findley,

(a) operational definition of the learning goal, (b) reduction of the learning goal into task steps, (c) preparation of a learning sequence on the basis of task fit; and (d) revision of the material on the basis of feedback to achieve more effectively the learning goal.

In order to operationally define learning goals the University of Georgia R & D Center, and other Centers, have had to address themselves to popular but ambiguous terms such as "discovery," "inquiry," "critical thinking," and "induction."

A critic of recent trends in social studies states:

Typically, discussions of the "inductive approach," etc., lack clarity. Current social studies theorists do not indicate in their suggested prescriptions for curriculum design and teaching practices whether they mean to imply under the label of induction that:
1. "Children learn inductively";
2. "Inductive processes of inquiry are a valid method for accumulating knowledge"; or
3. "Both or neither." [1]

In the R & D Centers a consensus as to the meaning of terms such as inquiry and induction seems to be arising. The definitions are based on the models of disciplines which theorists have posited.

In a discipline such as history, the neophyte learns the techniques historians apply to their data (internal and external criticism), the content of history (diaries, documents, memorials, and narratives), and the pro-

---

[1] Stephenie G. Edgerton, "Learning by Induction," *Social Education*, 31, no. 5 (May, 1967): 375.

ducts or outcomes of historians (statements of causal relationships and the imaginative reconstruction of the past). Another way of putting it would be to say that the student learns the syntactic and substantive structures of the discipline and the insights the interplay of these structures allows.

When educators speak of discovery, inquiry, and induction it is not clear whether they mean discovery by the student of the process, content, or product of the discipline. A student might be motivated and led to discover the process of history, i.e., external and internal criticism. He might also be taught this process of inquiry by other means and be led to discover the content of history. (Given certain methods of inquiry and certain outcomes where would you look to discover the source of the outcomes?) He might also be taught the methods and sources of historians and be led to discover the products of historians.

To further complicate the problem there is new inquiry and inquiry new to the student. The student might learn the techniques of the master by engaging in genuine research aided, of course, by wise tutoring; or the student might learn by repeating studies which have already been done but of which he has no knowledge. In the latter case the student can begin with very simple problems and progress to more complex ones, being able to compare his procedures and products with those of experts after he has finished each attempt.

Structuralists at the R & D Centers had to decide if discovery and induction meant that students were to create certain parts (or the whole) of the discipline for themselves—a strategy that might be termed a "full blown entry into life," or if the students were going to be led through materials organized in a psychologically valid pattern to gradually master the principles and practices in question—a strategy that might be termed "imitation of life."

The structuralists seem to be reaching a decision on this question. The following cogent analysis which was prepared as a precursor of a structurally oriented curriculum is offered at length as evidence of the resolution now developing.

The popularity of "structure" in curriculum making is perhaps due to a connotative ambiguity which permits advocates of both informal and formal teaching to subsume the category within preexistent approaches. This is perhaps inevitable, since Bruner, one of the great popularizers of the phrase "structure of knowledge," uses it ambiguously—sometimes to refer to a taxonomic organization of materials for instruction (1960) and at other times to refer to the process of inquiry (1964).
There is a revived respect for the taxonomic presentation of materials, since it is this type of organization which facilitates the integration of new with

old learning. Ausubel (1961, 1962) using the terms receptive and discovery has established a model in which new material is learned by subsumption under previously existent categories. The implication is that more effective learning takes place if the material is introduced in such a way that it relates quickly to the previous cognitive map, a conclusion reinforced by the discrimination studies of Simon and Feigenbaum (1964). While the language is different, these learning models might be regarded by a non-specialist as a revival of Herbartian apperception. (Herbart, 1900; Compayre, 1907).[2]

If discovery is going to mean anything, it is going to mean discovery of the generalizations of social scientists. The generalizations which will be discovered will not be new in the sense of being original; they will merely be new to the learner.

Discovery or induction will refer to a psychologically valid manner of learning rather than to a logically valid manner of acquiring or testing hypotheses. The distinction can be seen if we look at induction in terms of a Deweyan definition versus a structuralist definition as represented by Bruner or Fenton.

According to Dewey:

Were it stated that the man in question is brought face to face with particulars in the way which induces apprehension of general form as a result, there would be no logical difference between those cases in which it is said that the conclusion is induced. The process is in any case of natural education or eliciting, rather than of induction as it occurs in modern scientific method.[3]

Dewey's point was that the Baconian part to whole conception of induction was not the same concept of induction as held by modern scientists. Dewey objected to describing a Baconian view of induction as a logically valid manner of discovery or verification.

The structuralists' point is that the Baconian part to whole concept of induction appears useful psychologically because a person who learns a discipline in this manner apparently learns it in a superior fashion in terms of data retention (Ausubel) and future applications (Bruner). The answer, then, to Edgerton's question, according to the R & D Centers is, "Children learn inductively."

The Structure as a Stimulant Project at the University of Georgia Research and Development Center in Educational Stimulation has concluded that Ausubel's approach to structure is superior for their purposes.

---

[2] *Report of the Research and Development Center in Educational Stimulation,* p. 6.3.

[3] John Dewey, *Logic: The Theory of Inquiry* (New York: Holt, Rinehart & Winston, Inc., 1938), p. 424.

In history instruction this means, says the Center staff, that analytic skills can be taught by first teaching taxonomic abstraction and categorization.

This theory has been accepted by the Elementary Anthropology Project at the University of Georgia which will produce a taxonomy of key words, definitions, explanatory propositions, and expository idiosyncratic material to serve as the basis of their course of study. The Center may produce an elementary geography course also based on a taxonomy to articulate with the elementary anthropology course.

The Structure as a Stimulant Project's investigation of the productive properties of differing interpretations of the meaning of disciplinary structure is potentially of great significance for other curriculum makers. Its intelligent conclusions may bring increased clarity to the structuralist position, thereby making it operational in terms of daily classroom activities.

The Learning Institute of North Carolina

Before we present a synopsis of the social studies activities of the Regional Educational Laboratories, we will indulge in a worthwhile digression—a look at the intriguing work of the Learning Institute of North Carolina (LINC). This private, nonprofit corporation was founded in 1964 by the North Carolina State Board of Higher Education, Duke University, the University of North Carolina Fund. Its creation was enthusiastically encouraged by Governor Terry Sanford as described in his *But What About the People*.

Its first director was Harold Howe II, and a subsequent director, Gordon McAndrew, became superintendent of the embattled Gary Public Schools. LINC has aided the Regional Education Laboratory for the Carolinas and Virginia (RELCU) in the development of Individually Prescribed Instruction. Much of the planning for the formation of RELCU was done by LINC in 1965 and 1966.

LINC's first project and, to date, its most ambitious one was the establishment of the North Carolina Advancement School in Winston-Salem. The Advancement School was a residential institution for eighth-grade under-achieving boys. It was made possible by grants totaling 3.3 million dollars from the State Board Office of Education and the Carnegie Corporation. The Advancement School's purpose was to create materials and methods effective in Remedying under-achievement in North Carolina school children. The materials created, of course, have wide applicability.

Of the units developed, the Communications and Earth Science materials were adjudged by the State Department of Public Instruction to be the best. The Communications unit is intended for the language arts block of the total school curriculum, but many social studies classes include some work on the implications of language and expression, witness EDC's *Man: A Course of Study* curriculum which views language as a societal element appropriate for anthropological examination and treatment. The Department of Public Instruction's evaluators said of the Communications unit,

The Program is innovative, original, interesting and highly motivating; it proceeds on the theory that the best learning is self-directed discovery and it fully explores all avenues of communications as they open to the senses of sight, hearing, smell, taste, and touch.[4]

The review of the Earth Science unit (geology) stated, "This material could be used advantageously with any level eighth-grade student—but particularly with under-achievers and those of average or less than average ability. "[5]

Teachers can obtain a sample copy (which must be returned) of the units by having a principal or superintendent write the Learning Institute of North Carolina (1006 Lamond Avenue, Durham, North Carolina, 27701). The units are in the public domain and may be reproduced at will. [6]

The Regional Educational Laboratories

The Regional Education Laboratories are engaged in "a wide range of research, development, and dissemination programs, including basic and applied research, curriculum development and evaluation. . . ."[7]

For a very good short statement of the problems and potentialities of the Labs see Rankin and Blanke's article in the SEC *Newsletter*.[8]

Three Regional Laboratories are conducting significant programs in some aspect of social studies education. The three are: The Far West Laboratory for Educational Research and Development in Berkeley, the Central Midwestern Regional Educational Laboratory, Inc. in St. Ann, Missouri, and the Center for Urban Education in New York. Several others, including the Southwest Educational Development Laboratory in Austin, Texas, will soon be able to point with pride to new social studies

---

[4] "Advancement School Materials Evaluated," *The LINC Quarterly*, no. 10 (Winter, 1968), p. 3.

[5] Ibid., p. 3.

[6] Ibid., p. 4.

[7] *Guidelines For a National Program of Educational Laboratories*, Public Law 89–10, Title IV, OE–2240 c. p. 2.

[8] Stuart C. Rankin and Virgil E. Blanke, "RELS: Are They Here to Stay?" Strategies for Educational Change, *Newsletter*, vol. 2, no. 5 (April, 1968). (For issues of the SEC *Newsletter* write: Michael H. Kean, 314 Oxley Hall, 1712 Neil Avenue, Columbus, Ohio 43210).

materials or procedures. The Southwest Lab, for example, will produce social studies materials for elementary and junior high students which will emphasize the contribution of Negroes, Mexican-Americans, and Creoles to American life.

The Far West Lab (FWREL) has tackled teacher training and materials production. The Lab is producing a number of "minicourses" or short video tape programs for in-service training. Two of the "minicourses" are within our sphere of interest. "Appropriate Teacher Behavior for Teaching Urban Negro Secondary Students," will be relevant for all teachers; "Using Simulations and Games to Teach Secondary Social Studies," will be of particular interest to social studies teachers.

Five 30-minute television programs have been produced for use in an educational television series. Two handbooks complement the television offerings. The television program which is likely to be most appealing to social studies teachers is "All Working Together," a case study of a school involved in an attempt to improve the education of Negro students. The two handbooks are entitled *Mexican-Americans: A Handbook for Educators* and *Afro-Americans in the Far West: A Handbook for Educators.* The latter work, by Jack D. Forbes, assumes that, "The school must address itself to the task of bolstering the self-image of black pupils and adults in order to overcome the psychological effects of centuries of discrimination." [9]

The Central Midwestern Regional Educational Laboratory, Inc. (CEMREL) has maintained an association with Harold Berlak's Metropolitan St. Louis Social Studies Center and has benefited thereby. In social studies CEMREL has developed a Diffusion Project which involves analysis of curricular offerings, selection of exemplary products, and dissemination of this product through field-trials in selected schools. The diffusion model involves the training of teachers of six schools via cooperative efforts occurring in one of the schools. After training each participating team returns to its own school which, in turn, becomes a nucleus school for teachers and consultants from five other "unaffected" schools.

CEMREL is also involved in computer assisted instruction. Dr. Paul Wendt and Dr. Leslie Woeflin are designing a CAI program in geography for freshmen at Southern Illinois University. The CAI system will be built around an IBM 1500, cathrode ray tubes, earphones, typewriters, and lighted pens. Teachers who wish to keep informed regarding CEMREL efforts in social studies education should write for the CEMREL Social Studies Diffusion Project *Newsletter,* c/o Mrs. Verna Smith, 10646 St. Charles Rock Road, St. Ann, Missouri 63074.

[9] *Teaching and Learning Topics,* Far West Laboratory for Educational Research and Development, April, 1968.

The most exciting of the Regional Laboratories is the Center for Urban Education (CUE), New York. CUE is somewhat analogous to the Learning Institute of North Carolina. It was sponsored in 1965 by The City University of New York, Bank Street College of Education, Columbia University, Fordham University, New York Medical College, New York University, Teachers College of Columbia, and Yeshiva University as a private, nonprofit corporation to improve educational practice in urban areas. CUE was funded by the Carnegie Corporation, the Field Foundation, the New World Foundation, the Rockefeller Foundation, and the Alfred P. Sloan Foundation.

In 1966, CUE became a Regional Laboratory. Unlike the other Labs, which sometimes seem enamored of conventional wisdom, CUE scorns pedantry and its publications are sophisticated and innovative. In its Fact Sheet the CUE spokesman observes that ... "there has been expressed in the nation an increasing, and on the whole, healthy skepticism about the practices of urban educational systems. Most urban planners agree that a consideration of basic urban concerns is incomplete unless it includes education at the same time; some of the most unyielding educational reformers have come to sense that education is only one configuration in a complicated urban constellation and that reform cannot succeed in a vacuum surrounded by social disruption." [10]

CUE has sponsored a number of publications which will benefit teachers. *The Negro in Schoolroom Literature* by Minnie Koblitz provides references to appropriate literature dealing with Negro life for K-6 classes. Also included are films, records, and filmstrips which are free or inexpensive. Elementary school teachers will find the book a valuable guide to sources in Negro history. The author includes a background bibliography for teachers which cites works by Baldwin, Hughes, Hentoff, Lomax, and others.

One of the most significant of CUE publications is a book (excerpts available in Xerox copies) called *Planning for Change*.[11] This work was produced by the Architects' Renewal Committee in Harlem, Inc. (ARCH) and represents a good example of what can be done with such currently vacuous courses as community civics. *Planning for Change* begins by announcing:

This is a new kind of book. It is a book for people who know that there is something wrong with the world they live in and the neighborhood they live in. It is a book for students who want to change the way things are today.

---

[10] Center for Urban Education, *Fact Sheet,* 33 W. 42nd St., New York, N. Y. 10036, p. 3.

[11] "Planning for Change." Center for Urban Education, 33 W. 42nd St., New York, N.Y.

The students are encouraged to establish priorities among neighborhood problems. To do this they must survey their neighborhood (using census data and forms provided by the authors) and identify what they consider to be the most severe community difficulties. They are then instructed in the creation of land use and condition maps which serve as planning aids. In addition to their own opinions, the students interview workers in community service centers asking these people what problems in the neighborhood they consider most pressing. Gradually, the sampled population is enlarged so that the students talk with representatives of all major groups in the community, including population aggregates.

On the basis of the information they have gathered, the students make a plan for remediation of a selected problem or problems. Since the city of New York was the intended instructional area, *Planning for Change* describes the political and legal structure of the New York municipal corporation with the intention of providing the information that enlightened activists will need. Also provided is data on urban renewal and the means by which community organizations can obtain renewal funds. Students are reminded that.

Only with the Urban Renewal Program can a whole neighborhood be fixed up. But don't think you and your parents can't do anything right now. Besides using the legal tools you read about at the back of this book, people—even very poor people—can borrow money from the federal government in Washington to *buy and rehabilitate* their buildings instead of waiting for the landlord to fix them up. Here is how it is done: . . .

A future land use map is constructed at this point to provide an overview as to how the proposed changes will make the neighborhood look. A scale model may also be built.

Planning for Change includes an example of community sponsored neighborhood urban renewal and rehabilitation. The case study involving a neighborhood in East Harlem, as the rest of the "curriculum," frankly encourages students to acquire power in order to have the leverage to move sedentary officials and ossified organizations.

Planning for Change is designed for New York City, but its format can be adapted to apply to any Metropolitan area. Indeed, its *realpolitik* flavor will undoubtedly make it most attractive and perhaps, productive, for militant ghetto teachers. It should be noted that the interaction between school and society which *Planning for Change* envisions is progressivism resurrected.

In a very short time the R & D Centers and the Regional Labs have developed thrusts which are likely to make them future major forces in social studies education. The tension in these enterprises between national curriculum trends and regional requirements is likely to produce many avenues to quality education. Looking at the major social studies curriculum projects, foundation supported projects and government center based efforts, in perspective, it seems fair to say that high school social studies departments will, in a few years, have available many alternative programs of instruction and curriculum packages. If social studies teacher education programs provide practice in the use of the teacher behaviors called for by the new materials the quality of social studies instruction is likely to improve.

Bibliography

BOOKS

Angell, Robert C. *Directive on Teachers' Manual,* American Sociological Association, 1965.

Bane, Mary Jo; Donald Oliver and Fred M. Newmann. *Guide to Teaching.* Stamford, Conn.: Xerox Publishing Co., 1967.

Bendix, Peter. *Max Weber—An Intellectual Portrait.* Garden City: Doubleday & Company, Inc., Anchor, 1962.

Berger, Peter. *Invitation to Sociology: A Humanistic Perspective.* Anchor Books, 1963.

Bloom, B. S. and D. R. Krathwohl. *Taxonomy of Educational Objectives:* Handbook 1, Cognitive Domain. New York: David McKay Co., 1964.

Broek, Jan O. M. *Geography, Its Scope and Spirit.* Columbus, Ohio: Charles Merrill Books, 1965.

Bruner, Jerome S. *On Knowing.* Cambridge: Harvard University Press, 1962.

———. *The Process of Education.* Cambridge: Harvard University Press, 1960.

Bunge, W. *Theoretical Geography.* Lund-Gleerup, 1962.

Burston, W. H. and D. Thomson. *Studies in the Nature of Teaching of History.* New York: Humanities Press, 1967.

Cahnman, Werner J. and Alvin Boskoff (eds.). *Sociology and History— Theory and Research.* New York: Free Press of Glencoe, 1964.

Davis, Jefferson. *The Rise and Fall of the Confederate Government.* New York: Collier Books, 1961.

Dewey, John. *Democracy and Education.* New York: Macmillan, 1916.

———. *Lectures in the Philosophy of Education.* Reginald D. Archambault, ed., New York: Random House, 1966.

———. *Logic: The Theory of Inquiry.* New York: Henry Holt & Co., 1938.

Du Bois, W. E. B. *Black Reconstruction in America.* New York: Russell & Russell, 1953.

Elton, G. R. *The Practice of History.* New York: Thomas Y. Crowell Company, 1967.

Fenton, Edwin. *Developing a New Curriculum Rationale for the Holt Social Studies Curriculum.* New York: Holt, Rinehart & Winston, 1967.

———. *The New Social Studies.* New York: Holt, Rinehart & Winston, 1967.

———. *Teaching the New Social Studies: An Inductive Approach.* New York: Holt, Rinehart, & Winston, 1966.

Ginzberg, Eli and Alfred S. Eichner. *The Troublesome Presence—American Democracy and the Negro.* New York: Mentor Books, 1964.

Goodlad, John, with Maurice N. Richter, Jr. *The Development of a Conceptual System for Dealing with Problems of Curriculum and Instruction.* Contract No. SAE-8024, Project No. 454 with the University of

Chicago, Report processed and forwarded by the University of California, Los Angeles, and Institute of Educational Activities.

Gross, Richard E., Walter E. McPhie and Jack R. Fraenkel (ed.).*Teaching the Social Studies*. Scranton, Pa.: International Textbook Company, 1969.

Hidy, Ralph and Paul Cowein (eds.). *Case Studies in Business History and Economic Concepts, Individual Enterprise and National Growth*. Boston: D. C. Heath Company, 1967.

Holt, John. *How Children Fail*. New York: Pitman Co., 1964.

Homans, George. *The Human Group*. New York: Harcourt, Brace, 1950.

Hughes, H. Stuart. *History as an Art and a Science*. New York: Harper and Row, 1964.

Johnson, Harry M. *Sociology—A Systematic Introduction*. New York: Harcourt Brace & World, 1960.

Klein, Francis and Tyler, Louise L. *Recommendations for Curriculum and Instructional Materials*. Los Angeles: University of California, 1967.

Krug, Mark M. *History and the Social Sciences—New Approaches to the Teaching of Social Studies*. Waltham, Mass: Blaisdell Publishing Company, 1967.

Kuhn, Thomas S. *The Structure of Scientific Revolutions*. Chicago: The University of Chicago Press, 1962.

Logan, Rayford W. *The Negro in American Life and Thought: The Nadir, 1877—1901*. New York: Dial Press, 1954.

McWhitney, Grady (ed.). *Reconstruction and the Freedmen*. Chicago: Rand McNally Co., 1963.

Mayo, Elton. *The Human Problems of an Industrial Civilization*. New York: Macmillan Co., 1933.

Moore, Barrington, Jr. *Political Power and Social Theory*. New York: Harper Torchbooks, 1962.

Morison, Samuel Eliot. *The Oxford History of the American People*. New York: Oxford University Press, 1965.

———. *Vistas of History*. New York: Alfred A. Knopf, 1964.

Morrissett, Irving (ed.). *Concepts and Structure in the New Social Science Curricula*. Boulder, Colo.: Social Science Education Consortium, 1966.

Newmann, Fred M. *Negro Views of America*. Middletown. Conn.: Xerox Corporation, 1968.

———; Donald M. Oliver and Mary Jo Bane. *Guide to Teaching*. Stanford, Conn.: Xerox Publishing Co., 1967.

Oliver, Donald M.; Fred M. Newmann and Mary Jo Bane. *Guide to Teaching*. Stamford, Conn.: Xerox Publishing Co., 1967.

Phenix, Philip. *Realms of Meaning*. New York: McGraw-Hill Co., 1964.

Raymond, Henry J. (ed.). *The Life and Public Services of Abraham Lincoln —Together with his State Papers*. New York: Derby and Miller, 1864.

Saveth, Edward E. (ed.). *American History and the Social Sciences*. New York: 1964.

Schultz, Mindella. *Teachers Guide for Comparative Political Systems—An Inquiry Approach.*

Shaver, James P. and Donald W. Oliver. *Teaching Public Issues in the High School.* Boston, Houghton-Mifflin Company, 1966.

Sloan, Irving, *The Negro in American Modern Textbooks.* Washington, D.C.: American Federation of Teachers, AFL-CIO, 1967.

Southern, R. W. *The Making of the Middle Ages.* New Haven: 1967.

Stampp, Kenneth M. *And the War Came.* Chicago: University of Chicago Press, 1964.

Thornbury, Richard T. and Grace E. Johnson. Under the direction of Robert K. Burns, *A Look at Our Economy.* Chicago: Industrial Relations Center, 1965.

Tocqueville, Alexis De. *Democracy in America.* New York: Schocken Books, 1961.

Tyler, Louise L. and Francis Klein. *Recommendations for Curriculum and Instructional Materials,* Los Angeles: University of California, 1967.

Venable, Tom C. *Philosophical Foundations of the Curriculum.* Chicago: Rand McNally & Co., 1967.

Wilson, Henry. *History of the Rise and Fall of the Slave Power in America.* Boston: Walker Co., 1872—77.

Woodward, C. Vann. *The Strange Career of Jim Crow.* New York: Oxford University Press, 1955.

NEWSPAPER

Duberman, Martin. *New York Times Book Review.* August 11, 1968.

PAMPHLETS

Fact Sheet, Center for Urban Education. 33 W. 42nd St., New York, N.Y. 10036.

Guidelines For a National Program of Educational Laboratories. Public Law 89—10, Title 10, OE-2240 c.

Report of the Research and Development Center in Educational Stimulation. 6.3, Athens, Ga.: University of Georgia Press, 1967.

Sociological Resources for Secondary Schools Informational Materials. American Sociological Association, 1967.

Teaching and Learning Topics. Far West Laboratory for Educational Research and Development, April 1968.

ARTICLES

Allport, Gordon W., "The Psychology of Participation," *The Psychological Review,* Vol. 53, No. 3, May 1945.

Anderson, C. Arnold, "A New Frame for the Social Studies," *The School Review,* Winter 1964.

Angell, Robert C. and Lincoln Grahlfs, "The First National Trials of SRSS Episodes," A paper prepared for delivery at sixty-second annual meeting of the American Sociological Association, San Francisco, August 30, 1967, p. 7.

Anthony, Albert S., "The Role of Objectives in the New History," in *Social Education*, November 1967.

Beck, Clive, "The Question of Knowledge in Curriculum Inquiry," a paper delivered at the 1968 American Educational Research Association.

Bellack, Arno, "Structure in the Social Sciences and Implications for the Social Studies Program," in *The Social Studies: Curriculum Proposals for the Future*, Wesley Sowards, ed., Chicago: Scott, Foresman and Co., 1963.

Blanke, Virgil E. and Stuart C. Rankin, "RELS: Are They Here to Stay?" Strategies for Education Change, *Newsletter*, April 1968.

Bobrian, Haig, "The Councils on Economic Education... and how they work," New York: Joint Council on Economic Education, 1964.

Boch, G. L., "The State of Education in Economics," in Keith G. Lumsden, ed., *New Developments in the Teaching of Economics*, Englewood Cliffs, N.J., 1967.

Brown, Richard H., "History as Discovery: An Interim Report on the Amherst Project," *New Social Studies*. Amherst College, 1965.

Bruner, Jerome S., "Education or Social Invention," *Saturday Review*, February 19, 1966.

———, "Some Elements of Discovery," in *Learning by Discovery: A Critical Appraisal*, Lee S. Shulman and Evan R. Keisler, eds., Chicago: Rand McNally & Co., 1966.

Chase, Francis S., "The Distinctive Roles of Educational Laboratories," Keynote address at the annual membership meeting of the Central Regional Educational Laboratory, CAREL *Speaker*, February 1968.

———, "Excerpts From Educational Research and Development: Promise or Mirage?" *Journal of Research and Development*, Autumn 1968.

Collier, Malcolm, "A Question About Questions," *Social Education*, December 1965.

Cressey, George B., "Geography," in *High School Social Studies Perspectives*, Erling Hunt, ed., Boston: Houghton-Mifflin Co., 1907.

Edgerton, Stephenie G., "Learning by Education," *Social Education*, May 1967.

Etzioni, Amitai, "Social Analysis as a Sociological Vocation," *The American Journal of Sociology*, March 1965.

Farley, John V., "Developing Inquiry Skills With an Experimental Social Studies Curriculum," dittoed statement.

Farrell, Richard and James Van Ness, "A Thematic Approach to American History," in *Social Education*, December 1967.

Fenton, Edwin M., "Developing Inquiry Skills With an Experimental Social Studies Curriculum, dittoed statement.

Franklin, John Hope, "The New American History," *Negro Digest*, February 1967.

Gearing, Frederick O., "Why Indians," *Social Education*, February 1968.

Glock, Charles Y. and Rodney Stark, "Is There an American Protestantism?" *Trans-action*, November, December 1965.

Good, John M., "Developing Inquiry Skills With an Experimental Social Studies Curriculum," dittoed statement.

Goody, J. and J. Watt, "The Consequences of Literacy," Comparative Studies in *Society and History*, Vol. 5, pp. 304—45, 1963.

Grahlfs, Lincoln and Robert C. Angell, "The First National Trials of SRSS Episodes," A paper prepared for delivery at the sixty-second annual meeting of the American Sociological Association, San Francisco, August 30, 1967.

Gow, Steele, "Criteria for Appraising R and D Centers," a paper for the American Association of School Administrators, Atlantic City, February 13, 1967.

Haggard, E. A. and R. J. Rose, "Some Effects of Mental Set and Active Participation in the Conditioning of the Autokinetic Phenomenon," *Journal of Experimental Psychology*, Vol. 34, 1944.

Harris, Seymour E., "Economics," in *High School Social Studies Perspectives*, Erling Hunt, ed., Boston: Houghton-Mifflin Co., 1962.

Hering, William M. Jr. "Sociological Resources for Secondary Schools and the High School Curriculum," A paper delivered to the NDEA Summer Institute for State Supervisors of Social Studies, Carnegie-Mellon University, Pittsburgh, Pennsylvania, June 14, 1967.

Hughes, Helen MacGill, "Operation Paperback: Sociology in the High School Library," in *Indiana Social Studies Quarterly*, Muncie, Indiana. Ball State University, Winter 1967.

Kirkpatrick, Evron and Jeanne J., "Political Science," in *High School Social Studies Perspectives*. Erling Hunt, ed., Boston: Houghton-Mifflin Co., 1967.

Kohn, Clyde P., "Basic Concepts of Geography and Their Development in the Classroom in Teaching the New Social Studies," Edwin Fenton, ed., New York: Holt, Rinehart & Winston, 1966.

Krug, Mark M., "Bruner's New Social Studies—A Critique," *Social Education*, October 1966.

Lazarsfeld, Paul, "The American Soldier," *Public Opinion Quarterly*, Fall 1949.

Massialas, Byron C., "Teaching History as Inquiry," in *New Perspectives in World History*, Shirley H. Engle, ed., Thirty-fourth Yearbook of the National Council for Social Studies. Washington, 1964.

Mitsuhashi, S., "Conceptions and Images of the Physical World," *Comparative Education Review*, Vol. 6, pp. 142—47, 1962.

Morrissett, Irving and W. Williams Stevens, Jr., "Curriculum Analysis," *Social Education*, October 1967.

Newmann, Fred, "The Analysis of Public Controversy: New Focus on Social Studies, *School Review*, Winter 1965.

Newmann, Fred, "Questioning the Place of Social Science Disciplines in Education," *Social Education*, November 1967.

Oliver, Donald W., "The Selection of Content in the Social Sciences," in *Teaching the New Social Studies*, Edwin Fenton, ed., New York: Holt Rinehart & Winston, 1966.

———— and James P. Shaver, "Teaching Public Issues in the High School," Boston: Houghton-Mifflin Co., 1966.

Randall, James G., "The Blundering Generation," *Mississippi Valley Historical Review*, Spring 1940.

Rankin, Stuart C. and Virgil E. Blanke, "RELS: Are They Here to Stay?" Strategies for Educational Change. *Newsletter*, Vol. 2, No. 5, April 1968.

Rose, R. J. and E. A. Haggard, "Some Effects of Mental Set and Active Participation in the Conditioning of the Autokinetic Phenomenon," *Journal of Experimental Psychology*, Vol. 34, 1944.

Schwab, Joseph J., "The Concept of the Structure of a Discipline," *The Educational Record*, Vol. 43, July 1962.

————, "The Teaching of Science as Inquiry," in *The Teaching of Science*, Cambridge: Harvard University Press, 1964.

Stake, Robert E., "An Emerging Theory of Evaluation-Borrowings from Many Methodologies," a paper presented at a symposium on "The Role of Evaluation in National Curriculum Projects," 1967 Annual Meeting of the American Educational Research Association, New York.

Stark, Rodney and Charles Y. Glock, "Is There an American Protestantism," *Trans-action*, November-December 1965.

Stevens, W. William, Jr., "Curriculum Analysis," *Social Education*, Vol. XXXI, No. 6, October 1967.

Tyler, Ralph, "An Assessment: The Edge of the Future," *The Social Studies: Curriculum Proposals for the Future*, Wesley Sowards, ed., Chicago: Scott, Foresman and Co., 1963.

————, "New Dimensions in Curriculum Development," *Phi Delta Kappan*, Vol. XLVIII, No. 1, September 1966.

Van Ness, James and Richard Farrell, "A Thematic Approach to American History," *Social Education*, December 1967.

Watt, J. and J. Goody, "The Consequences of Literacy," *Comparative Studies in Society and History*, Vol. 5, pp. 304—45, 1963.

Wesley, Edgar B., "Let's Abolish History Courses," *Phi Delta Kappan*, September 1967.

Wilson, Everett K., "Inductive Methods in Teaching Sociology," Sociological Resources for the Social Studies *Newsletter*, American Sociological Association, No. 5, Summer 1968.

————, "Our Privileged Pariahs," *The Antioch Review*, Fall 1965.

————, "Notes for Building a High School Course in Sociology," *Indiana Social Studies Quarterly*, Muncie, Indiana: Ball State University, Winter 1967-1968.

Wilson, Everett K., "The Sociological Perspective: Some Basic Notions for the High School Student," A talk given at meetings of the Minnesota Council for the Social Studies, October 21, 1966.

———, "The SRSS Course in Sociology for High School Students," A paper prepared for delivery at the sixty-second annual meeting of the American Sociological Association, San Francisco, August 30, 1967.

———, "SRSS Presents a New High School Sociology Course," SRSS *Newsletter*, Fall 1967.

DIRECTORIES

"Directory of Research and Development Centers," Central Midwestern Regional Educational Laboratory, Inc.

Abbott, Max G., 303
Advisory Paper for Teachers Associated with the High School Geography
   Project. See geography
African Education Program, 243
Afro-American History. See history
Allport, Gordon W., 36, 117, 120, 127, 128
Almond, Gabriel, 268
American Council of Learned Societies, 251
American Creed. See Harvard Social Studies Project Materials
American Economic Association. See economics
American History and the Social Sciences, 24, 25, 27
Anachronism. See history
Analysis: criterion for, 17; economic, 143; linguistic, 309, 310; of public con-
   troversy. See Harvard Social Studies Project Materials; of rationales, 187
Anatomy of Revolution, The, 33
Anderson, C. Arnold, 40, 123
Anderson, Randall, 89
Angell, Robert, 126
Anthropology: as natural science, 34; as scientific history, 71; Elementary
   Anthropology Project, 319; feasibility of materials, 77; in precollegiate
   curriculum, 60—70 passim; in social studies, 59, 69, 70, 79; interests of, 34;
   physical anthropology, 34; race, 62—68; social anthropology, 35; stones and
   bones, 78
---Anthropology Curriculum Study Project: Anthropology Materials in Social
   Studies Courses: A Case Study -- Day One, 72; Great Tree and the Long
   House: Culture of the Iroquois, 74; History as Culture Change, 71, 75; Pat-
   terns in Human History, 71; Study of Early Man, 71
Archeology, 35
Areal association. See geography
Association of American Geographers. See geography
Ausubel, David, 318
Bach, George, 153, 180
Baliksi, Asen, 257, 259
Baltzel, E. Digby, 24
Bane, Mary Jo. 232
Behavioral Objectives: higher processes, 11; in anthropology, 69; in economics,
   156; in geography, 99; in teacher training, 304; knowledge, 12; recall and
   recognition, 11
Bellack, Arno, 17
Benson, Lee, 31
Berger, Peter, 132
Berlak, Harold, 321
Bernstein, Edgar, 192
Bierstedt, Robert, 23
Bilingual instruction. See Regional Educational Laboratories
Black history. See history
Blanke, Virgil E., 320
Bloom, Benjamin, 12
Boskoff, Alvin, 24, 25
Boulding, Kenneth, 133
Bridenbaugh, Carl, 200

THE BOOK MANUFACTURE

The New Social Studies: Analysis of Theories and Materials was typeset by Henkes-Holland N.V. Printing by offset and binding were performed at Kingsport Press, Inc. Internal design was by John Goetz; cover design by Evelyn Hansen. The paper is Perkins & Squier Company's Glatfelter Old Forge offset. The type in this book is Bembo.

Book Fair 10/7/99